First World War
and Army of Occupation
War Diary
France, Belgium and Germany

32 DIVISION
14 Infantry Brigade
Highland Light Infantry
15th (Service) Battalion (1st Glasgow)
1 October 1917 - 31 March 1919

WO95/2393B

The Naval & Military Press Ltd
www.nmarchive.com
Published in association with The National Archives

Published by

The Naval & Military Press Ltd

Unit 10 Ridgewood Industrial Park,

Uckfield, East Sussex,

TN22 5QE England

Tel: +44 (0) 1825 749494

www.naval-military-press.com

www.nmarchive.com

This diary has been reprinted in facsimile from the original. Any imperfections are inevitably reproduced and the quality may fall short of modern type and cartographic standards.

Contents

Document type	Place/Title	Date From	Date To
Heading	15 H L I Vol 24		
Heading	D.A.G G.H.Q 3rd Echelon		
War Diary	Wulpen	01/10/1917	03/10/1917
War Diary	St Georges	04/10/1917	06/10/1917
War Diary	Coxyde	07/10/1917	07/10/1917
War Diary	Petite Synthe	08/10/1917	25/10/1917
War Diary	Capelle St Sourent	26/10/1917	26/10/1917
War Diary	Rubrouck	27/10/1917	31/10/1917
Miscellaneous	Rubrouck	31/10/1917	31/10/1917
Miscellaneous	Appendix 1. Scud. Relief Orders.	03/10/1917	03/10/1917
Miscellaneous	Appendix 2 S K I H Relief Orders	03/10/1917	03/10/1917
Miscellaneous	Appendix 3 Defence Scheme Right Battalion St Georges Sector		
Operation(al) Order(s)	Operation Orders No. 12A		
Map			
Miscellaneous	Appendix 5		
Miscellaneous	15th H.L.I. Training Programme For 11th Oct. 1917	11/10/1917	11/10/1917
Miscellaneous	15th H.L.I. Training Programme For 12th Oct. 1917	12/10/1917	12/10/1917
Miscellaneous	15th H.L.I. Training Programme For Saturday 13th Oct. 1917	13/10/1917	13/10/1917
Miscellaneous	Training Programme For Monday 15th October 1917	15/10/1917	15/10/1917
Miscellaneous	Training Programme For Tuesday 16th October 1917	16/10/1917	16/10/1917
Miscellaneous	Training Programme For Wednesday 17th October 1917.	17/10/1917	17/10/1917
Miscellaneous	Training Programme For Thursday 18th October 1917.	18/10/1917	18/10/1917
Miscellaneous	Training Programme For Friday 19th October 1917.		
Miscellaneous	Training Programme For Saturday 20th October 1917	20/10/1917	20/10/1917
Miscellaneous	Training Programme For Monday 22nd October 1917	22/10/1917	22/10/1917
Miscellaneous	Training Programme For Tuesday 23rd October 1917	23/10/1917	23/10/1917
Miscellaneous	Training Programme For Wednesday 24th October 1917	24/10/1917	24/10/1917
Miscellaneous	Training Programme For Thursday 25th October 1917	25/10/1917	25/10/1917
Miscellaneous	Training Programme For Friday 26th October 1917	26/10/1917	26/10/1917
Miscellaneous	Training Programme For Saturday 27th October 1917	27/10/1917	27/10/1917
Miscellaneous	Training Programme For Monday 29th October 1917	29/10/1917	29/10/1917
Miscellaneous	Training Programme For Tuesday 30th October 1917	30/10/1917	30/10/1917
Miscellaneous	Battalion Orders by Lieut-Colonel V.B. Ramsden, M.C., Commanding 15th Bn. Highland Light Infantry.	16/10/1917	16/10/1917
Miscellaneous	Battalion Orders by Lieut-Colonel V.B. Ramsden, M.C., Commanding 15th Bn. Highland Light Infantry.	12/10/1917	12/10/1917
Miscellaneous	Battalion Orders by Lieut-Colonel V.B. Ramsden, M.C., Commanding 15th Bn. Highland Light Infantry.	13/10/1917	13/10/1917
Miscellaneous	Battalion Orders by Lieut-Colonel V.B. Ramsden, M.C., Commanding 15th Bn. Highland Light Infantry.	15/10/1917	15/10/1917
Miscellaneous	Battalion Orders by Lieut-Colonel V.B. Ramsden, M.C., Commanding 15th Bn. Highland Light Infantry.	16/10/1917	16/10/1917
Miscellaneous	Battalion Orders by Lieut-Colonel V.B. Ramsden, M.C., Commanding 15th Bn. Highland Light Infantry.	17/10/1917	17/10/1917
Miscellaneous	Battalion Orders by Lieut-Colonel V.B. Ramsden, M.C., Commanding 15th Bn. Highland Light Infantry.	18/10/1917	18/10/1917

Miscellaneous	Battalion Orders by Lieut-Colonel V.B. Ramsden, M.C., Commanding 15th Bn. Highland Light Infantry.	19/10/1917	19/10/1917
Miscellaneous	Battalion Orders by Lieut-Colonel V.B. Ramsden, M.C., Commanding 15th Bn. Highland Light Infantry.	20/10/1917	20/10/1917
Miscellaneous	Battalion Orders by Lieut-Colonel V.B. Ramsden, M.C., Commanding 15th Bn. Highland Light Infantry.	21/10/1917	21/10/1917
Miscellaneous	Battalion Orders by Lieut-Colonel V.B. Ramsden, M.C., Commanding 15th Bn. Highland Light Infantry.	22/10/1917	22/10/1917
Miscellaneous	Battalion Orders by Lieut-Colonel V.B. Ramsden, M.C., Commanding 15th Bn. Highland Light Infantry.	24/10/1917	24/10/1917
Miscellaneous	Battalion Orders by Lieut-Colonel V.B. Ramsden, M.C., Commanding 15th Bn. Highland Light Infantry.	15/10/1917	15/10/1917
Miscellaneous	Battalion Orders by Lieut-Colonel V.B. Ramsden, M.C., Commanding 15th Bn. Highland Light Infantry.	27/10/1917	27/10/1917
Miscellaneous	Battalion Orders by Lieut-Colonel V.B. Ramsden, M.C., Commanding 15th Bn. Highland Light Infantry.	28/10/1917	28/10/1917
Miscellaneous	Battalion Orders by Lieut-Colonel V.B. Ramsden, M.C., Commanding 15th Bn. Highland Light Infantry.	29/10/1917	29/10/1917
Miscellaneous	Battalion Orders by Lieut-Colonel V.B. Ramsden, M.C., Commanding 15th Bn. Highland Light Infantry.	30/10/1917	30/10/1917
Miscellaneous	Battalion Orders by Lieut-Colonel V.B. Ramsden, M.C., Commanding 15th Bn. Highland Light Infantry.	31/10/1917	31/10/1917
War Diary	Rubrouck	01/11/1917	11/11/1917
War Diary	Oudezeele	12/11/1917	12/11/1917
War Diary	Poperinghe	13/11/1917	16/11/1917
War Diary	Poperinghe Area	17/11/1917	24/11/1917
War Diary	Irish Farm	25/11/1917	25/11/1917
War Diary	Bellvue Support	26/11/1917	30/11/1917
Miscellaneous	Battalion Orders by, Lieut-Colonel V.B. Ramsden, M.C., Commanding 15th Bn. Highland Light Infantry	02/11/1917	02/11/1917
Miscellaneous	Battalion Orders by, Lieut-Colonel V.B. Ramsden, M.C., Commanding 15th Bn. Highland Light Infantry	03/11/1917	03/11/1917
Miscellaneous	Notice		
Miscellaneous	Battalion Orders by Lieut-Colonel V.B. Ramsden, M.C., Commanding 15th Bn. Highland Light Infantry	04/11/1917	04/11/1917
Miscellaneous	Battalion Orders by Lieut-Colonel V.B. Ramsden, M.C., Commanding 15th Bn. Highland Light Infantry	05/11/1917	05/11/1917
Miscellaneous	Battalion Orders by Lieut-Colonel V.B. Ramsden, M.C., Commanding 15th Bn. Highland Light Infantry	06/11/1917	06/11/1917
Miscellaneous	15th Bn The Highland Light Infantry.	07/11/1917	07/11/1917
Miscellaneous	Battalion Orders by Lieut-Colonel V.B. Ramsden, M.C., Commanding 15th Bn. Highland Light Infantry	07/11/1917	07/11/1917
Miscellaneous	Battalion Orders by Lieut-Colonel V.B. Ramsden, M.C., Commanding 15th Bn. Highland Light Infantry	08/11/1917	08/11/1917
Miscellaneous	Battalion Orders by Lieut-Colonel V.B. Ramsden, M.C., Commanding 15th Bn. Highland Light Infantry	09/11/1917	09/11/1917
Miscellaneous	Battalion Orders by Lieut-Colonel V.B. Ramsden, M.C., Commanding 15th Bn. Highland Light Infantry	10/11/1917	10/11/1917
Miscellaneous	Battalion Orders by Lieut-Colonel V.B. Ramsden, M.C., Commanding 15th Bn. Highland Light Infantry	13/11/1917	13/11/1917
Miscellaneous	Battalion Orders by Lieut-Colonel V.B. Ramsden, M.C., Commanding 15th Bn. Highland Light Infantry	17/11/1917	17/11/1917
Miscellaneous	Battalion Orders by Lieut-Colonel V.B. Ramsden, M.C., Commanding 15th Bn. Highland Light Infantry	18/11/1917	18/11/1917
Miscellaneous	Battalion Orders by Lieut-Colonel V.B. Ramsden, M.C., Commanding 15th Bn. Highland Light Infantry	22/11/1917	22/11/1917

Miscellaneous			
Miscellaneous	All Companies And R.S.M		
Miscellaneous	Battalion Orders by Lieut-Colonel V.B. Ramsden, M.C., Commanding 15th Bn. Highland Light Infantry.	23/11/1917	23/11/1917
Miscellaneous			
War Diary	Bellevue	01/12/1917	06/12/1917
War Diary	Hill Top Farm	07/12/1917	08/12/1917
War Diary	Seige Farm	09/12/1917	13/12/1917
War Diary	Irish Farm	14/12/1917	23/12/1917
War Diary	Hill Top Farm	24/12/1917	27/12/1917
Miscellaneous	Operation Order Capture Of Pill Box V. 28.b.0.8	29/12/1917	29/12/1917
War Diary	Hubner (In The Line)	27/12/1917	31/12/1917
War Diary	Irish Farm	01/01/1918	01/01/1918
War Diary	La Panne	02/01/1918	22/01/1918
War Diary	Dirty Bucket Camp	23/01/1918	30/01/1918
War Diary	Emile Camp	30/01/1918	31/01/1918
Miscellaneous	Battalion Strength		
Miscellaneous	Battalion Orders by Lieut-Colonel V.B. Ramsden, M.C., Commanding 15th Bn. The Highland Light Infantry. App III	02/01/1918	02/01/1918
Operation(al) Order(s)	15th Bn. The Highland Light Infantry. Operation Order No. 182		
Miscellaneous	15th Bn. The Highland Light Infantry Appendix I	12/01/1918	12/01/1918
Miscellaneous	15th Bn. The Highland Light Infantry.	14/01/1918	14/01/1918
Miscellaneous	15th Bn. The Highland Light Infantry.	15/01/1918	15/01/1918
Miscellaneous	15th Bn. The Highland Light Infantry.	16/01/1918	16/01/1918
Miscellaneous	15th Bn. The Highland Light Infantry.	18/01/1918	18/01/1918
Miscellaneous			
Miscellaneous	15th Bn. The Highland Light Infantry. Training Programme For Wednesday 23rd January 1918		
Miscellaneous	15th Bn. The Highland Light Infantry. Training Programme For Thursday	24/01/1917	24/01/1917
Miscellaneous	15th Bn. The Highland Light Infantry.	25/01/1918	25/01/1918
Miscellaneous	15th Bn. The Highland Light Infantry.	26/01/1918	26/01/1918
Miscellaneous	15th Bn. The Highland Light Infantry.	28/01/1918	28/01/1918
Miscellaneous	15th Bn. The Highland Light Infantry.	29/01/1918	29/01/1918
Operation(al) Order(s)	15th Bn. The Highland Light Infantry. Operation Order No. P.1. Appendix II		
Operation(al) Order(s)	General Instructions In Conjuction With Operation Order No. P.1		
Miscellaneous	Special Idea For Tactical Scheme Without Troops And Operation Order No. P.1		
Operation(al) Order(s)	15th Bn. The Highland Light Infantry Operation Order No. 181		
War Diary	Emile Camp	01/02/1918	01/02/1918
War Diary	Het Sas (Reserve)	02/02/1918	04/02/1918
War Diary	Baboon Camp	05/02/1918	05/02/1918
War Diary	Het Sas (Right Sect)	07/02/1918	08/02/1918
War Diary	Baboon Camp	09/02/1918	10/02/1918
War Diary	La Bergerie Camp	11/02/1918	19/02/1918
War Diary	Let Sas	20/02/1918	20/02/1918
War Diary	Het Sas (Support)	21/02/1918	23/02/1918
War Diary	Reserve	24/02/1918	24/02/1918
War Diary	Het Sas (Reserve)	25/02/1918	27/02/1918
Miscellaneous	Het Sas Sector Support	28/02/1918	28/02/1918
War Diary		28/02/1918	28/02/1918

Operation(al) Order(s)	15th Battalion The Highland Light Infantry. Operation Order 188 Appendix I	09/02/1918	09/02/1918
Miscellaneous	15th Battalion The Highland Light Infantry. Appendix 2	13/02/1918	13/02/1918
Miscellaneous	15th Battalion The Highland Light Infantry. Appendix 3	14/02/1918	14/02/1918
Miscellaneous	15th Battalion The Highland Light Infantry. Appendix 4	15/02/1918	15/02/1918
Miscellaneous	15th Battalion The Highland Light Infantry. Appendix 6	16/02/1918	16/02/1918
Miscellaneous	15th Battalion The Highland Light Infantry. Appendix 5	16/02/1918	16/02/1918
Operation(al) Order(s)	Operation Order No. 1 Issued by Major ? Commanding 15th Battalion The Highland Light Infantry. Appendix 7	17/02/1918	17/02/1918
Miscellaneous			
Operation(al) Order(s)	Operation Order No. 5. by Lieut-Colonel V.B. Ramsden, M.C. Commanding 15th Bn. The Highland Light Infantry Appendix II		
Operation(al) Order(s)	Operation Order No. 4. by Lieut-Colonel V.B. Ramsden, M.C., Commanding 15th Bn. The Highland Light Infantry. Appendix D		
Operation(al) Order(s)	15th Battalion The Highland Light Infantry. Operation Order No. 2	23/02/1918	23/02/1918
Miscellaneous	Operation Orders issued by Lieut. Col. V.B. Ramsden, M.C., Commanding 15th Battalion The Highland Light Infantry. Appendix 9	25/02/1918	25/02/1918
Miscellaneous	War Diary		
Miscellaneous	Operation Order To Attack Pill Box V28.Goo.8		
Miscellaneous	Acknowledge		
Heading	15th Battalion The Highland Light Infantry March 1918		
War Diary	Het Sas Sector Front Hill	01/03/1918	04/03/1918
War Diary	Het Sas Sector Support	05/03/1918	11/03/1918
War Diary	Het Sas Sector Right Front Hill	13/03/1918	13/03/1918
War Diary	Het Sas Sector Brigade in Reserve.	14/03/1918	16/03/1918
War Diary	Baboon Camp	17/03/1918	21/03/1918
War Diary	Bosinghe Sector Front Line	22/03/1918	24/03/1918
War Diary	Bosinghe Sector Reserve	25/03/1918	27/03/1918
War Diary	Seige Camp	28/03/1918	29/03/1918
War Diary	Manin	30/03/1918	30/03/1918
War Diary	Haute-Ville	31/03/1918	31/03/1918
War Diary	Purple Line Monchy Sector	31/03/1918	31/03/1918
Miscellaneous	Appendices		
Operation(al) Order(s)	Operation Orders 6. by Lieut-Colonel V.B. Ramsden, M.C. Commanding 15th Bn. The Highland Light Infantry Appendix 1		
Miscellaneous	Table A2 Appendix 1a		
Operation(al) Order(s)	Operation Order No. 11. by Lieut-Colonel V.B. Ramsden, M.C, Commanding 15th Bn. The Highland Light Infantry. Appendix 2	20/03/1918	20/03/1918
Miscellaneous	Administrative Instruction to Accompany Operation Order No. 11 Appendix 2a		
Miscellaneous	Amendment To Operation Orders No. 11 Appendix 2b	21/03/1918	21/03/1918
Operation(al) Order(s)	Operation Orders No. 13 by Lieut Colonel V.B. Ramsden, M.C. Commanding 15th Battalion The Highland Light Infantry.		
Operation(al) Order(s)	Operation Order No. 14. by Lieut-Colonel V.B. Ramsden, M.C, Commanding the 15th Bn. The Highland Light Infantry. Appendix 4	27/03/1918	27/03/1918
Miscellaneous	Table "A" Appendix 4a		

Operation(al) Order(s)	Operation Order No. 15. by Lieut-Colonel V.B. Ramsden, M.C., Commanding 15th Bn. The Highland Light Infantry.	30/03/1918	30/03/1918
Heading	15th Battn. The Highland Light Infantry April 1918		
War Diary	Adinfer Wood	01/04/1918	01/04/1918
War Diary	Douchy	02/04/1918	05/04/1918
War Diary	Purple Line F 8a Coy	05/04/1918	09/04/1918
War Diary	Front Line Right Sub-Sector Hqrs F9a84	10/04/1918	20/04/1918
War Diary	Purple Line F8A O Y	21/04/1918	24/04/1918
War Diary	Saulty	25/04/1918	30/04/1918
Miscellaneous			
Miscellaneous	Appendices 1 To 10		
Operation(al) Order(s)	Operation Order No. 16 by Lt Colonel V.B. Ramsden, M.C. Comdg The 15th Batt Light L.I.	01/04/1915	01/04/1915
Operation(al) Order(s)	Operation Order No. 17 by Lt Colonel V.B. Ramsden, M.C. Comdg The 15th Batt High L.I.	02/04/1918	02/04/1918
Miscellaneous	Addendum to Operation Order No. 17		
Miscellaneous	The Following Code Will be Used		
Operation(al) Order(s)	Operation Order No. 18 by Lt/Col V.B. Ramsden, M.C., Commanding 15th Bn.The Highland Light Inf.		
Miscellaneous	Report On Operation Carried Out By The 15th Batt H.L.I. On Night Of 2nd/3rd April 1918	03/04/1918	03/04/1918
Miscellaneous	Officer Commanding 15th H.L.I.	08/04/1918	08/04/1918
Miscellaneous	Capture Of Ayette By 14th Infantry Brigade On Night 2/3rd April 1918	04/04/1918	04/04/1918
Miscellaneous	VI Corps G.S. 29/4	13/04/1918	13/04/1918
Miscellaneous	VI Corps G.S. 29/6	17/04/1918	17/04/1918
Miscellaneous			
Miscellaneous	To Plump	08/04/1918	08/04/1918
Miscellaneous			
Miscellaneous	From O/C B Coy		
Miscellaneous	Plump		
Miscellaneous			
Miscellaneous	To Plump	03/04/1918	03/04/1918
Miscellaneous	A Form. Messages And Signals.	03/04/1918	03/04/1918
Miscellaneous	C Form. Messages And Signals.	03/04/1918	03/04/1918
Operation(al) Order(s)	Operation Order No. 19 by Lt/Colonel V.B. Ramsden, M.C. Comdg The 15th Batt H.L.I.	04/04/1918	04/04/1918
Operation(al) Order(s)	Operation Order No. 20 by Lt/Colonel V.B. Ramsden, M.C. Comdg The 15th Batt H.L.I.		
Operation(al) Order(s)	Operation Order No. 21 by Lt/Colonel V.B. Ramsden, M.C. Comdg 15th Bn High L.I.		
Miscellaneous	1st Dorset Regt Relief Orders.	19/04/1918	19/04/1918
Operation(al) Order(s)	Operation Order No. 22 by Major G.M. Cleghorn D.S.O. Commanding 15th Battn Light L.I.		
Miscellaneous	Appendix A		
Miscellaneous	Preliminary Orders.		
War Diary	Saulty	01/05/1918	10/05/1918
War Diary	Map Refe Boisleux	11/05/1918	13/05/1918
War Diary	Front Line	14/05/1918	30/05/1918
Miscellaneous	Purple Reserve	31/05/1918	31/05/1918
Miscellaneous	(2)		
Operation(al) Order(s)	Operation Order No. 25. by Lieut. Colonel V.B. Ramsden, D.S.O. M.C. Commanding 15th Battn The Highland L.I.	18/05/1918	18/05/1918

Operation(al) Order(s)	Operation Order No. 26. by Lieut. Colonel V.B. Ramsden, D.S.O. M.C. Commanding 15th Bn The High L.I.		
Operation(al) Order(s)	Operation Order No. 27. by Lieut. Colonel V.B. Ramsden, D.S.O. M.C. Commanding 15th Battn The Highland Light Infantry.	30/05/1918	30/05/1918
War Diary	Front Line	06/05/1918	12/05/1918
War Diary	Purple Reserve	13/05/1918	16/05/1918
War Diary	Front Line	17/05/1918	25/05/1918
War Diary	Purple Line	26/05/1918	30/05/1918
Miscellaneous			
Operation(al) Order(s)	Operation Order No. 30 by Major G.M. Cleghorn D.S.O. Commanding 15th Bn. High L.I.	11/06/1918	11/06/1918
Operation(al) Order(s)	Operation Order No. 31 by Major G.M. Cleghorn D.S.O. Commanding 15th Bn. Highland Light Infantry	16/06/1918	16/06/1918
Operation(al) Order(s)	Operation Order No. 23 by Lieut-Colonel V.B. Ramsden, DSO. MC. Commanding 15th Bn. The Highland Light Infantry.	10/05/1918	10/05/1918
Miscellaneous	Appendix 1		
Miscellaneous	Report On Lighting Patrol Of The 15th H.L.I. On Light Of 23rd/24th Inst		
Miscellaneous	15th Battalion The Highland Light Infantry Amendment To O.O. No. 33	22/06/1918	22/06/1918
Operation(al) Order(s)	15th Battalion The Highland Light Infantry Addendum To Operation Order No. 33	24/06/1918	24/06/1918
Operation(al) Order(s)	15th Battalion Highland Light Infantry Operation Order No 33		
Operation(al) Order(s)	15th Bn The Highland Light Infantry Operation Order No. 32	19/06/1918	19/06/1918
Operation(al) Order(s)	Operation Order No. 29 by Major W. White M.C. Commanding 15th Bn High L.I.		
Miscellaneous	Report On Fighting Patrol Of The 15th H.L.I. On Night Of 23rd/24th Inst.	24/06/1918	24/06/1918
Miscellaneous	To 32nd Div	24/06/1918	24/06/1918
Miscellaneous	M		
Miscellaneous	Report On Lighting Patrol The 15th H.L.I. On Night Of 23rd/24th Mist		
Miscellaneous			
Operation(al) Order(s)	Operation Order No. 34 By Major G.M. Cleghorn D.S.O. Commanding 15th Bn High L.I.		
Miscellaneous	Headquarters. VI Corps.	25/06/1918	25/06/1918
Miscellaneous		24/06/1918	24/06/1918
Miscellaneous	Report In Raw		
Operation(al) Order(s)	15th Bn. The Highland Light Infantry Operation Order No. 38	06/08/1918	06/08/1918
Miscellaneous			
Miscellaneous	Messages And Signals.		
Miscellaneous			
Operation(al) Order(s)	Operation Order No. 42 By Major G.M. Cleghorn D.S.O. Commanding 15th Batt High L.I. App V		
Operation(al) Order(s)	Operation Order No. 41 Major G.M. Cleghorn D.S.O. Commanding 15th Battalion Highland Light Infantry. App IV		
Operation(al) Order(s)	15th Bn. The Highland Light Infantry Operation Order No. 40. App III	17/08/1918	17/08/1918
War Diary	Purple Line	01/07/1918	05/07/1918

War Diary	Saulty	06/07/1918	18/07/1918
War Diary	Bambecque	19/07/1918	31/07/1918
Miscellaneous			
Operation(al) Order(s)	Operation Order No. 55. By Major G.M. Cleghorn D.S.O. Commanding 15th Bn High L.I.		
Miscellaneous			
Operation(al) Order(s)	Operation Order No. 37 by Lieut-Colonel V.B. Ramsden, D.S.O. M.C., Commanding 15th Bn. Highland Light Infantry.		
Miscellaneous	Table "A"		
Map			
Map	Redan		
Map	K.11. M.23		
War Diary	Bambecque	01/08/1918	07/08/1918
War Diary	Gentelles	08/08/1918	08/08/1918
War Diary	Beaucourt	09/08/1918	09/08/1918
War Diary	Bouchoir	10/08/1918	11/08/1918
War Diary	Bouchoir Folies Beaucourt	12/08/1918	12/08/1918
War Diary	Beaucourt Domart	13/08/1918	13/08/1918
War Diary	Domart	14/08/1918	17/08/1918
War Diary	Domart Harbonnieres	18/08/1918	18/08/1918
War Diary	Harbonnieres	19/08/1918	28/08/1918
War Diary	Deniecourt	29/08/1918	29/08/1918
War Diary	Villers Carbonnel	30/08/1918	30/08/1918
Miscellaneous			
Miscellaneous	Table "A" To Accompany 15th Bn. H.L.I. Operation Order No. 38		
War Diary	Barleux	05/09/1918	08/09/1918
War Diary	Barleux Somme	08/09/1918	08/09/1918
War Diary	Brie Area	08/09/1918	08/09/1918
War Diary	Brie Area	06/09/1918	06/09/1918
War Diary	Bouvincourt	07/09/1918	07/09/1918
War Diary	Tertree	08/09/1918	11/09/1918
War Diary	Trefcon	12/09/1918	14/09/1918
War Diary	Bussy-Les-Daours	15/09/1918	17/09/1918
War Diary	Athies	18/09/1918	23/09/1918
War Diary	Larris Wood	24/09/1918	28/09/1918
War Diary	Cooker Quarry	29/09/1918	30/09/1918
Miscellaneous			
Operation(al) Order(s)	15th Bn. The Highland Light Infantry Operation Order No. 42. App I	16/09/1918	16/09/1918
Miscellaneous			
Operation(al) Order(s)	15th Bn. The Highland Light Infantry Operation Order No. 43 App II		
Miscellaneous	Narrative Of Events From 29th September 1918 To 6th October 1918 App III		
War Diary	Le Tronquoy	01/10/1918	01/10/1918
War Diary	Sequehart	02/10/1918	03/10/1918
War Diary	Liahcourt	04/10/1918	04/10/1918
War Diary	Vendelles	05/10/1918	05/10/1918
War Diary	Bouvincourt	06/10/1918	17/10/1918
War Diary	Bellenglise	18/10/1918	19/10/1918
War Diary	Bohain	20/10/1918	29/10/1918
War Diary	St Souplet	30/10/1918	30/10/1918
War Diary	Le Quenoplet	31/10/1918	31/10/1918
Miscellaneous			

Operation(al) Order(s)	The 15th Bn. Highland Light Infantry. Operation Order No. 15A. Appendix IV		
Miscellaneous	Training Programme For Thursday Appendix I	01/11/1917	01/11/1917
Miscellaneous	Training Programme For Saturday 3rd November 1917		
Miscellaneous	15th Bn.The Highland Light Infantry. Appendix II	05/11/1917	05/11/1917
Miscellaneous	15th Bn. The Highland Light Infantry.	06/11/1917	06/11/1917
Miscellaneous	15th Bn.The Highland Light Infantry.	08/11/1917	08/11/1917
Miscellaneous	15th Bn The Highland Light Infantry.	09/11/1917	09/11/1917
Operation(al) Order(s)	15th Bn. The Highland Right Infantry. Operation Order No. 16A Appendix III		
Operation(al) Order(s)	The 15th Bn. Highland Light Infantry. Operation Order No. 15A. Appendix V		
Miscellaneous	Duplicate Copy		
Miscellaneous			
Diagram etc			
War Diary	Le Quenellet Farm	01/11/1918	03/11/1918
War Diary	Ors	04/11/1918	04/11/1918
War Diary	East Of Ors	05/11/1918	05/11/1918
War Diary	Favril	06/11/1918	06/11/1918
War Diary	La Basse Haroilles	07/11/1918	07/11/1918
War Diary	Le Foyaux	08/11/1918	09/11/1918
War Diary	Avesnelles	10/11/1918	13/11/1918
War Diary	Sains Du Nord	14/11/1918	19/11/1918
War Diary	Sivry	20/11/1918	20/11/1918
War Diary	Froidchapelle	21/11/1918	24/11/1918
War Diary	Daussois	25/11/1918	30/11/1918
Miscellaneous			
Operation(al) Order(s)	Operation Order No. 48. App I	06/11/1918	06/11/1918
Operation(al) Order(s)	15th Bn.The Highland Light Infantry Operation Order No. 50 App 2		
Miscellaneous	Operation Order by Lieut Col. V.B. Ramsden, DSO. MC. Commanding 15th Battalion The Highland Light Infantry. Appx 3	12/11/1918	12/11/1918
Operation(al) Order(s)	Battalion Operation Order No. 1 App No 4	17/11/1918	17/11/1918
Miscellaneous	15th Battalion The Highland Infantry. App No. 5		
Operation(al) Order(s)	15th H.L.I. Battalion Operation Order No. 2 App No 6	19/11/1918	19/11/1918
Miscellaneous	15th Battalion The Highland Light Infantry App No.44		
War Diary	Daussois	01/12/1918	12/12/1918
War Diary	Biesmeree	18/12/1918	18/12/1918
War Diary	Denee	14/12/1918	18/12/1918
War Diary	Godinne	19/12/1918	31/12/1918
War Diary	Godinne	25/12/1918	31/12/1918
Miscellaneous			
Miscellaneous	Battalion Orders by Lieut-Colonel V.B. Ramsden, M.C. Commanding 15th. Bn. Highland Light Infantry Appendix VI	01/11/1917	01/11/1917
Operation(al) Order(s)	Battalion Operation Order No. 5 App 2	12/12/1918	12/12/1918
Operation(al) Order(s)	Battalion Operation Order No. 6	17/12/1918	17/12/1918
Operation(al) Order(s)	Battalion Operation Order No. 4	11/12/1918	11/12/1918
Diagram etc			
Heading	15th Bn High'd Lt Infy Jan-May 1919		
War Diary	Godinne	01/01/1919	28/01/1919
War Diary	Nameche Germany	29/12/1918	30/12/1918
War Diary	Bonn Germany	31/01/1919	31/01/1919
Operation(al) Order(s)	15th Bn The Highland Light Infantry Operation Order No. 7		

War Diary	Beuel Germany	01/02/1918	26/02/1918
War Diary	Solingen Germany	27/02/1918	28/02/1918
Operation(al) Order(s)	15th Battalion The Highland Light Infantry Operation Order No. 8		
Miscellaneous	Special Order Of The Day	24/02/1918	24/02/1918
War Diary	Solingen Germany	01/03/1919	22/03/1919
War Diary	Solingen	23/03/1919	31/03/1919

24.0
55 sheets

14/33

On His Majesty's Service.

SECRET.

SECRET.

D.G.

G.H.Q.

3rd Echelon

637

Original

Instructions regarding War Diaries and Intelligence Summaries are contained in F. S. Regs., Part II. and the Staff Manual respectively. Title pages will be prepared in manuscript.

WAR DIARY
or
~~INTELLIGENCE~~ SUMMARY.

(Erase heading not required.)

Army Form C. 2118.

HEADQUARTERS G206/2 -2 NOV 1917 [illegible]th INFANTRY BRIGADE

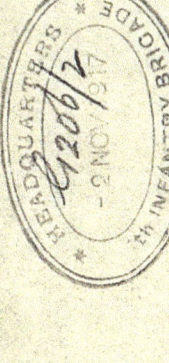

Place	Date 1917	Hour	Summary of Events and Information	Remarks and references to Appendices
WULPEN	OCTOBER 1		Battalion in Reserve. In Billets. There was again slight shelling of the billets in the early hours of the morning; no damage was caused and no casualties suffered. At night the battalion was engaged on working parties in the line. Weather bright and fine.	
	2.		Battalion in Reserve. In Billets: The day was quiet in Reserve and at night the battalion was as usual engaged on working parties. There was no shelling of the billets during the night. Weather bright and clear. 2/LT. C. L. TIMONY returned from Leave.	
	3		Battalion in Reserve. In Billets. At 4 P.M. the battalion left WULPEN to proceed to the line to relieve 1st DORSET REGT. in ST GEORGES Right subsector; the battalion marched by Companies in the following order D, A, B, C, Headquarters, platoons at 200 yards interval. A and D companies took over the front line positions; A on the right in NEGRO TRENCH and HASTY TRENCH to its junction with NORA SAP; D on the left in NORA SAP and ~~[illegible]~~ NICE ALLEY to its junction with NICE AVENUE; B company in Support, C company in Reserve both companies in dug outs in NIEUPORT - BRUGES ROAD. There was little shelling and relief was complete by 10.20 P.M. The day was overcast and the long spell of good weather shews signs of breaking. 2/LT W. L. G[illegible]DING while acting as Bombing Instructor at the Corps Reinforcement Camp was wounded in a bombing accident. 2/LT W. M. RITCHIE proceeded on leave.	APPENDIX 1 Do. 2 Do 3.

A5834 Wt. W4973/M687 750,000 8/16 D. D. & L. Ltd. Forms/C.2118/13.

Army Form C. 2118.

Instructions regarding War Diaries and Intelligence Summaries are contained in F. S. Regs., Part II. and the Staff Manual respectively. Title pages will be prepared in manuscript.

WAR DIARY
or
~~INTELLIGENCE SUMMARY~~.
(*Erase heading not required.*)

Place	Date 1917	Hour	Summary of Events and Information	Remarks and references to Appendices
ST GEORGES	October 4	X.	Battalion in the line. The day was uneventful and there was little activity on either side. The Reserve Company (C Company) on the completion of work for the night moved into Brigade Reserve in GROOT LABOUR FARM. The weather was wet with a strong blustery wind. 2/LT SAWERS returned from convalescence and 2/LTS RODGER and McCAIG reported for duty.	
	5.		Battalion in the line. At 12.10 A.M. the enemy successfully raided one of our posts - NORA POST - and took three prisoners; 4 O.R. were also wounded. A fourth man who was taken prisoner succeeded in eluding his captors and jumping into the canal swam back to our lines. 1 German was killed. It was established that the raid had been made by a party from a MATROSEN REGT. The remainder of the day passed quietly although there was some sharp shelling of the right company front between 5.30 P.m and 7 P.m. Retaliation was asked for and received. The advance party of the relieving Brigade arrived at 10 P.m. The weather was unsettled with heavy showers.	
	6.		Battalion in the line. The day was quiet. The battalion was relieved by the 9th Bn MANCHESTER REGT at 11.55 P.m.; subsequently companies marched independently to billets at COXYDE where all were in by 2 A.m. (Greenwich Time) The weather was wet and cold. SUMMER TIME ceased at midnight. COL. RAMSDEN returned from leave.	APPENDIX 4.
COXYDE	7.		The Battalion left COXYDE at 11.15 A.m. and proceeded by road to ADINKERKE a halt being made near there for dinners. The battalion then embarged and proceeded by canal as far as ROSENDAEL which was reached at 8.50 P.m; thence by road.	

A5834 Wt. W4973/M687 750,000 8/16 D. D. & L. Ltd. Forms/C.2118/13.

Army Form C. 2118.

Instructions regarding War Diaries and Intelligence Summaries are contained in F. S. Regs., Part II. and the Staff Manual respectively. Title pages will be prepared in manuscript.

WAR DIARY

or

~~INTELLIGENCE SUMMARY.~~

(Erase heading not required.)

Place	Date 1917	Hour	Summary of Events and Information	Remarks and references to Appendices
COXYDE	October 7.		via Dunkirk to PETIT SYNTHE which was reached at 10.30 P.m. The weather was bad there being a heavy rainstorm and a high wind and conditions were very trying. On the way 2/Lt McBain rescued a man who had fallen into the canal 2/Lts THOMSON and HODGE rejoined from courses.	
PETITE SYNTHE	8"		Battalion in billets. The days was spent cleaning up. Weather was unpropitious, the sky being overcast, heavy rain fell in the afternoon and evening.	
"	9"		Battalion in billets Training according to programme. Weather. Cold + showery.	
"	10"		Battalion in billets. Training according to programme. Weather. cold - showery.	appendix 5.
"	11"		Battalion in billets. Training according to programme. Weather cold. dry. 2/LIEUT E.L. WOOD rejoined from 257 TUNNELLING Coy.	
"	12"		Battalion in billets Training according to programme Weather fine	
"	13"		Battalion in billets. Training according to programme Weather fine	
"	14"		Battalion in billets Training according to programme Weather showery. cold	

Instructions regarding War Diaries and Intelligence Summaries are contained in F. S. Regs., Part II. and the Staff Manual respectively. Title pages will be prepared in manuscript.

WAR DIARY
or
INTELLIGENCE SUMMARY.
(Erase heading not required.)

Army Form C. 2118.

Place	Date	Hour	Summary of Events and Information	Remarks and references to Appendices
Petite Synthe	1917 October 15		Battn resting. In billets. Weather fair. Bn witnessed an instructive Gas Demonstration in the morning, training as per programme followed. Officers & NCOs lectured on Anti-Gas measures in the evening by Div. Gas Officer.	
do	16th		Battn resting. In billets. Weather fair between showers. The day was spent bathing at Zuydcoote, Bn proceeded there by double trips in barges, in the morning, returning in the afternoon. Training programme cancelled.	
do	17th		Bn resting. In billets. Heavy rain in the morning clearing up in the afternoon, Training as per programme. Officers & NCOs lectured in the evening, on the Attack, by Brigade Major. Capt G.A.R. McCay the M.O. & 2nd Lt Cain, proceeded on leave to England.	
do	18th		Bn resting. In billets. Weather fair between showers, heavy rain about 4:30 pm. Training as per programme in the morning, dinner in the field, carried out Attack Scheme in the afternoon with contact aeroplane & M.G. support, Night operations postponed owing to inclement weather. Enemy air raid in vicinity of billets about 8 pm. Capt. Davies left for duty with 4th Army Musketry School. 2nd Lt Pitcher returned from leave.	

A5834 Wt. W4973 M687 750,000 8/16 D. D. & L. Ltd. Forms/C.2118/13.

Instructions regarding War Diaries and Intelligence Summaries are contained in F. S. Regs., Part II. and the Staff Manual respectively. Title pages will be prepared in manuscript.

WAR DIARY
or
INTELLIGENCE SUMMARY.
(Erase heading not required.)

Army Form C. 2118.

Place	Date	Hour	Summary of Events and Information	Remarks and references to Appendices
	1917. October			
Petite Synthe	19th		Bath resting. In billets. Weather fair. Training as per programme in the morning. A night assembly in gas masks was practised in the evening. Lt H. Brown left for duty with Base Paymaster. 2nd Lt. Gooding returned from Hospital.	
do	20th		Bn. resting. In billets. Weather fair. Training per programme in the morning. Football match against the 3rd Manchester Regt. in the afternoon – Result, 15th HLI 3 – Manchesters 0. Air raid about 7.30 pm, no casualties.	
do	21st		Bn. resting. In billets. Weather fair. Church Parade at 11.30 am. Enemy air raid at night, bombs dropped in vicinity of billets – no casualties.	
do.	22nd		Bn. resting. In billets. Weather fair. Training. Bn. attack through strong points under Brigade arrangements. Other programme cancelled. 2nd Lt D. Pryde proceeded to B.F. course at St. Pol. 2nd Lt Gooding to Hospital, sick.	
do.	23rd		Bn resting. In billets. Very wet in the morning, clearing about mid-day. Bn practised an assembly from shell hole positions in the early morning, and attacked at dawn. Heavy rain fell throughout.	

A5834 Wt. W4973/M687 750,000 8/16 D. D. & L. Ltd. Forms/C.2118/13.

Instructions regarding War Diaries and Intelligence Summaries are contained in F. S. Regs., Part II. and the Staff Manual respectively. Title pages will be prepared in manuscript.

WAR DIARY
or
INTELLIGENCE SUMMARY.
(Erase heading not required.)

Army Form C. 2118.

Place	Date	Hour	Summary of Events and Information	Remarks and references to Appendices
Petite Synthe	1917. October. 24th		Battn resting. In billets. Weather fair. Inspection of clothing and equipment by Comdg Officer in the morning. Billeting party left on cycles for Chapelle St Laurent. 2nd Lt Pitchie left for 2nd Corps School of Instruction.	
do	25th		Battn marched to billets in Chapelle St Laurent reaching there about 1.30pm. Motor transport was provided for packs. Weather fair.	
Chapelle St Laurent	26th		Battn marched to billets in Rubrouck area. Ref sheet 27. B+H. Billets very scattered but accomodation fairly good. Weather showery.	
Rubrouck.	27th		Bn resting. In billets. Weather fair. Inspection of feet + equipment, followed by Gas drill under Coy arrangements. 2nd Lt Gooding returned from Hospital. 2nd Lt Hepburn returned from Lewis Gun course at Le Touquet. 2nd Lt Harrison proceeded to 18th Corps L.G. course.	
do	28th		Bn. resting. In billets – weather fair between showers – ~~[illegible]~~ Two companies were bathed at Arneke, other training cancelled. 2nd Lt Sawers left the Bn. on ~~attachment~~ to R. F. C.	
do	29th		Bn resting. In billets. Weather showery. Practised an attack scheme in the morning, and a night assembly in Gas masks in the evening.	

Instructions regarding War Diaries and Intelligence Summaries are contained in F. S. Regs., Part II. and the Staff Manual respectively. Title pages will be prepared in manuscript.

WAR DIARY
or
INTELLIGENCE SUMMARY.
(Erase heading not required.)

Army Form C. 2118.

Place	Date 1917.	Hour	Summary of Events and Information	Remarks and references to Appendices
Rubrouck.	October 30th.		Battn. resting – in billets – weather showery – proceeded to training area to carry out a scheme of attack. Owing to inclement weather we returned to billets early.	
do.	31st.		Bn resting – in billets – weather fair – practised attack scheme on training area in the morning – Night operations were cancelled – The Comdg Officer held a tactical exercise with all officers & selected NCOs in the afternoon. Capt. W.A.R. McCay the M.O. returned from leave.	

Army Form C. 2118.

Instructions regarding War Diaries and Intelligence Summaries are contained in F. S. Regs., Part II. and the Staff Manual respectively. Title pages will be prepared in manuscript.

WAR DIARY
or
INTELLIGENCE SUMMARY.
(Erase heading not required.)

Place	Date 1917	Hour	Summary of Events and Information	Remarks and references to Appendices
Rubrouck	October 31st			

	1st October	31st October
Commanding Officer's Strength	748	863

Fighting Strength.	1st October	31st October
Officers.	35	37.
O.R.	938	987

Casualties. - Total for month.	Officers	O.R.
	2	21.

W. Ramsden Lieut. Col.
Comdg 15th (Service) Bn
The Highland Light Infantry

A5834 Wt. W4973/M687 750,000 8/16 D. D. & L. Ltd. Forms/C.2118/13.

SECRET. APPENDIX 1. 1

Operations

Copy No. 8

S C U D.
RELIEF ORDERS.

- - - - - - - - - - - - - -

1. The Battalion will relieve SKIN in the right SUB Sector, ST GEORGES SECTOR on the night of 3rd/4th October.

2. D. Coy. SCUD will relieve B. Coy. SKIN on the left.
A. " " " " C. Coy. " " " right.
B. Coy. " " " D. Coy. " in support.
C. Coy. " " " A. Coy. " in Brigade Reserve.

3. Completion of relief will be reported to Battalion Headquarters in code as follows:-
RELIEF COMPLETE.................HOME.
MUCH SHELLING...................YOUR.
LITTLE SHELLING.................FATHER.

4. All trench stores, maps, defence schemes, etc. will be taken over and receipts in duplicate forwarded to Battalion Headquarters. Special care will be exercised in taking over details of all anti-gas arrangements.

5. The two A.A. Positions at present held by A. Coy. will be relieved this afternoon by teams from SKIN. A.A. positions in the line will be taken over by companies on relief.

6. The Battalion will march to the trenches by companies in the following order:- D. Coy., A. Coy., B. Coy., C. Coy. & Battalion Headquarters. Starting Point...Battalion H.Q. D. Coy. will pass starting point at 7 p.m.. 200 yds. interval between platoons will be maintained throughout the march. Route:- From Battalion Headquarters by main road to S 8 b 2.3 - S 9 a 25.65 - S 9 a 9 9 - RAMSCAPELLE ROAD to S 10 b 45.25 - S 11 a 9.9.

7. GUIDES:- Guides 1 per Coy. H.Q's. & 1 per Platoon will be at MAISON BLANCHE at 8.30 p.m.

8. Limbers for Lewis Guns, ammunition, Mess Stores, Signalling Equipment & Orderly Room Boxes will be at X 17 a 9 8 - WULPEN BRIDGE at 6.30 p.m. All stores will be at the BRIDGE ready to be loaded up at 6.30 p.m. Route for limbers:- NIEUPORT ROAD - S 3 c 65.25 - RAMSCAPELLE - MAISON BLANCHE.

9. All billets in WULPEN must be left scrupulously clean. C.O. will inspect billets, beginning with B. Co. at 5 p.m.

10. Limbers to take Officers Valises to Q.M. Stores will be at WULPEN BRIDGE at 5 p.m. ALL VALISES must be across the bridge by 5 p.m.

11. Work will be started immediately after relief.

12. ACKNOWLEDGE.

[signature]
Lieut. & A/Adjt.,
S C U D.

3/10/17.

Copy No. 1 C.O.
" " 2 SCAM
" " 3-6 O.s.C. Coys.
" " 7 SKIN.
" " 8 Adj.
" " 9 Q.M.
" " 10 T.O.
Copy No. 11 R.S.M.
" " 12 FILE.
" " 13 War Diary.
" " 14 2/Lt. W.S.O'MAY.

APPENDIX 2.
APPENDIX ~~Ind~~ 2.

War Diary

S K I E. Copy No. 2.

RELIEF ORDERS.

1. SKIE will be relieved in the right Subsector by SCUD on night of 3/4th October, 1917.

2. On relief, Companies will withdraw independently to Divisional Reserve at WULPEN.

3. ROUTE. ST. GEORGE - RAMSCAPELLE ROAD - S.11.a.9.9. - S.10.b.45.25. RAMSCAPELLE ROAD - S.9.a.9.9. - S.9.a.55.55. - S.8.b.2.8. - main Road to WULPEN.

4. Completion of Relief will be reported to Battalion H.Q. in code as follows:-

Relief complete....... STAYNER.
Much Shelling......... ALDERMAN.
Little Shelling....... BALL.

5. As much work as possible will be carried on before Relief.

6. Great care will be paid to the handing over of all Trench Stores, information about the line, Maps, Details re work, receipts being obtained for same and sent to Battalion Headquarters.

7. O.C. Coys will see that Trenches and Dug Outs are left scrupulously clean.

8. Gas Helmets will be worn in Gas Alert position at WULPEN and O.C. Coys will post a sufficient number of Gas Sentries, 2/Lieut RICHARDS arranging Battalion Headquarters.

9. GUIDES. (a) Details re which Companies of SCUD are relieving ours and Guides are required for SCUD will be issued later.
When (b) Q.M. will arrange for Guides for Battalion Headquarters and Companies ~~will~~ to be at entrance to WULPEN on main WULPEN - NIEUPORT Road.

10. Sgt WARNER will arrange for all Cooking Pots and Dixies to be ready for loading on Limber at Cookhouse at 7.0.p.m.

11. R.S.M. will arrange for Hot Food Containers to be brought to Battalion Headquarters for handing over.

12. L/Cpl WILLIS and Coy Gas N.C.O's will hand over all Gas Stores etc obtaining receipts for same.

13. Q.M. will issue his own orders re taking over Billets, moving, Officers Valises etc, to WULPEN.

14. (a) T.O. will arrange for Limbers to be at Cookhouse for Cooking Pots and Officers Trench Kits at 8.0.p.m.
(b) Officers Mess Stores at Cookhouse at 9.0.p.m.
(c) Limbers for Lewis Guns and Signalling Equipment to be at HOGGE BRIDGE at 9.0.p.m.
(d) Officers Chargers to be on RAMSCAPELLE Road at S.9.a.9.9. at 10. 0. p.m.
(e) C.O. 2nd i/c and Adjutant's Chargers as arranged verbally

(contd)

15. On arrival at FULNEN an Officer will be on the Telephone night and day as Battalion will be at 1 Hours notice to move. Officers for Telephone duty as below:-

2/Lieut WILKINS	10.0.p.m.	to	2.0.a.m.	4/5th Oct.	
2/Lieut R.E.C.GOFF.	2.0.a.m.	to	6.0.a.m.	5th	"
Lieut R.S.FAULKNER.	6.0.a.m.	to	10.0.a.m.	5th	"
2/Lieut W.H.DAVIES.	10.0.a.m.	to	2.0.p.m.	5th	"
2/Lieut H.C.BELL.	2.0.p.m.	to	6.0.p.m.	5th	"
Lieut J.H.WATSON.	6.0.p.m.	to	10.0.p.m.	5th	"
Lieut D.E.PLATT.	10.0.p.m.	to	2.0.a.m.	5/6th	"
2/Lieut E.C.V.YOUNG.	2.0.a.m.	to	6.0.a.m.	6th	"
2/Lieut A.G. BIRKS.	6.0.a.m.	to	10.0.a;m;	6th	"
2/Lieut W.H. CHAMBERLAIN.	10.0.a.m.	to	2.0.p.m.	6th	"
2/Lieut F.E. PELGRIFT.	2.0.p.m.	to	6.0.p.m.	6th	"
2/Lieut A.R. FENTON.	6.0.p.m.	to	10.0.p.m.	6th	"
2/Lieut J.H.V. HAINSONE.	10.0.p.m.	to	2.0.a.m.	6/7th	"
2/Lieut H.A. FORD.	2.0.a.m.	to	6.0.a.m.	7th	"
2/Lieut W.V. RICHARDS.	6.0.a;m;	to	10.0.a.m.	7th	"
2/Lieut H.S. WOOD.	10.0.a.m.	to	2.0.p.m.	7th	"
2/Lieut R.E.H. EXHARDON.	2.0.p.m.	to	6.0.p.m.	7th	"

16. A C K N O W L E D G E.

Captain,
Adjutant SKIN.

3. 10. 17.

Copy No. 1.	C.O.		Copy No. 10.	2/Lieut W.V.RICHARDS.
" " 2.	COMD.		" No. 11.	R.S.M.
" " 3.	2nd.i/c SKIN.		" No. 12.	Sgt JANAWAY.
" " 4.	Adjutant, SKIN.		" No. 13.	Q.M.
" " 5 to 8.	O.C. Coys, SKIN.		" No. 14.	T.O.
" " 9	2/Lieut H.A.FORD.		" No. 15.	FILE.

A P P E N D I X "A"

"A" Company will find the three A.A. positions. Details etc as to positions and taking over will be issued later; These Teams should be told off. The Officer Commanding "A" Coy will ensure that only men who know how to use the A.A. Sight be put on these Posts.

Instruction should be given these men as to the marking on the Aeroplanes and how they may distinguish hostile aircraft.

SECRET

APPENDIX 3.

DEFENCE SCHEME
RIGHT BATTALION ST. GEORGES SECTOR.

Ref. SECRET TRENCH MAP Nº 5. 1/10,000
SHEETS 12.S.W. } 11.S.E. } 1/20.000

1/ The Battalion is holding a front extending along the line of the RIVER YSER (NICE ALLEY) from M.30.d.8.1 NAMELESS House – VERTESQUE FARM – DORIS POST – NORA POST – NASTY TRENCH – NASTY SAP – NEGRO POST – NEGRO TRENCH to the BEVER DIJK CANAL at T.1.a.75.95.

2/ MAINLINE The main line of resistance is the front line trench NICE ALLEY – DORIS POST – NORA POST – NASTY TR. – NEGRO TR. This line must be held at all costs.

3/ DISTRIBUTION The Battalion front is held by two Companies. The LEFT Coy. holds NICE ALLEY – DORIS POST – NORA POST to junction of NASTY TR. —— The RIGHT Coy. holds NASTY TR – NASTY SAP – NEGRO TR. and the posts in front of that trench. Nº 3 Coy (less 2 sections on posts) is in Battn. Reserve in shelters in NASTY AVENUE at M.36.a.2.3.
Nº 4 Coy is in Brigade Reserve at GROOTE LABOUR FARM 37.a.95.80.

4/ METHOD OF HOLDING

RIGHT Coy.
H.Q. in NEGRO TR. at N.31.d.20.65.
3 Platoons in NEGRO TR – NEGRO SWITCH. + NASTY TR. to N.31.b.38.57.
and NIGGER POST
PAULINE "
NEGRO "
NASTY "
1 Platoon in NEGRO WALK.

LEFT Coy
H.Q. in NASTY AVENUE at M.36.b.35.60.
1 Platoon in NASTY TR. + NORA POST.
2 " on N. BANK of YSER Canal in NICE ALLEY from DORIS POST to M.30.d.50.17.
1 Platoon in NASTY WALK

SUPPORT Coy
H.Q in NASTY AVENUE at M.36.a.1.3.
2 Platoons (less undermentioned liaison posts) in dugouts along BRUGES ROAD about M.35.b.9.3.
LIAISON. POSTS at HOOGE BRIDGE about M.35.d.50.35
KETTELERSDAM BRIDGE at M.36.d.75.70.
H.Q. Belgian Battalion at about S.5.c.6.5.

RESERVE Coy (IN BRIGADE RESERVE)
H.Q. ~~Groote Labour Farm~~ ~~[illegible]~~. WHITE HOUSE.

5/ ACTION IN CASE OF ENEMY RAID. (1) ~~[illegible]~~ In the event of enemy raiding parties gaining possession of any portion of our front line trench, the garrison of the next line in rear – (less a few posts left to hold the line) will at once counter-attack – without further orders and drive back the raiders while bombing parties on the flanks of trenches occupied will immediately commence bombing attacks against the raiders flanks.

5/ continued
(2) The saps & advanced posts are held by rifle sections and they are covered by rifle grenade sections at the trench end of sap in the case of the RIGHT Coy. & half way up the saps in the LEFT Coy. & Lewis Gun section situated in the trench & on a flank.
(3) In the event of an alarm RIFLE GRENADE Sections will barrage NO MANS LAND in front of his posts, & continue until ordered to cease. Bombing Parties will immediately move up the saps - If enemy are encountered - will attack & drive them out.

6/ ACTION IN CASE OF HOSTILE ATTACK ON LARGE SCALE
(1) The front line Coys will hold their ground to the last, all points being defended whether the flanks are turned or not.
(2) Troops will not fall back from any post or line to any other line under any circumstances.
(3) Coy Commanders on flanks of the enemy will at once communicate by every means possible with Battalion Headquarters stating how much of our line the enemy is occupying & his estimated strength.
(4) By night all men working in the front line will hold this line if attacked.

7/ BATTLE & NIGHT STATIONS
1 Platoon from NEGRO WALK moves to NEGRO SWITCH
1 " " NASTY " reinforces the garrison in NICE ALLEY.
Support Coys (less 2 sections) from M.35.b.9.3. will move to NASTY & NEGRO WALKS.
The 2 Platoons of Support Coys in NASTY WALK will come under orders of O.C. LEFT Coy who will be responsible for establishing blocks in NASTY WALK & the trench running along Southern bank of Canal - UP & DOWN TRENCH.
The 2 Platoons in NEGRO WALK will be under command of O.C. Support Coy. who will be responsible for establishing a block at junction of track in the neighbourhood of KETTELERSDAM BRIDGE.
Coys in Brigade Reserve at GROOTE LABOUR FARM — STANDS TO - and awaits orders to move.

8/ MACHINE GUNS
The Battalion front is covered by 4 Guns of the 11th Machine Gun Coy. Their position & S.O.S. lines are as shewn on special map attached.

9/ TRENCH MORTARS.
There are 4 3" Stokes Mortars and 3 6" Mortars in the Battalion Sector.
Their positions are as shewn on special map attached

10/ ANTI-AIR-CRAFT
Two Machine Guns are detailed for anti aircraft duties. Their position are as shewn on map
Three Lewis Guns Sections are detailed for similar duties by day. They fire from positions at M.30.d.65.10. & M.31.a.40.99. & M.31.b.5.8.

11/ NEIGHBOURING TROOPS.
A Belgian Battalion is on the right. Their nearest post join our line at BEVER DIJK CANAL at T.1.a.60.95.
Their Battn. H.Qrs. is at S.6.a.90.00.
No 2 (LEFT) Battalion of the Brigade is on our left
The point of junction is in NICE ALLEY at M.30.a.8.1.

11/ Continued

: They also hold POLDER FARM and ROODE POORT FARM by night. Their RIGHT Coy Headquarters is in NICE ALLEY at M.30.d.3.3.
Their Battalion Headquarters is at the SARDINERIE M.34.b.77.90.

COMMUNICATION & LIAISON

12/. LIAISON 1 N.C.O + 2 men are attached to the H.Qrs of the Right Battalion (Belgian)
A Belgian Liaison Officer is attached to Battalion Headquarters.
COMMUNICATION Communication is by telephone
The left Company has one forward station in NORA SAP about M.31.b.8.7. and one at Coy. H.Qrs. communicating with Battalion Headquarters.
The RIGHT Coy has a station at Coy H.Qrs connected with Battn. H.Qrs. + Battn H.Qrs is connected with the Headquarters of both the right (Belgian) + left Battalion H.Qrs.
The Battalion H.Qrs is connected with Brigade H.Qrs by four lines. by Wireless + by pigeons.

13/ S.O.S. The S.O.S. is variation "B" rifle grenade bursting into two red + two green lights. One man at each Coy H.Qrs. + one man in each Coy front line will be permanently detailed by day + night to give the S.O.S. signal.

14/ aid POST The Aid-Post is near Battn H.Qrs. on the BRUGES ROAD at about M.36.a. central.

15/ LOCATION OF 14th INF. Bde. The 14th Inf. Bde. H.Qrs. are at VILLA JULIET. X 4.a.4.7.

16/ ACKNOWLEDGE

R M Grant
Lieut
a/Adjt. for Major
Commanding 15/H.L.I.

APPENDIX 4.

SECRET. SCUD COPY No 10

OPERATION ORDERS:- No 12A

1 The Battalion will be relieved by the 9th Manchester Regiment in the right sub-sector RIGHT (St GEORGES) Sector on the night 6/7th October.

2. A. Coy SCUD will be relieved by C Coy 9th MANCHESTER
B . . do . B . do
C . . do . A . do
D . . do . D . do

3 All Defence Schemes, Information about the line details of patrols, work in progress, aeroplane photographs Trench Dumps and Stores, fixed rifle rests, Grenade Stores, A.A. Gun Mountings etc will be handed over and receipts obtained. Two copies will be forwarded to Battn Hdqrs forthwith.

Special care will be excercised in handing over details of all ANTI-GAS arrangements. AA pivot mountings will not be handed over but will be brought out of the line on relief

4. Advance parties consisting of 1. OFFICER per Battn Hdqrs, 1. officer per Coy & 1 N.C.O. per platoon will report at Battn Hdqrs at 10 P.M. on Oct 5th.

5.(a) Guides for the incoming Battalion will be as follows:-

1 per platoon, 1. per Coy Hdqrs & 1 per Batt HQrs to be at BRIDGE HOUSE (M 35. d 45. 30) at 8. 30 PM. They must not stand about on the road, but will wait behind house S.W. of BRIDGE.

They will report to 2/Lt. PATON at Battn HQrs at 7-45 PM

(B) The route for incoming Battalions (9th & 10th Manchesters) is via WULPEN BRIDGE - S. 8. b. 2.3 - S. 9. a. 3.6. - S. 9. a. 9.9 - RAMSCAPPELLE ROAD to S. 10 b. 45. 35. - Track to S. 11. a. 9.9. thence up main road Two guides (from Battn Hdqrs) will be at S. 10. b 45. 35. to ensure that incoming platoons do not miss the turning

They will remain there until all incoming platoons of both Manchester Battalions have passed.

As much use as possible will be made of track running from M 35 d 55. 65 to M 36. a. 23

All guides must know this track.

6. The following personel will be left behind for 24 hours after relief:-

1. OFFICER per Coy
1 OR per platoon
1 Runner per Coy HQrs
2 Runners per Battn Hdqrs.

7. Completion of Relief will be reported to Battn HQrs in code as follows:-

RELIEF COMPLETE	VERY
MUCH SHELLING	GOOD
LITTLE SHELLING	SIR.

8. On relief Companies will march independently to Billets in COXYDE_ ROUTE - RAMSCAPELLE ROAD S.11.a.99.- S.10.b.45.35.- S.9.a.99.- S.8.b.2.3.- WULPEN - COXYDE - 200 yards interval will be maintained between platoons and strict march discipline will be ~~maintained~~ observed.
9. Billeting parties consisting of CAPT HERBERT and all CQM Sergeants will report to STAFF CAPTAIN at TOWN MAJORS Office COXYDE at 10 AM. Oct 6th
10. Limbers for Lewis Guns, Mess Stores, Signalling Stores etc will be at WHITE HOUSE at 11 PM.
11. OFFICERS Chargers to be at S.9.a.99 at 12 midnight
12. Hot meals will be served on arrival in Billets
13. On 7th Oct. - Battalion will proceed to Billets in LAPANNE_ Starting Point ROAD opposite CANADA CAMP_ TIME 2. PM.

    Details will be issued later.
14. Billeting parties 2/Lieut PATON. 1. N.C.O. per Coy will report to STAFF CAPTAIN at AREA COMMANDANTS Office LAPANNE at 9-30 AM on 7th inst.
15. ACKNOWLEDGE.

Copies to

1. C.O
2. Adjt
3. SCAN
4. 7 Coys
8. T.O.
9. Q.M.
10. 2/Lt O'may
11. 2/Lt Paton
12. RSM
13. FILE
14. WAR. DIARY.

[signature]
Lieut &
Adjt.
SCUD

6/10/17.

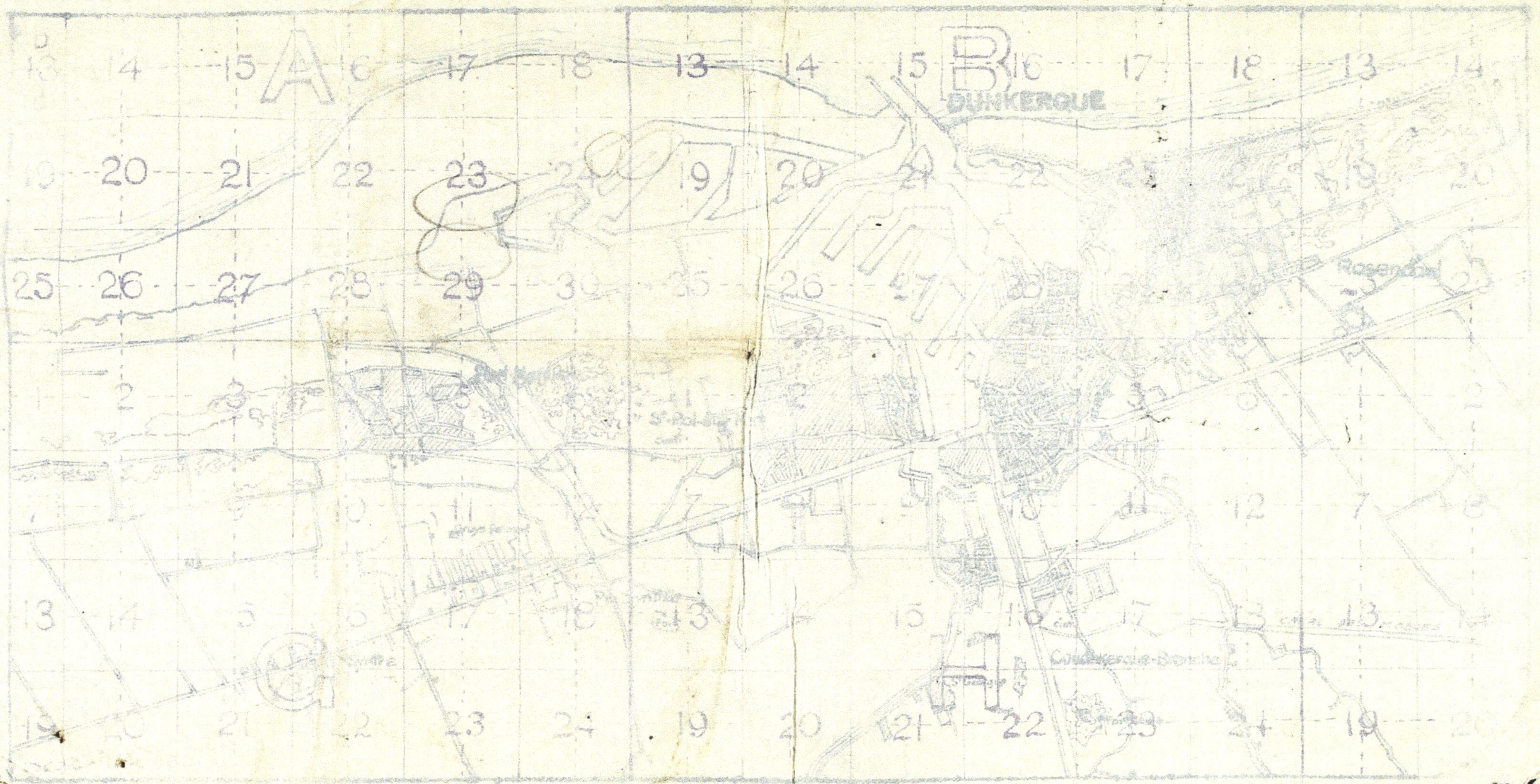
A
B
DUNKERQUE
Rosendaël

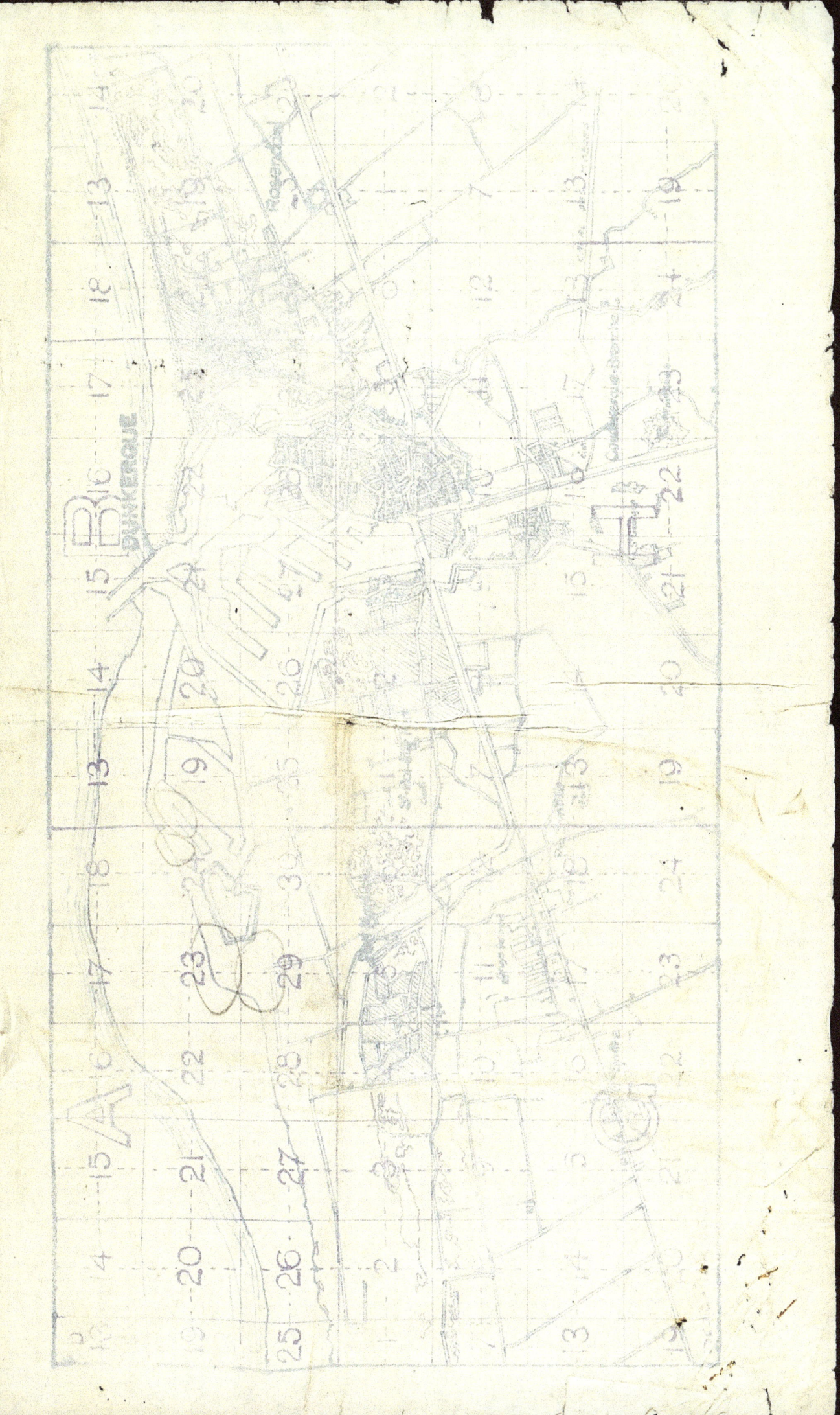

APPENDIX 5.

[illegible] 10th [illegible] 1917

COY.	TIME	[illegible]	TRAINING	[illegible]	REMARKS.
All Coys & [illegible]	7/ 7-30 am.	10 Off & 900 OR.	P. T.	Billets.	
All Coys	9-30 10 am	6 Off 300 OR.	Saluting drill		
" "	10-10 11 am		Musketry	[illegible]	Under 2nd L/C.
" "	11-30 12 noon		Gas instruction and Lecture. Lecture on Gas by O. C. Coys.		
	12-12-30		Coy drill & Saluting parade.		
C. Coy.	9-11 am	4 Off 100 OR.	Inspection by O. C.		
	11-12-30.		Gas instruction by Sgt., R. C. O.	Vicinity of Billets.	
D. Coy.	9-11 am	4 Off 150 OR	Gas Instruction by Sgt., R. C. [illegible]		
	11am 12- 4 pm		Inspection by O. C.		

Special Classes.

a/ [illegible] under [illegible] at present with Battn.

b/ [illegible].

(1).
A & B Coy [illegible] to parade under orders of [illegible] for training.

(2).
A class of 6 men per coy under 2nd Lieut., [illegible] (who have not been trained previously) to assemble at Battn Hd Qr. at [illegible].
[illegible] will select instructors for this.

[signature] Lieut. [illegible]
for Lieut-Colonel.
Comm'dg. [illegible]

15th. H. L. I. TRAINING PROGRAMME FOR 11th OCT.1917.

COYS	TIME	NOS ON PARADE	NATURE OF TRAINING	LOCALITY	REMARKS.
All Coys.	7am 7-30.	16 Off 700 O.R.	P. T.	Billets.	
A.	9-15 12-45.	4 Off. 160 O. R.	Musketry.	Range.	Coy S. M. to A. Coy only.
B. C. & D.	9-15 10-15.	4 Off 540 O. R.	Coy extended order drill.		~~[illegible]~~.
	10-30 11-15.		Musketry. Rapid Loading, Fire Control, Indication & Recog., of targets by unit Commanders	Training area.	
	11-30 12 noon.		Specialist Section Training.		
	12-5. 12-30.		Close Order Drill.		
All Off & N.C.O's	5-15.	27 Off 100 N.C.O's	Lecture. 'The Attack'.		

SIGNAL. CLASSES. A. & B. as for Wednesday.

R. M. Grant Lieut. 5/Bn.
for Lieut- Colonol.
Comm'dg. 15th Battn. High. L. I.

16th H. L. I. TRAINING PROGRAMME FOR 12th OCTOBER 1917

[illegible] ON [illegible]

COYS.	TIME.	PARADE.	TRAINING.	LOCALITY.	REMARKS.
All Coys.	7am 7-30.	15 Off. 700 O.R.	P.T. or B.F.	Billets.	O.C. [illegible] GREY to B.Coy.
All Coys	9-45 11am.		Demonstration in attack on strong points by "B" Coy. Remainder to [illegible] as spectators.		
A.C.D. Coys.	11-15 12-30.	14 Off. 500 O.R.	platoons in practice attack on strong points.	"	-do-
B. Coy.	11-12.3	Off & 150 O.R.	Musketry.		
All Off & N. C. O.s	5-15.	37 Off & 150 N.C.O.s.	Lecture. Employment of Lewis Guns in the attack.		

[illegible] Classes. A.C.S.

R M [illegible] Lieut & A/Adj

for Lieut-Colonel.
Comm'dg. 18th Battn. High. L. I.

Rumford Lieut. Maj.

TRAINING PROGRAMME for Monday 15th October 1917.

15/H.L.I.	Time.	Nos on parade.	Nature of training	Locality	Remarks.
All Cos. & Hdqrs.	6.[illegible] - 7.10 a.m.	4 Off. 780 O.R.	P.T. & B.F.	Billets	Stf.Sgt. to "A" Coy.
Battn. (including all classes & as many Transport Sect. as available)	Morning	26 Off. 780 O.R.	Gas demonstration Co. & Bn. Drill for remainder of time.	G.6.d.	
All Officers & N.C.Os.	[illegible].15 p.m.	26 Off. 110 N.C.Os.	Lecture by Divl. Gas Officer.		

Regimental Classes:-

(a) SIGNALLERS:-
A & B Classes 32 9 - 1 p.m.
under S.O.

(b) LEWIS GUNNERS:-
6 per Co. under 2Lt. [illegible]
9 - 1 p.m.

(c) N.C.Os.
12 N.C.Os for Advd. Course
P.T. & B.F. under Stf.Sgt.
Gray 9 - 1 p.m.

(d) SUBALTERN OFFICERS
Communication & Saluting
Parades 7 - 7.30 a.m.

NOTES.

(1) All classes will attend
Gas demonstration.

(2) Box Respirators & P.H.
Helmets will be worn by
all ranks for Gas demonstration.

(3) Above (2) also applies for Lecture
walking out dress.

Lieut-Colonel,
Commanding 15th Bn. High. L. I.

TRAINING PROGRAMME FOR TUESDAY 16th October 1917.

16/H.L.I.	Time.	Nos on parade.	Nature of Training	Locality	Remarks.
All Coys. & Hdqrs.	6.45 - 7.15 a.m.	4 Off. 757 O.R.	P.T. & B.F.	Billets	Att. Sgt. Gray to "D" Coy.
A Coy.	9 - 12.45 p.m.	4 Off. 170 O.R.	Musketry	Range Area	
B.C.D. Cos.	9.30 - 10.30 a.m.	14 Off. 520 O.R.	Cos. forming up for "Trench to Trench Attack" (32nd Divl. Standard Pattern) and practising same.	A 29 a & b and 23 c & d	
	10.30 - 12		Cos. debouching from "Close Assembly Formation" into same open Warfare attack formation.		
	12.15 - 12.45		Musketry and Gas Drill or Repetition of above		
All Officers & N.C.Os.	5.30 - 6.30 p.m.	26 Off. 110 N.C.Os	Lecture "The Attack"		

Regimental Classes:-

A, B, C, & D.

Note

All trained Lewis Gunners to Fire on Beach.
Limbers to take all Guns and Ammunition.

Lieut-Colonel,
Commanding 16th Bn. High. L. I.

TRAINING PROGRAMME for WEDNESDAY 17th October 1917.

15/H.L.I.	Time.	Nos on parade.	Nature of training	Locality	Remarks.
All Cos. & Hdqrs.	6.45 - 7.15 a.m.	4 Off. 750 O.R.	P.T. & B.F.	Billets	Stf. Sgt. Gray to "C" Co.
"B" Co.	9 - 12.45 p.m.	4 Off. 170 O.R.	Musketry	Range	
"A,C,D" Cos.	9.30 - 11 a.m.	14 Off. 580 O.R.	Practice attack on Strong Points by Coys.	A 29 a & b and 23 c & d	
	11.20 - 12.30		Platoon & Co. Training of:- (a) Specialist sections (b) Rapid wiring squads * (under R.E. supervision)		

Regimental Classes:-

A,B,C,D.

*Limbers to take out material.

Lieut-Colonel,
Commanding 15th Bn. High. L. I.

[illegible] Programme for Thursday 18th October 1917.

13/R.W.F.	Time.	Nos on parade.	Nature of training.	Locality	Remarks.
All Coys. & Hdqrs.	6.45 – 7.45 a.m.	4 Off. 750 O.R.	P.T. & B.F.	Billets	[illegible] Sgt. [illegible] to "[illegible]" Coy.
"C" Coy.	9 – 12.45 p.m.	4 Off. 170 O.R.	[illegible]	Range	
"A, B, Coys. + D 60	11 – 12 noon	14 Off. 520 O.R.	Platoon [illegible]. (a) Specialist sects. [illegible] (b) [illegible] firing squads under [illegible] supervision		
	12.15 – 1.15 p.m.		[illegible] handling arms and Close Order Drill		
All Officers	12.15 – 1.15 p.m.	20 Off.	Instruction in Compass (a) for day and (b) setting for night		
	Dinners on Area				
All Coys. & Classes	2.45 – 4.45 p.m.	20 Off. 750 O.R.	Bn. in attack on position organised in depth		
	Teas on Area				
Bn.	6 – 10 p.m.	20 Off. 750 O.R.	NIGHT [illegible]. 1st Phase. Platoon Commanders lead platoons on a compass bearing to position of assembly to represent night relief prior to dawn attack. 2nd Phase. [illegible] up in depth in [illegible] trench to trench attack [illegible] formation [illegible] will be sent later. 3rd Phase. Coy. led by [illegible] on compass bearing to a second rendezvous. March home	[illegible] [illegible] not yet [illegible]	Suppers in barracks.

Regimental [illegible].
(a) [illegible]
(b) Billets
(c) Billets till 12 noon
(d)

[illegible]
[illegible]

[illegible]

Date & Serial.	Time.	Nos on parade.	Nature of training	Locality & Remarks
[illegible]	[illegible] - 12.45 p.m.	[illegible] off. 170 O.R.	[illegible]	[illegible]
[illegible]	10 - 11 a.m.	[illegible] off. [illegible] O.R.	[illegible] (a) Specialist sect. [illegible] (b) [illegible] in firing [illegible] [illegible]	
	11.15 - 12.15 p.m.		Company Training. (a) [illegible] order drill (b) [illegible] drill	
11 Officers [illegible]		[illegible] off. 180 O.R.	[illegible] (a) Criticism of previous days operations (b) Lecture by Capt. [illegible] on "Results of his visit to Compen(?) School"	

Regimental Boards.

N.I.L.(?)

[illegible] Lieut-Colonel,
Commanding 1/5th [illegible]

__Training Programme for Saturday [illegible] October 1917.__

15/H.L.I.	Time	Nos on parade.	Nature of Training	Locality	Remarks.
All Cos. & Hdqrs.	6.45 - 7.45 am	4 Off. 750 O.R.	P.T. or B.F.	Billets	Stf.Sgt. Gray as wanted.
"A"	9-10 am		C. Os. Inspection		All classes will attend parade Cos. to be drawn up in New Organisation Formation.
"B"	10-11 am	16 Off. 750 O.R.	In F. S. M. O.	Billets	
"C"	11-12		(Inspection will include all service stores)		
"D"	12- 1				

__Remaining Hours.__

¾ hr. Musketry
¾ " Specialist Sect. Training
¾ " Arms and Close Order Drill.

Lieut-Colonel,
Commanding 15th Bn. High. L. I.

War Diary

TRAINING PROGRAMME for Monday 22nd October 1917.

16/H.L.I.	Time.	Nos. on parade.	Nature of Training	Locality	Remarks.
All Coys. & Hdqrs.	6.45 – 7.15am	16 Off. 740 O.R.	P.T.	Billets	
"D" Co.	9-1 pm	4 Off. 165 O.R.	Musketry	Range	Lewis Gunners Observers Trgn. Traing. of Gunne
"A", "B" & "C" Cos.	11-12pm	12 Off. 495 O.R.	Specialist Sect. Train.	Train. Area.	
	12-15 – 1 p.m.		Practice Coy. attacks on Strong Points.		
	1.30 – 2.30 pm.				Dinners
Bn.	3-5 pm.	20 Off. 740 O.R.	Batt. attack on a position organised in depth.	G.6.d.	Contact to be arranged. Packs to be carried.
	5.30pm.				Teas in same position.
	8 p.m.		Practice forming up on tape line from shell hole positions.		(In Gas Helmets

[signature]
2/Lieut.,
A/Adjt. 16th Bn. High. L. I.

TRAINING PROGRAMME for Tuesday 23rd October 1917.

15/H.L.I.	Time	Nos on parade.	Nature of Training	Locality	Remarks.
Bn.	10-2pm	20 Off. 740 O.R.	Route March. Practice deploying from column of Route.		F.S.M.O.
All Off. & N.C.Os.	5.30pm	20 Off. 118 N.C.Os	Lecture.		

[illegible]
2/Lieut.,
A/Adjt. 15th Bn. High L. I.

TRAINING PROGRAMME for Wednesday 24th October 1917.

15/H.L.I.	Time	Nos on parade.	Nature of Training	Locality	Remarks.
Bn.	6.45 - 7.15am	20 Off. 750 O.R.	P.T.	Billets.	
XXXXXX.	XXXXXX	XXXX. XXXXXXX.	XXXXXXXX	XXXXXX	
"A" "B" &"C" Cos "D"	10-11	12 Off. 498 O.R.	Platoon Specialist Trg. Musketry. Intensive Digging. Bombers. Rifle Grenadiers & Lewis Gunners Co-operating. Bayonet Fighting.	Area.	Beach.
	11-20 - 12.20 pm.		Bn. Close Order Drill under R.S.M.		
All Off. & Senior NCOs		20 Off. & 30 Sen. NCOs.	Tactical Exercise without troops.		Writing of messages etc.

[illegible] 2/Lieut.,
for A/Adjt. 15th Bn. High. L. I.
for O. C.

TRAINING PROGRAMME for Thursday 25th October 1917.

15/H.L.I.	Time	Nos on parade.	Nature of Training	Locality	Remarks.
Bn.	6.45 - 7.45am	20 Off. 740 O.R.	P.T.	Billets	All Lewis Gunners on Range.
Bn.	10-11.30 a.m.	"	Coy. Training. Coys. in attack of Strong Points.	Area	
Bn.	11.50 - 12.30 pm.	"	Ceremonial	Area	

Jas. D. Rae
2/Lieut.,
for A/Adjt. 15th Bn. High. L. I.
for O.C.

TRAINING PROGRAMME for Friday 26th October 1917.

15/H.L.I.	Time	Nos on parade.	Nature of Training	Locality	Remarks.
Bn.	6.45 - 7.15 am	20 Off. 740 O.R.	P.T.	Billets	
Bn.	10-12.30 p.m.	"	**Movements in Bn:-** Movements from Close Assembly into Artillery Formations. Open warfare attack Practice, on an enemy in position.	Area.	All Lewis Gunners. Firing on Range.
All Off. & NCOs.	5.30 p.m.	20 Off. & 115 NCOs.	Lecture.		

[illegible] 2/Lieut.,
for A/Adjt. 15th Bn. High. L.I.
for O.C.

TRAINING PROGRAMME for Saturday 27th October 1917.

15/H.L.I.	Time	Nos on parade	Nature of Training	Locality	Remarks.
Bn.	6.45 - 7.15am.	20 Off. 740 O.R.	P.T.	Billets	
"A"	9-10am		C. Os. Inspection		All classes will. attend parade.
"B"	10-11am	16 Off. 750 O.R.	in F. S. M. O.	Billets	Cos. to be drawn up in New Organ-isation
"C"	11-12 noon 12-1 pm.		(inspection will include all service stores)		Formation.

Remaining hours.

¾ hr. Musketry
¾ hr. Specialist Sect. Training.
¾ hr Arms and Close Order Drill.

[illegible] 2/Lieut.,
for A/Adjt. 15th Bn. High L. I.
for O.C.

TRAINING PROGRAMME for Monday 29th October 1917.

Cos.	Time.	Nos on parade.	Nature of Training	Locality	Remarks.
All Cos. & Hdqrs.	6.45 - 7.15 am.	22 Off. 700 O.R.	B.F.	Billets.	
All Coys.	9-10 am.		Musketry	Billets.	
	10.10 - 11.		March to Area		
	11.15 - 1.pm.		Co. & Platoon Training. Coys. in attack on Strong Points.	Area	
All Coys.	7 pm.		(i) March from Billets to an Assembly Point on Area. (ii) From Assembly Point march in Gas Helmets into taped lines and form up for attack.	H.5.	

R M Grant Capt. & Adj.
for Lieut-Colonel,
Commanding 15th Bn. High. L. I.

TRAINING PROGRAMME for Tuesday 30th October 1917.

Coys.	Time	Nos on parade.	Nature of Training	Locality	Remarks.
All Coys. & Hdqrs.	6.45 - 7.15 am.	22 Off. 700 O.R.	B.F.	Billets.	
All Coys.	9.15- 10.15 am.		Coys. forming up in various attack formations.		
	10.15 - 10.45 am.		Lecture by Coy. Commanders to their Coys. on the attack.		
	11. - 12.15 pm.		2 Coys. in attack on Strong Points. 2½ Coys. to act as enemy remaining ½ Coys. to spectate & criticize.	Area	
	12.15 - 1.30 pm.		Vice Versa.		

R M Grant Captn. & Adjt.
for Lieut-Colonel,
Commanding 15th Bn. High. L. I.

TRAINING PROGRAMME for Wednesday 31st October 1917.

Coys.	Time.	Nos on parade.	Nature of Training	Locality	Remarks.
All Coys. & Hdqrs.	6.45 - 7.15 am.	22 Off. 700 O.R.	B.F.	Billets.	
All Coys.	9.15 - 10.15 am.		Platoon Specialist Training.	Area	
	10.15 - 10.45 am.		Gas Drill	"	
Bn.	10.45 - 1 pm.		Bn. in attack practice. 2 Coys. to "Leap frog".		
Bn.	7 pm.		(i) 2 Coys. to relieve 2 Coys. in shell hole positions. (ii) The whole to form up on taped line in Gas Helmets.	Area	

R M Grant Captn. & Adjt.
for Lieut-Colonel,
Commanding 15th Bn. High. L. I.

Batt'n. Orders. October

Battalion Orders
by Lieut-Colonel V.B. RAMSDEN, M.C.,
Commanding, 15th. Bn. Highland Light Infantry.
11th. October 1917.

---

1. Reveille .... 6 .15 a.m.
Breakfast .... 7. 45 a.m.
Sick Parade .... 8. 15 a.m.
C.O's Orderly Room .... 2. 30 p.m.
Co. on duty .... "C" Co.
Orderly Officer .... 2/Lieut. HODGE.

2. Training will be carried out as per programme issued herewith.

3. Religious Service. Rev. D. HIRSCH Jewish Chaplain, Hd. Qrs. 4th. Army will hold a special Service for JEWS at the Synagogue, Rue De Chateau 30, DUNKIRK on Friday evening 12th. inst. at 5.30 p.m. All ranks wishing to attend will parade at Orderly Room at 4.30 p.m.

4. ACTS of COURAGE:-

During disembarkation on the night of the 7/8th. October No.36651 Pte. J. HALL, "D" Co. fell overboard from the barge into the DUNKIRK CANAL in full marching order.

2/Lieut. W. McCAIG, "D" Co. without a moment's hesitation, jumped into the canal and supported Pte. HALL in the water, until further assistance was rendered.

Both were then pulled on board an adjoining barge.

2/Lieut. McCAIG's prompt action undoubtedly saved the man's life, as he was fully equipped and was being borne down by the weight of the pack.

On the night of September 29th. during a hostile aircraft attack on DUNKIRK, a bomb was dropped on GHYVELDE CAMP, killing and wounding several officers, 2/Lieut. MECHAN, though wounded himself by a splinter, most gallantly helped to carry the wounded officers under cover, and later in the evening during a further bombardment assisted wounded officers to walk to the hospital, returning alone himself to the camp.

The Commanding Officer congratulates the above mentioned officers heartily on their gallant bearing, and thanks them for the credit they have brought to the battalion and to the Highland Light Infantry.

The above order will be read out to all Cos. and units in the battalion on parade.

R.M. Grant Lieut.,
A/Adjutant, 15th. Bn. High. L.I.

Battalion Orders
by Lieut-Colonel V.B.RAMSDEN, M.C.,
Commanding, 15th.Bn.Highland Light Infantry.
12th. October 1917.

---

1. Reveille............................6.15 a.m.
   Breakfast...........................7.45 a.m.
   Sick Parade.........................8 a.m.
   C.O's Orderly Room..................2.30 p.m.
   Co. on duty.........................."D" Co.
   Orderly Officer.....................2/Lieut.THOMSON.

2. Parades:-
   Physical Training 6.45 a.m. - 7.15 a.m.
   Programme of training has already been issued.
   "A" & "B" Cos. will parade at the same rendezvous as this morning at 8.45 a.m., "B" Co. leading.
   "C" & "D" Cos will be on same parade ground as this morning at 9.45 a.m.

3. Troop Trains:- Considerable quantities of S.A.A. have been found in troop trains after detrainment.
   Officers i/c Parties travelling by troop trains will see that carriages and trucks are cleared of all S.A.A., Equipment etc., on detrainment, before the troops leave the station yard.

Lieut.,
A/Adjutant, 15th.Bn.High.L.I.

War Diary

Battalion Orders
by Lieut-Colonel V.B. RAMSDEN, M.C.,
Commanding, 15th Bn. Highland Light Infantry,
13th October 1917.

12th.

1. Reveille............................6.15 a.m.
Breakfast............................7.45 a.m.
Sick Parade..........................8 a.m.
C.O's Orderly Room...................2.30 p.m.
Co. on duty..........................."A" Co.
Orderly Officer......................2/Lieut. J.D. Muir.

2. Parades.
Hour and rendezvous at the same time as 12th inst.
Training will be carried out as per programme issued.

3. The following 32nd Div. No. G.1. 592/1/1 of 9-10-17 will be read out to all companies on parade.

Small coal-gas balloons may from time to time be found in the Fourth Army Area, containing information of military value placed in a special envelope attached to the balloon.

Instructions are printed in English, French and Flemish on each label concerning the disposal of the message.

Please issue instructions to all troops concerned that such balloons should be taken by them to the nearest military authority for transmission to this Office.

K. Mc[illegible]

Lieut.,
A/Adjutant 15th High. L. I.

NOTICE.

Postponed.

A football match will be played between the 2nd Manchester Regt., and the 15th H.L.I. on the ground near Transport Lines tomorrow 13th inst. at 3.30 p.m.

A programme will be given by the "[illegible]" on Saturday 13th inst., at 6 p.m. in the Hall at "B" Coys., Billet.

The above two notices to be read out on parade.

2nd Lt. Nichan. returned from Signalling course

War Diary

Battalion Orders
by Lieut-Colonel V.B. [illegible], M.C.,
Commanding 15th Bn. Highland Light Infantry.
13th October 1917.

Sat.

---

1. Reveille.............................7 a.m.
Breakfast...........................8 a.m.
Sick Parade.........................9 a.m.
Co. on duty.........................."B" Coy.
Orderly Officer.....................2/Lieut. J. [illegible]SON.

2. DIVINE SERVICES.

C. of E. Service at 10.15 a.m. place to be intimated later.

Presbyterian. Parade service for "C" and "D" Coys., in "C" Coy's Billet at 11 a.m.
Parade service for H.Qrs., "A and B" Coys. in "B" Coy's. Billet at 12 noon.
Voluntary service in "C" Coy's Billet at 5.30 p.m.

R.C. Parade Service at Church of Saint Antoine for "A and B" Coys., at 8 a.m. Mass.
Parade service at Church of Saint Nicolas for "C" and "D" Coys., at 8 a.m.
Voluntary service in the Parish Church of PETITE [illegible] at 9 a.m.

There will probably be a Brigade Parade on Sunday Morning. If this Parade is ordered the Church Parades will be cancelled. Companies must be ready to parade on short notice.

[illegible signature]

Lieut.,
A/Adjt. 15th Bn. High. L. I.

Mr. Baer + ~~[illegible]~~ JR Robertson

War Diary

Battalion Orders by
Lieut-Colonel V.B. RAMSDEN, M.C.,
Commanding 15th BN. Highland Light Infantry.
15th October 1917.

---

1. Reveille.......................................6.15 a.m.
   Breakfast.....................................7.45 a.m.
   Sick Parade...................................8 a.m.
   C. Os. Orderly Room...........................2.30 p.m.
   Co. on duty...................................."C" Coy.
   Orderly Officer...............................2/Lieut. J.B. PATON.

2. Hdqrs. "A" and "B" Coys. will parade at Orderly Room at 9.30 am. and proceed to G.6.d.
   "C" and "D" Coys. will join the column as arranged.

   Dress. Drill Order with Box Respirators, P.H. Helmets and Steel Helmets.
   No classes will be held tomorrow except (D) see programme already issued.
   Reference class (D) Officers of "A" and "B" Coys., will parade at Medical Inspection Room. Officers of "C" and "D" Coys., at "C" Coy's Billet.

3. G.R.O. No.2683 Cleaning rifles and revolvers.
   Precaution against accident.
   "Before any attempt is made to clean a rifle, either outside or inside, the bolt will be first removed and then the magazine.
   After cleaning, the bolt will always be replaced and closed, springs eased, and safety catch applied, before magazine is reattached.
   Revolvers are not to be cleaned, either internally or externally, without being first unloaded".
   This order to be read out periodically on Coy. parades.
   G.R.O. No. 2684 Leave.
   Before a new paybook (A.B. 64) is issued to a soldier an entry will be made in it showing the dates of the last grant of Leave.

[illegible] Lieut.
A/Adjt. 15th BN. High. L. I.

2nd Lt. Meehan left for duty as instructor at Div signalling school.

3 Killed 1 died of wounds 2 wounded. Other 3 wounded & remained on duty.

War Diary

Battalion Orders by,
Lieut-Colonel V.B. RAMSDEN, M.C.,
Commanding 15th Bn. Highland Light Infantry,
16th October 1917.

1.	Reveille)		5 a.m.
	Breakfast) "A" and "B" Coys.	5-30	a.m.
	Reveille)		6. a.m.
	Breakfast) Hdqrs. "C" and "D" Coys.	6.30	a.m.
	Sick Parade..............................		8 a.m.
	Co. on duty..............................		"D" Coy.
	Orderly Officer..........................		2/Lieut. ROGER.

2. The Battalion will proceed to PONT DE GHYVELDE for baths tomorrow by barge from H.5.c. as follows:-

"A" and "B" Coys. will leave Orderly Room at 6 a.m. and embark at H.5.c. at 7 a.m.

"C" and "D" Coys. will leave Orderly Room at 8 a.m. and embark at 9 a.m.

Hdqrs. and all oddments including men from sick parade etc., will leave at 10 a.m. and embark at 11 a.m.

There will be no classes or training tomorrow.

Company Commanders are responsible that all their men have baths and that they proceed with their companies as far as possible.

Dress - Walking out dress with great coats and towels.

R.M. Grant
Lieut.,
A/Adjt. 15th Bn. High.L. I.

War Diary

Battalion Orders by,
Lieut-Colonel V.B. RAMSDEN, M.C.
Commanding 15th Bn. Highland Light Infantry.
17th October 1917.

1. Reveille.............................. 6.15 a.m.
Breakfast.............................. 7.45 a.m.
Sick Parade............................ 8 a.m.
Co. on duty............................ "B" Coy.
Orderly Officer........................ Lieut. Brown.

2. Training for Thursday 18th inst.
(a) No P.T. or B.F. in the morning
(b) Regimental Classes (b) and (c) only. All signallers will parade with their companies.
(c) Band, Hdqrs., "A" and "B" Coys. will parade at Orderly Room at 9 a.m. and proceed to area.
"C" and "D" Coys. will be on Training Area by 10 a.m.
Coys. will parade at full strength.
Dress:- Battle Order including Steel Helmets, Gas Equipment and all shovels in possession of Coys. to be carried.
"B" Coy. will take up the two rattles.
Training as per programme will be carried out.
"E" Coy. will proceed at once to range.
Limbers required for all Lewis Guns, Bombs, including Smoke Bombs and Rifle Grenades of all descriptions, Flares, Tape, Lamps, Targets - Landscape and Small will be carried in a Limber.
Cookers will be at O.6.c.9.1. at 1 p.m. will meals prepared. Teas will also be served on the ground.

Lieut.,
A/Adjt. 15th Bn. High. L. I.

N O T I C E.

A Recreation Room has been opened for the use of the troops in the RUE DE L'AVENIR. It will be open daily from 2 - 4 p.m. and from 5 - 8 p.m.

FOUND. Near Orderly Room a cheque book (Sir C.R.McGRIGOR and Coy.). Owner can have same on applying at Orderly Room.

File

Battalion Orders by,
Lieut-Colonel V.B. RAMSDEN, M.C.,
Commanding 15th Bn. Highland Light Infantry.
18th October 1917.

---

1. Reveille.................................. 6.15 a.m.
Breakfast.................................. 7.45 a.m.
Sick Parade................................ 8 a.m.
C.O's Orderly Room........................
Co. on duty................................ "C" Co.
Orderly Officer............................ 2/Lieut. SAWERS.

2. Programme for Friday 19th inst.

No P.T. or B.F.

Band, "A" and "B" Coy. will parade at Orderly Room at 8.15 am and proceed to area. "C" and "D" Coys. will be on area at 9.15 " "C" Coy. will proceed to range.

Class (b) will parade under Sgt. DUNCAN with "A" and "B" Coys and proceed to range on arrival at area.

Training 9.30 a.m. Demonstration of platoon ("B" Coy) attack on small Strong Point. Remainder will watch.

10.30 a.m. Demonstration of platoon ("A" Coy.) attack on unknown Strong Point. Remainder will watch.

11.30 a.m. Demonstration of organisation and consolidation of Coy. ("D" Coy.) position in depth.

3.30 p.m. Band, "A" and "B" Coys. will parade at Orderly Room and proceed to area. "C" and "D" Coys. will be at this evening's rendezvous at 4.15 p.m.

Practice forming up on tape line from crater positions:

Platoon Commanders instruction in leading their platoons on a selected point at night by compass bearing.

The lecture detailed on programme is postponed.

Regimental Classes (a) and (c) will carry on as usual.

Limbers will be detailed for Lewis Guns, Landscape and small targets, Bombs (including Smoke Bombs). Sgts. DUNCAN and BEATTIE will be responsible that these stores are properly loaded up.

3. All captured electrical signalling apparatus, especially Wireless Stores, will be sent to Divisional Signal Co., with a view to forwarding to G.H.Q.

It is very important to find out what substitutes are being used by the enemy for various materials used in the construction of apparatus in order to assist the authorities at home, who are dealing with the Blockade question.

4. APPOINTMENT No. 13586 Sgt. A. BRESLIN, C. Co. apptd. A/CSM., with effect from 11/9/17 vice C.S.M. ROSS.

R M Grant

Capt.,
A/Adjt. 15th Bn. High. L. I.

War Diary

Battalion Orders by
Lieut-Colonel V.B. RAMSDEN, M.C.,
Commanding 15th Bn. Highland Light Infantry,
19th October 1917.

---

1. Reveille.............................. 7 a.m.
   Breakfast............................ 7.45 a.m.
   Sick Parade.......................... 8.15 a.m.
   C.O's. Orderly Room.................12.30 p.m.
   Co. on duty.......................... "D" Co.
   Orderly Officer...................... 2/Lieut. W.M. RITCHIE.

2. Training for tomorrow 20th inst.
   No P.T. or B.F.
   All Coys. under Coy. Sgt. Majors in vicinity of billets.
   10.30 a.m. to 11.15 a.m. Musketry.
   11.30 a.m. to 12.15 p.m. Close Order Drill.
   All Officers and 8 N.C.Os per Coy. will meet the C.O. at same rendezvous as this afternoon at 9.30 a.m. - Walking out dress - Waterproof sheets.
   All Officers and N.C.Os. to have note books, pencil, and special maps issued for yesterday's operations.
   As many compasses as possible to be brought.

Jas. S. Paton 2/Lieut.,
for A/Adjt. 15th Bn. High. L. I.

N o t i c e.

Owing to numerous complaints by panic stricken civilians, immediately the siren blows for the approach of enemy air-craft all lights in billets will be extinguished.
Numerous complaints have been received regarding petty thefts in the neighborhood during hostile air-raid. None of these so far have been traced to this battalion. The C.O. hopes that no more complaints of this nature will be lodged against this battalion.

A football match has been arranged for tomorrow against the 2nd MANCHESTER REGT. on their ground. The kick off is at 3.30 p.m. it is hoped a large number of men will turn out to support the Regimental Team.

War Diary

Battalion Orders by,
Lieut-Colonel V.B. RAMSDEN, MC.
Commanding 15th Bn. Highland Light Infantry.
20th October 1917.

1.	Reveille....................................	7 a.m.
	Breakfast....................................	7.45 a.m.
	Sick Parade....................................	9 a.m.
	Co. on duty....................................	"A" Co.
	Orderly Officer....................................	2/Lieut.W.C.BLACK.

2. Divine Services:-

Presbyterians. Parade Service for all Coys. on"C" Coy's parade ground at 11.30 a.m.

Church of England.

7.45 a.m.	Holy Communion	- in Church Army Hut. No.14 Rue Victor Hugo.
10. 0 a.m.	Church Parade	- in Men's Club.
6.30 p.m.	Evensong	- in Church Army Hut.
7.15 p.m.	Holy Communion	- in Church Army Hut.

R. C. Service.
Mass at PETITE SYNTHE Parish Church at 9 a.m.

3. C. O. will inspect Transport Lines at 11 a.m.

4. Saluting.
The following are the distinguishing flags affixed to motor cars:-

G.H.Q.	- Red and Blue.
Army	- Red and Black
Corps	- Red and White
Division	- Red.

A flag flown on a car denotes that a General Officer is in the car, and must, therefore, be saluted in accordance with the salute given to a General Officer by guards and sentries. Individual Officers, soldiers, or parties must be on the look out for a flag on a motor car and salute smartly in the usual manner before the car has passed.

The above order to be read out on parade.

Jas. B. Paton
2/Lieut.,
A/Adjt.for O.C.,15th Bn. High. L. I.

War Diary

Battalion Orders by,
Lieut-Colonel V.B. RAMSDEN, M.C.,
Commanding 15th Bn. Highland Light Infantry,
21st October 1917.

---

1. Reveille.................................. 6.15 a.m.
   Breakfast .... 7.45 a.m.
   Sick Parade............................... 8 a.m.
   C.O's. Orderly Room.......................
   Co. on duty............................... "B" Co.
   Orderly Officer........................... 2/Lieut. E.L. WOOD.

2. No P.T. or B.F.
   Hdqrs. "A" and "B" Coys will parade at Orderly Room at 9 a.m.
   "C" and "D" Coys to be on the road in rear of tape by 9.30 a.m.
   "C" Coy. to ta ke four red flags and two rattles.
   Dress. Drill Order - Tools - 70 shovels per Coy. to be carried.
   Coys. will parade as strong as possible.
   Parade States to be taken on to the ground.
   All regimental classes will attend parade.

3. From this date the Orderly Officer will attend at Orderly Room at 5 p.m., to supervise the stamping of the letters of the out-going mail.

   All letters must be in Orderly Room by 4 p.m.

Jas. S. Paton
2/Lieut.,
A/Adjt. for O.C.15th High. L. I.

War Diary

Battalion Orders by,
Lieut-Colonel V.B. RAMSDEN, M.C.,
Commanding 15th Bn. Highland Light Infantry.
22nd October 1917.

---

1. Reveille under Coy. arrangements.
Sick Parade.................................. 9 a.m.
C.O's. Orderly Room.......................... 9.30 a.m.
Co. on duty.................................. "C" Coy.
Orderly Officer.............................. 2/Lieut. M. BARR.

2. Parade. Hdqrs. "A" and "B" Coys. will parade at the Orderly Room ~~and~~ at 3 a.m.
"C" and "D" Coys. will arrange to be on this morning's training area at 3.30 a.m.
Coys. will arrange to give the men tea etc., before moving.

3. Dress:- Drill Order, Tools, Tape, also Smoke ~~Bombs~~ Grenades to be carried.

4. Lewsi Gun Limbers will carry L.Gs. and ammunition.
"C" Coy. will arrange to take flags as this morning.

5. The whole operation will be carried out on this morning's scheme.
On one G. being sounded Coys. will adjust Gas Helmets and commence forming up in ~~same~~, on the tape line.
Zero 5.45 a.m. Watches to be synchronised at 5 a.m.

6. Breakfast in barracks about 8 a.m.
Remainder of day to be spent cleaning up.

Jas B Paton.
2/Lieut.,
A/Adjt. for O.C.15th Bn.High.L.I.

War Diary

Battalion Orders by,
Lieut-Colonel V.B. RAMSDEN, M.C.,
Commanding the 15th Bn. Highland Light Infantry.
24th October 1917.

---

1. Reveille.................................. 5.15 a.m.
Breakfast.................................. 7 a.m.
Sick Parade.................................. 6 a.m.
Co. on duty.................................. "A" Coy.
Orderly Officer.................................. 2/Lieut. HOWIESON.

2. The Battalion will move to ERINGHEM on the 25th October 1917, passing the starting point G.12.d.3.0. at 9 a.m.
Order of March. Hdqrs., "A" Coy. "B" Coy., Band, "C" Coy., "D" Coy., and Transport.
Dress. - See separate instructions already issued.

3. Hdqrs. "A" and "B" Coys. will parade at Orderly Room at 8.25 a.m. "C" and "D" Coys. will parade on side road beside their large billet and be ready at 8.55 a.m. to join the column behind the Band.

4. Packs, Blankets Etc.
(a) Hdqrs. "A" and "B" Coys.
Packs to be labelled and stacked beside Church at 6.15 a.m.
Blankets to be rolled in bundles of ten and stacked beside Church at 6.45 a.m.
Officers' Valises to be at Q.M. Stores at 8 p.m. this evening.
Officers' Mess Stores (i.e. breakfast necessaries only) will be stacked outside respective Messes at 7.15 a.m. They will be collected by the Mess Cart.
(b) "C" and "D" Coys.
Packs to be labelled and stacked in front of large billet at 6.45 a.m.
Blankets to be rolled in bundles of ten and stacked in front of large billet at 7.15 a.m.
Officers' Valises to be outside "C" Coy's Officer's Mess at 6 a.m. tomorrow 25/10/17.
Officers' Mess Stores (i.e. breakfast necessaries only) to be stacked outside Mess at 7.30 a.m.

Note. It is of the utmost importance that all times stated above be strictly adhered to.

5. The C.O. will inspect billets of Hdqrs., "A" and "B" Coys., commencing with "B" Coy. at 7.30 a.m.
Major CLEGHORN will inspect "C" and "D" Coys. billets commencing at 8.15 a.m.

[signature]
Captain,
A/Adjt. 15th Bn. High. L. I.

War Diary

Battalion Orders by,
Lieut-Colonel V.B. [illegible], M.C.
Commanding 15th Bn. Highland Light Infantry.
[illegible]th October 1917.

---

1. Reveille.. 5.45 a.m.
Breakfast... 6.45 a.m.
Sick Parade... 7.30 a.m.
Co. on duty... "B" Coy.
Orderly Officer..................................... 2/Lieut. [illegible].

2. The Battalion will move to [illegible], north west area.
Starting Point - Q.M. Stores.
All Coys. - except "D" Coy., will be at starting point at 9.30 am.
"D" Coy. will parade on road outside billets and join the column as it passes.
Order of March - Hdqrs. "B" "C" Band "D" and "A" Coys.
Dress Full Marching Order.
Particular attention will be paid to the shaping and correct adjustment of packs. Steel Helmets will be worn.
The Divisional Commander remarked this morning that he had nothing but praise to offer for the general turn out and smart appearance of the Battalion. The C.O. desires that this reputation will be upheld tomorrow.
The March will only be 6 - 7 miles long.

3. Billeting Party. (one N.C.O. per Coy). will report to 2/Lieut. McCAIG at Q.M. Stores at 7 a.m.

4. All blankets will be rolled in bundles of ten and stacked on road outside billets - one stack per Coy. - by 6.30 a.m.
T.O. will detail one limber per Coy., to take blankets to Q.M. Stores by 7 a.m.

5. The Mess Cart will pick up all Mess Stores beginning with "B" Coy. at 7 a.m.

6. Officers valises will be picked up outside respective Coy. Messes - beginning with "B" Coy., at 7 a.m.

7. The Q.M. will report to Orderly Room without fail in the event of any stores not being ready by times stated.

Captain,
a/Adjt. 15th Bn. High. [illegible]. I.

War Diary

Battalion Orders, by
Lieut-Colonel V.B. RAMSDEN, M.C.,
Commanding 15th Bn. Highland Light Infantry.
27th October 1917.

---

1. Reveille................................ 6.30 a.m.
Breakfast.............................. 7 a.m.
Sick Parade............................ 8.15 a.m.
Co. on duty............................"D" Coy.
Orderly Officer........................ 2/Lieut. ROGER.

2. The Battalion will parade as strong as possible at their billets at 9 a.m.
"A" and "B" Coys. (to whom maps have been sent) will proceed direct to Training Area at H.5.b.0.3.
The 2nd in Command will conduct "C" Coy., to rendezvous and C.O. will conduct Hdqrs. and "D" Coy.
Stretcher Bearers will parade with their Coys.

3. Dress:- Drill Order.

4. O.C. Signals will arrange to take out 40 flags.

5. Sgt. BEATTIE will arrange to take out 10 ground Sheets, 2 rattles, 5 shovels, and 500 yards tape.

6. T.O. will send out L.G. Limbers to Coys. by 8.30 a.m.

7. Coy. Commanders will bring with them latest diagrams of Assembly Formations - sheets A and "B.

B/21198 Cpl. WATERFIELD, "D" Coy., reverts to the ranks at his own request.

R.M. Grant
Captain,
A/Adjt. 15th Bn. High. L. I.

War Diary

Battalion Orders by,
Lieut-Colonel V.B. RAMSDEN, M.C.,
Commanding 15th Bn. Highland Light Infantry,
28th October 1917.

---

1. Reveille.................................... 6 a.m.
Breakfast - Under Company arrangements.
Sick Parade.................................... 8 a.m.

2. Training will be carried out as per programme except for "B" Coy., and Hdqrs., who will proceed to Baths as arranged.

3. Company Officers will bring compasses with them on parade.

4. T.O. will detail L.G. Limbers to report to "C" and "D" Coys., at 9.30 a.m.

R M Grant
Captain,
A/Adjt.15th Bn. High. L. I.

War Diary

Battalion Orders by,
Lieut-Colonel V.B. RAMSDEN, M.C.,
Commanding 15th Bn. Highland Light Infantry,
29th October 1917.

---

1. Reveille.................................... 6 a.m.
Breakfast under Company arrangements.
Sick Parade.................................. 8 a.m.

2. Training will be carried out as per programme.

3. All Officers and 8 N.C.Os. per Company will meet C.O. at Cross-roads (H.11.c.8.4.) opposite C.C.S. at 2.30 p.m. with small maps issued with orders (10 per Coy.).

R M Grant Captain,
A/Adjt. 15th Bn. High. L. I.

NOTICE.

The Regimental Canteen has been opened near Medical Inspection Room, near billet of No. 16 platoon.

War Diary

Battalion Orders by,
Lieut-Colonel V.B. RAMSDEN, M.C.,
Commanding 15th Bn. Highland Light Infantry,
30th October 1917.

---

1. Reveille.................................... 6 a.m.
Breakfast - Under Company arrangements.
Sick Parade.................................. 8 a.m.

2. Inspection of Brigade is cancelled.

3. Training will be carried out as per programme.

4. Until further orders, companies will hold feet rubbing parades and feet inspections daily.

5. Company Commanders are reminded that parade states are to be rendered to Orderly Room by 9 a.m. daily. These must agree with ration indents.

R M Grant
Captain,
A/Adjt.15th Bn. High. L. I.

War Diary

Battalion Orders by,
Lieut-Colonel V.B. RAMSDEN, M.C.,
Commanding 15th Bn. Highland Light Infantry,
31st October 1917.

---

1. Reveille.. 6 a.m.
Breakfast - Under Company Arrangements.
Sick Parade.. 8 a.m.

2. Companies will rendezvous at 8.45 a.m. on road behind the right of first objective taken this morning.
Every possible man will be on parade including stretcher bearers.

3. Dress:- Drill Order with waterproof sheets - no gas equipment will be carried.

4. O.C. Hdqrs. Coy. will march Band, with instruments, and Signallers to rendezvous at 8.30 a,m.
Sgt. BEATTIE will arrange to gather sufficient stakes for three Strong Points and take waterproof sheets for same, 400 yards tape, all flags for barrage and rattles.
T.O. will detail a Limber.
Detailed orders for Battalion Scheme will be issued.

5. No P.T. or B.F.

6. Company Commanders will explain the Scheme to their Companies before moving off to rendezvous. Particular attention is to be paid to this explanation and to the General turn out as the Major General will visit the Battalion during operations.

R M Grant
Captain,
A/Adjt. 15th Bn. High. L. I.

REGIMENTAL CANTEEN.

Balance Sheet as at 31/10/17.

Liabilities.		Assets.	
Canteen Fund.	500	Stock	500.00
Profit & Loss Account.		Cash	120.55
		Sundry A/Cs	40.00
Balance	160.55		
	660.55		660.55

Instructions regarding War Diaries and Intelligence Summaries are contained in F. S. Regs., Part II. and the Staff Manual respectively. Title pages will be prepared in manuscript.

WAR DIARY
or
INTELLIGENCE SUMMARY.
(Erase heading not required.)

15th H.L.I. Original Vol 25

Army Form C. 2118.

Place	Date	Hour	Summary of Events and Information	Remarks and references to Appendices
	1917. November			
Ruprouck	1st.		Batt. resting - In billets - weather fair. - Practised a scheme of Attack in the morning as per training programme. 2nd Lt. Carthew reported to the Battn for duty & was posted to A Coy.	Appendix II
do.	2nd.		Bn. resting - in billets - weather cold and dry. Carried out a Tactical Exercise with the 1st Dorset Regt in the morning, we were inspected in same by the Divisional Commander. Other training programme cancelled.	App. III
do.	3rd.		Bn resting - in billets - weather fair between showers - Attack practice by double companies in the morning. Football match against K.O.Y.L.I. in the afternoon, result - K.O.Y.L.I. 5 goals 15th H.L.I. 1 goal. The men received an advance of pay. 2nd Lt. Gooding went to Hospital - Sick.	
do	4th.		Bn resting, in billets, weather cold and dry. Church Parade in the morning football match against the 17th H.L.I. in the afternoon, result 17th 2. - 15th 1. Massed bands of the 15th 16th + 17th Battns. provided an excellent entertainment in the afternoon. ~~2nd Lt Little proceeded on leave to Scotland~~.	

A5834 Wt. W4973/M687 750,000 8/16 D. D. & L. Ltd. Forms/C.2118/13.

25.0.
41 sheets

Instructions regarding War Diaries and Intelligence Summaries are contained in F. S. Regs., Part II. and the Staff Manual respectively. Title pages will be prepared in manuscript.

WAR DIARY
or
INTELLIGENCE SUMMARY.
(Erase heading not required.)

Army Form C. 2118.

Place	Date	Hour	Summary of Events and Information	Remarks and references to Appendices
Rubrouck.	5th		Battn. resting - in billets - weather fair between showers - training :- attack practice as usual as per programme. 2nd Lt Steele proceeded on leave to Scotland.	Appendix II
do	6th		Battn. resting - in billets - weather showery - training as per programme	
do	7th		Battn resting . in billets - weather again showery - usual training per programme.	
do .	8th		Bn. resting - in billets - weather fair - Attack practice under Brigade arrangements in the morning - All Box-respirators tested in the afternoon. 2nd Lt Pryde returned from course at St Pol.	App IV
do	9th		Bn resting - in billets - weather showery, heavy rain in the morning - Training programme cancelled. 2nd Lt Cairn returned from leave.	
do	10th		Bn. resting - in billets - weather showery, training as per programme.	
do .	11th		Bn resting - in billets. Heavy rain in the morning, clearing slightly in the afternoon. Bn marched to Oudezeele and remained overnight under canvas. 2nd Lt Cathro proceeded to 5th Army Inf School. 2nd Lt Howlson rejoined	

A5834 Wt. W4973/M687 750,000 8/16 D. D. & L. Ltd. Forms/C.2118/13.

Instructions regarding War Diaries and Intelligence Summaries are contained in F. S. Regs., Part II. and the Staff Manual respectively. Title pages will be prepared in manuscript.

WAR DIARY
or
INTELLIGENCE SUMMARY.
(Erase heading not required.)

Army Form C. 2118.

Place	Date 1917	Hour	Summary of Events and Information	Remarks and references to Appendices
Rubrouck	November 11th (contd)		from Lewis Gun course.	
Oudezeele	12th		Bn on the march - weather fair. Marched to Poperinghe area, and took over Tunnelling camp. 2nd Lt Paton to hospital - sick.	
Poperinghe	13th		Bn resting - under canvas - weather cold but dry. Kits were inspected in the morning by the Comdg. Officer. Capt Davies returned from 4th Army Musketry Camp. 2nd Lts. Simony and McArthur rejoined from Inf. course.	
do	14th		Bn resting - under canvas. Training as per programme. Football match in the afternoon - Officers v Sergts, result Officers 4. Sergts 0. Weather fair during the day, showery in the evening.	
do	15th		Bn Resting - under canvas. Training as per programme practice attacks. Weather fair. Capt Davies to Brigade H.Q. for ~~duty as assist~~ instruction in Staff duties	Appendix V
do	16th		Bn Resting - under canvas, weather dry but cloudy. - training as programme tactical exercise.	

A5834 Wt. W4973/M687 750,000 8/16 D. D. & L. Ltd. Forms/C.2118/13.

Instructions regarding War Diaries and Intelligence Summaries are contained in F. S. Regs., Part II. and the Staff Manual respectively. Title pages will be prepared in manuscript.

WAR DIARY
or
INTELLIGENCE SUMMARY.
(Erase heading not required.)

Army Form C. 2118.

Place	Date 1917.	Hour	Summary of Events and Information	Remarks and references to Appendices
	Nov.			
Poperinghe area	17th.		Bn. resting - under canvas - weather showery - training as usual. Lt Lane reported for duty in re-inforcement.	
do.	18th.		Bn. resting - under canvas - weather cold, dry and cloudy. Church Parade in Camp at 11.am.	
do	19th.		Bn. resting - under canvas - weather fair between showers - training as per programme. 2nd Lt. Kevin reported for duty, as reinforcement.	
do.	20th.		Bn. resting - under canvas - weather fair between showers - training under Coy arrangements. Lt. J.D. Muir detached to School of instruction R.F.C.	
do	21st.		Bn resting - under canvas - weather fair - training as usual - Coy officers reconnoitred new position in the line west of Passchendaele.	
do	22nd.		Bn resting - under canvas - weather cloudy but dry. training under Coy. arrangements.	
do.	23rd.		Bn resting - under canvas - weather fair - training programme cancelled - Divisional Commander addressed the Battn. with the other Battns of the Brigade at Ha	

Instructions regarding War Diaries and Intelligence Summaries are contained in F. S. Regs., Part II. and the Staff Manual respectively. Title pages will be prepared in manuscript.

WAR DIARY
or
INTELLIGENCE SUMMARY.
(Erase heading not required.)

Army Form C. 2118.

Place	Date 1917.	Hour	Summary of Events and Information	Remarks and references to Appendices
Popperinghe	Nov 24th		Bn resting - under canvas - weather cold, dry. - Battn moved to Irish Farm. Ref Sheet 28. N.W. C 27 a 3.6. Capt Doughty and Lt Howison detached to 5th Army Musketry Camp.	
Irish Farm	25th		Battn in reserve - under canvas and in huts - weather cold, fair between showers. Battn moved to Support position in Bellvue. Ref. Sheet 28 D.4.d9.6 Lt Lane to 5th Army Scouting School of instruction.	
Bellvue Support.	26th		Battn. in Support - Shell hole positions - weather fair between showers - conditions very trying. 2nd Lt Thomson appointed Divl. Burial Officer.	
do	27th		Battn. in Support - shell hole positions - weather showery - Battn provided carrying parties to front line under very trying conditions	
do	28th		Battn in Support - in shell hole positions - weather cloudy but dry - Carrying parties again provided - conditions very trying on the whole, but improving.	
do	29th		Battn in Support - in shell hole positions - weather cloudy slight showers - carrying parties again provided throughout the day - men suffering from bad conditions, with swollen feet etc. 2nd Lt. E.S. Wood Sick.	
do	30th		Battn in support - in shell hole positions - weather fair between slight showers, carrying parties were again provided in preparation for Divl. attack on the morning of 1/12/17.	

A5834 Wt. W4973/M687 750,000 8/16 D. D. & L. Ltd. Forms/C.2118/13.

War Diary

Battalion Orders by,
Lieut-Colonel V.B. RAMSDEN, M.C.,
Commanding 15th Bn. Highland Light Infantry.
2nd November 1917.

---

1. Reveille.. 6 a.m.
Breakfast - Under Company Arrangements.
Sick Parade..................................... 8 a.m.
C.O's. Orderly Room............................. 3 p.m.

2. Route March for tomorrow is cancelled.

3. All Companies will do B.F. - 6.45 am. - 7.15 a.m.

4. Companie s will parade independently at 9.30 a.m. at same rendezvous as where Coy. attacks were made yesterday morning after Battalion attack was finished.
"A" Coy. will co-operate with "B" Coy.
"C" Coy. will co-operate with "D" "
"A" Coy. will arrange to have the usual strong points erected on their ground by 9.15 a.m.
"C" Coy. will make similar arrangements for same time.

5. Dress:- Drill Order with waterproof sheets.

6. O.C. Signals will send 15 flags to "A" and "C" Coys. by 8.30 a.m.

Captain,
A/Adjt. 15th Bn. High. L. I.

War Diary

Battalion Orders by,
Lieut-Colonel V.B. RAMSDEN, M.C.,
Commanding 15th Bn. Highland Light Infantry,
3rd November 1917.

---

1. Reveille.................................... 7 a.m.
Breakfast.................................... 8 a.m.
Sick Parade.................................... 9 a.m.

2. DIVINE SERVICES:-
(1) Presbyterian. Parade Service in field opposite blacksmith's shop near 13th C.C.S. (H.11.c.7.8.) at 10 a.m.
C of E.
Parade Service in Scottish Churches Tent at ARNEKE Station at 10.30 a.m.
R.C.
Mass at 13th C.C.S. at 8.30 a.m.

3. The Commanding Officer wishes to point out that three cases have occured in one Company of men overstaying their leave. It must be clearly understood that the granting of leave is a ~~privilage~~ privilage which can be very easily taken away by Higher Authority if abused. In order to bring it home to the remainder of the men in "A" Coy. and also as an example to the rest of the Battalion, the Commanding Officer feels reluctantly compelled to cancel all leave to U.K. from "A" Coy. for one fortnight from this date.

Part 2.

1. REVERSION. No. 13079 Cpl. H. WYPER, "D" Coy. reverts to the ranks at his own request 2/11/17.
APPOINTMENTS. The following men are appointed unpaid L/Cpls. as from 27/10/17.

No.4648	Pte.	A.DRUMMOND	"A" Coy.
39141	"	H. KNIGHT.	" "
42544	"	J. NICOL.	"B" "
38489	"	A.PITT.	"B" "
13202	"	D.R. HALLIDAY	"B" "
41300	"	J. CARNELL	"B" "
42065	"	W.LINDSAY	"C" "
350305	"	J.WICKWAR	"C" "
33224	"	J. FERRIER	"C" "
40245	"	J. MOWATT	"C" "
25646	"	D.FERGUSON	"D" "
13874	"	R. RITCHIE	"D" "
3053	"	T. CRAWFORD	"D" "
40964	"	R. NEILSON	"D" "
40620	"	R. UNDERWOOD	"D" "
40585	"	W. BLACKBURN	"D" "
45185	"	W. RAE	"D" "
18582	"	J. McLARTY	"D" COY.
42789	"	J. SIMPSON	"D" "
353141	"	W. HUTTON	"D" "

R.M. Grant
Captain,
A/Adjt. 15th Bn. High. L. I.

NOTICES P.T.O.

N O T I C E.

A footba ll match will be played tomorrow afternoon against the 17th H. L. I. at 2.15 p.m. The place will be intimated later.

After the match there will be competitions for the Pipe Bands and individual Pipers of the three H. L. I. Battalions in the Division, concluding with a performance by the Massed Band.

File B.O.

Battalion Orders by,
Lieut-Colonel V.B. RAMSDEN, M.C.,
Commanding 15th Bn. Highland Light Infantry.
4th November 1917.

---

1. Reveille.. 6 a.m.
   Breakfast - Under Company Arrangements.
   Sick Parade... 8 a.m.
   COs. Orderly Room..................................... 3 p.m.
2. Training will be carried out as per programme already issued.

3. Coys. will do Close Order Drill and handling of arms from 9 - 9.30 a.m. at their billets after which they will proceed to same area as for Saturday morning.
   "A" and "C" Coys. will be responsible for erecting two Strong Points each ~~under~~ on their respective areas. These Strong Points will be completed by the time Coys. arrive at area.

4. All Signallers will parade under Signalling Officer at Hdqrs.billet at 9.15 a.m.

5. T.O. will send a Limber to Pipers billet at 8 a.m. to collect tins for barrage purposes. The Limber will then proceed to "A" and "C" Coys., and leave half with each Coy. They will be taken out to area.

Captain,
A/Adjt.15th Bn. High. L. I.

War Diary

Battalion Orders by,
Lieut-Colonel V.B. RAMSDEN, M.C.,
Commanding 15th BN. Highland Light Infantry,
5th November 1917.

---

1. Reveille.................................. 6 a.m.
Breakfast - Under Company Arrangements.
Sick Parade.................................. 8 a.m.
C.O's Orderly Room.......................... 2.30 p.m.

2. Training will be carried out as per programme.
Coys. will rendezvous in order "A","B","C","D" and Hdqrs. at cross-reads B.29.d.6.7. at 10.15 a.m.
The Band and Stretcher Bearers and two O.R. per Coy. will rendezvous at above point at 9.45 a.m.
2/Lieut. PATON will arrange to take down sufficient men to carry stakes and waterproof sheets for Four Strong Points and 800 yards tape.

R.M. Grant
Captain & Adjt.
15th Bn. Highland L. I.

War Diary

Battalion Orders by,
Lieut-Colonel V.B. RAMSDEN, M.C.,
Commanding 15th Bn. Highland Light Infantry.
6th November 1917.

---

1. Reveille.. 6 a.m.
Breakfast - Under Company Arrangements.
Sick Parade..................................... 8 a.m.
C.O's. Orderly Room............................. 2.30 pm.

2. The Route March for tomorrow is cancelled.

3. B.F. 6.45 - 7.15 a.m.

4. Coys. will parade at same rendezvous as today at 9.30 a.m.
The same attack practice will be carried out as for today, except that "C" & "D" will be the first line Coys. and "A" & "B" will leap-frog.
An enemy will be in position and unexpected situations will arise.

5. 4 Lewis Gun Paniers will be carried by team Nos. where available. One full magazine will be carried in each panier and all paniers will be strapped to the equipment, vide S.S.194. recently issued.

6. 2 Sections per Coy. will be detailed for enemy, these will be at the rendezvous by 9 a.m.
2/Lieut. PATON will arrange details as for today.

7. All Signallers will parade under S.O. at Hdqrs. Billet at 9.15 am.

8. Observers to be at rendezvous at 9 a.m. to erect Strong Points etc. after which they will parade independently under B.I.O.

R.M. Grant
Captain & Adjt.,
15th Bn. Highland Light Infantry.

15th. Bn. The HIGHLAND LIGHT INFANTRY.

INSPECTION INSTRUCTIONS.

1. The II Corps Commander will inspect the Brigade Group in the field at H.6.b.9.5. at 10 a.m. tomorrow Thursday 8th inst.

11. DRESS:-
Drill Order (without rifle covers) belt, braces, pouches, bayonet and frog, caps.
No. anti-gas equipment, haversacks or waterbottles.
Officers will carry sticks and wear gloves.
Dress for Officers as per special letter already issued.
Coy. Commanders are mounted Officers.

111. If the Corps Commander wishes to address the Brigade after the inspection, the Brigade will close in. The word of command will be given by the Brigade Commander as follows:-

The Brigade will unfix bayonets

" Unfix - Bayonets"

The Brigade will close - Move.

On the above command all platoons will first close up to 2 paces distance. Brigade H.Q. and T. M. Battery will then move in rear of 90th Field Ambulance and M.G. Coy. respectively and the Right half battalion of the 1st DORSET REGT., and the Left half battalion of 2nd MANCHESTER REGT. will move by the most direct route to the rear of their Left and Right half battalions respectively.

On completion of above move all units on right and left flanks will move on the word of Command to be given by C.O. 5/6th ROYAL SCOTS and 15th H. L. I. respectively, to position as shown in diagram.

IV. 2 Markers and R.S.M. will be on the ground at 9.10 a.m.

V. Band will form up in rear of centre of the battalion.

Vl. Transport will be Brigaded in three lines on South West side of field. Pack animals will be loaded, vehicles empty.

Vll. Coys. will rendezvous at H.5.b.2.0. (battalion rendezvous for night operations) at 9.15 a.m. and not earlier.
2 Markers per Coy. to be at above rendezvous at 9.5 a.m. under C.S.M. BEAUCHAM. Markers to bring strength of strongest platoons.

Vlll. Coys. will make their leading platoons the strongest.

lX. Battalion will parade at full strength. Minimum of men to be left off.

X. Special attention will be paid to the hair and shaving.
No hair must show under the bonnet.
Stretcher Bearers must have clean and ironed brassards.

Xl. Coys. will render Parade States for tomorrow's parade to Orderly Room as early as possible to night.

[illegible] Captain & Adjt.,
7/11/17. 15th Bn. Highland Light Infantry.

War Diary

Battalion Orders by,
Lieut-Colonel V.B. RAMSDEN, M.C.,
Commanding 15th Bn. Highland Light Infantry.
7th November 1917.

---

1. Reveille.. 6 a.m.
Breakfast - Under Coy. arrangements..
Sick Parade.. 8 a.m.

2. No B.F.
Instructions for inspection are issued separately.
"B" Coy. will put all material for barrage etc. (left in their charge today) in house where their cooker is - to be ready for use after inspection.

3. There will a test of Box-respirators on Friday at 2nd MANCHESTER REGT. Hdqrs. All Coys, will send a runner tomorrow afternoon to reconnoitre route to and position of gas chamber.

R.M. Grant.
Captain & Adjt.
15th Bn. High. L. I.

N O T I C E S.

BRIGADE FOOTBALL TOURNAMENT. The 15th H.L.I. will play 1st DORSET REGT. in the 2nd round at 2.30 p.m. tomorrow 8th inst. at H.8.c.2.2. - past Brigade Hdqrs.

LOST. On Training Area on 6th inst. a briar pipe. Finder will please return same to Orderly Room.

War Diary

Battalion Orders by
Lieut-Colonel V. B. RAMSDEN, M.C.,
Commanding, 18th. Bn. Highland Light Infantry.
6th. November 1917.

---

1. Reveille.................................. 6 a.m.
Breakfast - under Co. arrangements.
Sick Parade.................................. 8 a.m.

2. Cos will rendezvous at same place as this morning at 10 a.m. in the following order:- "A", "B", "C", "D" & Hd. Qrs.
Operation Orders are issued separately.
T.O. will detail a limber to take to each Co. by 8 a.m. 32 shovels and Flares, Smoke Bombs and Rifle Grenades as detailed in Operation Orders - Sergt. BEATTIE will arrange.
Another limber will report to 2/Lieut. McCAIG at Orderly Room at 8 a.m. to take out all flags including the battalion flag and tins for barrage. 2/Lieut. McCAIG will report to Captain SMYTHES on area at 10 a.m. with barrage party of Stretcher-Bearers and Band. O.C. "D" Co. will detail 8 O.R. to report at Band billet at 8.30 a.m. to join barrage party. Dress - Walking out dress, caps and waterproof sheets.

3. Respirator Test. Cos will parade at Gas Chamber near Manchesters Hd. Qrs. to-morrow as follows:-
"B" Co. at 2 p.m.
"A" Co. 2.30 p.m.
"C" Co. 3 p.m.
"D" Co. 3.30 p.m.
Hd. Qrs. 4 p.m.
1 Gas N.C.O. per Co. will report to Sergt. RIPPON at Gas Chamber at 1.45 p.m. prompt. Dress - Walking Out Dress with water-proof sheets, Box Respirators and P.H. Helmets.

[illegible signature] Captain & Adjt.,
18th. Bn. Highland Light Infantry.

Diary

Battalion Orders by,
Lieut-Colonel V.B. RAMSDEN, M.C.,
Commanding 15th Bn. Highland Light Infantry.
9th November 1917.

---

1. Reveille.. 6.30 a.m.
   Breakfast - Under Company Arrangements.
   Sick Parade.. 9 a.m.
   C.O's. Orderly Room.................................12 noon.

2. No training will be done during the day. Time will be spent in cleaning up billets and generally preparing for march on 11th inst.

   Billets will be ready for inspection by the C.O. at 10 a.m.

Captain & Adjt.,
15th Bn. Highland L. I.

War Diary

Battalion Orders by,
Lieut-Colonel V.B. RAMSDEN, M.C.,
Commanding 15th Bn. Highland Light Infantry,
10th November 1917.

---

1. Reveille.) Under Company Arrangements.
Breakfast)
Sick Parade.. 7 a.m.

2. The Battalion will march to an area N.W. of OUDEZEELE on Sunday November 11th.

3. Band, Hdqrs., "D" & "C" Coys. and Transport will rendezvous at cross roads VIOLON D'OR H.11.c.8.5. at 10.30 a.m.
"B" & "A" Coys. and Cookers will rendezvous under Major Cleghorn at cross-roads at B.29.d.6.7. at 11 a.m. and will proceed to Battalion starting point - Road Junction I.8.a.6.8. at 12.18 p.m.

4. Order of March:- Hdqrs., "D" "C" Band "B" "A" and Transport.
Route. LEDRINGHEM - WORMHOUDT - Road Junction C.17.b.0.5.- STEENVOORDE Road.

5. Coy. Commanders will ensure that their Coys. arrive at rendezvous exactly at times stated - or at most 5 minutes before.

X 6. Dress:- Marching Order with packs; steel helmets will be worn, waterproof sheets as usual under flap of pack.

7. O.C. "A" Coy. will detail a Brigade Stragglers Party of 1 Officer 1 N.C.O. and 6 O.R. to march 100 yards in rear of 14th T.M. Battery after road junction I.8.a. The Officer detailed will send in a report to Brigade Hdqrs. at end of march on any stragglers collected en route.
<u>Note</u>. Brigade Order of March after 15th H. L. I. is Brigade Hdqrs. 14th T.M. Battery.

8. <u>OFFICERS VALISES</u>. A limber will report to "A" and "B" Coys. for Officers valises and Mess Stores at 8 a.m. Baggage wagon will collect "C" "D" & Hdqrs. Officers valises and Mess Stores at 8 a.m.

9. Band's packs will be at Q.M. Stores at 8 a.m.

10. Blankets will be rolled in bundles of 10 labelled and stacked outside billets (1 stack per Coy) by 7.30 a.m. Jerkins will be labelled and stacked similarly in bundles of 20 by 7.30 a.m.

11. C.O. will inspect "C" & "D" Coy. billets - commencing with "C" Coy. at 9.30 a.m; Major Cleghorn will inspect "A" and "B" Coy. billets - commencing with "A" Coy. at 10 a.m.

R M Grant
Captain & Adjt.,
15th Highland Light Infantry.

Jargicamp

Battalion Orders by,
Lieut-Colonel V.B. RAMSDEN, M.C.
Commanding 15th Bn. Highland Light Infantry.
13th November 1917.

---

1. Reveille.. 6 a.m.
Breakfast.. 7.30 a.m.
Sick Parade.. 8 a.m.
C.O's. Orderly Room.................................... 12.30 p.m.
Co. on duty.. "A" Coy.
Orderly Officer.. 2/Lieut. D. PRIDE.

2. Training will be carried out as follows:-
Bn. 6.45 - 7.15 am. P.T. or B.F. Billets. "A" "B" & "C" Coys. 9 am. Lewis Gunners on range F.20.d.9.2. 9 - 9.45 am. Coy. Drill. 9.45 - 10 Handling Arms. 10 - 10.15 am. Gas Drill. "D" Coy. & Hq. bathing. All Coys. 10.30 - 11.30 a.m. Gas Test. F.27.a. central. 11.30 - 12 noon Close Order Drill. F.27.a central. All Coys. 6. pm. 2 Coys. marching on compass bearings, ~~2xCoysxxxdxx~~. F.28.d. & 29 b.
2 Coys. marching on Compass Bearings F.27.c. & d.
Hdqrs. and "D" Coys. will be intimated later re times to proceed to Baths.

3. The Divisional Gas Officer will give a lecture in Officers Mess at 2.30 p.m. tomorrow. All Officers who have attended a Gas Course and all Gas N.C.Os. will attend.

4. Excerpt from Camp Standing Orders - Braziers are on no account to be taken into or placed near tents.
Dress:- All Ranks will wear P.H. Helmets at all times when on present area.

R.M. Grant
Captain & Adjt.
15th Bn. High. L. I.

War Diary

Battalion Orders by,
Lieut-Colonel, V.B. RAMSDEN, M.C.,
Commanding 15th Bn. Highland Light Infantry.
17th November 1917.

---

1. Reveille.. 7 a.m.
Breakfast.. 8 a.m.
Sick Parade.. 9 a.m.
Co. on duty.. "A" Coy.
Orderly Officer.. 2/Lieut. HODGE.

DIVINE SERVICES.

2. Presbyterian. Parade Service on Football Field at 11 a.m.
Greatcoats will be worn.
The Sacrament of the Lord's Supper will be dispensed in the Officers Mess Marquee at 11.45 a.m.
Parade Service for Transport Section in Transport Lines at 2.3 0 p.m.

DIVINE SERVICES.

C. of E. Parade Service on 2nd Manchesters Parade Ground at 10 a.m. Parade at Guard Tent at 9.30 a.m. 2/Lieut. CAIN will be in command.

R.C. Service. Notice will be given later.

3. DISCIPLINE. The Hop Fields opposite the camp are strictly out of bounds to all ranks.
Several cases have occurred recently of men committing a nuisance in the Camp Lines. Any more found guilty of this offence will be severely dealt with.

Excerpt from 32nd Divisional Routine Orders dated 16th Novr.1917.
RAILWAYS - DAMAGE TO.
Considerable damage is being done to Light Railway tracks by troops making use of them as thoroughfares, also by artillery and transport vehicles crossing the lines indiscriminately instead of at the proper crossing places.
Onno account are troops permitted to walk on the tracks except those actually employed on the railway.
Vehicles are not allowed to cross except at the proper crossing places.
Unit Commanders will take severe disciplinary action should any breach of these orders occur in future.
It is of the utmost importance that the efficiency of the railway service should not in any way be impaired. Special police measures should be organized by Corps and Divisions to prevent misuse of railway tracks, and to insure disciplinary action being taken in cases where the above orders are contravened.

Part 2.

APPOINTMENTS.
No. 971 C.Q.M.S. J. LOCHRIE, D. Co. to be acting R.Q.M.S. 12/11/17 vice 13477 R.Q.M.S. J. PHILLIPS transferred to Base 11/11/17.
No.13651 Sgt. G. COCKBURN, C. Co. to be A/C.Q.M.S. of D. Co. 12/11/17. vice No. 971 LOCHRIE.
No 353150 Pte. G. McLELLAN, D. Co. to be unpaid L/Cpl. 17/11/17.

SUMMARY PUNISHMENTS.
No. 13446 Pte. A. MATHIE, Hq. Co. offence "Drunkenness" fined 7/6d
33332 Pte. A. BOWDEN, C. Co. offence "Absent of Leave" from 6/11/17 to 10/11/17 awarded 28 days F.P. No. 1, forfeits 4 days pay by R.W.

R M Grant
Captain & Adjt.,
15th Bn. High. L. I.

Battalion Orders by,
Lieut-Colonel V.B. RAMSDEN, M.C.,
Commanding 15th Bn. Highland Light Infantry.
18th November 1917.

---

1. Reveille.................................... 6 a.m.
Breakfast - Under Company arrangements.
Sick Parade.................................... 8 a.m.
C.'Os Orderly Room............................. 12.30 p.m.
Co. on duty.................................... "B" Co.
Orderly Officer................................ 2/Lieut. J.R. ROBERTSON

2. Training will be carried out as per programme.
Coys. will arrange to serve hot tea and biscuits before the C.O's parade at 7 a.m.
Dress for this parade - Drill Order - No gas equipment will be worn.
Any web equipment which is not thoroughly dry need not be worn on parade tomorrow.

3. All Company Commanders (mounted) and one subaltern and two sergeants per Coy. will report to C.O. outside Guard Tent at 9.15 a.m. ALL compasses in possession of Coys., will be brought on this parade.
Arrangements for inspection of model of front line in Town Hall POPERINGHE tomorrow afternoon will be intimated later.

R.M. Grant Captain & Adjt.,
15th Bn. High. L. I.

War Diary

War Diary

Battalion Orders by,
Lieut-Colonel V.B. RAMSDEN, M.C.,
Commanding 15th Bn. Highland Light Infantry.
22nd November 1917.

---

1. Reveille.. 6 a.m.
Breakfast.. 6.15 a.m.
Sick Parade.. 7 a.m.
C.O's. Orderly Room.. 12.30 p.m.
Co. on duty... "B" Co.
Orderly Officer... 2/Lieut. W.C.BLACK.

2. Traing programme is cancelled. No training will be carried out tomorrow.

3. The Divisional Commander will probably address the Battalion about 11 a.m.
Company Commanders will take special precautions that all ranks are well turned out.

4. RETURN OF STORES.
Extra blankets (i.e. one per man) will be rolled in bundles of ten, labelled and carried down to wagons at Q.M. Stores at 7 a.m. Great coats will be tied up securely in bundles of five, labelled and carried down to Q.M. Stores at 7.30 a.m. Haversacks containing personal kit housewife etc. to be at Q.M. Stores at 7.45 a.m. This does not apply to details. Separate instructions are being issued for them.
NOTE.
All cleaning and shaving kit will be taken in the pack.
Officers surplus kit to be at Q.M. Stores at 8 a.m. Kitsto be taken up the line are limited to 45 lbs.

5. DISCIPLINE - S.A.N.L.C. CHINESE AND EGYPTIAN LABOUR COYS.
G.R.O. 2828 is republished :-
(1) All camps in which S.A.N.L.C. Chinese and Egyptian Labour Coys. are accommodated are out of bounds to British N.C.Os and men except those on duty.
(2) Employers to whom such labour is allotted, will, as far as possible so lay out their work that British personnel when employed on the same task as the Natives, shall be supervisors only.
(3) Undue familiarity which is derogatory to discipline is forbidden by British N.C.Os and men and the S.A.N.L.C. Chinese and Egyptian between Coolies at all times whether at work or not.
(4) British N.C.Os and men are not to offer any articles to the S.A.N.L.C. Chinese and Egyptian Coolies either by way of gift, sale or barter or receive, buy or exchange articles from those Natives.

Captain & Adjt.,
15th Bn. High. L. I.

After Order.

Ref. para 3 supra. The Divisional Commander will address the Brigade Group on the Camp Football Ground at 11 a.m. tomorrow. Dress: Drill Order with rifles(no breach covers) belt, braces, pouches, bayonet and frog, caps and P.H. Helmets. No other equipment will be worn.
All Officers will be dismounted. There will be no General Salute.
Mounted officers will wear boots or leggings and spurs: (Coy. Commanders are mounted officers)

P.T.O.

Unmounted officers will wear puttees. All Officers will wear khaki breeches, no sticks or canes will be carried.

Coys. will parade at 10.10 a.m. on Coy. Parade Ground.

Further orders will be issued later.

ALL COMPANIES AND R.S.M.

All blankets of men who are going to details camp will be rolled in bundles of ten and labelled; jerkins will be rolled in bundles of five and labelled; these stores will all be carried down to Proven Road - end of duck board track and loaded on lorries at 7 a.m. tomorrow. "A" Coy. will detail two O.R. to proceed with these stores to HOUTERQUE - they will take two days rations with them. These two men will be detailed from "A" Coy's details list .

Captain & Adjt.,
16th Bn. High. L. I.

22-11-17.

War Diary

[illegible]ion Orders by,
Lieut-Colonel [illegible], M.C.,
Commanding 15th Bn. Highland Light Infantry.,
23rd November 1917.

---

1. Reveille.. 6 a.m.
   Breakfast.. 6.45 a.m.

2. The Battalion less details will parade on Football Ground beside Headquarters Huts at 9 a.m. and proceed to entrain at [illegible] for IRISH FARM.
3. DRESS:- Marching order with packs; steel helmets will be worn; blanket will be carried in packs; jerkins will be worn. Haversack rations will be carried by all ranks.
4. Officers valises will be handed in to Q.M. Stores at 7 a.m. Details for HOUTERQUE will be on road opposite SCHOOL CAMP(WATOU ROAD)at 10 a.m. 2/Lieut. CALDERWOOD will be in command and will issue necessary orders. Details Blankets will be rolled in bundles of 10; jerkins in bundles of five, labelled and carried to end of duck board track - [illegible] ROAD by 7.30 a.m.
   R.S.M. will detail a party to load up these stores on lorry and proceed with lorry to HOUTERQUE.
   2/Lieut. CALDERWOOD's valise will also be taken by this lorry.
5. Camp will be inspected by C.O. at 8.15 a.m. Dinners will be served in arrival at IRISH FARM.

Captain & Adjt.,
15th Bn. High. L. I.

Instructions regarding War Diaries and Intelligence Summaries are contained in F. S. Regs., Part II. and the Staff Manual respectively. Title pages will be prepared in manuscript.

WAR DIARY
or
INTELLIGENCE SUMMARY.
(Erase heading not required.)

Army Form C. 2118.

Place	Date	Hour	Summary of Events and Information	Remarks and references to Appendices
				Appendix VI Battn. Orders.

	1st Nov.	30th Nov.
Comdg. Officer's Strength.	871	788.

Fighting Strength.	1st Nov.	30th Nov.
Officers.	38	38
Other ranks.	990	961

Total casualties for month.	Officers	Other ranks
Killed and died of wounds	-	16.
Wounded	-	24
Missing	-	1

WMcL

[signature] Lt. Colonel
Comdg. 15th (Service) Battn.
The Highland Light Infantry

A5834 Wt. W4973/M687 750,000 8/16 D. D. & L. Ltd. Forms/C.2118/13.

Instructions regarding War Diaries and Intelligence Summaries are contained in F. S. Regs., Part II. and the Staff Manual respectively. Title pages will be prepared in manuscript.

14/32

WAR DIARY
or
INTELLIGENCE SUMMARY.
(Erase heading not required.)

15 HLI
Vol 26

Army Form C. 2118.

Place	1917. Date	Hour	Summary of Events and Information	Remarks and references to Appendices
BELLEVUE	December 1st		Bn. in support in shell hole positions – weather cold but clear. Carrying parties were again provided.	WH
do	2nd		Bn in support during Divisional attack. During night 1st-2nd heavy enemy barrage put down on Bn. area. Artillery very quiet during forenoon.	WH
do	3rd		Bn in support. Preparations made for accomodating 2nd Manchesters in Bn area. Whole Bn. occupied positions of A+B Coys. 2nd Manchesters occupied C+D Coys area.	WH
do	4th		Bn in support. Bn. re-occupied former positions when 2nd Manchesters moved forward to TOURNANT FM.	WH
do	5th		Bn in support. Weather frosty & clear. Work done improving shell hole positions. A+B Coys moved to HILL TOP	WH
do	6th		Bn. relieved by 2nd Manchesters and moved back to HILL TOP FM. where day was spent resting.	WH
HILL TOP FARM	7th		Bn billetted. 2 companies in readiness to move at 15 min. notice. 2 Coys provided carrying parties.	WH
do	8th		Bn in billets. Resting and cleaning up. Carrying parties as 7th inst.	WH
SEIGE FARM	9th		Bn. moved back to SEIGE CAMP. Day spent cleaning up. C.O. left to attend course	WH
do	10th		Bn in billets. Cleaning up and improving conditions in camp	WH
do	11th		Bn in billets. Coy parades and cleaning up. Weather good but cold	WH
do	12th		Bn in billets. Bn. at baths. A+B Coy. inspected by MAJOR CLEGHORN. Detail rejoined Bn. 2/Lt KEWAN joined Bn.	WH
do	13th		Bn in billets. C+D Coy inspected by MAJOR CLEGHORN	WH
IRISH FARM	14th		Bn. moved to IRISH FARM where day was spent settling down. A Coy billetted in VIEW FARM.	WH
do	15th		Bn in billets. Bn on working parties – salving – carrying and working in forward area	WH
do	16th		Bn in billets Bn on working parties. 2/Lt MANSON & 2/Lt BARR wounded in VIEW FARM.	WH

26.0
10 sheets

A5834 Wt. W4973/M687 750,000 8/16 D. D. & L. Ltd. Forms/C.2118/13.

Instructions regarding War Diaries and Intelligence Summaries are contained in F. S. Regs., Part II. and the Staff Manual respectively. Title pages will be prepared in manuscript.

WAR DIARY
or
INTELLIGENCE SUMMARY.
(Erase heading not required.)

Army Form C. 2118.

Place	1917 Date	Hour	Summary of Events and Information	Remarks and references to Appendices
IRISH FARM	December 17th		Bn in billets. Working parties consisting of whole Battalion again employed. CAPT. DOUGHTY and A/Cpt. HOWISON returned off course. LT HOWISON left for Brigade as Brigade Gas Officer.	[illegible]
do	18th		Bn in billets. Working parties as usual. Lt. Col. Ramsden returned from Paris leave	[illegible]
do	19th		Bn. supplied working parties as usual. Lt Lane & 2/Lt Carthew returned from courses 2/Lt Ferguson left on leave to England	[illegible]
do	20th		Bn in billets in Irish Farm where the usual working parties were found	[illegible]
do	21st		Bn in billets. Working parties handed over to 96th Brigade	[illegible]
do	22nd		~~Bn~~ Whole Battalion employed making Corps main line of Defence	[illegible]
do	23rd		Bn moved to Hill Top Farm. 'C' Coy moved to Corps main line. Details under 2Lt MacArthur moved back to Reigersburg.	
HILL TOP FARM	24th		Bn in Brigade reserve. 'D' Coy moved into Corps main line.	[illegible]
do	25th		Bn in Brigade reserve. 'A' Coy relieved 'C' Coy in Corps main line. 'C' moved back to HILL TOP FM	[illegible]
do	26th		Bn in Brigade reserve. 'B' Coy relieved 'D' Coy in Corps main line. "SOS." sent up by Division on our right and Battalion occupied Corps line until SOS. cancelled at 10 pm. when 'C' & 'D' Coys returned to HILL TOP FM. 2/Lt BLACK left on course	[illegible]
do	27th		Bn relieved 1st DORSET REGT. in left sub. sector. Front occupied by 'B' & 'C' Coy. Front extended from V 28 a 35·50 to ~~V 21a~~ V 21 c 2·0. 'D' Coy in support at BURNS HOUSE V 20 d 4·6. 'A' Coy in reserve at WINCHESTER at D 2 b 5·4.	[illegible]

A5834 Wt. W4973/M687 750,000 8/16 D. D. & L. Ltd. Forms/C.2118/13.

SECRET

OPERATION ORDE[R]

CAPTURE OF PILL BOX AT V.28.b.0.8.

1/ Previous instruction are cancelled.

2/ INFORMATION It has been ascertained definately by patrols that
occupies a post about 80° N.W of pill box.

3/ INTENTION

(a) 2/LT. ROBERTSON + a party of 6 O.R. will occupy by 5·30 AM. a point
from the pill box which he will select by reconnaissance tonight
From this point he will watch the enemy carefully.

(b) If the post mentioned in para 2. is seen to withdraw to the [illegible]
in rear + it is considered that no apparent sign of occupation [illegible]
pill box exists the party will approach carefully + occupy it.

(c) If the garrison of the post (estimated at 3) withdraws to the pill box
and there are no indications of further reinforcements in the pill box he
will at once attack + endeavour to capture it by surprise.

(d) If there are indication of a garrison in the pill box + if the garrison
of the post mentioned above is larger than estimated. O.C. party will withdraw his party carefully to front line. This will only be done if
he considers that the forces against him are too large and the attack
too hazardous.

4/ COMPOSITION OF Nº 1 PARTY. 2/LT. ROBERTSON, Cpl MARTIN + 5 O.R, 1 Signaller from
H.Q. + two runners from 'C' Coy.

5/ ACTION ON CAPTURE OF POSITION

(a) When the position has been captured O C party will immediately
order the signaller to signal back to Nº 2 post a series of dots by flash
lamp: this will be the only indication of success, by signal. At the
same time the two runners will immediately return to Nº 2 post with
accurate information. Those 2 runners will co-operate 75x in ~~front~~ rear of
the Nº 1 party.

(b) On receipt of above signal or runner message at Nº 2 post O.C 'C' Coy
will dispatch immediately runners, who will have been previously
established there, to Bn H.Q. + H.Q 5/6 R.S. The information will
also be transmitted by phone to Bn H.Q.

6/ INSTRUCTION FOR ASSEMBLY OF TROOPS SUPPORTING ATTACK.

(a) Nº 2 party as detailed in previous orders ie Sgt. LYONS + 6 O.R. + 1 L.G.
will move up + occupy Nº 3 post by 5-30 AM. O.C. 'C' Coy will place
existing garrison of this post in SOURD Fm

(b) O.C 'C' Coy will detail garrison for 2 additional posts (each of 1 N.C.O + 4
men) to be held in readiness in Nº 3 post + SOURD Fm

7/ ACTION [illegible] OF SUPPORTING TROOPS AFTER CAPTURE OF POSITION FOR

THE EVENT OF THE PILL BOX BEING CAPTURED BY 6·30 AM.

(a) On receipt of success signal or runner message. Nº 2 party + post
garrison as detailed in para 6(b) will immediately move out and occupy
posts to link up the new position to the existing Nº 3 post.

(b) Nº 2 party will split up into two groups. One group will occupy
a post (with L G.) 50x from the pill box and the other party another
post 50x away from that. The 'C' Coy parties will divide the
distance from Nº 2 parties left post to the present Nº 3 post. O.C 'C'
Coy. will point out the approximate position of these posts previously
to Sgt. LYONS + his own parties.

8/ ACTION IN EVENT OF THE POSITION BEING CAPTURED AFTER 7 AM.

(a) All garrisons detailed in new posts will be held in readiness to
move out at any time to occupy new posts if mist or fog permits
O.C 'C' Coy will decide.

(b) Above garrison will move out as soon as dusk permits.

(c) O.C. Nº 1 party will be prepared to defend the new position during
day-light at all costs.

9/ O.C 5/6. R.S. will arrange to keep a careful watch + co-operate with
fire action against any enemy counter-attack. At dusk he will
link up his line with the new position.

10/ DRESS & EQUIPMENT

As previously ordered. Garrisons detailed for posts will carry
shovels.

29/12/17.

[illegible] Lt Col

[illegible]

Instructions regarding War Diaries and Intelligence Summaries are contained in F. S. Regs., Part II. and the Staff Manual respectively. Title pages will be prepared in manuscript.

WAR DIARY
or
INTELLIGENCE SUMMARY.

(Erase heading not required.)

Army Form C. 2118.

Place	Date	Hour	Summary of Events and Information	Remarks and references to Appendices
HUBNER (in the line)	December 27th	(Cont)	Battalion Headquarters at HUBNER D1c 47. The relief was completed by 8.30pm without casualties. Immediately after relief, work was commenced wiring the posts. There was very little activity on the enemy's part although the night was clear and fine.	WK
do	28th		Battalion in the line. The enemy's artillery was active during the day, the favourite targets being the Corps main line, Triangle and the tracks in rear of Bn. Hqrs. Very little shelling took place in advance of Bn. Hqrs. 2Lt. Robertson remained in ~~left~~ right company front line to observe a pill box at V28 b 0.8. No movement of any kind was observed and there was no activity from machine guns in the pill box	WK
			2 patrols left our post on left company frontage to endeavour to locate enemy's position 2 shell-hole posts were discovered at V21 d 53 and V21 a 30. Three of the enemy were seen in each of these posts.	
			Capt Jeffries and 1 O.R. patrolled in vicinity of V28 b 08 and found the enemy established in shell holes in front of pill box.	
			Capt Jeffries + Lt Robertson patrolled in vicinity of V28 b 0.8 and found enemy in vicinity dressed in white	
			Operation Orders were drawn up for attack on pill box V28 b 08	Copy of O.O. attached
do	29th		Battalion in line. Artillery activity very slight. During night work was done wiring front line. Patrols went out from 'B' Coy to verify map reference of posts previously mentioned. These are now at V21 c 9.4 and V21 d 2.3. Operation orders were drawn up cancelled previous ones ~~which~~ owing to the weather conditions not being favourable.	WK Copy attached

Instructions regarding War Diaries and Intelligence Summaries are contained in F. S. Regs., Part II. and the Staff Manual respectively. Title pages will be prepared in manuscript.

WAR DIARY
or
INTELLIGENCE SUMMARY.

(Erase heading not required.)

Army Form C. 2118.

Place	Date	Hour	Summary of Events and Information	Remarks and references to Appendices
HUBNER (In the line)	Decemb 1917 30th ~~29th (cont)~~		Battalion in line. Before daybreak 2Lt Robertson with No 1 party left our posts and went in direction of V29 b 08 and found 3 posts around the pill box. He remained there with enemy under observation till 7 am and there was no sign of enemy withdrawing, so he withdrew to our line. Enemy artillery was active on Corps line and Triangle but otherwise fairly quiet. Battalion relieved by 16th Rifle Brigade and moved back to IRISH FARM	
	31st		Bn in IRISH FARM. B & C Coys had their feet treated in French method. All feet ~~[illegible]~~ are in excellent condition. Bn. rested during the day.	

	1st Decr	31st Decr
Comdg Officers Strength	780	674

Fighting Strength	1st Decr	31st Decr
Officers	38	33
OR	960	840

Casualties for month	Officers	OR
Wounded	3	
Sick	2	
Killed & died of Wounds		13
Wounded		51

[signature] Lt Col
Comdg 15th [illegible]
4/1/18

A5834 Wt. W4973/M687 750,000 8/16 D. D. & L. Ltd. Forms/C.2118/13.

ructions regarding War Diaries and Intelligence Summaries are contained in F. S. Regs., Part II. and the Staff Manual respectively. Title pages will be prepared in manuscript.

WAR DIARY
or
INTELLIGENCE SUMMARY.
(Erase heading not required.)

Army Form C. 2118.

15 HLI

Vol 27

Place	Date	Hour	Summary of Events and Information	Remarks and references to Appendices
IRISH FARM.	1st Jan	1918.	The Battalion entrained, along with 1st DORSETS at St JEAN railhead at 4 p.m. Travelled thence to ADINKERQUE, & from there by route march to LA PANNE where Batt. was billetted.	
LA PANNE	2nd "		Battalion resting in billets. C.O. inspected billets. Billets fairly good, weather cold, with severe frost. Coy. Commanders met C.O. in the evening to discuss training programmes & New Year celebrations.	
"	3rd "		Coys cleaning up & improving billets. Snow fell during the day. C.O. P.M.C. & 2/Lt CALDERWOOD went to CALAIS to order provisions for dinners for the men.	
"	4th "		Forenoon devoted to drill. T.O. proceeded to CALAIS to bring back provisions bought the previous day. 2/Lt W. McCAIG admitted to hospital suffering from P.U.O. 2/Lt FERGUSON returned from leave. Weather clear, cold & frosty.	
	5th "		Bn. in billets. Forenoon spent in cleaning-up, & arm drill. 2/Lt McARTHUR left on leave.	
	6th "		Xmas & New Year dinner given to the men in Company billets. 2/Lt PRYDE left on leave.	
	7th "		Inspection of Battalion by Brigadier. Cold frosty weather continues.	
	8th "		Heavy snowfall during the day. Bde. group was to be inspected by the Corps Commander at 2.45 p.m. but inspection was cancelled owing to the weather. In evening, Sergeants' dinner & Officers' dinner. 2/Lt McGILL joined the Bn.	

A5834 Wt. W4973/M687 750,000 8/16 D. D. & L. Ltd. Forms/C.2118/13.

Instructions regarding War Diaries and Intelligence Summaries are contained in F. S. Regs., Part II. and the Staff Manual respectively. Title pages will be prepared in manuscript.

WAR DIARY
or
~~INTELLIGENCE SUMMARY.~~
(Erase heading not required.)

Army Form C. 2118.

Place	Date	Hour	Summary of Events and Information	Remarks and references to Appendices
LA PANNE	9th Jan		Batt in billets. Training as per programme from 10 am. 2/LT McCAIG returned from hospital.	App. Gnib
	10		"B" + D Coys trained as per programme. A + C Coys inspected by C.O.	" Gnib
	11		B + D Coys inspected by C.O. Remainder trained as per programme. Weather not so cold as thaw set in	" Gnib
	12.		A + B Coys on range – grouping + application practices. Ground very soft underfoot owing to thaw	" Gnib
	13.		Sunday. Church Parades	Gnib
	14.		Bn in billets. Weather very wet. Training as per programme.	" Gnib
	15.		Training as per programme. C + D Coys on range.	Gnib
	16.		Range practices cancelled owing to wet weather. C.O. proceeded to G.H.Q. Major CLEGHORN + Capt O'MAY returned from leave.	Gnib
	17.		Weather still wet. Range practices again cancelled. C.O. returned from G.H.Q.	Gnib
	18.		Training – Route march as detailed in Bn. orders, in place of training programme.	App. Gnib

Gnib

A5834 Wt. W4973/M687 750,000 8/16 D. D. & L. Ltd. Forms/C.2118/13.

Instructions regarding War Diaries and Intelligence Summaries are contained in F. S. Regs., Part II. and the Staff Manual respectively. Title pages will be prepared in manuscript.

WAR DIARY
or
~~INTELLIGENCE SUMMARY.~~
(Erase heading not required.)

Army Form C. 2118.

Place	Date	Hour	Summary of Events and Information	Remarks and references to Appendices
LA PANNE	19th Jan.		Bn. bathed at RECQUES. When not at baths, Coys trained as laid down in programme. Weather dull but dry.	app I [illegible]
	20th		Sunday. Church Parades. Weather dry.	[illegible]
	21st		The day was spent scrubbing equipment & cleaning up generally. Advance party as detailed in Op. order No 181 left for new area by train from Audruicq	[illegible] app. II
	22.		Bn. less transport marched to Audruicq & entrained for ELVERDINGHE – thence by road to billets at DIRTY BUCKET Camp.	" [illegible]
DIRTY BUCKET Camp.	23.		Training as laid down in programme. C.O. & 2/LT WOOD proceeded on leave. 2/LT MacARTHUR returned from leave, & 2/LT PRYDE.	app I [illegible]
	24.		Training as per programme. Weather fair & warmer.	" [illegible]
	25		Training as per programme. Special lecture to Lewis Gunners by Brigade Major.	" [illegible]
	26.		Training as per programme except that "B" Coy trained as laid down for A Coy & range was devoted to Lewis Gun work. C.O. Adjt, Capt D'AMAY & 2/LT CALDERWOOD proceeded to new sector taken over by Division at BOESINGHE & became acquainted with the area.	app III [illegible]

[illegible]

A5834 Wt. W4973/M687 750,000 8/16 D. D. & L. Ltd. Forms/C.2118/13.

Instructions regarding War Diaries and Intelligence Summaries are contained in F. S. Regs., Part II. and the Staff Manual respectively. Title pages will be prepared in manuscript.

WAR DIARY
or
INTELLIGENCE SUMMARY.
(Erase heading not required.)

Army Form C. 2118.

Place	Date	Hour	Summary of Events and Information	Remarks and references to Appendices
Dirty Bucket Camp.	27th Jan.		Bn. bathed at SEIGE CAMP. Church parade cancelled. Weather continued fine.	[illegible]
"	28th Jan.		Bn. trained as per programme, ~~Lewis Gunners fired on range~~ In the afternoon the Bn. received an advance of pay. Weather fine. Major CLEGHORN proceeded to MILLAIN to visit II Corps School.	App I [illegible]
	29th		Bn. trained in accordance with programme. Party of four officers & four NCO.s proceeded up the line to reconnoitre the new sector to be taken over.	App II [illegible]
	30th		Batt. moved from DIRTY BUCKET Camp to EMILE Camp, near ELVERDINGHE.	App III [illegible]
EMILE Camp.			In the afternoon, all men had their feet treated in the French method, for protection against Trench feet. In the evening a draft of four officers & twenty OR reported to the Bn. Officers were Major W.W. WHITE. Lt. J REID, 2/Lt. W GEORGESON & 2/Lt J. CROMBIE	
	31		Bn. in Divisional ~~Rest~~ Reserve in Emile Camp. The men again had their feet treated & physical & arm drill was done under Coy. arrangements. Weather was very misty & frost again set in. Advance party of one officer & 8 OR left to take over from the 2nd KOYLI, 97th Bde, in Bde. Support.	[illegible]

[illegible]

A5834 Wt. W4973/M687 750,000 8/16 D. D. & L. Ltd. Forms/C.2118/13.

Instructions regarding War Diaries and Intelligence Summaries are contained in F. S. Regs., Part II. and the Staff Manual respectively. Title pages will be prepared in manuscript.

WAR DIARY
or
INTELLIGENCE SUMMARY.
(Erase heading not required.)

Army Form C. 2118.

Place	Date	Hour	Summary of Events and Information	Remarks and references to Appendices
			Battalion Strength.	

	1st Jan	31st Jan
C. Os. Strength.	673	675.
Fighting Strength. — Officers	33	42
" " O.R.	844	857
Casualties	Nil.	

[signature] Cunningham Major
Commdg 15th [illegible]

31/1/18.

A5834 Wt. W4973/M687 750,000 8/16 D. D. & L. Ltd. Forms/C.2118/13.

War Diary

App III

Battalion Orders by,
Lieut-Colonel V.B. RAMSDEN, M.C.,
Commanding 15th Bn. THE HIGHLAND LIGHT INFANTRY.
2nd January 1918.

---

1. Reveille)
Breakfast) Under Coy. Arrangements.
Dinner)
Sick Parade.. 9.30 a.m.
Orderly Officer......................................2/Lieut. D.C. HODGE.
Battalion Orderly Sergeant.........................Sgt. RIACH.
Co. on duty.. "C" Co.

2. Precautions against fire.
Copies of S.S. 611 have today been issued to all Coys. These orders must be strictly complied with and will be read on Co. parades at least once a month. Certificates that this has been complied with will be rendered to Orderly Room on the penultimate day of each month. S.S. 611 will be posted in all billets containing straw or other inflamable material.

3. 32nd Division Instructions No. 17.
These have today been issued to Coys. for information.

4. Extract from 14th Infantry Brigade Letter 24-12-17 "Brigadier received a letter from the Divisional Commander in which he wishes the 14th Infantry Brigade best Christmas Wishes and he also states he owes the Brigade a great dept of gratitude for all the good work the Battalions have done and the credit which they have brought to the Division. He expresses a desire that the contents of his letter be communicated to all ranks and wishes them all every possible good luck and continuation of their successes in 1918".

2 /Lieut.,
A/Adjt. 15th Bn. High. L. I.

Adj. War Diary

S E C R E T.

Copy No......

15th Bn. THE HIGHLAND LIGHT INFANTRY.

Operation Order No. 182.

1. The 15th Bn. H. L. I. will move from DIRTY BUCKET CAMP to EMILE CAMP B.9.c.6.6. (BOESINGHE No. 3 Area) on Wednesday 30th inst.

ROUTE. Hospital Farm and ELVERDINGHE.

2. The Battalion will parade in DIRTY BUCKET CAMP at 10.15 a.m. ready to move in the following order:- H.Q. "B" "C" "D" "A" and Transport. The following intervals will be observed on the march. 100 yards between Coys. Transport 100 yards in rear of "A" Coy.

3. DRESS. Full marching order, shrapnel helmets will be worn, leather jerkins strapped on pack.

4. The Commanding Officer will inspect the huts at 9.30 a.m. the usual certificates will be rendered to Orderly Room.

5. BILLETING PARTY. 1 N.C.O. per Coy. will report to 2/Lieut. CALDERWOOD at Orderly Room at 7.30 a.m. This party will proceed on bicycles to EMILE CAMP, report to Camp Adjutant at 8.30 a.m., take over billets, and meet the Battalion at B.9.c.1.3.

6. BLANKETS. Blankets will be stacked in bundles of 10 at Q.M. Stores at 7 a.m. One blanket man per Coy. will remain with blankets. O.C. B. Co. will detail 1 N.C.O. to remain in charge of this party.

VALISES. On roadside at Hqrs. at 8.30 a.m.

7. Cookers, two Lewis Gun Limbers and two water carts will proceed in rear of the Battalion.

8. The Mess Cart and Lewis Gun Limbers, Orderly Room material and Medical Stores will be loaded at 9 a.m.

9. While the Battalion is in the line, Transport Lines and Q.M. Stores will be located in BOESINGHE No. 3 Area at A.12.a.2.6.

[signature] 2/Lt

for Major,
Commanding 15th Bn. High. L. I.

C.O.
Adj.
2 O.
H Q
A
B
C
D
QM.
T.O.
SM
File

Appendix I.

15th Bn. THE HIGHLAND LIGHT INFANTRY.

Amended Training Programme for Saturday 12th January 1918.

Coys.	Time.	Nature of Training.	Locality.	Remarks.
"A" Coy.	8 - 10.30 am.	Musketry.	Range.	
	11.30 - 12 noon	Gas Drill	Billets.	
	12.15 - 12.45 pm	Rapid Wiring.	"	
"B" Coy.	9 - 9.45 am.	Gas Drill.	Billets.	
	10.30 - 1 pm.	Musketry.	Range.	
"C" Coy.	9 - 9.35 am.	Gas Drill.	Billets.	
	9.45 - 10.45 am	Rapid Wiring	"	
	1 - 3.30 pm.	Musketry.	Range.	
"D" Coy.	9 - 9.45 am.	B.F.	Billets.	
	10-10.45 am.	Platoon extended order drill.		
	11 - 11.45 am.	Rapid Wiring.		
	12 - 12.45 pm.	Musketry.		

REGIMENTAL CLASSES:- as per original programme.

(b) Lewis Gunners to fire on range with their Coys.

(d) One target will be allotted throughout the day.

Lieut-Colonel,
Commanding 15th Bn. High. L. I.

War Diary

15th Bn. THE HIGHLAND LIGHT INFANTRY.

TRAINING PROGRAMME FOR MONDAY 14th JANUARY 1918.

Coys.	Time.	Nature of Training.	Locality.	Remarks.
Bn.	9 - 9.45 am.	C.O's. Parade.	Bn.Parade Ref. J.24.a.4.7.	
	10 - 12.30 pm.	Bn.practice in trench to trench attack with barrage.	do:	
	2.15 - 4 p.m.	Tactical Scheme without troops.	Training Area.	All Off. & Sgts.

REGIMENTAL CLASSES DAILY 9 - 1 p.m.

(a) Signallers under S.O.

(b) Lewis Gunners (6 per Coy.) under L.G.O.

(c) N.C.Os. Class (4 per Co.) under R.S.M.

(d) Observers & Snipers under I.O.

[signature] for Lieut-Colonel,
Commanding 15th Bn. High. L. I.

[illegible] Bn. THE HIGHLAND LIGHT INFANTRY.

TRAINING PROGRAMME FOR TUESDAY 15th JANUARY 1918.

[illegible]

Coys.	Time.	Nature of Training.	Locality.	Remarks.
"A" Coy.	9 - 9.30 am.	Gas Drill	J.23b.6.5.	
	10.30 - 1 pm.	Musketry.	Range	
"B" Coy.	9 - 9.30 am.	Gas Drill		
	9.30 - 11.15 am	Co. practice in open warfare formation	J.30a.4.7. Bn. Parade Ground.	
	1 - 3.30 PM	Musketry	Range.	
"C" Coy.	9 - 9.45 am.	B.F.		
	10-11.45 am	Co. practice in open warfare formation	J.24a.8.4.7. Bn. Parade Ground	
	12.15-12.45 pm	Gas Drill	J.29.a.7.6.	Inspection by B.G.C.
"D" Co.	8 - 10.30 am	Musketry	Range.	
	12-12.40 pm	Gas Drill	J22.b.6.3.	
All Off. & 5 NCOs per Co.	5.30 pm	Lecture by B.G.C.		

(signature)

(signature) Lieut-Colonel,
Commanding 15th Bn. High. L. I.

18th Bn. THE HIGHLAND LIGHT INFANTRY.

TRAINING PROGRAMME FOR WEDNESDAY 16th JANUARY 1918.

Coys.	Time.	Nature of Training.	Locality.	Remarks.
Bn.	9 - 11 a.m.	Bn. in open warfare attack practice.	Training Area.	
	11.15 - 1 pm.	Bn. in position organised for defence in depth.	do:	

for Lieut-Colonel,
Commanding 18th Bn. High. L. I.

18th Bn. THE HIGHLAND LIGHT INFANTRY.

TRAINING PROGRAMME FOR THURSDAY 17th JANUARY 1918.

Coys.	Time.	Nature of Training.	Locality.	Remarks.
"A" Coy.	9 - 9.45 am.	B.F.	J.23.b.6.5. Billet Ref.	
	10 - 12 noon	Coy. practice in open warfare movements.	Bn. Parade Ref. J.24.a.4.7.	
	12.15 - 12.45 pm.	Coy. Close order Drill.	Billet Ref. J.23.b.6.5.	
"B" Coy.	8 - 10.30 am.	Musketry	Range.	
	12 - 12.45 pm.	Coy. Close order drill.	Billets.	
"C" Coy.	9 - 9.30 am.	Gas Drill		
	10.30 - 1 pm.	Musketry.	Range.	
"D" Coy.	9 - 11 am.	Coy. practice in open warfare formation.	Bn. Parade Ref. J.24.a.4.7.	
	1 - 3.30 pm.	Musketry.	Range.	

for Lieut-Colonel,
Commanding 18th Bn. High. L. I.

SECRET

15th Bn. THE HIGHLAND LIGHT INFANTRY.

TRAINING PROGRAMME FOR FRIDAY 18th JANUARY 1918.

Coys.	Time.	Nature of Training.	Locality.	Remarks.
"A" "B" "C" "D" Cos.	9 - 9.30 am.	Co. Close Order Drill	J.23.b.6.5. J.23.c.1.9. Billet Refs. J.29.a.7.6.	
Bn.	12.30 p.m.	Bn. Field Firing Scheme.	J.22.b.4.3.	Scheme to be submitted later.

Lieut-Colonel,
Commanding 15th Bn. High. L. I.

15th Bn. THE HIGHLAND LIGHT INFANTRY.

TRAINING PROGRAMME FOR SATURDAY 19th JANUARY 1918.

Coys.	Time.	Nature of Training.	Locality.	Remarks.
"A" Co.	9 - 9.45 am.	P.T.	J.23.b.6.5. Billet Ref.	
	10.-10.45 am.	Platoons rapid wiring competition.		
	11.15-11.45 am.	Visual Training.	Bn. Parade Ground Ref. J.24.a.4.7.	
"B" Co.	9 - 9.45 am.	P.T.	Billet Ref. J.23.c.1.9.	
	10 -10.45 am.	Judging distance & composition of Range Charts.	Bn. Parade Ground Ref.	
	11-11.45 am.	Platoons rapid wiring competitions.		
"C" Co.	9 - 9.45 am.	P.T.	Billet Ref. J.29.a.7.6.	
	10-10.45 am.	Visual Training & judging distance, composition of Range Charts.	Bn. Parade Ground Ref.	
	11-11.45 am.	Platoons specialists training.	do:	
"D" Co.	9 - 9.45 am.	B.F.	Billet Ref. J.22.b.4.3.	
	10-10.45 am.	Visual Training & J.D. composition of range charts.	do:	
	11-11.30 am.	Gas Drill.		
Bn.	12 -12.45 pm.	C.O's. Parade.	Bn. Parade Ground Ref.	

Lieut-Colonel.
Commanding 15th Bn. H. L. I.

Training programme for 7th January.

Duplicate.

War Diary.

15th Bn. THE HIGHLAND LIGHT INFANTRY.

TRAINING PROGRAMME FOR WEDNESDAY 23rd JANUARY 1918.

Coys.	Time.	Nature of Training.	Locality.	Remarks.
"A" Coy.	9 - 10 am.	Close order drill	Camp.	
	10.15 - 11.15 am.	Platoon Specialist Training.	"	
	11.45-12.45 pm.	Platoon Rapid Wiring Squads. Gas Drill.	"	
"B" Coy.	9 - 10 am.	Platoon Rapid Wiring Squads. Gas Drill.		
	10.15-11.15 am.	Close order drill.		
	11.45-12.15 pm.	B.F. Assault Course.		
	12.15-12.45 pm.	Saluting Parade.		
"C" Coy.	9 - 9.45 am.	B.F. Assault Course.		
	10 - 11 am.	Platoon Rapid Wiring Squads. Gas Drill.		
	11.30 - 12.15 pm	Platoon Specialist Training.		
	12.15-12.45 pm	Handling Arms.		
"D" Coy.	9 - 1 pm.	Range.		

REGIMENTAL CLASSES:-
(a) Signallers under S.O.
(b) Lewis Gun Class (6 per Coy) under L.G.O.
(c) N.C.Os. Class (4 per Coy)
(d) Observers and Snipers under I.O.
DAILY.
B.F. supervised by Bde. C.S.M.I.

[signature]

E/Lieut.,
for O.C. Commanding 15th Bn. High. L. I.

15th Bn. THE HIGHLAND LIGHT INFANTRY.

TRAINING PROGRAMME FOR THURSDAY 24th JANUARY 1918.

Coys.	Time.	Nature of Training.	Locality.	Remarks.
"A" Coy.	9 - 9.45 am.	B.F. Assault Course.	Camp.	
	10 - 11 am.	Platoon Specialist Training.		
	11.30 - 12 noon	Platoon Rapid Wiring Squads.		
	12 - 12.45 pm.	Musketry.		
"B" Coy.	9 - 10 am.	Close order drill.		
	10.15 - 11.15 am.	Platoon Specialist Training.		
	11.45 - 12.45 pm.	Musketry.		
"C" Coy.	9 - 1 pm.	Range.		
"D" Coy.	9 - 10 am.	Platoon Rapid Wiring Squads. Gas Drill.		
	10.15 - 11 am.	B.F. Assault Course.		
	11.30 - 12 noon	Close order drill.		
	12 - 12.45 pm.	Platoon Specialist Training.		

[signature] 2/Lieut.,
for O.C. Commanding 15th Bn. High. L. I.

15th Bn. THE HIGHLAND LIGHT INFANTRY.

TRAINING PROGRAMME FOR FRIDAY 25th JANUARY 1918.

Coys.	Time.	Nature of Training.	Locality.	Remarks.
"A" Coy.	9 - 1 pm.	Range.	Camp.	
"B" Coy.	9 - 9.45 am.	B.F. Assault Course.		
	10 - 11 am.	Platoon Specialist Training,		
	11.30 - 12.15 pm	Musketry.		
	12.15 - 12.45 pm	Close order drill.		
"C" Coy.	9 - 10 am.	Platoon Rapid Wiring Squads. Gas Drill.		
	10.15 - 11.15 am.	Platoon Specialist Training.		
	11.30 - 12.15 pm	B.F. Assault Course.		
	12.15 - 12.45 pm	Close order drill.		
"D" Coy.	9 - 9.45 am.	Close order drill.		
	10 - 11 am.	B.F. Assault Course.		
	11.30 - 12.15 pm	Platoon Rapid Wiring Squads. Gas Drill.		
	12.15 - 12.45 pm	Saluting Parade.		

[signature]

2/Lieut.,
for O.C. Commanding 15th Bn. High. L.I.

15th Bn. THE HIGHLAND LIGHT INFANTRY.

TRAINING PROGRAMME FOR SATURDAY 26th JANUARY 1918.

Coys.	Time.	Nature of Training.	Locality.	Remarks.
"A" Coy.	9 - 9.45 am.	P.T.	Camp.	
	10 - 11 am.	Platoon Specialist Training.		
	11.30 - 12 noon	Platoon Rapid Wiring Squads.		
	12 - 12.45 pm.	C.O's. Parade.		
"B" Coy.	9 - 1 pm.	Range.		
"C" Coy.	9 - 10 am.	Platoon Rapid Wiring Squads.		
	10.15 - 11 am.	B.F. or P.T.		
	11.30 - 12 noon.	Gas Drill.		Supervised by Bde.Gas. Off.
	12-12.45 pm.	C.O's. Parade.		
"D" Coy.	9 - 10 am.	Platoon Specialist Training.		
	10.15 - 11 am.	Platoon Rapid Wiring Squads.		
	11.30 - 12 noon	Gas Drill.		do:
	12-12.45 p.m.	C.O's. Parade.		

2/Lieut.,
for O.C. Commanding 15th Bn. H.L.I.

15th Bn. THE HIGHLAND LIGHT INFANTRY.

TRAINING PROGRAMME FOR MONDAY 28th JANUARY 1918.

Coys.	Time.	Nature of Training.	Locality.	Remarks.
"A" Coy.	9 - 10.45 a.m.	Platoon Rapid Firing Squads.	Vicinity of Camp.	
	11 - 11.30 a.m.	P.T. & B.F.		
	11.30 - 12 noon	Handling of Arms		
	12.15 - 12.45 p.m.	Saluting Drill.		
"B" Coy.	9 - 9.30 a.m.	P.T. & B.F.	do:	
	9.30 - 10 a.m.	Saluting Drill		
	10.15 - 11.15 a.m.	Handling of Arms.		
	11.30 - 12.45 pm.	Platoon Rapid Firing Squads.		
"C" Coy.	9 - 10 a.m.	Handling of Arms and Close order drill.	do:	
	10.15 - 11.15 am.	Musketry.		
	11.30 - 12 noon.	P.T. & B.F.		
	12 - 12.45 pm.	Saluting Drill.		
"D" Coy.	9 - 9.30 a.m.	Handling of Arms.	do:	
	9.30 - 10 a.m.	Saluting Drill.		
	10.15 - 10.45 am.	P.T. & B.F.		
	10.45 - 11.45 am.	Musketry.		
	12 - 12.45 pm.	Handling of Arms and Close order drill.		

REGIMENTAL CLASSES:-

(a) Signallers under S.O.
(b) Lewis Gun Class (6 per Co.) under L.G.O.
(c) N.C.Os. Class (4 per Co.)
(d) Observers and Snipers under I.O.
(e) Bombers and Rifle Grenadiers as per Bn. Orders.

Major,
Commanding 15th Bn. High. L. I.

15th Bn. THE HIGHLAND LIGHT INFANTRY.

TRAINING PROGRAMME FOR TUESDAY 29th JANUARY 1918.

Coys.	Time.	Nature of Training.	Locality.	Remarks.
"A" Coy.	9 - 9.30 a.m.	P.T. & B.F.		
	9.30 - 10 am.	Gas Drill.		
	10.15 - 11.15 am	Musketry.	Vicinity	
	11.30 - 12 noon	Handling of Arms.	of	
	12 - 12.45 pm	C.O's. Parade.	Camp.	
	(9 - 9.30 am.	Lewis Gunners on Range)		
"B" Coy.	9 - 10 a.m.	Musketry.		
	10.15 - 10.45 am	Handling of Arms.		
	10.45 - 11.15 am	Gas Drill.	do:	
	11.15 - 11.45 am	P.T. & B.F.		
	12 - 12.45 pm.	C.O's. Parade.		
	(9.30 - 10 am.	Lewis Gunners on Range)		
"C" Coy.	9 - 10.45 am.	Platoon Rapid Wiring Squads.		
	11 - 11.45 am.	P.T. & B.F.		
	12 - 12.45 pm.	C.O's. Parade.		
	(10 - 10.30 a.m.	Lewis Gunners on Range)		
"D" Coy.	9 - 9.45 a.m.	P.T. & B.F.		
	9.45 - 10.30 am.	Gas Drill.		
	10.45 - 12 noon	Platoon Rapid Wiring Squads.		
	12 - 12.45 pm.	C.O's. Parade.		
	(10.30 - 11 am.	Lewis Gunners on Range.)		

W McLang Capt

for Major.
Commanding 15th Bn. High. L. I.

APP. II

SECRET. War Diary Copy No. 1.

15th Bn. THE HIGHLAND LIGHT INFANTRY.

Operation Order No. P.1.

INTENTION.

1. The 15th Bn. H. L. I. will relieve the _______ Bn. in the line on the night of the 16/17th (imaginary)
The line to be held runs on a general line along the ridge P.8.c., P.8.a. - P.2.c.

SYSTEM OF DEFENCE.

2.
(a) After relief the defensive position will be reorganized and the positions held as follows.
The front system about 700 yards will be held by three Coys. each Coy. having one platoon in the front line (the outpost line) Two platoons in the main line of resistance about 150 yards in rear and the remaining platoon of each Coy. in reserve about 200 yards in rear of the main line of resistance.
The fourth or reserve Coy. will be about 400 yards in rear of the reserve platoons.
(b) Front line Coys., (from right to left) "A" "B" "C" and "D" Coy. in reserve.

"A" Coy. will hold from P.8.a.05.15 - 35.40
"B" Coy. will hold from P.8.a.35.40 - 6.9.
"C" Coy. will hold from P.8.a.6.9. -P.2.c.9.3.

The reserve Coy. will dig in in selected positions along the tracks in P.1.b. & d.
Bn. Hqrs. in Quarry in J.31.d.

ACTION IN EVENT OF HOSTILE ATTACK.

3.
(a) The posts in the front line system will hold out at all costs and break up the enemy attack.
If the front line posts are overwhelmed the garrison of the main line of resistance will likewise hold out to the last.
Directly any indication of an enemy attack shows itself the reserve platoons of front line Coys. will go forward to either reinforce the main line of resistance or to counterattack in the event of the main line of resistance becoming penetrated in any place.
If the enemy's attack is not in strength and has only gained out front system of posts half the garrison of the main line of resistance will counter attack immediately and drive the enemy from the post system.
The reserve Coy. will similarly move forward on any indication of a hostile attack and will be prepared to either reinforce the main line of resistance or counter attack on its own initiative in the event of the enemy penetrating this line in any place.
(b) Directly a hostile attack becomes evident Unit Commanders will send forward patrols to ascertain the situation or if known will immediately inform Bn. Hqrs. by Runners.
Each Unit, however small, when in the front line system will endeavour to ascertain the situation and will report same to its immediate commander.
Information gained must be transmitted by every means available to Bn. Hqrs.

ARTILLERY.

4. The normal artillery support (for open warfare) can be expected.

MACHINE GUNS & T.Ms.

5. Definite information to be communicated later.
The framework of the defensive system must be built without their co-operation at first.

GENERAL INFORMATION.

6. The enemy is not considered to be in strength but has a fair amount of artillery.
The left flank will be in the air for some hours. The_____ Bn. will be linked up on the right.
Two Coys. of the______Bn. will be in general reserve at TOURNEHEM.

Lieut-Colonel,
Commanding 15th Bn. High. L. I.

General Instructions in conjunction with

Operation Order No. P.1.

---

1. On the afternoon of Monday the 14th inst., all Officers and Sergeants or Platoon N.C.Os will carry out the above scheme without troops.

Coy. Commanders will decide how to dispose of their commands: platoon commanders will definitely locate posts and detail their strength, paying special attention to the location of L.Gs. and their arcs of fire and the location of R.G. Posts.

2. Platoon and Coy. Commanders will submit detailed schemes with sketches and instructions given to Bn. Hqrs. Sketches to be put on the special issued maps.

3. O.C. Signals will submit detailed scheme of communication by all means available.

4. Officer I/C. Observers and Snipers will site Snipers and Observers and will submit scheme and location of same.

5. Officer I/C. Lewis Guns will submit scheme for siting of Lewis Guns and formation of ammunition dumps.

6. During the period that the Bn. is holding the line Coy. Commanders etc. will question sentries and N.C.Os in charge of posts as to the situation and as to their operation in the event of any possible eventuality arising.

7. A definite signal will be arranged which will signify that the enemy is actually attacking.

8. On the morning of the 17th (subject to alteration) the attack will be carried out with troops (as per Special Idea attached) and afterwards the line will be organized in depth as per Operation Order No. P.1. and defensive scheme proposed by Coys. and approved by Bn. Hqrs. on Monday.

9. Definite instructions as regards co-operation of M.Gs. and T.Ms. will be issued later.

10. The attack practice will be carried out against a flagged and skeleton enemy.

11. The attack will be carried out on orders issued on the spot from information gained by scouts.

12. The attack will not be carried out (without troops) on Monday, the ground will be merely reconnoitred.

13. For the purpose of the <u>whole</u> scheme Coys. will be arranged into platoons of three sections i.e. 1 L.G., 1R.G., 1 R.S. section.

14. The N.C.Os. class will attend under Sgt. GRANT, for instruction, on both days.

Lieut-Colonel,
Commanding 15th Bn. High. L. I.

SPECIAL IDEA
FOR TACTICAL SCHEME WITHOUT TROOPS
AND OPERATION ORDER NO. P.1.

Reference Sheet RECQUES AREA (EAST) 1,10,000.

1. On arrival at TOURNEHEM (day to be notified later) _____ Bde. received orders to attack the enemy in position on the ridge running through P.8.c. P.8.a. - P.2.c.

2. The attack was successfully carried out and the enemy driven S.E. of the FORET-DE-TOURNEHEM.

3. The 15th Bn. H. L. I. and the _____ Regt. were ordered to relieve the attacking BnS. on the night of the 16/17th inst. and organize the position for defence in depth.

4. The 15th Bn. H. L. I. were ordered to hold and defend the line from P.2.c.8.4. - P.8.a.1.3. and the dispositions as ordered in Operation Order P. 1. were taken up.

NOTE.

For instructional purposes the 15th Bn. H. L. I. will also carry out the attack against the enemy in position on the ridge.

Lieut-Colonel,

Commanding 15th Bn. High. L. I.

SECRET.

15th Bn. THE HIGHLAND LIGHT INFANTRY.

Operation Order No. 181.

1. The Battalion less Transport as per para 12 will move by train from AUDRUICQ to ELVERDINGHE on Tuesday 22nd inst.

2. BLANKETS.
One blanket will be carried on the man, the remainder will be stacked in bundles of ten, properly labelled at Q.M. Stores by 10 a.m. 21st inst. One blanket man per Coy. will go with blankets to AUDRUICQ. Lewis Guns and S.A.A. will be stacked beside blankets at Q.M. Stores at same time.

3. O.C. "D" Coy., will detail one N.C.O. to remain with Lewis Guns. He will stay with Camp Guard at AUDRUICQ and will be fully equipped and carrying one blanket. Guns will be drawn at AUDRUICQ Station and carried to destination.

4. DUMP GUARD.
One N.C.O. and three men will be detailed by O.C. "D" Coy. They will take charge of baggage dumped at AUDRUICQ Station. This Guard will parade at Q.M. Stores at 1 p.m. 21st inst. fully equipped and carrying one blanket, and will proceed with first lorry to AUDRUICQ.

5. On arrival at ELVERDINGHE the Battalion will move to billets in the following order: H.Q. "A" "B" "C" and "D" Coys. 100 yards interval will be observed between platoons and Coys.

6. PARADE. Time of parade will be notified later.

7. DRESS. Field Service Marching Order, blanket, jerkin and steel helmet strapped on pack. Blanket carefully folded to size of pack.

8. DISCIPLINE. The strictest march and train discipline will be observed; previous instructions issued for train journey will be complied with.

9. SUPPLY ARRANGEMENTS.
(1) For personnel entraining: Issue on morning of 19th for consumption on 20th inst.
Issue on afternoon of 19th for consumption on 21st inst.
Issue on morning of 20th for consumption on 22nd inst.
Issue on afternoon of 20th for consumption on 23rd inst.
Rationed in forward area for 24th inst.
(2) Personnel with Transport.
Rations for the 21st inst. on the man.
Rations for the 22nd inst. on first line Transport.
Rations for the 23rd on Train Wagons.

10. ADVANCE PARTY.
2/Lieut. FERGUSON and 1 N.C.O. per Coy. on bicycles will move by ordinary train service from AUDRUICQ on 21st inst. N.C.Os. will report at Bn. H.Q. time will be notified later. This party will report to Area Commandant, Hospital Farm Area and will meet the Bn. at Elverdinghe at 2.40 p.m. 22nd inst.

11. MOVEMENT OF STORES.
1 lorry will be at the disposal of Bn. on afternoon of 21st inst. Valises will be stacked by 4 p.m. on afternoon of 21st inst., at Q.M. Stores. The Q.M. will make the necessary arrangements for the movement of stores and loading parties, which will go to VLAMERTINGHE on Omnibus Train leaving AUDRUICQ at 10.10 a.m. arriving

15th H.L.I.

15 HLI

Vol 28

Instructions regarding War Diaries and Intelligence Summaries are contained in F. S. Regs., Part II. and the Staff Manual respectively. Title pages will be prepared in manuscript.

WAR DIARY
or
INTELLIGENCE SUMMARY.
(Erase heading not required.)

Army Form C. 2118.

Place	Date	Hour	Summary of Events and Information	Remarks and references to Appendices
EMILE CAMP.	February 1st	1918.	Battalion preparing to go into the line during the day. In the evening it moved up and took over from the 2nd K.O.Y.L.I. in support in the HET SAS sector. It was very quiet and the weather very fine.	W.D.
HET SAS (Reserve)	2nd		The line very quiet. The battalion was employed in working and carrying parties, and on improving the posts in the corps line.	W.D.
"	3rd		The battalion again working and carrying. Very quiet; practically no enemy activity.	W.D.
"	4th		The battalion was relieved by the 17th H.L.I. of the 97th Brigade. On relief we moved back to BABOON CAMP CANAL BANK. An advance party went up to take over from 16th Lanc. F. in the right sector.	W.D.
BABOON CAMP	5th		Relieved the 15th Lanc. F. in the right sector. The battalion was disposed as follows A Coy on the right; D Coy on the left, B and C Coys in support with Batt H.Q. at EGYPT HOUSE.	A W.D.
HET SAS (RIGHT SECT)	6th		Fairly quiet with a certain amount of enemy machine gunning going on.	
"	7th		The battalions front was extended to the left, B Coy going up and taking over from a company of the 1st DORSET RGT. on the left of D Coy. The weather was still fine but the night was very dark	W.D.
"	8th		There was very little shelling during the day. In the evening the battalion was relieved by the 5th/6th ROYAL SCOTS during which time there was very little machine gun fire, but LES 5 CHEMINS was shelled periodically. On relief the battalion withdrew to BABOON CAMP.	W.D.
BABOON CAMP	9th		The day was spent in cleaning up. In the afternoon a large draft from the 17th H.L.I. arrived; it included Capt J.G. STEPHEN, Lieut FLETCHER, 2nd Lt D.D. MARTIN and 2nd Lieut LONGLEY	W.D.

A5834 Wt. W4973/M687 750,000 8/16 D. D. & L. Ltd. Forms/C.2118/13.

28.0

21 sheets

Instructions regarding War Diaries and Intelligence Summaries are contained in F. S. Regs., Part II. and the Staff Manual respectively. Title pages will be prepared in manuscript.

WAR DIARY
or
INTELLIGENCE SUMMARY.
(Erase heading not required.)

Army Form C. 2118.

Place	Date	Hour	Summary of Events and Information	Remarks and references to Appendices
	~~January~~ February	1918		
BABOON CAMP	10th		The battalion moved back to LA BERGERIE CAMP by train. The accomodation consisted of huts and shelters which were quite comfortable though scattered.	APPENDIX 1 WW.
LA BERGERIE CAMP	11th		Parades in the morning by companies. In the afternoon the battalion bathed at WOESTEN. The weather was very fine though cold.	WW
"	12th		Parades were carried out in the morning ~~A Coy being on the range~~. In the afternoon Box Respirators were tested in the gas chamber at WOESTON. Capt J.H. Stephen took over the duties of A/Adjutant from 2nd Lieut W. McCAIG.	WW
"	13th		Companies paraded according to the training programme in the morning. In the afternoon work was done on the range and one company had foot treatment. 2nd Lieut W. McCAIG went on leave. The weather was fine and not very cold.	APPENDIX 2 WW.
"	~~14~~ 14th		Parades were as per programme in the morning D Coy being on the range. In the afternoon a party work on the Lewis gun range, and another on the new Bullet and Bayonet course. Weather fine.	APPENDIX 3 WW.
"	15th		In the morning companies paraded, C Coy shooting on the range. In the afternoon D Coy had the use of the range. Work was again done on the Lewis gun range and on the bullet and bayonet course. A very fine day ~~but~~ with frost in the early morning.	APPENDIX 4 WW.
"	16th		During the morning parade an attack practice where also carried out by companies. B Coy fired on the range. The Lewis gun range and the bullet and bayonet course were again worked on. The company commanders reconnoitred the army line. Fine with a little frost.	APPENDIX 5 APPENDIX 6 WW

A5834 Wt. W4973/M687 750,000 8/16 D. D. & L. Ltd. Forms/C.2118/13.

Instructions regarding War Diaries and Intelligence Summaries are contained in F. S. Regs., Part II. and the Staff Manual respectively. Title pages will be prepared in manuscript.

WAR DIARY
or
INTELLIGENCE SUMMARY.
(Erase heading not required.)

Army Form C. 2118.

Place	Date	Hour	Summary of Events and Information	Remarks and references to Appendices
	February	1918.		
LA BERGERIE CAMP.	17th		The battalion worked on the army line companies going up by train to CHARPENTIER CROSS ROADS where they were met by the R.E. guides. They returned by train in the afternoon. The officers left behind attended a lecture at WOESTON by Brig General F. LUMSDEN V.C. D.S.O. In the evening a voluntary service was held which was well attended. 2nd Lt Dunlop and 2nd Lt Canavan joined the battalion	mw.
"	18th		The battalion again worked on the army line, companies being taken up and brought back by train. There was a little rain in the morning but it cleared up about mid-day.	
"	19th		Companies paraded for inspection prior to going up the line. In the evening the battalion relieved the 16th H.L.I. in the HET SAS sector. The battalion was disposed as follows A Coy and 2 Platoons of D Coy in the CORPS LINE at GOURBI FARM, two platoons of D Coy at LES LILAS, C Coy in support at CHAUME FARM, B Coy in support at TILLEUL WOOD, and Battalion H.Q. at MONDOVI FARM. The night was very fine and quite quiet. B and C companies work under the RE at MANGELARE, HOUCHARD, and PAPEGOED POSTS in the forward zone. 2nd Lieut SOUTHERLAND joined the battalion.	APPENDIX 7. mw.
HET SAS	~~20th~~ 20th		A and D Coys worked on the CORPS LINE under the R.E. during the morning. B and C Coys worked on the POSTS in the forward zone in the evening. Very quiet. The weather was cold but fine. Lieut A. LANE and 2nd Lieuts HODSON, GLEN, CAIN rejoined the battalion from courses. Capt W DOUGHTY went on leave to England.	mw.

Instructions regarding War Diaries and Intelligence Summaries are contained in F. S. Regs., Part II. and the Staff Manual respectively. Title pages will be prepared in manuscript.

WAR DIARY
or
INTELLIGENCE SUMMARY.
(Erase heading not required.)

Army Form C. 2118.

Place	Date	Hour	Summary of Events and Information	Remarks and references to Appendices
	February 1918			
HET SAS (SUPPORT)	21st		The battalion was in support A and D Coys worked on the CORPS LINE and B and C coys worked forward posts again in the evening. In the afternoon B Coy moved from TILLEUL WOOD to CAMELIA and VOLTIGEUR FARMS. The day was clear and fine with practically no artillery activity.	W.W.
"	22nd		Working parties exactly the same as the day before. 2nd Lt RITCHIE and 2nd Lieut McARTHUR left to go on a 5 weeks course.	W.W.
"	23rd		In the morning A and D Coys worked on the CORPS LINE. B and C Coys worked on the forward posts in the evening. The battalion was relieved by the 5/6th ROYAL SCOTS and withdrew to reserve, A Coy going to STATUETTE FARM, B Coy to the CANAL BANK at J.1. BRIDGE, C Coy to CANAL BANK at J.2 BRIDGE, D Coy to TILLEUL WOOD, and Battalion H.Q. to BOCHE CROSS-ROADS 2nd Lieuts D.D. MARTIN and RODGER left the battalion to go to the Indian army.	APPENDIX 8. W.W.
(RESERVE)	24th		All four companies worked on the ARMY LINE under the R.E. One officer per company reconnoitred their battle positions in the ARMY LINE. A very fine day. Lieut. Col. V.B. RAMSDEN rejoined the battalion and assumed command.	W.W.

Instructions regarding War Diaries and Intelligence Summaries are contained in F. S. Regs., Part II. and the Staff Manual respectively. Title pages will be prepared in manuscript.

WAR DIARY
or
INTELLIGENCE SUMMARY.
(Erase heading not required.)

Army Form C. 2118.

Place	Date	Hour	Summary of Events and Information	Remarks and references to Appendices
HET SAS (RESERVE)	February 25th	1918.	All four companies out working on the ARMY LINE for 5 hours in the morning. In the afternoon C Coy and one platoon of B Coy were suddenly ordered to relieve the left company of the 1st DORSET RGT and a platoon in MANGELARE respectively. These two units came under the command of the OC. 1st DORSETS RGT on the completion of the relief. The morning was very wet with a strong north wind. Conditions improved in the afternoon, and at night it froze again. Major W.W. WHITE was appointed acting Adjutant, and Capt J.C. STEPHEN was appointed Assistant Adjutant.	APPEDIX 9. WWW
"	26th		Battalion in reserve with one company and one platoon attached to 1st DORSET RGT. The remainder of the battalion did 6 hrs work on the army line in the morning. A fine day with strong wind blowing. 2nd Lieut Brough rejoined from a course.	WWW
"	27th		The two and 3/4 companies that remained in reserve worked on the ARMY LINE in the morning. In the evening D company relieved a company of the DORSETS in close support. A Company and B Company relieved the 5th/6th Royal Scots in CHAUME Fme and CAMELIA FARM respectively. Batt HQ relieved the Royal Scots at MONDOVI FARM. The relief was completed by 6.50 pm. At 7.50 pm. our guns opened to support a raid made by the ROYAL SCOTS and 1st DORSET REGT. The enemy replied by shelling the posts in front of PAPEGOED and MANGELARE wounding two of our sergeants, 2 lance corporals and 4 privates. The artillery quietened down about 10 pm.	APPENDIX 10. WWW

Instructions regarding War Diaries and Intelligence Summaries are contained in F. S. Regs., Part II. and the Staff Manual respectively. Title pages will be prepared in manuscript.

WAR DIARY
or
INTELLIGENCE SUMMARY.
(Erase heading not required.)

Army Form C. 2118.

Place	Date	Hour	Summary of Events and Information	Remarks and references to Appendices
HET SAS sector SUPPORT.	February 28th.		A and B companies worked on the CORPS LINE during the morning. In the evening the battalion relieved the 1st DORSET REGT in the line, the dispositions being as follows:— B Coy on the right with Coy H.Q. at HOUCHARD, A Coy in the centre with Coy HQ at FRIANT, C and D Coys the same as the day previous, Battalion H.Q. at EAST end of BRIE BRIDGE. A raid was launched by the division on the right while the relief was going on, which caused the enemy to retaliate with their artillery on the right of the battalion line. After this there was very little activity.	APPENDIX H WW

Army Form C. 2118.

WAR DIARY
or
INTELLIGENCE SUMMARY.
(Erase heading not required.)

Instructions regarding War Diaries and Intelligence Summaries are contained in F. S. Regs., Part II. and the Staff Manual respectively. Title pages will be prepared in manuscript.

Place	Date	Hour	Summary of Events and Information	Remarks and references to Appendices
	February 28th			

	1st Feb.	28th Feb.
Commanding officer strength.	668	657
Fighting strength		
Officers	42	49
Other Ranks	857	990
	Officers	O.R.
Total casualties for the month		
Killed and died of wounds	–	1
Wounded	–	24
Missing	–	–

W. Warnock Lieut Col
Commanding 15th H.L.I.

A5834 Wt. W4973/M687 750,000 8/16 D. D. & L. Ltd. Forms/C.2118/13.

War Diary

APPENDIX I

SECRET.

15th Battalion The Highland Light Infantry.
Operation Order 188.
9/2/18.

- - - - - - - - - - - - - - - - - -

1. The Battalion will move by train to LA BERGERIE, T 19.d. Transport Lines and Q.M. Stores will remain in present position.

2. The Battalion will parade in BABOON CAMP at a time to be notified later in the following order H.Q's. A,B,C,& D Coys.

3. DRESS. F.S.M.O. Blanket, Jerkin & Steel Helmet strapped on pack. Blanket will be carefully folded to size of pack. The strictest March and Train discipline will be observed.

4. Billeting party. Orders have been issued separately.

5. Lewis Guns. Lewis Guns will be loaded on L.G. Limbers at 11 a.m. and will proceed by road when the Battalion moves from BABOON CAMP.

6. BLANKETS. One Blanket will be carried on the man. Q.M. will arrange to send remaining blankets to LA BERGERIE.
VALISES will be loaded at 1.30 p.m. and will proceed immediately to the new area.
MESS CART. will be loaded at 1.30 p.m., Orderly Room, Signalling & Medical Stores will also be loaded at this time and will immediately proceed to the new area.
Cookers and Water carts will also move at this time.
Rations for the 11th inst. will be issued on arrival in new area.

7. ACKNOWLEDGE.

W McCaig

2/Lieut. A/Adjt.,
15th High. L.I.

APPENDIX 2

15th Battalion The Highland Light Infantry.

- -

Training Programme for WEDNESDAY, 13th Feb., 1918.

Coy.	Time.	Nature of Training.	Location	Remarks.
A.	8.30 a.m. - 12 noon.	Musketry.	Range.	
	12 noon - 12.45 p.m.	Coy. or Battn. Training.		
B.	9 a.m. - 9.30 a.m.	Physical Training & Bayonet Fighting.		
	9.30 a.m. - 10 a.m.	Section Training.		
	9 a.m - 10 a.m.	(Two Squads Wiring Drill).		
	10 a.m.- 11. a.m.	Platoon Training.		
	11 a.m. - 12 noon.	Anti-gas Drill.		
	12 noon - 12.45 p.m.	Coy. or Battn. Drill.		
C.	9 a.m. - 9.30 a.m.	P.T. & B.F.		
	9.30 a.m. - 10 a.m.	Section Training.		
	10 a.m. - 10.45 a.m.	Anti-gas Drill.		
	11 a.m. - 12 noon.	Platoon Training.		
	12 noon - 12.45 p.m.	Coy. or Battn. Drill.		
D.	9 a.m. - 9.45 a.m.	Anti-gas Drill.		
	9.45 a.m. - 10.15 a.m.	P.T. & B.F.		
	10.15 a.m.- 10.45 a.m.	Section Training.		
	10 a.m. - 11 a.m.	(Two Squads Wiring Drill).		
	11.15 a.m. - 12 noon.	Inspection by C.O. Dress:- F.S.M.O.		
	12 noon - 12.45 p.m.	Coy. or Battalion Drill.		

All officers' Servants will parade with their Coys. at 11 a.m.

5.30 p.m. - 6.30 p.m. Lecture and discussion by C.O. or Adjutant.

<u>DAILY CLASSES.</u>

- Lewis Guns. 6 men per Coy. under Lewis Gun Officer.
- N.C.O's. Class. 4 N.C.O's. per Coy.
- Signallers. under Signalling Officer.
- Snipers & Observers under Intelligence Officer.

All training will be carried out in vicinity of camp. Exact locations will be forwarded to-morrow.

APPENDIX 3.

15th Battalion The Highland Light Infantry.

Training Programme for Thursday, 14th Feb., 1918.

Coy.	Time.	Nature of Training.	Location.	Remarks.
A.	9 a.m.- 9.30 a.m.	Physical Training & Bayonet Fighting.		
	9.30 a.m.- 10 a.m.	Section Training.		
	9 a.m.- 10 a.m.	(Two Squads wiring drill).		
	10 a.m.- 11 a.m.	Platoon Training.		
	11.15 a.m.- 12 noon.	Anti-gas drill.		
	12 noon - 12.45 p.m.	Coy. or Battn. Drill.		
B.	9 a.m.- 9.30 a.m.	P.T. & B.F.		
	9.30 a.m.- 10 a.m.	Section Training.		
	10 a.m. - 10.45 a.m.	Anti-gas Drill.		
	11 a.m. - 12 noon.	Platoon Training.		
	12 noon - 12.45 p.m.	Coy. or Battn. Drill.		
C.	9 a.m. - 9.45 a.m.	Anti-gas Drill.		
	9.45 a.m. - 10.15 a.m.	P.T. & B.F.		
	10.15 a.m. - 10.45 a.m.	Section Training.		
	10 a.m. - 11 a.m.	(Two Squads wiring Drill).		
	11.15 a.m. - 12 noon.	Inspection by C.O. Dress:- F.S.M.O.		
	12 noon - 12.45 p.m.	Coy. or Battn. Drill.		
D.	8.30 a.m. - 12 noon.	Musketry	Range.	
	12 noon - 12.45 p.m.	Coy. or Battn. Training.		

APPENDIX 4.

15 th Battalion The Highland Light Infantry.

Training Programme for FRIDAY, 15th Feb., 1918.

Coy.	Time.	Nature of Training.	Location.	Remarks.
A.	9 a.m.- 9.30 a.m.	Physical Training & Bayonet Fighting.		
	9.30 a.m.- 10 a.m.	Section Training.		
	10 a.m.- 10.45 a.m.	Anti-gas Drill.		
	11 a.m. - 12 noon.	Platoon Training.		
	12 noon - 12.45 p.m.	Coy. or Battn. Drill.		
B.	9 a.m.- 9.45 a.m.	Anti-gas Drill.		
	9.45 a.m.- 10.15 a.m.	P.T. & B.F.		
	10.15 a.m.- 10.45 a.m.	Section Training.		
	10 a.m. - 11 a.m.	(Two squads wiring Drill).		
	11.15 a.m. - 12 noon.	Inspection by C.O. Dress - F.S.M.O.		
	12 noon - 12.45 p.m.	Coy. or Battn. Drill.		
C.	8.30 a.m.- 12 noon.	Musketry.	Range.	
	12 noon - 12.45 p.m.	Coy. or Battn. Training.		
D.	9 a.m. - 9.30 a.m.	Physical Training & Bayonet Fighting.		
	9.30 a.m.- 10 a.m.	Section Training.		
	9 a.m. - 10 a.m.	(Two squads wiring drill).		
	10 a.m.- 11 a.m.	Platoon Training.		
	11.15 a.m.- 12 noon.	Anti-gas drill.		
	12 noon - 12.45 p.m.	Coy. or Battn. Drill.		

APPENDIX 6

War Diary

1[illegible]th Battalion the [illegible] Light Infantry.

Amended Training Programme for [illegible], 10th Feb., 1916.

Coy.	Time.	Nature of Training.	Location.	Remarks.
A.	9 a.m.– 10.30 a.m.	Attack practice.		
	10.40 a.m.– 12.10 p.m.	One squad wiring practice.		
	10.40 a.m.– 12.15 p.m.	Section & platoon drill including musketry exercises.		
	12.15 p.m.– 12.45 p.m.	Coy. Drill.		
B.	8.30 a.m.– 12.45 p.m.	Musketry – [illegible].	Range.	
	2 p.m. – 4 p.m.	Range practice.		
C.	9 a.m. – 9.30 a.m.	Physical Training.		
	9.30 a.m.	Bayonet fighting.		
	9.30 a.m. – 10 a.m.	Section training.		
	9 a.m. – 10 a.m.	One squad wiring drill.		
	10 a.m. – 11 a.m.	Platoon training.		
	11.10 a.m.– 12 noon.	Anti-gas drill.		
	12 noon – 12.45 p.m.	~~[illegible]~~ Coy. Drill.		
	2 p.m.–5 p.m.	Attack practice.		
D.	9 a.m. – 9.30 a.m.	[illegible]		
	9.30 a.m.– 10 a.m.	Section training.		
	10 a.m. – 10.40 a.m.	Anti-gas drill.		
	10.40 a.m. – 12 noon.	Attack practice.		
	12.15 p.m.– 12.45 p.m.	Coy. Drill.		

Lewis Gun teams will report to Lewis Gun Officer on range as under:-

C. Coy. 2 sections [illegible] at 8.30 a.m.

A. Coy. 2 sections [illegible] at [illegible] a.m.

N.C.O's., signallers, [illegible] classes will be continued as before.

J.G. Stephen Capt A/Adj

Major,
Commanding [illegible]

Please Return

APPENDIX 5.

15th Battalion The Highland Light Infantry.

Training Programme for SATURDAY, 16th Feb., 1918.

Coy.	Time.	Nature of Training.	Location.	Remark
A.	9 a.m.- 9.45 a.m.	Anti-gas Drill.		
	9.45 a.m.- 10.15 a.m.	Physical Training & Bayonet Fighting.		
	10.15 a.m. - 10.45 a.m.	Section Training.		
	10 a.m. - 11 a.m.	(Two squads wiring Drill.)		
	11.15 a.m. - 12 noon.	Inspection by C.O. Dress:- F.S.M.O.		
	12 noon - 12.45 p.m.	Coy. or Battn. Drill.		
B.	8.30 a.m. - 12 noon.	Musketry.	Range.	
	12 noon - 12.45 p.m.	Coy. or Battn. Training.		
C.	9 a.m. - 9.30 a.m.	P.T. & B.F.		
	9.30 a.m. - 10 a.m.	Section Training.		
	9 a.m. - 10 a.m.	(Two squads wiring drill).		
	10 a.m.- 11 a.m.	Platoon Training.		
	11.15 a.m. - 12 noon.	Anti-gas Drill.		
	12 noon - 12.45 p.m.	Coy. or Battn. Drill.		
D.	9 a.m. - 9.30 a.m.	P.T. & B.F.		
	9.30 a.m. - 10 a.m.	Section Training.		
	10 a.m. - 10.45 a.m.	Anti-gas Drill.		
	11 a.m. - 12 noon.	Platoon Training.		
	12 noon - 12.45 p.m.	Coy. or Battn. Drill.		

J. G. Stephen Capt.

Major,
Commanding 15th Bn. The High. L.I.

APPENDIX 7

14

[illegible]

Operation Orders [illegible]

[illegible]

[illegible]

Operation Order No. 189 [illegible]

[illegible]

[illegible]

Coys. will [illegible] as under:-

B9b [redacted] [illegible]

[redacted] [illegible] do. do.

A & D. [illegible]

B9b. [redacted] [illegible]

[illegible]

[illegible]

[illegible]

RATIONS. Contd.

A. Coy.	)	
D. Coy.	)	BONDOVI FARM U 8 d 0.7.
H.Q. Coy.	)	
Medical Stores.	).	
B. Coy.	)	Road junction U 24 d 9.6
C. Coy.	).	do. do. U 19 a 5.4

One limber will take up 2 days rations for A. & D. Coys.
One do. do. do. B. & C. Coys.
Mess cart do. do. do. Battn. H.Q.

These limbers to be at Coy. Ration dumps about 6.30 p.m.

Battn. H.Q.

Will be at BONDOVI FARM U 14 b 2.9.

DEFENCE SCHEME.

All defence schemes, maps, work schemes & all other information to be taken over.
A.A. sight will not be taken over. All A.A. Sights in possession will be taken into the line.

Relief complete to be reported by wire, in code (as issued to coys) and by runner.

Copy of trench store list to be sent to Battn. H.Q. with morning intelligence report.

Major,
Commanding 15th Battn. The High. L.I.

Copy issued to Comdg. Offr. No.1.
do. 2nd in Command. No.2.
do. Adjutant No.3.
do. O.C. A. Coy. No.4.
do. O.C. B. Coy. No.5.
do. O.C. C. Coy. No.6.
do. O.C. D. Coy. No.7.
do. O.C. H.Q. No.8.
do. Brigade. No.9.
do. 16th H.L.I. No.10.
do. T.O. No.11.
do. Q.M. No.12.
do. File. No.13.
do. War diary. No.14.

~~[illegible]~~

~~[illegible]~~

War Diary

APPENDIX II

SECRET.

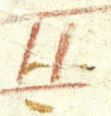

OPERATION ORDER No. 5.
by Lieut-Colonel V.B. RAMSDEN, M.C.,
Commanding 15th Bn. THE HIGHLAND LIGHT INFANTRY.

1. INTENTION. Map Reference Sheet A. 2 1/10,000.

15th Bn. H. L. I. (less two Coys.) will relieve 1st DORSET Regt., (less two Coys.) in forward Zone tonight 28th February 1st March.

2. INFORMATION.

"B" Coy. 15th ~~XX~~ H.L.I. will relieve "B" Coy. 1st DORSET Regt. in right Coy. front.

"B" Coy. will then be disposed as follows:-

Hqrs. - HOUCHARD Post.
5 sections - Outpost Line.
1 Platoon - MANGELARE Post.
1 Platoon - HOUCHARD Post.
3 sections - MORTIER Post.

"A" Coy. 15th H. L. I. will relieve "A" Coy. 1st DORSET Regt. in centre Coy. front and will be disposed as follows:-

Hqrs., - FRIANT Post.
1 Platoon - Outpost Line.
3 Platoons - FRINAT Post.
Battalion Hqrs. - U.8.d.4.3.

3. GUIDES.

1 Guide per platoon and 1 for Coy. Hqrs., will be at Battalion Hqrs. - U.8.d.4.3. at 5.45 p.m.

1 Guide per platoon and 1 for Coy. Hqrs., will be left at Battalion Hqrs., by 15th H. L. I. to guide platoons of 1st DORSET Regt., back to billets vacated by them.

4. MOVES AND ROUTES.

Coys. will proceed with Coy. Hqrs., leading and 5 minutes intervals between platoons.
ROUTE:- via MONDOVI - BRIE BRIDGE; "B" Coy. leading.

5. All Defence Schemes, Maps, Schemes of work will be carefull y taken over and all officers will make certain that they are perfectly acquainted with all details of their posts and its defence before reporting the relief complete.

6. All A.A. Mountings and positions will be carefully taken over and receipts showing patterns taken over will be ~~handed~~ taken and two copies sent to Battalion Hqrs.

7. RATIONS.

Rations will be dumped each night at 6 p.m. at MONDOVI DUMP.

Coy. Commanders will arrange to have hot food supplied ~~each~~ twice each night. Hot Food containers are available at the Cookhouses at the dump.

Water tins can be filled at the watercarts which will be left at the dump.

8. Completion of relief will be reported in code:-

Relief Complete - A
Little Shelling - GREAT
Much Shelling - SUCCESS.

Major,
A/Adjt., 15th Bn. High. L. I.

7. RATIONS.

Rations for "D" Coy. will be dumped at CARREFOUR de LONDRES at 6 p.m.

Hot Food will be supplied under Coy. arrangements of DORSET REGT.

Rations for Hqrs. Coy. at MONDOVI DUMP at 6 p.m., for "B" Coy. at CAMELLIA FARM at 6 p.m. and for "A" Coy. at CHAUME FARM at 6 p.m.

All waterbottles will be filled before leaving.

Coys. will take with them the 10 water tins at present in their possession.

BAGGAGE. One Limber will be at Battalion Hqrs., at 5 p.m. to convey Officers kit, Mess, Orderly Room, and Signal Stores to MONDOVI DUMP.

8. Completion of relief will be reported by wire and runner, ("D" to both Hqrs., 1st DORSET Regt., and Hqrs., 15th H. L. I.) in following code:-

Relief complete	-	THE
Little Shelling	-	BETTER
Much Shelling	-	HOLE

9. Acknowledge.

W White
Major,
A/Adjt., 15th Bn. H. L. I.

Copies issued to:-

1. C.O.
2. O.C. "A" Coy.
3. O.C. "B" Coy.
4. O.C. "C" Coy.
5. O.C. "D" Coy.
6. Signal Officer.
7. Quartermaster.
8. War Diary.
9. File.
10. 1st DORSET Regt.

APPENDIX 7.D

Mar 21/57

SECRET.

OPERATION ORDER No. 4.
by Lieut-Colonel V.B. RAMSDEN, M.C.,
Commanding 15th Bn. THE HIGHLAND LIGHT INFANTRY.

Map Reference BIXSCHOOTE Sheet 20 S.W. 4. 1/10,000.

1. INTENTION.

The following reliefs will take place tonight 27/28th inst.

2. INFORMATION.

(a) "D" Coy. 15th H. L. I. will relieve No. 4 (D) Coy. 1st DORSET Regt. in forward Zone and will be disposed as follows:-

Coy. Hqrs. and 2 Platoons - CATINAT Post.
1 Platoon - ISLANDE Post.
1 Platoon - VICTORY Post.

On completion of relief this Coy. comes under Command of C.O. 1st DORSET Regt.

Relief to be completed by 6 p.m.

(b) "A" Coy. 15th H. L. I. will relieve No. 3 Coy. 5/6th Royal Scots in Support System of forward Zone.

Hqrs. - CHAUME Fm.

"B" Coy. 15th H. L. I. will relieve No. 4 Coy. 5/6th Royal Scots in Support System.

Hqrs. - CAMELIA Fm.

Battalion Hqrs., will relieve Hqrs., 5/6th Royal Scots in MONDOVI Fm. Reliefs to be completed by 7 p.m.

(c) No. 3 and 4 Coys., 1st DORSET Regt., will relieve Nos. 1 and 2 Coys., 5/6th Royal Scots respectively in the Support System and on completion of relief will come under Command of C.O. 15th H. L. I.

3. GUIDES.

1 Guide per Platoon and 1 for Coy. Hqrs., will meet "D" Coy., at MONDOVI DUMP at 5.15 p.m.

4. MOVES & ROUTES.

"D" Coy. will move with 100 yards intervals between platoons, leading platoon to leave CORMORAN DUMP at 4.30 p.m.
ROUTE:- LANCIER Cross Roads - U.13.b.5.3.
"B" and "A" Coys. will move with similiar intervals, first platoon of "B" Coy., leaving CORMORAN DUMP at 5 p.m.

5. LEWIS GUNS.

A.A. Lewis Gun~~x~~ positions and mountings will be taken ~~over~~, receipts for mountings showing pattern will be taken over and a copy forwarded to Battalion Hqrs.

A.A. Sights will NOT be handed over.

6. DEFENCE SCHEMES.

Defence Schemes, Maps, Log Books, Schemes of work and all other information about the line will be taken over carefully.

Great care must be taken in taking over a Post and the relieving Officer will not report relief complete until he is satisfied that he understands his Post, dispositions and defence.

Copy No.....

SECRET.

15th Battalion The Highland Light Infantry.

- -

FILE

OPERATION ORDER No. 2. 23/2/18.

Ref. Map:- BIXSCHOOTE 1/10,000.

1. **INFORMATION.** There will be an Inter-battalion relief to-night 23rd/24th. February as follows:-
   1st DORSET REGT. will relieve 5/6 Royal Scots in the LINE.
   5/6 ROYAL SCOTS do. 15th H.L.I. in Support.
   15th H.L.I. moves back to Reserve.

2. **INTENTION.** The battalion will move back to Reserve on being relieved by 5/6 Royal Scots as follows:-

A.(No.1) Coy.	will go to	STAYUETTE FARM		T 24 d	90.15
B.(No.3) Coy.	do.	CANAL BANK	about	T 29 d	00.30.
C.(No.4) Coy.	do.	do. do.	do.	T 23 d	00.30.
D.(No.2) Coy.	do.	TILLEUL WOOD	do.	T 24 d	80.80.
Battn. H.Qrs.	do.	BOCHE X Roads	do.	T 24 d	25.60.
AID POST	do.	do.	do.		do.

3. **ADVANCE PARTY.** The Advance Party consisting of the following will be sent:-
   1 N.C.O. per Coy. & 1 man per platoon.
   1 N.C.O. & 1 signaller from Battn. H.Q.
   1 man from each of two L.G. teams of A. Coy.
   This party will be under 2/Lieut. T.W. HEPBURN and will report at LANCIER X ROADS at 1.30 p.m. sharp.
   The party will find all available accomodation & take over stores & will return to meet their platoons at LANCIER X Roads and guide them down. The representatives from each L.G. team from A. Coy. will give receipts for taking over A.A. Mountings & positions and will also get receipts from 1st Dorset Regt.

4. **MOVE.** A. & D. Coys. will wait in present positions till relief by 5/6 Royal Scots. O.C. Coys. will be particular to let advance parties of opposite unit know exactly where each post in Corps Line is. They will then go down to new position by road all the way.
   B. & C. Coys. will work as usual reporting at MONDOVI DUMP at 5.30 p.m. They will leave their equipment at a place to be chosen by O's.C. Coys. under double sentry. On completion of work they will go back by road, pack up kit and go straight to new position. O.C. Coys. are to instruct their advance parties as to what time they are to be at LANCIER X ROADS.

5. **TRANSPORT ARRANGEMENTS.** One Limber will be at MONDOVI DUMP at 6.30 p.m. to collect A,D & H.Q. Coy's. Cooking utensils.
   One Limber will be at Road Junction U 13 b 50.35 at 6.30 p.m. to collect B. Coy's. Cooking utensils & Officer's Mess Kit. It will then go to C. Coy's. ration dump at CHASSE FARM and pick up cooking & Officer's Mess kit. All cooks will go with these limbers. They will take each Coy's. material to Coy's. new ration dumps which are as follows:-
   A. Coy. T 24 d 8.0. B. Coy. J 1 BRIDGE.
   C. Coy. T 23 c 65.40 (J 2 bridge).
   D. Coy. T 24 d 9.6. Battn.H.Q. BOCHE X ROADS.
   The Mess cart will be at MONDOVI DUMP at 8 p.m. to take H.Qrs., A. & D Coys. Officer's Mess Kit & Orderly Room Box back to new areas. The Maltese Cart cart will be at MONDOVI DUMP at 8 p.m. to collect Medical Stores.
   Rations will be brought up to Coy's new ration dumps to be there at 9 p.m.

6. **COOKERS.** Ration Limbers will also bring up Officer's Valises. Cooks and all servants must be at dumps in time to receive rations and valises.
   The cookers for A,C & D. Coys. will be brought up at the same time as rations. B. Coy. will cook in its cook-house.

7. WATER. The Water-cart will fill the water-containers at CAMES DE LONDRES as usual, then come back, refill, and be left at J 2 BRIDGE.

Coys. can draw water as follows:-

A, D & H.Q. Coys:- CHARPENTIER X ROADS.
B. Coy.:- BOESINGHE
C. Coy.:- Water-cart, J 2 BRIDGE.

8. SALVAGE. All Salvage will be sent down and dumped at Road Junction U 13 d 7.8 by 12 noon.

9. LEWIS GUNS. All Lewis Guns and magazines to be carried out by the teams. Receipts stating kind of mountings are to be obtained for each A.A. Position handed over. These are to be handed into Orderly Room by 12 noon next day 24th. A.A. Sights are not to be handed over.

10. HANDING OVER. The greatest care must be taken in handing over posts. Stores, Defence Schemes, Log Books (If issued), Schemes for work and all other information about the Line will be handed over.

11. Coy. Commanders are reminded that they are to be very careful that no battle stores or equipment of any kind is left behind.

12. WIRING SQUAD. Members of the Wiring Squad at present at Battalion H.Q. will return to their Companies on completion of work to-night. However they still compose Battalion Wiring Squad.

13. A.A. POST. C. Coy. Lewis Gun A.A. Position at U 13 d 35.15 will be relieved by the 5/6 ROYAL SCOTS on 24/2/18 before 12 noon.

14. Completion of relief of A. & D. Coys will be reported to Battalion H.Q. in code by runner and wire.

Relief Complete with little shelling:- No DUST.
Relief Complete with much shelling:- DUST FLYING.

15. Coys. will report in the same code by wire when they are settled in their new billets.

W. Stephen

Capt. & A/Adjt.,
16th Battn. The High. L.I.

Copies issued:- No. 1 O.C. A. Coy.
" 2 O.C. B. Coy.
" 3 O.C. C. Coy.
" 4 O.C. D. Coy.
" 5 Signal Officer.
" 6 C.O.
" 7 2nd in Command.
" 8 Adjt.
" 9 14th Inf. Bde.
" 10 1st DORSET REGT.
" 11 5/6 ROYAL SCOTS.
" 12 FILE.
" 13 Q.M.
" 14 T.O.

APPENDIX 9.

Copy No. 8.....

SECRET.

Operation Orders issued by
Lieut. Col. V.B. R A M S D E N, M.C.,
Commanding 15th Battalion The Highland Light Infantry.

OPERATION ORDER No. 5.191 25/2/18.

Map Reference Sheet A 2 1/10,000.

1. The following reliefs will take place to-night 25th/26th. inst.

2. C. Coy., 15th H.L.I. will relieve C. Coy., 1st DORSET REGT. in Left Coy. Front.
1 Platoon B. Coy., 15th H.L.I. will take over garrison of MANGELARE POST from Platoon of 1st DORSET REGT.

3. O.C. C. Coy. will arrange to take over the following posts:-
No. 9 U.3 b 5.0. . . . . .1 Sect.
No.10 U 3 b 0.5. . . . . .1 Sect.
No.11 U 3 a 9.3. . . . . .1 Sect.
INTERNATIONAL POST N. of CORVERBEEK. . . . .1 N.C.O. & 2 O.R's.
do. do. S. of do. . . . . .1 N.C.O. & 2 O.R's.
PAPEGOED POST. . . . .1 Platoon (Permanent Garrison).
do. do.. . . . .1 Platoon (Counter attack).
do. do.. . . . .3 Sections.
INTERNATIONAL POST. . .U 8 b 85.15......1 N.C.O. & 8 O.R's.

4. Units will move from present billets at 12.30 a.m. and proceed with intervals of 100 yds. between platoons via. CHARPENTIER X ROADS - MONDOVI to CATINAT POST.

5. One Guide per platoon and one for Coy. H.Q. will meet C. Coy. at CATINAT POST at 2 a.m. One Guide will meet Platoon of B. Coy. at CATINAT POST at 2.15 a.m.

6. Rations will be dumped at CARREFOUR DE LONDRES commencing to-morrow night 26th inst.

7. Hot food will be cooked in SOYER STOVES at CARREF DE LONDRES and carried forward in Hot food containers already there.
All water-bottles will be filled before leaving present billets.

7. All defence schemes, trench stores, etc. will be taken over carefully by commander of each post.

8. OnCompletion of relief both Units will come under command of O.C. 1st DORSET REGT.

9. Completion of Relief will be reported by wire, both to C.O. of 15th H.L.I. and to C.O. of 1st DORSET REGT. in the following code:-
Relief complete:- VERY JUMBLED.

10. ACKNOWLEDGE.

Major & A/Adjt.,
15th High. L.I.

Copies issued:- No. 1. C.O.
" 2. O.C. A. Coy.
" 3. O.C. B. Coy.
" 4. O.C. C. Coy.
" 5. O.C. D. Coy.
" 6. Signal Officer.
" 7. Q.M.
" 8. War Diary.
" 9. File.
" 10. 1st DORSET REGT.

WAR: DIARY 6

SECRET

Operation Order

To attack Pill Box V.28.b.00.85.

1/ ATTACKING TROOPS

PARTY No 1

2/Lt ROBERTSON Cpl MAXON.

5. O.R.

PARTY No 2.

Sgt. LYONS 6 O.R including the Lewis Gun.

2/ ASSEMBLY

2/Lt Robertson's party will assembly in No 2 post

Sgt Lyons' party in No 3 post

3/ METHOD of ATTACK

a/ Capt Jeffry will decide as to whether the operation can be carried out or not (i.e weather conditions permitting).

b/ 2/Lt Robertson will settle details of attack

c) Sgt Lyons' party will move 75x in rear and will be prepared to reinforce quickly in event of the position being captured or to cover the withdrawal by fire at the loophole if necessary.

d). OC 'C' Coy will have ~~5~~ groups of ~~5~~ men told off to establish posts on the ridge between the new position & No 2 post.

(e) OC 5/6 Royal Scots will similarly push out posts to link up the new post to his line.

f) OC 'D' Coy will detail 1 platoon to move up to C Coy HQ to replace 'C' Coy's support.

4/ COMMUNICATIONS.

When the post has been gained, rapid communication must be established between No 2 party, No 1 post & OC C Coy. For this purpose the following methods will be employed.

a). If the post is taken without ~~[illegible]~~ noise 3 rounds rapid will be fired from a rifle from the post.

b/ 2 good runners from C Coy will accompany No 1 party keeping 50x in rear. These runners will return immediately to No 1 post to report progress.

OC 'D' Coy will detail 2 good runners to accompany No 2 party. These runners will work in cooperation with the runners of No 1 party.

c) A telephone post & 3 linesmen will be established in No 2 post to OC C Coy & thence to OC B Coy.

d) OC 'C' Coy will get in touch with OC Coy ~~[illegible]~~ Reserve Coy on his right to ensure rapid communication with OC 5/6 R.S. by telephone & runner.

f) In the event of the position being captured in spite of opposition OC party will carry 2 Very Pistols loaded which will be discharged together as a signal of success. They must be fired towards our line at a low altitude

5) General ~~Instructions~~

a) If weather conditions appear favourable at 7 am; a definite zero hour will be settled by the C.O. PLUMP in conjunction with OC C Coy. This hour will be communicated to OC 5/6 R.S.

e) OC 'C' Coy will detail runners to be posted at ~~[illegible]~~ NOS 1, & 3. posts, one to take verbal messages to the phone in No 2 post. & one to proceed direct to Coy HQ.

b) On the signal being given or on definite report being received that the post has been captured posts will immediately be pushed out.

(c). It must be carefully explained to the runners accompanying Nos 1 & 2 parties that their ~~acts~~ resolute the ultimate success of the operation depends largely on their resolute action in getting back to No 2 post with definite & accurate reports as to the results of the enterprise.
OC 'C' Coy will explain carefully to the runners the chain of communication & their own responsibility.

d) Nos 1 & 2 parties will remain in their present position until fetched by 2Lt Robertson who will be at 'C' Coy HQ from 6 am – 8 am.

[illegible]

White fatigue
2 Bandoliers
2 Bombs

ACKNOWLEDGE

32nd Division.

14th Infantry Brigade.

15th BATTALION

THE HIGHLAND LIGHT INFANTRY

MARCH 1 9 1 8

Attached :- Operation Orders.

15th H.L.I.

Army Form C. 2118.

WAR DIARY
or
INTELLIGENCE SUMMARY.
(*Erase heading not required.*)

Instructions regarding War Diaries and Intelligence Summaries are contained in F. S. Regs., Part II. and the Staff Manual respectively. Title pages will be prepared in manuscript.

March 1918.

Vol 29

Place	Date	Hour	Summary of Events and Information	Remarks and references to Appendices
HET SAS Sector, front line	1st		[illegible]	
	2nd		[illegible]	
"	3rd		The day was again very quiet, though enemy artillery was active, some of their shells falling a little short and very near our posts. At dusk a complete reconnaissance of the wire along the whole battalion front was carried out.	
"	4th		Fairly quiet. In the evening the battalion was relieved by the 5th/6th Royal Scots. Owing to the rain falling in the earlier part of the night and the extreme darkness the relief was delayed considerably. On relief the battalion moved back to support, the dispositions being as follows:— A Company in CAMELIA Fm and VOLTIGEUR FARM, B Company in COURBI FARM (Coy. line) C Coy in CHAUME FARM, D Company in GORBI FARM (Coy. line) and Battalion H.Q. at HANDAYL FARM	APPENDIX 1

A5834 Wt. W4973/M687 750,000 8/16 D. D. & L. Ltd. Forms/C.2118/13.

29. O. 21 sheets

Army Form C. 2118.

WAR DIARY
or
INTELLIGENCE SUMMARY.
(*Erase heading not required.*)

Instructions regarding War Diaries and Intelligence Summaries are contained in F. S. Regs., Part II. and the Staff Manual respectively. Title pages will be prepared in manuscript.

Place	Date	Hour	Summary of Events and Information	Remarks and references to Appendices
HET SAS SECTOR Support.	March 5th		In the morning there took place a ceremonial parade near RICHMOND CAMP at which the Corps commander presented the Belgian Legion of Honour to those to whom it had been awarded for their work in recent raids. Two platoons of C Company attended this parade. B and D Coys worked on the Corps line during the day and A and C Coys worked on the forward posts at night. 2nd Lieut W. McCAIG took over command of C Company	WM
"	6th		A beautiful day, and the artillery was very quiet. In the morning B and D Coys worked on the breastwork in the Corps line, and at night A and C Coys worked on the forward posts, MANGELAIRE and FRIANT respectively. In the afternoon all officers and N.C.Os. reconnoitred their battle positions in the Corps line. Lieut Robertson proceed to England on leave.	WM
"	7th		The enemies artillery was more active than usual especially in the back areas such as LANCIE CROSS ROADS. In the morning B and D Coys worked on the Corps line, and at night A and C Coys worked on the forward posts. About 4 am. the 35th Division on the right raided the enemy who retaliated heavily on our sector. In the afternoon the officers and NCOs reconnoitred the ARMY LINE. In the evening the battalion was relieved by the 5/6th Royal Scots. On the completion of relief the battalion moved back to reserve, companies being disposed as follows A Coy. STATUETTE FARM B Coy CANAL BANK J1 BRIDGE C Coy CANAL BANK J2 BRIDGE D Coy, TILLEUL WOOD and Batt H.Q. at BOCHE CROSS ROADS.	WM

A5834 Wt. W4973/M687 750,000 8/16 D. D. & L. Ltd. Forms/C.2118/13.

Instructions regarding War Diaries and Intelligence Summaries are contained in F. S. Regs., Part II. and the Staff Manual respectively. Title pages will be prepared in manuscript.

WAR DIARY
or
INTELLIGENCE SUMMARY.
(Erase heading not required.)

Army Form C. 2118.

Place	Date March	Hour	Summary of Events and Information	Remarks and references to Appendices
HET SAS Sector RESERVE	8th		The weather was excellent. The battalion was put on ¼ hrs notice to move to the "G" Army Zone. The move was cancelled owing to an attack on the Brigade on our right and the Battalion stood to battle stores being issued. The Battalion stood down at 2.30 pm. The enemies artillery was very active all morning, but quietened down in the afternoon. His aeroplanes were also very busy.	WM
"	9th		The weather was again very fine. All companies bathed, the rest of the time being spent in cleaning up. Aerial activity was considerable but the guns were quieter.	WM
"	10th		Weather fine. The morning was spent in training under company arrangement. In the evening the battalion moved up the line again and took over as follows:— A Coy relieved C Coy of the 10th Argylls in front line on the right of the brigade sector, about U 10 b 2 3. C Coy relieved D Coy of the 10th Argylls in support about U.10 a 2 2. B Coy relieved a company of the 5/6th Royal Scots at GOURBI FARM U.8.a.7.5. D Coy relieved a company of the 5/6th Royal Scots at CAMELIA FARM U 12 b 5 7. Batt H.Q. relieved ~~the~~ 10th Argylls in CALEDONIAN CLUB. Relief completed by 1.30 am. After relief A Coy reorganised the front line posts. Aerial activity below normal.	WM
"	11th		Weather fine all companies worked on the construction of 3 new posts and on strengthening their own posts. The enemy was extremely quiet.	WM

A5834 Wt. W4973/M687 750,000 8/16 D. D. & L. Ltd. Forms/C.2118/13.

Instructions regarding War Diaries and Intelligence Summaries are contained in F. S. Regs., Part II. and the Staff Manual respectively. Title pages will be prepared in manuscript.

WAR DIARY
or
INTELLIGENCE SUMMARY.
(Erase heading not required.)

Army Form C. 2118.

Place	Date March	Hour	Summary of Events and Information	Remarks and references to Appendices
HET SAS Sector Right Front-line	12th		Weather fine. The day was very quiet, and also the night when the companies all worked on posts, and wired. Our aeroplanes and artillery were fairly active. 2nd Lieut A.G. GLEN was wounded.	WM
"	13th		Weather fine. Both our artillery and that of the enemy was quiet. In the evening the battalion was relieved by the 16th Lancashire Fusiliers. During the relief the enemy put down a heavy "strafe" on the Brigade on our right. The relief was cancelled for half an hour while every one stood to. On completion of relief the battalion moved back to BABOON CAMP.	WM
HET SAS. Sector Brigade in reserve	14th		Weather again fine the morning was spent in cleaning up and improving the camp. Companies also went in turn to foot treatment. In the evening the enemy shelled the camp. 2nd Lieut Ritchie returned from a general course.	WM
"	15th		Weather fine. The morning spent in company and platoon training each company going to the range in turn. 2nd Lieut Langley went on a course of Chinese Dummy figures	WM
"	16th		During the morning companies went in turn to the baths after which they continued training. In the afternoon company boxing competitions took place. 2nd Lieuts N.C. McArthur and J.B. Allan reported to the 5th/6th Royal Scots for temporary duty with that unit. 2nd Lieut Black proceeded on leave	WM

Army Form C. 2118.

Instructions regarding War Diaries and Intelligence Summaries are contained in F. S. Regs., Part II. and the Staff Manual respectively. Title pages will be prepared in manuscript.

WAR DIARY
or
INTELLIGENCE SUMMARY.
(Erase heading not required.)

Place	Date	Hour	Summary of Events and Information	Remarks and references to Appendices
BABOON CAMP	March 17th		Weather fine. Companies practiced forming up for an attack. At noon all companies went to church parade with the exception of A Coy which was firing on the range. There was football and boxing in the afternoon. Capt J.H. Stephen returned from Intelligence course.	WM
"	18th		Weather fine. One company worked under the R.E. constructing shelters on the canal. One company in the range and two companies did the attack practice. In the afternoon inter company football matches were played, and the divisional band performed in camp. The 14th Inf. Brigade rugby team, of which 5 members belonged to the 15th H.L.I., defeated the Divisional Headquarters team.	WM
"	19th		The weather broke down and rained hard all morning. One company was working on the canal bank, and one company fired on the range. Training for the other two companies was cancelled; they spent the morning cleaning up and being lectured to by their officers. 2nd Lieut D. Hodge returned from hospital. 2nd Lieut R.C.L. Timony returned from IV Army School	WM

A5834 Wt. W4973/M687 750,000 8/16 D. D. & L. Ltd. Forms/C.2118/13.

Instructions regarding War Diaries and Intelligence Summaries are contained in F. S. Regs., Part II. and the Staff Manual respectively. Title pages will be prepared in manuscript.

WAR DIARY
or
INTELLIGENCE SUMMARY.
(Erase heading not required.)

Army Form C. 2118.

Place	Date	Hour	Summary of Events and Information	Remarks and references to Appendices
	March			
BABOON CAMP.	20th		It rained in the early morning and cleared up about 10 a.m. One company was working on the canal bank, one firing on the range and the other two practised the attack. In the afternoon the battalion played the 16th H.L.I. at football. About midnight an advance party left to go up the line preparatory to the battalion taking over the next day. Two of this party were killed and 1 wounded	MM
BABOON CAMP	21st		Weather fine. The morning was spent in preparing for the line. In the evening the battalion relieved the 11th Border Regt in the BOSINGHE SECTOR front line, companies being disposed as follows. "C" Company in the front line on the right, D Company in the front line on the left, B Company in support, and A Company in reserve. Battalion H.Q. were at PASCAL FARM. The relief was carried out with comparatively little shelling, but during the remainder of the night the enemy's machine guns and trench mortars were fairly active. Only 3 men were wounded. The enemy started their great offensive in the South.	APPENDIX 2 " 2.a MM
BOSINGHE SECTOR Front line.	22nd		At 4.30 am our artillery fired a counter preparation shoot which lasted half an hour, to which the enemy replied slightly on our left company front. The day time was very quiet and the weather was beautiful and very warm. In the evening three patrols were sent out, one of which under 2nd Lieut W. McCaig came in contact with	MM

A5834 Wt. W4973/M687 750,000 8/16 D. D. & L. Ltd. Forms/C.2118/13.

Instructions regarding War Diaries and Intelligence Summaries are contained in F. S. Regs., Part II. and the Staff Manual respectively. Title pages will be prepared in manuscript.

WAR DIARY
or
INTELLIGENCE SUMMARY.
(Erase heading not required.)

Army Form C. 2118.

Place	Date	Hour	Summary of Events and Information	Remarks and references to Appendices
	March 22nd	(Continued)	a hostile machine gun which fired at it from 25 yds range killing one man and wounding 2nd Lieut W McCay and the other man. This officer succeeded in bringing in the wounded man though wounded in the leg himself. During the night the posts were reorganised. 2nd Lieut W. Fergeson proceeded to England as a war weary soldier for 6 months light duty.	
BOSINGHE SECTOR (Front-line)	23rd		The day was very quiet and again very fine. In the evening and during the night the hostile machine guns and trench mortars were fairly active causing several casualties. The reserve company worked under the R.E. and the other companies worked on their own posts during the night. Short bursts of artillery were fired on the enemy's known machine guns with a view to keeping them quiet, but this had little or no effect. In the early morning B Coy relieved D Coy and A Coy relieved C Coy.	
"	24th		The day was again very fine and fairly quiet. In the evening the battalion was relieved by the 5th/6th Royal Scots. During the relief the enemies machine guns and trench mortars were again active but did little damage. The battalion moved back into Brigade reserve, companies being disposed as follows. A Company in HUNTERS BREASTWORK, B Coy GRUYTERSZALE FARM. C Company in	APPENDIX 3

A5834 Wt. W4973/M687 750,000 8/16 D. D. & L. Ltd. Forms/C.2118/13.

Instructions regarding War Diaries and Intelligence Summaries are contained in F. S. Regs., Part II. and the Staff Manual respectively. Title pages will be prepared in manuscript.

WAR DIARY
or
INTELLIGENCE SUMMARY.
(Erase heading not required.)

Army Form C. 2118.

Place	Date (March)	Hour	Summary of Events and Information	Remarks and references to Appendices
	24th continued		COLONEL'S FARM, ~~and~~ D Coy ~~and~~ Battalion H.Q. at LA CHAUDIERE. Total casualties for the tour were 1 officer and 24 O.R.	
BOSINGHE SECTOR Reserve.	25th		Weather much colder. Three companies were employed as working parties under the RE. In the evening the enemy "strafed" the front posts and the brigade on our right. A and B Companies were shelled slightly.	[illegible]
"	26th		Three companies again working for the RE. In the evening B Coy sent two platoons to breastwork near their head quarters and A Company Company H.Q. moved with one platoon to LEOPARD HUTS. During the night there was a considerable amount of artillery activity especially on the right.	[illegible]
"	27th		Fine day and quite quiet. Three companies again worked for the R.E. In the evening the battalion was relieved by the 3rd Belgian Regiment. After the relief the battalion moved back by train to SEIGE CAMP which was reached by the last company at [illegible] am 28/3/17.	APPENDIX 4 4a. [illegible]
SEIGE CAMP	28th		The day was spent in cleaning up and preparing for the next day's journey. The advance party left in the afternoon to take over billets in the new area. D Coy marched to PESELHOEK station preparatory to entraining.	[illegible]

A5834 Wt. W4973/M687 750,000 8/16 D. D. & L. Ltd. Forms/C.2118/13.

Army Form C. 2118.

Instructions regarding War Diaries and Intelligence Summaries are contained in F. S. Regs., Part II. and the Staff Manual respectively. Title pages will be prepared in manuscript.

WAR DIARY
or
INTELLIGENCE SUMMARY.
(Erase heading not required.)

Place	Date	Hour	Summary of Events and Information	Remarks and references to Appendices
SEIGE CAMP	29th		D Company entrained at 1 a.m. and after a [illegible] hours journey detrained at TINQUES where it marched to MANIN where it was billeted. The remainder of the battalion entrained at PESELHOEK at 1 p.m. and [illegible] at MANIN at 10 p.m. The billets were [illegible] [illegible] in billets at MANIN at 10 p.m. [illegible] early morning [illegible]	
MANIN	30th		The commanding officer, [illegible] company commanders and two HQ officers went up the line to reconnoitre the new sector. Rain commenced to fall at about 11 a.m. and continued all day. At 4 p.m. the battalion [illegible] marched to new billets in HAUTEVILLE	APPENDIX 5 [initials]
HAUTEVILLE	31st		The battalion marched out of the village at 2 p.m. on its way up to the line. The battalion relieved the 10th EAST YORKSHIRE REGIMENT in the line [illegible]. The battalion halted for [illegible] the PURPLE LINE north of ADINFER [illegible] on the way to have tea. The relief was completed by about 11 p.m. Companies were disposed as follows:- A Coy and B Coy in the purple line on the right and left respectively. C and D Coys being in support [illegible] ADINFER WOOD with Bn H.Q. in the Wood. The relief of the night was very quick.	[initials]
PURPLE LINE MONCHY SECTOR				

A5834 Wt. W4973/M687 750,000 8/16 D. D. & L. Ltd. Forms/C.2118/13.

Instructions regarding War Diaries and Intelligence Summaries are contained in F. S. Regs., Part II. and the Staff Manual respectively. Title pages will be prepared in manuscript.

WAR DIARY
or
INTELLIGENCE SUMMARY.
(Erase heading not required.)

Army Form C. 2118.

Place	Date	Hour	Summary of Events and Information	Remarks and references to Appendices
	March			

—	March 1st	March 31
Commanding officers strength	668	821.
Fighting Strength.		
Officers	50	44
O.R.	1000	1227

Total casualties for month.	Officers	O R
Killed and died of wounds		10
Wounded	2	13
Missing.		1

[illegible] Lt Col
Commanding.
15th R.I.R.

A5834 Wt. W4973/M687 750,000 8/16 D. D. & L. Ltd. Forms/C.2118/13.

A P P E N D I C E S

1
1a
2
2a
2b
3
4
4a
5

APPENDIX 1

SECRET. C.O.

[illegible] No. 6.
by Lieut-Colonel [illegible], M.C.,
Commanding 15th Bn. THE HIGHLAND LIGHT INFANTRY.

Map Reference BIXSCHOOTE Sheet 20 S.E. 4 1/10,000.

1. The 5/6th Royal Scots will relieve the 15th H. L. I. tonight, 4/5th March in the FORWARD ZONE.
On relief the 15th H. L. I. will withdraw to the SUPPORT SYSTEM of the FORWARD ZONE and will relieve the 1st DORSET Regt.

2. Moves will take place in accordance with attached table A.
The greatest care must be taken in handing over and taking over all posts. The Officer Commanding Coy. will not withdraw until he is satisfied that the relieving Officer understands his post, dispositions, and defence.

3. All Defence Schemes, Maps, Log Books, Schemes of work, and Trench Stores will be handed over and receipts obtained, one copy being forwarded to Bn. Hqrs.

4. A.A. Lewis Gun Positions and Mountings will be handed over, receipts for Mountings, showing pattern will be taken and two copies forwarded to Bn. Hqrs.
A.A. Sights will not be handed over.

5. An advance party as under will proceed at 2 p.m. to take over from 1st DORSET Regt.
"A" Coy. 1 Officer and 2 N.C.Os.
"B" Coy. 1 Officer and 2 N.C.Os.
"C" Coy. 1 Officer and 2 N.C.Os.
"D" Coy. 1 Officer and 1 N.C.O. per Platoon.
Battalion Hqrs. 1 N.C.O.

6. Completion of relief will be reported to Battalion Hqrs. in code by wire and Runner.
Relief Complete - Bo.
Little Shelling - Here.
Much Shelling - Wire.
Coys. in billets by code - BOR.

7. Acknowledge.

mwhite
Major,
A/Adjt., 15th Bn. High. L. I.

APPENDIX 1a

T a b l e "B"

15/H.L.I. Coy.	Royal Scots Coy. relieving.	1st Dorset Coy. relieved.	Location & completion of relief.	Times and Guides.
"A"	"D"	"B"	Hqrs.& 3 Pltns. at CAMELIA Fm. 1 Pltn. at VOLTIGEUR Fm.	"A" Coy.5/6th Royal Scots will be at Carref-de Londres at 4.30 pm. No Guides. "C" & "D" Coys.will arrive at CARREFOUR de LONDRES at 5.30 pm. No Guides. "B" Coy.15/H.L.I. will send 1 Guide per pltn. and 1 for Coy.H.Q. to Bn. H.Q. at 5.30 p.m. for "B" Coy.5/6th Royal Scots. O.C. Coys.will arrange that advance parties act as Guides for their Coys. on relief.
"B" Coy.	"B"	"D"	2 Pltns.at Gourbi 2 Pltns.at [illegible] Hqrs. GOURBI.	
"C"	"A"	"A"	[illegible] Fm.	
"D"	"C"	"C"	GOMEZ [illegible] Hqrs. GOURBI	
Hqrs.	Hqrs.	Hqrs.	MONDOVI.	

APPENDIX 2.

SECRET. Copy No.......

OPERATION ORDER No.11.
by Lieut-Colonel V.B. RAMSDEN, M.C.,
Commanding 15th Bn. THE HIGHLAND LIGHT INFANTRY.
20th March 1918.

Map Reference BIXSCHOOTE S.W. 1. 1/10,000.

1. The 15th H. L. I. will relieve the 11th BORDER Regt, in the right Battalion Front of the right Brigade Sector on the night of 21/22nd March.

2. (a) The Companies will on completion of relief, bedisposed as follows:-
"C" and "D" Coys. in front line.
"B" Coy. in Support.
"A" Coy. in reserve.

(b) DISTRIBUTION OF COMPANIES.

No. 1. "C" Coy. Right.

1 Rifle Section - Post 1.
1 L.G. Section - Post 3.
1 L.G. " - Post 4.
1 L.G. " - Post 6.
1 Rifle " - Post 8.

1 Platoon (Officer) - AVOCA Post.

Coy. H.Qrs and Remainder. - TRANQUIL House.

No. 2. "D" Coy.

1 Rifle Section. - Post 9.
1 L.G. " - Post 10.
1 Rifle Section - Post 11.
1 L.G. " - Post 12.
1 Rifle " - Post 14.
1 " " - Post 15.
1 " " - Post 16.
1 L.G. " - Post 17.
1 Rifle Section. - Post 18.
1 L.G. Section. - Post 19.

One Officer at COLOMBO HOUSE. 1Officer at ANGLE POINT.
Coy. H.Q. and remainder - EGYPT HOUSE.

No. 3. "B" Coy. SUPPORT.

1 N.C.O. and 6 O.Rs. - Post 1a.
do: - Post 2a.
do; - Post 3a.
do: - Post 4a.
3 N.C.Os. (- Post 5a
&16 O.Rs. (- Post 6a (2 Officers)

1 N.C.O. & 11 O.Rs. - Egypt House (L.G.)
1 N.C.O. & 6 O.Rs. - CAIRD HOUSE (L.G.)
Coy. H.Qrs. - EGYPT House.
1 Platoon(Officer) - TRANQUILE House.

No.4. "A" Coy. Reserve.

1 Platoon at PASCAL FM.
2 Platoons & Coy. H.Qrs. at VEE BEND.
1 Platoon (less 1 L.G. Section) at HEY CROSS ROADS.
1 L.G. Section at TRANQUILE House.
Bn. H.Qrs. - PASCAL FM.

(c) A.A. Lewis Gun Positions will be taken over as under:-
U.12.b.35.45.)
U.6.c.0.1.) No. 3 Co.

APPENDIX 2

U.12.c.5.3.) No. 4 Coy.
U.11.d.2.6.)

Details regarding these will be issued separately.

3. Receipts will be given for all A.A. Mountings taken over and a duplicate copy forwarded to this Office immediately after relief.
A.A. Sights will <u>not</u> be taken over.

4. Defence Schemes, Maps, Schemes of work, Trench Stores and all information about the line will be carefully taken over.

5. The greatest care will be exercised in taking over each post. The Officer taking over a post will not report relief complete until he is satisfied that he understands the post, its location and defence scheme and has obtained all information concerning it.

6. ADVANCE PARTIES.
Advance Parties consisting of 1 Officer and two Runners for Bn. H.Qrs. and 1 Officer and 1 N.C.O. per platoon, 1 Lewis Gunner per team, and 1 Runner for each Coy. willreport at H.Qrs. 11th BORDER Regt. PASCAL Fm. at 2 a.m. on 21st inst.
Careful instructions will be given to these advance parties.

7. GUIDES.
Guides at the rate of 1 per Bn. and Coy. H.Qrs. and 1 per platoon will be at junction of HUNTERS ST. Track with Langemarck - BIXSCHOOTE Road (U.21.d.50.95.) at 6.30 p.m. on 21st inst.

8. ROUTES AND TIMES.
(a) Route for all Coys.:- BABOON CAMP - RUGBY CORNER - HUNTERS ST. Track.
Movement will be with intervals of 100 yards between platoons.
(b) Coys. will move off at the following times from BABOON CAMP:-
"C" Coy. - 5.40 p.m.
"D" Coy. 5.50 p.m.
"B" Coy. - 6 p.m.
"A" Coy. - 6.10 p.m.
H.Qrs. 6.15 p.m.

9. ADMINISTRATIVE.
These will be issued separately.

10. Relief must be completed by 11 p.m.

11. Relief complete will be reported to Bn. Hqrs. by wire and Runner in following code:-
Relief Complete - SIX
Little shelling - MONTHS
Much Shelling - Leave.

12. ACKNOWLEDGE.

mwhite
Major,
A/Adjt., 15th Bn. High. L. I.

APPENDIX 2a

ADMINISTRATIVE INSTRUCTIONS

to accompany

OPERATION ORDER No.11.

---

1. DRESS Haversacks, leather jerkins and water proof sheets will be carried.

2. BAGGAGE.
Packs, blankets, officers ~~xxxxxxx~~ valises etc. will be dumped at J.1 Bridge at 2.30 p.m.

3. RATIONS.
Two days rations will be taken. One day's rations will be on the man and the next days will be taken by limber up to the dump at NEY CROSS ROADS at 8.30 p.m.

4. WATER
The watercarts will be at NEY CROSS ROADS nightly.
In addition 10 water tins per Coy. will be dumped at the ration dump with the rations tonight.
These will be brought down and filled nightly thereafter.

5. HOT FOOD.
As many Tommy Cookers as possible will be supplied to the Coys. in front and in Support.
C.Q.M.Ss. will arrange that these go to the proper sections.
Tea and Soup will be cooked in Soyers Stoves and large kettles at NEY CROSS ROADS and will be carried from there in food containers twice nightly.
No open fires will be lit at posts.

6. SALVAGE.
The collection of this will be carried on continuously and a return showing amount salved and where dumped will be rendered by Coys. at 8 p.m. each night.
Ration carrying parties will take as much salvage as possible down to the ration dump each night from where it will be taken on the limbers to RUGBY CORNER Salvage Dump.

7. SANITATION.
All Hqrs., posts and their surroundings will be cleaned up daily.

8. RESERVE RATIONS.
There is a reserve of rations and water in all the main line posts.
A separate receipt will be exchanged for this on taking over and a duplicate copy forwarded to this office.
Coys. will render a certificate by 9 a.m. on 24th inst., that all reserve water in their area has been turned over.

9. AMMUNITION.
The following establishment will be maintained.
(a) Front line posts.
1 box - S.A.A.
1 " - No. 5 Grenades.
1 " - No. 23 "
2 Red Flares.
(b) Main Line posts.
5 boxes - S.A.A.
5 " - No. 5 Grenades.
5 " - No.23 "
Proportion of S.O.S. Grenades.

APPENDIX 2.A.

(c) Coy. Hqrs.
15 boxes - S.A.A.
15 " - No. 5 Grenades.
15 " - No.23 Grenades.
6 S.O.S. Signals.

(d) Battalion Hqrs.
40 boxes - S.A.A.
50 " - No. 5 Grenades.
30 " - No.23 Grenades.
12 " - Very Lights 1"
12 S.O.S. Signals.

The Coys. in Support will have a similar establishment.
Coys. will report by 9 a.m. on 22nd inst. if their establishment is complete.
Coys. going into the front line will take with them from BABOON CAMP.
(a) 1 biscuit tin for each outpost. This tin will be placed in the parapet and Grenades contained in it. [will be sent up with rations]
(b) One box of grenades per post.
(c) 4 Sandbags per man.
A report that this has been done will be forwarded to reach this Office by 10 a.m. on 20th inst.

10. MEDICAL ARRANGEMENTS.
R.A.P. - Egypt House.
Relay Posts - VEE BEND.
NEY FM.

11. STORES etc.

The complete list of stores etc., taken over will be forwarded in duplicate to Battalion Hqrs. by 9 a.m. on 22nd inst.

12. All Orderly Room, Signal, and Officers Trench Stores, will be placed in Limbers at 5 p.m. today.

13. ACKNOWLEDGE.

mWhite
Major,
A/Adjt., 15th Bn. High. L. I.

APPENDIX 26.

AMENDMENT TO OPERATION ORDERS No. 11.

Paras 7 and 8 are amended as follows.

7. GUIDES.

Guides for Right Front Coy., Bn. H.Q., Platoon of Reserve Coy for PASCAL Fm., Reserve Coy. Lewis Gun team for TRANQUIL HOUSE and SUPPORT Coy., Platoon for TRANQUIL HOUSE will be at junction of Railway Track with the WIJENDRIFT ROAD at 7 p.m.

(Right front Coy. will arrive in order of posts from right to left, platoon at AVOCA HOUSE and Coy. H.Qrs. and remainder)

Guides for the Left front Coy., arriving in order of posts from right to left, the support Coy. in order of posts and for the reserve Coy. (less PASCAL FM. Platoon) will be at junction of HUNTER ST. with WIJENDRIFT Road at 7 p.m..

8. TIMES.

Coys. will leave BABOON CAMP as under and move via RUGBY CORNER, Railway and HUNTER Tracks respectively with 5 minutes intervals between platoons.

"C" Coy. 1st Platoon 5.30 p.m.	
Bn. H.Q. and "A" Coy's platoon for PASCAL FM.	- 5.50 p.m.
"A" Coy. L.G. Team for TRANQUIL HOUSE	- 5.55 p.m.
"B" Coy. Platoon for TRANQUIL HOUSE	- 6 p.m.
"D" Coy's 1st Platoon.	- 6.5 p.m.
"B" Coy. (less 1 platoon)	- 6,20 p.m.
"A" Coy. (less 1 platoon)	- 6.30 p.m.

Lewis Guns will be placed in Limbers at 5 p.m., one each to ~~be at~~ proceed to junction of HUNTER Track with WIJEN DRIFT Road and ~~at~~ to junction of Railway Track with WIJEN DRIFT Road respectively. At 6.30 pm.

Coy. Commanders will ensure that their guns are put in the proper Limbers.

21- 3-18.

Major,
A/Adjt., 15th Bn. High. L. I.

Operation Orders No 13
By Lieut-Colonel V. D. Ramsden M.C.
Commanding 15th Battalion The Highland Light Infantry.

1. The 5/6th ROYAL SCOTS will relieve the 15th H.L.I. in the RIGHT BATTALION FRONT OF THE BOESINGHE SECTOR tonight the 24/25th inst.
On completion of relief the 15th H.L.I. will withdraw into Support and take over positions vacated by the 5/6th ROYAL SCOTS.
The Battalion will then be disposed as follows;–

H. Q's.		LA CHAUDIERE (U 14 c 6 0.)
No. 1 (B) Coy.		PERMANENT GARRISON OF SUPPORT SYSTEM, FORWARD ZONE
		H.Q. HEY FARM.
No. 2 (A) Coy.	" "	H.Q. GRUYTERSZALE FM.
No. 3 (D.) Coy.	"	LA CHAUDIERE
No. 4 (C) Coy.		COLONEL'S FM.

2. The greatest care must be taken in handing over and taking over all posts. The Officer Commanding a post will not leave it until he is satisfied that the Relieving Officer understands his post and its position, defences, and role of its Garrison.

3. A.A. Lewis Gun Positions will be handed and taken over with great care. Relief of these to be completed by 10 P.M.
Seperate receipts for A.A. Mountings will be taken and duplicate copies forwarded to Battn. H.Qs by 9 A.M. on 25th inst.

4. Defence Schemes, Schemes of Work, Trench Store Lists and all other information about the line will be carefully handed over.
Seperate receipts will be obtained for reserve rations.

5. **ADVANCE PARTIES.** Advance parties of 1 Officer per Coy. and 1 N.C.O. per platoon & 1 Officer for Battn. H.Q. will proceed to H.Q.s of the 5/6th ROYAL SCOTS at 2 P.M. this unit to take over.
Advance parties of 1 Officer and 1 N.C.O. per Coy from 5/6th ROYAL SCOTS will report at each Coy. H.Q's at 3 P.M. tonight to take over.

6. **GUIDES.** One per platoon and one for Coy. H.Q's for A Coy and one for Battn. H.Q's will be at JUNCTION OF RAILWAY STREET with WIJENDRIFT ROAD at 7-30 P.M.
Guides on same scale for remainder (B. D. & C. Coys). [redacted] at JUNCTION OF HUNTER'S TRACK with KOEKUIT ROAD at 8 P.M.
COY Commanders will arrange for post guides to new Coy. H.Q's.
Guides to take relieved platoons to new positions will be at Station [illegible] at 9 P.M.

7. **RATIONS & WATER** in new dispositions will be conveyed to LA CHAUDIERE for C. D. and H.Qs. Coys and for A. & B. Coys to HEY CROSS ROADS

8. Completion of Relief will be reported by wire and runner in code
RELIEF COMPLETE = HIS. LITTLE SHELLING = LAST. MUCH SHELLING = KICK

9. ACKOWLEDGE

White
Major, A/Adjt.
15th Battn. High. L. I.

War Diary

APPENDIX 4.

SECRET.

OPERATION ORDER No. 14.
by Lieut-Colonel V.B. RAMSDEN, M.C.,
Commanding the 15th Bn. THE HIGHLAND LIGHT INFANTRY.

Map Reference BIXSCHOOTE 1/10,000.

1. The 14th Infantry Brigade will be relieved by the 18th Belgian Regiment in the right Brigade Sector tonight the 27/28th March 1918

2. The 15th Bn. H. L. I. will be relieved by Units of the 18th Belgian Regiment as in Table "A" attached.

3. The greatest care will be taken in handing over all posts. The Officer commanding a post will not leave it until he is satisfied that the relieving Officer thoroughly understands his post, its position, defences and means of communication.

4. A.A. Posts will be most carefully handed over. Mountings, but not sights will be handed over.
Separate receipts in triplicate will be forwarded to this office immediately after relief.

5. Defences Schemes, Maps, Schemes of work, and all information about the line will be handed over on relief.

6. Trench Store lists will be most carefully prepared and handed over. Triplicate copies will be forwarded to this Office on completion of Relief.

7. Officers Kits, cooking utensils, Medical and Signal Stores etc., will be collected at Ration Dumps at 10 p.m. tonight.
Lewis Guns will be carried by the L.G. Sections.

8. Completion of relief will be reported by wire and runner in code as follows:-

Relief Complete - ALWAYS.
Little shelling - KEEP.
Much shelling. - SMILING.

9. On completion of relief "A" and "B" Coys. will withdraw to vicinity of LA CHAUDIERE and "C" and "D" Coys. will remain at their present locations. Orders will be issued from Bn. H.Qrs. as to when Coys. may be moved off to entraining point at RUGBY CORNER from where Bn. will move to SEIGE CAMP.

10. Billeting party, consisting of 1 Officer and of 2 N.C.Os. per Coy., will proceed to SEIGE CAMP from Bn. Hqrs. at 12 noon and will report to Camp Adjutant there.

11. ACKNOWLEDGE.
27-3-18.

Major,
A/Adjt., 15th.Bn. H. L. I.

Copies issued to:-

1. C.O.
2. O.C. "A" Coy.
3. O.C. "B" Coy.
4. O.C. "C" Coy.
5. O.C. "D" Coy.
6. Signal Officer,
7. Q.M.
8. File.
9. War Diary.
10. 14th Inf. Bde.

APPENDIX 4 a.

TABLE "A".

Coy.	Relieved by.	Guides at Rugby Corner at:-	Route.
"A"	1 Coy. No. 2 Bn. 18th R.I.	9 p.m.	RAILWAY TRACK - LEOPARD HUTS.
"B"	1 Coy. No. 2 Bn. 18th R.I.	9 p.m.	CLARGES STREET - GRUYTERSZALE Fm.
"C"	1 Coy. No. 3 Bn. 18th R.I.	10 p.m.	Road - Colomel's Fm.
"D" ~~Kxy~~	do:	10 p.m.	Road - LA CHAUDIERE.
Hqrs.	Hqrs. No. 3 Bn. 18th R.I.	10 p.m.	do:

1. GUIDES.

1 per Coy. H.Q. and 1 per platoon) To meet Units.
1 per Bn. Hqrs.) "A" and "B" will each send 1 Off. in addition. Captain STEPHEN will superintend all arrangements at RUGBY CORNER.

2. All movement east of the CANAL will be by platoons at 100 yards interval.

APPENDIX 5

S E C R E T. Copy No.......

OPERATION ORDER No. 15.
by Lieut-Colonel V.B. RAMSDEN, M.C.,
Commanding 15th Bn. THE HIGHLAND LIGHT INFANTRY.
30th March 1918.

Map Reference Sheet 51 C. 1/40,000.

1. The 15th Bn. H. L. I. will move to billets in the LATTRE - HAUTEVILLE Area today the 30th inst.

2. All companies will be paraded on the road outside their billets, complete with battle stores, ready to move off at 4 p.m. The order to move will be given when paraded.

3. Steel helmets and leather jerkins will be worn.

4. A billeting party of 1 Officer and 1 N.C.O. per Company will report to Town Major, HAUTEVILLE at 2 p.m. for billets.

5. Officers valises will be dumped outside Company Headquarter billets at 2 p.m.

6. Blankets, tightly rolled up in bundles of 10 will be dumped at Q.M. stores at 2 p.m.

7. Lewis Guns, with ammunition, will be at wagon lines by 2 p.m. One L.G. N.C.O. per Company will accompany each L.G. Limber.

8. All mess kit will be in mess cart by 3 p.m. Signal and Orderly Room Stores will be packed on Limber by the same time.

9. Quartermaster will arrange direct with the Transport Officer as to the carriage of all stores.

10. ACKNOWLEDGE.

M White
Major,
A/Adjt., 15th Bn. High. L. I.

Copies issued to:-

1. C.O.
2. O.C. "A" Coy.
3. O.C. "B" Coy.
4. O.C. "C" Coy.
5. O.C. "D" Coy.
6. Signal Officer.
7. Q.M.
8. T.O.
9. File.
10. War Diary.

14th Inf.Bde.
32nd Div.

WAR DIARY

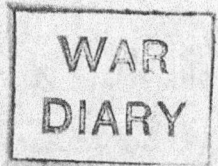

15th BATTN. THE HIGHLAND LIGHT INFANTRY.

A P R I L

1 9 1 8

Attached:

Appendices 1 to 10.

1918

Instructions regarding War Diaries and Intelligence Summaries are contained in F. S. Regs., Part II. and the Staff Manual respectively. Title pages will be prepared in manuscript.

WAR DIARY
or
INTELLIGENCE SUMMARY.
(Erase heading not required.)

15th H. L. I. 14/37

Army Form C. 2118.

Map Reference FRANCE Sht 57D N.E. 51c S.E. 1/10.000

Place	Date	Hour	Summary of Events and Information	Remarks and references to Appendices
ADINFER WOOD	April 1.	–	A quiet day was spent in the PURPLE LINE. Operation Order No 16 issued. The relief of the 2nd Battn MANCHESTER Regt was carried out as ordered without any unusual incidents. Immediately on completion of relief, D and C Coys each sent forward enterprising patrols to ascertain the strength in which the enemy was holding the village of AYETTE immediately in front of our lines. They found that the enemy were in considerable strength in the village and very active with machine guns.	APPENDIX I
DOUCHY	2	–	Preparations for the attack of AYETTE were then hastened and Operation Order No 17 was issued. The C.O. held a conference of Coy Commanders at 9 am at Bn HQrs DOUCHY and the details of the arrangements were thoroughly gone into. The enemy displayed little activity during the day and the preparatory work proceeded smoothly, all ranks displaying great energy and determination. The arrangements for artillery and M.G. support were most carefully made by 14th Inf Bde and these arrangements made known to all ranks. ~~The actual operation was carried~~	APPENDIX [illegible]

VA 30

57.C. 57 sheet 6

A5834 Wt. W4973/M687 750,000 8/16 D. D. & L. Ltd. Forms/C.2118/13.

Army Form C. 2118.

Instructions regarding War Diaries and Intelligence Summaries are contained in F. S. Regs., Part II. and the Staff Manual respectively. Title pages will be prepared in manuscript.

WAR DIARY
or
INTELLIGENCE SUMMARY.
(Erase heading not required.)

15 H. L. I

Map. Ref. FRANCE Sht 57D N.E. 51c S.E. 1/10

Place	Date April.	Hour	Summary of Events and Information	Remarks and references to Appendices
DOUCHY	2		Orders were received that after completion of operation, the frontage held by D and B Coys of the 15th H. L. I would be taken over by the 5/6th Royal Scots. Operation Order No 18 was issued.	APPENDIX 3.
"	3		The operation was carried through in the most enthusiastic and determined fashion, all ranks being inspired with the greatest dash and gallantry and the village captured despite the large number of the enemy found to be in it.	
			A special report of the operation is appended.	APPENDIX 4.
			It was subsequently discovered that a Battalion and a M.G. Battn of the enemy were in the village, the Battalion Commander and Adjutant being amongst the prisoners.	
			The report of the G.O.C. 14th Inf Bde, with the remarks of the CORPS and ARMY Commanders attached, on the operation is appended.	APPENDIX 5.
			The original messages received from the platoon commanders and Company commanders during the operation are appended.	APPENDIX 6.
			Owing to the length of time taken to mop up the many cellars and dug-outs in the village the relief of D and C Coys by the 5/6th ROYAL SCOTS had to be carried out during the fighting, but this was successfully done thanks to the fine spirit shown by the relieving troops.	

A5834 Wt. W4973/M687 750,000 8/16 D. D. & L. Ltd. Forms/C.2118/13.

Instructions regarding War Diaries and Intelligence Summaries are contained in F. S. Regs., Part II. and the Staff Manual respectively. Title pages will be prepared in manuscript.

WAR DIARY
or
~~INTELLIGENCE SUMMARY.~~

(Erase heading not required.)

Army Form C. 2118.

15. H. L. I.

Map Ref FRANCE Sht 57D N.E. 1/20,000 51C S.E.

Place	Date April	Hour	Summary of Events and Information	Remarks and references to Appendices
DOUCHY	3	–	Our casualties were slightly heavier than at first thought Officers – Killed 2/Lt W. GEORGESON Died of Wounds A/Capt. W. S. O'MAY Wounded { 2/Lt T. KEWIN Lt A LANE Missing – Lt J. REID O.R. Killed – 22 Wounded – 150 Missing – 8.	MW.
			The remainder of the day was fairly quiet; the village of AYETTE being shelled fairly heavily from 9am to 9.30 am. causing us a few casualties. At 9pm B. Coy went forward and relieved C Coy in the village which was under command of 2/Lt CALDERWOOD, the latter withdrawing into reserve in our old front line.	MW WM
	4	–	The night was uneventful, the heavy rain which fell probably accounting for the unusual quietness. Operation Order No 19 was issued	Appendix 7. WM
	5		The 1st DORSET Regt relieved the battalion which withdrew into positions as ordered. Relief was completed without incident by 1am on 5th inst.	MW WM

A5834 Wt. W4973/M687 750,000 8/16 D. D. & L. Ltd. Forms/C.2118/13.

Instructions regarding War Diaries and Intelligence Summaries are contained in F. S. Regs., Part II. and the Staff Manual respectively. Title pages will be prepared in manuscript.

WAR DIARY
or
INTELLIGENCE SUMMARY.
(*Erase heading not required.*)

Army Form C. 2118.

15. H. L. I.

Map Reference FRANCE Sheet 57D NE 51 SSE 1/10,000

Place	Date April	Hour	Summary of Events and Information	Remarks and references to Appendices
PURPLE LINE F8 a C4	5	–	By 4am the battalion had all settled down into its new positions in reserve in the PURPLE LINE. The weather was wet and the men were not well accommodated and had little chance of resting or recuperating. 2/Lt R. M. McARTHUR, having injured his back during the operations of the 2nd/3rd inst., went to hospital. The companies in the PURPLE LINE were subjected to considerable enemy shelling from 2pm to 3pm but no damage was done. Lt J. G. A. JEFFREY was transferred to C. Coy and took over command from 2/Lt CALDERWOOD.	[illegible]
"	6	–	The weather remained wet and cheerless. A few casualties were caused by enemy shelling of the PURPLE Line. Enemy shelling was however only slight.	[illegible]
"	7	–	The dull weather continued. The usual indiscriminate shelling of the PURPLE Line and the valley in F8 took place with little hurt to us.	[illegible]
"	8	–	The enemy artillery was extremely active against our batteries in the SUNKEN Road about F2c from 4am to 7am causing many casualties to the personnel of the batteries and a few gas casualties to us.	[illegible]

A5834 Wt. W4973/M687 750,000 8/16 D. D. & L. Ltd. Forms/C.2118/13.

Instructions regarding War Diaries and Intelligence Summaries are contained in F. S. Regs., Part II. and the Staff Manual respectively. Title pages will be prepared in manuscript.

WAR DIARY
or
INTELLIGENCE SUMMARY.
(Erase heading not required.)

15 H.L.I.

Army Form C. 2118.

Map References Sht 57 C N.E. 1/20,000 51C S.E.

Place	Date April	Hour	Summary of Events and Information	Remarks and references to Appendices
PURPLE LINE F8a07	9	–	The usual cheerless day was spent in the PURPLE LINE. The activity of the enemy artillery was however less than usual. Operation Order No 20 was issued. The relief of the 5/6th ROYAL SCOTS, as detailed in this order was carried out without unusual enemy activity. The front held by the battalion extended from F11c95, along the SUNKEN ROAD just E. of AYETTE, to F11b86 with 2 platoons A Coy, 1 platoon C Coy and 2 Platoons B Coy in the front line, the remaining platoons of these Companies being in close support in the village and D Coy in reserve in the old GERMAN trench about F9b. During the day there was very little shelling of the battalion area.	APPENDIX 8. mw WA
FRONT LINE Right Sub-Sector HQs F9a84	10	–	The morning started very quiet till 7AM when the enemies artillery opened out with 5.9's and Minenwerfer's and kept same up till 7.30AM. We had two casualties 2Lt HODSON & SERGT DIXON both wounded. the rest of the day passed very quietly. The two companies carried out wiring and work on posts during the night. a patrol under SERGT McGARVIER captured one prisoner. The night was also quiet.	[illegible] WM

A5834 Wt. W4973/M687 750,000 8/16 D. D. & L. Ltd. Forms/C.2118/13.

Army Form C. 2118.

Instructions regarding War Diaries and Intelligence Summaries are contained in F. S. Regs., Part II. and the Staff Manual respectively. Title pages will be prepared in manuscript.

WAR DIARY
or
INTELLIGENCE SUMMARY.
(Erase heading not required.)

15TH H.L.I.

Map Reference Sheets: 57D NE, 51C SE 1/10000.

Place	Date April	Hour	Summary of Events and Information	Remarks and references to Appendices
FRONT LINE Right Sub Sector HQ F9a8.4	11		A Coy took over the platoon frontage of C Coy. From 6.30AM till 7AM enemy artillery active shelling the village and back area. During the day enemy aircraft were active. The weather conditions good, sunshine. Working on posts and wiring carried on at night as usual. 2nd LT J.B. ALLAN att ROYAL SCOTS went down the line with Gas poisoning from shells.	PB.
	12.		Enemy opened out artillery fire at same time as morning before and dropped them also on the village and back areas. During the day line was very quiet, weather good. At night companies carried out wiring and enlarging posts. Our artillery putting over bursts of shell fire every fifteen minutes. 2nd LT. W. THOMSON. died of wounds received from a shell which burst near his shelter. 2nd LT. F.B. GAIN seriously wounded.	MI PB
	13.		At 3.30AM enemy artillery opened out and continued till 4.30AM with a Gas Shell bombardment through which the Battalion suffered very heavily our casualties through same amounted to 8 officers & 250 other ranks. Officers Gassed LIEUT J.G.A. JEFFREYS. MC. 2ND LT. H MEEHAN. " W. ROGER " P.R.H. LONGLEY. " R.M. CALDERWOOD. MC. " W.O. BLACK. " W.M. RITCHIE " J.A. DUNLOP att TMB's 2nd Lt F.B. GAIN died from wounds received the day before, amongst the cases admitted to hospital	MI

A5834 Wt. W4973/M687 750,000 8/16 D. D. & L. Ltd. Forms/C.2118/13.

Army Form C. 2118.

Instructions regarding War Diaries and Intelligence Summaries are contained in F. S. Regs., Part II. and the Staff Manual respectively. Title pages will be prepared in manuscript.

WAR DIARY
or
INTELLIGENCE SUMMARY.
(Erase heading not required.)

15TH H L I

Map Reference Sheet 57 D NE 51 B SE 1/10000

Place	Date	Hour	Summary of Events and Information	Remarks and references to Appendices
FRONT LINE Right sub Sector	April 13.		were about two thirds of our pipe band which we are all sorry to lose after being trained to a band's highest pitch of perfection. During the remainder of the day the artillery shelled back area's. Work carried out in the line as previous evenings. The body of LT. J REID, and his runner was found on the B Coy front.	RB
H.Q. F9a84.				WM
	14.		Enemy artillery had its usual half hour strafe on the village, weather good for observation and both his and our own aircraft were very active all day otherwise everything was very quiet.	RB
	15.		The effects of the Gas bombardment on the 13TH began to be felt and other two officers and also our Commanding Officer had to go down the line for treatment. LT. COL. V.B. RAMSDEN. DSO, MC. CAPT. J.G. STEPHEN. MC. LT. B.G. FLETCHER. We received a reinforcing draft of 100 O.R. The weather was very dull no observation otherwise very quiet. At 5.30 p.m. enemy artillery opened out on the village for fifteen minutes. Work done in line same as previous evenings.	WM RB
	16.		Very quiet day in the line. Enemy artillery active on back area. Work carried out on posts putting turf on parapet & parados. The weather was showery and had a mist on the front which cleared about 10 a.m.	WM RB

A5834 Wt. W4973/M687 750,000 8/16 D. D. & L. Ltd. Forms/C.2118/13.

Instructions regarding War Diaries and Intelligence Summaries are contained in F. S. Regs., Part II. And the Staff Manual respectively. Title pages will be prepared in manuscript.

WAR DIARY
or
INTELLIGENCE SUMMARY.
(*Erase heading not required.*)

Army Form C. 2118.

15th H. L. I.

Map Reference Sheet 57 D NE / 51 B. SE 1/10000

Place	Date April	Hour	Summary of Events and Information	Remarks and references to Appendices
Front line right sub sector	17		The enemy's artillery was very quiet all day. We received a draft of 47 O.R. 2nd Lt T. W. HEPBURN rejoined the Battalion having been attached to Brigade as Gas Officer. The weather was clear & dry.	RB WM
H Q Fq a 8.4	18.		The decorations for the capturing of AYETTE to the N.C.O's & men were published. 25 Military Medals and one Bar. The enemy's artillery was active all day but as usual mostly on the rear. Brigade Wiring party wired the B Coy front under the supervision of the R.E. Officer. Report from front companies about our artillery firing short.	RB WM
	19		Enquiry was held on the falling short of our own shells and Brigadier General Lumsden VC. DSO. watched from the front line the Batteries firing on their own Barrage Lines. Enemy artillery was very busy all day and a few dropped very near B. H. Q. Operation Order issued No 21. The relief by the 1st DORSET. REGt. was carried out without any unusual occurences on the completion of the relief A & B Companies went back to rest at Monchy. The enemy dropped a few Gas Shells around Battalion Headquarter's.	Appendix 9 WM
	20.		The enemy's artillery were active on the ADINFER wood and PURPLE LINE. A & B Companies carried out Bathing at the Divisional Baths at MONCHY. A draft of 27 O.R. arrived at the Battalion and posted to C. Coy. Weather dry and fine. Aerial activity on both sides. The night was very quiet.	WM

A5834 Wt. W4973/M687 750,000 8/16 D. D. & L. Ltd. Forms/C.2118/13.

Instructions regarding War Diaries and Intelligence Summaries are contained in F. S. Regs., Part II. and the Staff Manual respectively. Title pages will be prepared in manuscript.

WAR DIARY
or
INTELLIGENCE SUMMARY.
(Erase heading not required.)

Army Form C. 2118.

15TH H L I.

Map Reference Sheets 57 D NE, 51 B SE 1/10000

Place	Date	Hour	Summary of Events and Information	Remarks and references to Appendices
PURPLE LINE F8 A 0.7	April 21		Enemy artillery active Battalion Headquarters heavily shelled and the Aid post blown in nobody being wounded this bombardment lasted for nearly three hours. The list of honours for the capture of AYETTE for Officer's & NCO's Men. 2 DSO's 7 MC's & 6 DCM's 1 Military Medal. The following Officers received Decorations LT COL. V.B. RAMSDEN. MC. } DSO's MAJOR G.M. CLEGHORN. } CAPT. J.F. MUIR. } " J.G. STEPHEN. } " W. DOUGHTY. } LT. J.G.A. JEFFREY. } MC's 2ND LT. J.R. ROBERTSON. } " W. THOMSON. } " T. KEWIN. }	RB
			Inspection parades were carried out by A & B Coys at MONCHY. The night passed very quiet in the PURPLE LINE. The Companies carried on strengthening firing positions & shelters. CAPT. J.C. THOMSON ATT. 97 BRIGADE went down the line for treatment of Gas Poisoning by shelling.	
	22.		A & B Coy's relieved C & D companies to enable C & D Companies to go to Bathe, as on no account was the PURPLE LINE to be left without a garrison. The weather dull & cold. The day was spent cleaning up the lines.	RB WH

A5834 Wt. W4973/M687 750,000 8/16 D. D. & L. Ltd. Forms/C.2118/13.

Instructions regarding War Diaries and Intelligence Summaries are contained in F. S. Regs., Part II. and the Staff Manual respectively. Title pages will be prepared in manuscript.

WAR DIARY
or
INTELLIGENCE SUMMARY.
(Erase heading not required.)

Army Form C. 2118.

15TH H.L.I.

Map Reference Sheet. 57D NE 57C SE 1/10000.

Place	Date	Hour	Summary of Events and Information	Remarks and references to Appendices
	April			
PURPLE LINE & 8 a.0.7.	23.		Got official word that we would be relieved by the 2ND GRENADIER GUARDS. Another large Draft arrived to the Battalion including one Officer + 299 O.R. 2ND LT J.L. BRODIE. MC. joined the Battalion for duty. MAJOR WHITE proceeded to POMMIER to inspect the new draft. Weather fine & mild.	
			Operation Order's No. 22. issued	WM
	24.		The 14th Infantry Brigade was relieved by the 1st GUARDS BRIGADE on the night of the 24/25th A & B. Coys were relieved by the 2ND GRENADIER'S GUARDS about 6 p.m. The relief was carried out without unusual enemy activity. The Battalion came back to rest at SAULTY.	Appendix 10. WM
SAULTY.	25.		The Battalion carried out Bathing Parades and cleaning parades. Working party of 50 O.R. under 2ND LT HEPBURN proceeded to V 3 a. to build a Battalion Musketry Range a similar party under 2ND LT CANAVAN carried out work on the new BRIGADE RANGE. The weather cold & Dull. LT COL. V B. RAMSDEN rejoined the Battalion after being treated for GAS POISONING	WM
	26.		Received a reinforcing draft of 12 Officers ~~who~~ whom were posted to different companies for duty	
			CAPT. R.B.H. ALEXANDER.	
			" A.G. McNAUGHTON	
			LIEUT. A.C. BRUCE	
			" R.N. THOMSON	
			" D.W. KEITH.	
			" A. FLETCHER.	
			LIEUT. A.M. BROWN	
			" A.W. CAVE	
			" H.A. AGNEW	
			2ND LT A. MIDDLETON	
			" J.C. AIRLIE	
			" W. GAGE	

Army Form C. 2118.

WAR DIARY
or
INTELLIGENCE SUMMARY.
(Erase heading not required.)

15TH H L I

51C SE 1/10000

*Instructions regarding War Diaries and Intelligence Summaries are contained in F. S. Regs., Part II. and the Staff Manual respectively. Title pages will be prepared in manuscript.

Place	Date	Hour	Summary of Events and Information	Remarks and references to Appendices
	April			
SAULTY	26		The companies carried out work & training as per programme. Weather wet & cold.	RB
	27		C Coy carried out Musketry and Bombing on the BATTALION RANGE the other two companies carrying out work as per programme. Weather cold & wet. The last and only original charger BEAUTY which had come through the campaign since the battalion landed in France died at SAULTY of which both OFFICERS & MEN were very sorry to hear about.	RB
	28.		B Coy carried out Musketry & Bombing on the range the other three companies carried out the Open Warfare attack formations. The Battalion Football team played the 5/6th ROYAL SCOTS at football and after an exciting game the finish saw us one goal up the final score being H.L.I. 1 ROYAL SCOTS NIL. Weather cold & dull. 2Lt H. FRASER & 2Lt H J YOUNGER joined the Battalion for duty.	RB
	29.		The Battalion carried on training as per programme. The weather again cold & wet. The Commanding Officer held a lecture for all the new officers in the CHATEAU GROUNDS.	RB
	30		D. Coy carried out Musketry & Bombing on the range, C. Coy carried out Musketry on the BRIGADE RANGE at P33 d1.5 We had a visit from MAJ GEN. CAMPBELL. the Divisional Commander on the range. The weather was very wet.	RB

Instructions regarding War Diaries and Intelligence Summaries are contained in F. S. Regs., Part II. and the Staff Manual respectively. Title pages will be prepared in manuscript.

WAR DIARY
or
INTELLIGENCE SUMMARY.
(*Erase heading not required.*)

April 1918

Army Form C. 2118.

Place	Date	Hour	Summary of Events and Information	Remarks and references to Appendices
			(table below)	

	1st April	30th April
Commanding Officer's Strength.	852.	928.
Fighting Strength.		
Officers	44	38
Other Rank's	1022	997
	Officers	Other Rank's
Total. Casualties for the Month.		
Killed & Died of Wounds.	5.	36
Wounded	15	390
Missing		5.

W. Saunders[?] Lieut. Col. D.S.O. M.C.
Commanding 15th H.L.I.

A P P E N D I C E S

1 to 10.

Secret. Operation Order. No. 16. No I

by Lt/Colonel. V.B RAMSDEN. M.C.

Comdg. the 15/ Batt High. L. I.

MAP REFERENCE.

Sheets 51c. SE. & 57.d NE.
1/20000 1/20000

No. 1. a/ The 14th Infantry Bde will relieve the 96th Infantry Bde in the front line, from approximately F10 d.9.7. to approximately F.5. b.6.3.

b/ The 15th H.L.I. will be relieved in Purple Line by 1st Dorset Regt. and will relieve the 2nd Manchester Regt. from COJEUL River F.5. c 45.20 to F.5. b.5.3.

c/ The Batt will be distributed on a two Company front with D Coy on the Right from COJEUL RIVER to F.5. c.8.6. and "C" Coy on the left from F.5. c 8.6 to Road at F.5. c.6.3.

B" Coy will be in Support in trenches about F.4. d.7.5. and A Coy in Reserve from F.4. b.20. to F.4. c.7.6.

Batt H Qrs will be at F.4. c 7.6.

No. 2. All Defence Schemes, defensive arrangements and information about the line will be most carefully taken over and made known to all.

No. 3. Companies will report immediately on completion of relief that their flanks are in touch.

No. 4.

No. 4. Guides for C & D. Coys at the rate of 1 per platoon, and 1 for Coy. H. Qrs. will be at point where Purple line cuts the ADINFER DOUCHY ROAD. X.17.d.9.1. at 8-20 p.m.
"C" Coy to arrive at this point first, with 100 yds interval between ~~platto~~ platoons

No. 5. A & B. Coys will previously reconnoitre positions to be occupied by them and move to these positions as soon as they have been relieved in the PURPLE LINE by 1st DORSET REGt.
"B" Coy will send Guides, 1 per platoon and 1 per Coy H. Qrs. to junction of PURPLE LINE with Sunken Road. F.2.d.30.75. at 9-45 p.m. to meet relieving Company.
Relief of "A" Coy will commence at 9.30 pm.

No 6. Completion of Relief to be notified to Batt. H. Qrs by Runner in Code as under.

Relief Complete .... ALL.
Little Shelling - - - - FOOLS.
Much Shelling - - - - - DAY.

No 7. Acknowledge.

1/4/18.

M White Major.
a/Adjt. 15/ Batt H. L. I.

Secret.

Operation Orders. No. 17.
by Lt/Colonel .B. RAMSDEN. M.C.
Comdg. 15/ Batt. High. L. I.

Copy No: No 2

Map REFERENCE.
Sheets.. 57.d N.E. 1/10,000 51.C. S.E. 1/10,000.

(1) Intention.

The 15/ Bn. H. L. I. will attack and capture the village of AYTTE on the night of 2nd/3rd inst; and to establish a line of posts on the general line of the enclosure East of the Road.

(2) Information.

It is thought that the enemy push forward at night & occupy the village in some strength.

Enemy Machine Guns have been located at F.5.d.5.6. F.11.a.5.6. (on either side of the Cross Roads.)

Enemy posts have been located in the old Bosche Trench, in F.11 a. Central, and at F.11 a 5.5. and at F.5 d.6.6.

(3). Objectives

First objective, Main Road through the Village from F.5 d: 4.7 to F.11.a.7.2.. — Second Objective, Eastern edge of the enclosure from F.5.d:6.6 to F.11 b.1.1.

(4) Distribution of Troops.

Attacking Troops will form up in the Standard Attack formation laid down by the 32nd Division.

All Waves must be closed up on the assembly point, and will get their distance as the attack proceeds.

The attacking force will be composed of three Companies. "C" Coy on the Left. B. Coy. in the Centre, D. Coy. on the Right. A. Coy. will be in Reserve.

(5) Forming up.

"C" Company. (Left attack company) will form up in the old Bosche Trench, from F.5.C 5.5 to F.5.C.2.2.

No. 5.

5) B. Coy (centre attack Coy.) will form up in the old German Trench from F.5.C.2.2. to F.11.a.2.9. D. Coy. (Right attack Coy.) will form up in the Old German Trench from F.11.a.2.9. to F.11.a.0.5. A. Coy. will have three platoons thirty yards behind the old German trench from F.5.C.3.2. to F.11.a.1.6. and one platoon behind the trench from F.5.C.3.3. to F.5.C.6.5.

6). Method of Attack.

(a) At Zero. (hour to be notified later) an intense Shrapnell and H.E. Barrage will commence, under cover of which, the attacking troops will at once creep forward and get as close to the Barrage as possible

A. Coy will move forward 100 yds from the assembly position, and remain ready for any emergency.

(B) ~~Coy~~. The creeping barage will advance at the rate of 50 yds in three minutes, and must be closely followed by the attacking troops up to the final objective

("C") ~~Coy~~. On reaching the final objective a post line will be established on the outskirts of the enclosure on the East side of the Village, and under cover of the protective barrage. Companies will reorganise and consolidate in depth

(7). Responsibility

On gaining the final objective "C" Coy will be responsible for the defence and consolidation, from F.5.d.7.7. to F.11.b.7.7.
B. Coy. from F.11.b.7.7. to F.11.b.45.40. (i.e.) inclusive of sunken road running through F.11.b.)
D. Coy. from F.11.b.4.4. to F.11.b.1.0.

(8) Action of Supporting Coy.

A. Coy. will follow the advance at 150 yds. distance, but will halt on reaching the enclosures on the West side of the Road keeping close touch with the attacking troops.

Jo. 8.

(8) If the attack is held up in any place; O.C. A Coy. will at once reinforce the attackers, and make every endeavour to capture the obstacle.

(9) Consolidation

On reaching the final objective, a series of posts will be established along the Eastern Edge of the enclosure, East of the Village.
This outpost line will be occupied by two platoons per Company the remaining two platoons of each Company will consolidate in depth to the Main Road running through the Village.
The support Coy will consolidate on a general line of the Western Edges of the enclosure West of the Village.
Consolidation must be pressed on at the greatest speed

(10) ~~Counter Attacking T.~~

Counter – Counter Attacking Troops.

The rear platoon of each attacking Coy. and the support Coys will be the Counter attacking troops, and must push forward directly an enemy Counter attack develops.
O/C. D. Coy will ensure that the road at F.11 a.7.2. is adequately guarded.
O/C. B. Coy will arrange similarly for defending the Road in F.11 b.
The 5/6 Royal Scots & the 96th Brigade will assist in linking the new position to the South
A Section of R.E. will also assist in the consolidation; details as to outside assistance will be issued later.

~~(11)~~ The line will be carried Northwards from the North Edge of the Village up to the old German Trench in F.5.d central.

(11) Machine Guns & R.A. Co-operation

To be issued later: a barrage map will also be issued.

No 12

No 12. T.M.B's. will be sited to develop intense fire on Cross Roads at F.11.a.5.6. in augmentation of the Shrapnel barrage & will lift with the artillery and barrage the enemy trench in F.11.a.7.2. One of these Guns will engage the Machine Guns & snipers on either side of the Cross Roads, the other will operate against the barricade at F.11.a.4.7. One T.M.B will engage enemy Machine Gun at F.5.d.3.5. and afterwards conforming to R.A. Barrage-Table will barrage the main Road and enclosures in rear.

13. Communications.

O/c. Signals will lay a line from present Batt. H.Qrs to advanced Batt. H.Qrs at F.5.C.3.5. and also from F5.C.3.5 to Quarry at F.5.d.6.8. Lamp communication will be established from F.5.C.3.5. to X.28.C.05.65. Runner communication from Coys. to Batt. H.Qrs. will be maintained

Tapes will be laid to Coy. H.Qrs during the advance. Runner Relay Stations. Batt. H.Qrs. at present Location.

14/ Equipment

Fighting Order. 170 Rds S.A.A. for Riflemen, 120 for Bombers & Rifle Grenadiers; Each man to carry two Bombs, bombers six, & Rifle Grenadiers six Rifle grenades. Each Man will carry a pick or shovel between the braces of the equipment.

15/ Advanced Dressing Station.

Medical Officer will arrange ~~to have~~ an advanced Aid post, at advanced Batt. H.Qrs. R.A.P will be at present Batt. H.Qrs.

16/. Support A. Coy. of the 1st Dorset Regt will relieve "B" Coy of the 15th H.L.I. in the Support Line.

17/.

17. Prisoners
All prisoners taken will be sent down to present Batt H. Qrs. where they will be counted & despatched to Bde. H. Qrs.

18. Acknowledge.

2-4-18.

W White. Major.
A/Adjt: 15/Batt H.L.I.

Copies issued to

(1) C.O.
(2) O.C. A. Coy.
(3) O.C. B Coy
(4) O.C. C. Coy.
(5) O.C. D. Coy.
(6) Signal officer.
(7) File
(8) War Diary.
(9) 14th Inf Bde.
(10) 5/6th Royal Scots
(11) 1st DORSET Regt.
(12) 14th T.M. Bty.
(13) M.G. Coy.

Secret.

Addendum to Operation Order No 17.

para. 4. Two platoons of 5/6 Royal Scots will be attached to the Batt and will co-operate, on the Right of D. Company.

para. 5. The two platoons of 5/6 Royal Scots will form up in Old German trench from F11. a 05. to F10 b 9.3.

para. 7. The platoons of 5/6 Royal Scots will be responsible for consolidation in depth of line F11. b.10. to F11. c 9.5.
The 96th Infantry Bde. will adjust its line to get into touch with 5/6 Royal Scots. at F11. c 9.5.

para 11. Four Vickers Machine Guns. will be attached, and will be in position behind right attacking company at 1.A.M. and will be available for garrisoning new line taken up.
The Artillery Barrage. will be on line F5 d 05; 55 – F11. a 33. at Zero.
At Zero + 5 minutes. the creeping barrage. will lift and advance at the rate of 50 yds per three minutes
At Zero + 27 minutes this barrage will become protective along the line F6 a 3.6. – F12. a. 0.8. – F.11. d. 20 – F17. b. 02. until Zero + 50.

para 15 Two extra Stretcher Bearer parties will be at present Bn. H. Qrs. Lieut. F. W. McLaughlan. will be advanced Aid Post, and Capt Skinner, 1st Dorset Regt at R.A.P. at present Bn. H. Qrs.

Signals In the event of a hostile counter attack developing, a counter barrage will be asked for. by sending up Green. Very Lights in rapid succession.

Rations & Hot Food.

Rations will be issued to the men. before moving off. to the assembly. Rum & hot food. will also be given them
A Water party of four O.R's per Coy. will be detailed to carry forward. eight Tins of Water per Coy to final positions.
Men will move off. with Water Bottles full.

W White.
Major
a/Adjt 15/Bn. H.L.I.

The following code will be used -

Succession of

A	means	Assembly complete -
AZ	-	Assembly complete much shelling
AX	-	do. little do.
B	-	Village entered
C	-	Hard fighting in progress
D	-	Heavy Machine Gun fire.
E	-	Hostile barrage heavy on -
F	-	- do - weak -
G	-	Objective reached.
H	-	Consolidation commenced
K	-	Prisoners captured.
L	-	Machine guns captured
M	-	Casualties heavy.
N	-	do light.
O	-	Counter attack expected.
P	-	- do - repulsed
Q	-	In touch on flanks -
R	-	Reorganization complete.

SECRET No 3 (3)

Operation order No 18.
by Lt/Col V. B Ramsden M.C
Commanding 15th Bn The Highland Lt Infy.

(1). On completion of operations the following reorganisation will take place.

(2). The 5/6th Royal Scots will take over the front from F11 c 96 to Southern Edge of Copse at F11 b 87. The 15th H. L. I. will hold the line from F11 b 87 to where it joins the old line.

(3). A. Coy 5/6th Royal Scots will relieve B. Coy. 15th H. L. I. and will be at point F11 b 39 at 3.30 am.

(4). D Coy 5/6th Royal Scots will relieve D Coy 15th H. L. I on right and will be at road-junction F11 a 83 at 3.45 am.

(5) Os C. B and D Companies will send back parties to bring in these Companies to new positions. Also Os. C. 5/6th ROYAL SCOT Companies will send forward reconnoitring parties to find out positions of Companies being relieved

(6). On relief B. Coy will withdraw with two platoons to previous positions & 2 platoons & Coy Hqrs to position previously occupied by D Coy 15th H. L. I.

C Coy 15th H. L. I will remain in positions occupied and will carry on with consolidation with greatest energy.
A Coy 15th H. L. I will move to the left and take over line previously held by C Coy 15th H. L. I.
Companies to be in final positions by 5 a.m.

(7). Final and exact positions of Companies will be reported to Bn HQrs by runner without delay.

(8). Acknowledge.

2/4/18

W White Maj
A/Adj

No. 4 4

Report on Operation carried out by the 15th Batt H.L.I.
on night of 2nd/3rd April. 1918.

Map. Reference. Sheet 57.d. NE.
1/10.000.

---

1. The general Idea of the Operation was to improve our position by capturing the Village of EYETTE.
Objectives were allotted as follows.
1st Objective .... Main Road through village
2nd Objective .... Eastern Edge of Enclosures, on. East side of Village of EYETTE.

2. In accordance with Orders issued, Companies moved to their assembly positions as under, at 12.30 A.M. on 3rd Inst. and were ready for assault by 1.30 A.M.
2 Platoons 5/6 Royal Scots attached. .... F.10.b.9.1. — F11. c.0.5.
"D" Coy. — in old German Trench — F11.a.2.9. - F11.a.0.5.
"B". Coy. — in old German Trench — F11.a.2.9 - F5.c.2.2.
"C" Coy. — in old German Trench — F5.c 2.2. - F.5.c.5.5.
"A". Coy — 3 platoons. 30.yds. in rear of Centre Coy.
1 platoon. 30 yds in rear of Centre of Left Coy.
2 platoons of 5/6 Royal Scots (attached)
D.B & C. Coys were assaulting Troops.
A. Coy. the fourth Coy. was ordered by Bde. to occupy the Old. Front Line, immediately the attack had commenced, and the assaulting Troops were clear of it.
(This Coy had previously been ordered in Batt. Orders to move forward in close support to attacking Companies.)
The assaulting Companies were formed up in 32nd Divisional standard Attack formation.
Conditions for the forming up were very good and no difficulties were experienced in spite of the fact that the Enemy in

front of Bunhi Copse ... 150 yds away and very active and on the alert.

While the forming up was in progress at 1-15 A.M., a little uneasiness was caused amongst the Troops by a heavy Rifle & Machine Gun fire opening opposite our Right Flank.

It transpired that this was caused by the fact that five Machine Gunners, who were to co-operate with assaulting Companies, having lost their way during forming up were captured by the Enemy. This burst of fire lasted for two minutes after which all was quiet until Zero hour.

At Zero hour 2 A.M. the Machine Gun and Artillery Barrage commenced, and the assaulting Troops moved forward up to barrage, and waited for the first lift.

Directly the barrage was put down the enemy opened considerable Machine Gun fire and sent up large numbers of white Very Lights almost immediately a Red Flare was sent up by the enemy and these were sent at frequent intervals afterwards. Within a minute his Artillery had opened out, but was not heavy, and was all on our original front line or in Rear of it.

Green Lights, the meaning of which is not known, were also sent up later by the enemy.

The rate of the barrage advance, viz 50 yds in 3 Minutes was found to be slow (this rate was settled to make allowance for the natural obstacles known to exist & for mopping up, but the Troops overcame these with more ease than anticipated.) otherwise the barrage was splendid and gave great confidence to the Troops.

The two Right Companies experienced little difficulty in following the barrage ~~throughout~~, and reaching the first objective despite a considerable short range Machine Gun and Rifle fire.

The left Company however met trouble from a M. Gun. post in the North East corner of the Ruin which seriously affected its left flank.
The right platoon of this company however reached its final objective up to time.
Our troops pursued the retreating enemy up to the protective barrage and inflicted casualties on the enemy on the ridge beyond the final objective. — Standing patrols were there established, and remainder withdrawn with the idea of consolidating. On return to the village about 3 A.M., it was apparent that the mopping up had been very incomplete, the consolidating troops being harassed by Rifle and M. Gun. fire from their Rear, such as to render consolidation impossible. Owing to the darkness the mopping up of these concealed posts and dugouts was found very difficult, and most of the consolidating troops had to be used by the Officers in charge of mopping up. The assistance of the R.E. Section under its Officer was even called on in this work and was joyfully given
Most of the casualties suffered were incurred during this period, but the work of clearing the village, as far as the two right Companies were concerning was splendidly accomplished and organised consolidation commenced about 4-30 A.M.
Mean while the left Coy. had been heavily engaged and unable to compete with the opposition, and it was considered essential to throw in the fourth Coy. to clear the North of the Village. At 3-45 A.M. three platoons of this Coy. were moved forward between Road F.5.c.3.2. — F.5.d.3.3. and road from into village from F.11.a.4.6 — F.11.b.3.9. these three platoons then moved in a N.E. direction & were met by a stubborn resistance, rapid progress was made and numerous prisoners taken,
At the same time the fourth platoon of this Coy. was thrown in from the old German Trench at F.5.b.3.1. and ordered to attack the N.W. corner of the Village in advancing in S.E. direction

a few posts in the northern corner of village could not be located and occasioned a great deal of trouble, and could not be put out of action, until after dawn. The whole of the village in F6d was eventually cleared and consolidation was in progress by 6. A.M.

It would have been quite impossible for the left attacking Coy. to have dealt with the situation on its flank, and also to consolidate on its final objective, without the energetic assistance rendered by the fourth company.

At 4. 30 A.M. on the 4th inst the 5/6 Royal Scots commenced the relief of the Sector from the Sunken Road F11 b.5.3. to the South. This sector was handed over by 5-45 A.M.

The total prisoners taken during the attack were. 4 Officers and 174. O.R. — 10 Machine Guns (of which 4 were Heavy) have already been brought in.

Our Casualties.

1 Officer - Killed
1 " died of Wounds.
2 " Wounded.

17. O.R. Killed
102 O.R. Wounded.

As a result of this operation, it would appear that it is essential, for village fighting at night, to have a force of ½ the Strength of the attacking troops detailed to follow up the attack to Mop up: This force should be detailed to mop up (definite areas) and is more necessary at night than by day, owing to the difficulty of accurately locating the nests and dug outs.

[illegible]

Lieut/Colonel.

Comdg. the 15th Batt High. L.I.

No 5 (5)

14th Inf. Bde. No. G. 214/0/11.

Officer Commanding,

15th H. L. I.

HEADQUARTERS
INFANTRY BRIGADE

Herewith copy of G.O.C's. report on capture of AYETTE, for your information.

M H Crum

Captain,

8th April 1918. Brigade Major, 14th Infantry Brigade.

CAPTURE OF A Y E T T E

by 14TH INFANTRY BRIGADE on

night 2/3rd April, 1918.

Reference Map Tracing "A" attached.

1. The 14th Infantry Brigade under the Command of General F. W. LUMSDEN, V.C., D.S.O., attacked and captured the Village of AYETTE on the night of the 2/3rd April, 1918.

The 96th Infantry Brigade under the Command of General A. GIRDWOOD, D.S.O., co-operated with the 14th Infantry Brigade by attacking with one Company a trench on the right flank, (vide Yellow dotted line on attached Tracing "A").

Three Companies 15th H.L.I. under Command of Lieut.-Colonel V. B. RAMSDEN, M.C., attacked the Village having as our objective the general line running Cross roads F.11.c.9.8. along road to cross roads F.5.d.65.20. - thence to trench F.5.d.35.90. - thence to original line at F.5.b.55.20. , (vide Green dotted line on attached Tracing "A").
The fourth Company was held in support.

Two platoons of the 5/6th Royal Scots under the Command of Lieut.-Colonel G. D. A. FLETCHER, M.C., attacked the Sunken road running from F.11.c.9.8. to F.11.central (vide Green dotted line on attached tracing "A").

2. ASSEMBLY AND FORMING UP.

The attacking forces consisted of three Companies of 15th H.L.I and two platoons of the 5/6th Royal Scots assembled in and immediately in rear of our front line trench.

Companies took up a frontage of about 200 yards, the left flank on a point about F.5.c.9.5..
The 2 platoons of 5/6th Royal Scots formed up with its left and right flanks resting on the 15th H.L.I. and 16th Lancashire Fusiliers (96th Infantry Brigade) respectively.

The troops assembled noiselessly and in perfect order. The whole movement was carried out rapidly under cover of standing patrols pushed out in front.

All were in position at zero minus 30 minutes in accordance with 14th Infantry Brigade Operation Order No. 204.

The /-

The night was very dark at this time, and the difficulties of moving over the ground quickly and noiselessly were great; the enemy were known to be alert as 5 men of the M.G. Battalion at 1.15 am. walked into the German line and were captured.

3. ARTILLERY ACTION.

The barrage came down at zero well together, but it was irregular in intensity, and consequently difficult to follow.

4. MACHINE GUN FIRE.

Machine Gun Fire commenced a few minutes before zero; its effect could not be estimated.

5. STOKES MORTAR BARRAGE.

3 Guns fired intense from zero to zero plus 5 on 3 specially selected targets. On the final objective being reached, 2 Guns were brought up to cover the consolidation and search the COURCELLES and ABLAINZEVELLE Roads.

6. THE ATTACK.

The troops advanced to the ATTACK in perfect order, (for formation see attached Tracing "A").

The night was light only during the short periods when the moon shone from behind dense clouds, the obstacles to maintaining good direction were many and difficult, but in spite of these the line of attack was well maintained.

The leading platoons carried out their orders implicitly, pushing right forward to the final objective in spite of a heavy machine gun and rifle fire, dealing with those who directly opposed their advance.

Although the enemy appeared at first to be taken by surprise, the leading platoons had heavy and severe fighting. He contested the ground yard by yard, and it was only due to the indomitable courage and inexhaustible energy that the final objective was eventually reached, the enemy holding the road ejected, and consolidation commenced; patrols being sent forward to the protective barrage.

In the meantime the rear lines were fighting in the Village.

The enemy were in strength and the fighting was close and severe. Four Machine Guns were rushed and the teams killed and Guns captured. Germans who were continually appearing from the houses were all either killed or captured.

The Village is long and straggling and the mopping up lasted until dawn.

Two machine guns in the N.E. corner of the Village held up

the left of the attack for some time causing great inconvenience to the operations being completed.

Special parties were told off to outflank these guns. In both cases the teams were killed and the guns captured.

By dawn the troops were tired from the extreme severity of the fighting, but elated with victory and the joy of conquest.

7. ATTACK OF 5/6TH ROYAL SCOTS.

The 2 platoons of the 5/6th Royal Scots advanced with the 15th H.L.I., keeping close to the barrage then the River COJEUL and reached the sunken road running N.E. from P.11.c.4.6. Here the enemy put up a stubborn fight, However, they were overcome, and one prisoner captured.

The Battalion on the 5/6th Royal Scots right flank had failed to advance, and as these platoons were so weakened by the fighting, the right flank was thrown back to get touch with the 18th Lancashire Fusiliers.

Several prisoners were captured and two machine guns.

8. RE-ORGANISATION.

The re-organisation of the line, and the relief of the 15th H.L.I. by 5/6th Royal Scots Company was quickly carried out.

The fourth Company of 15th H.L.I. which had been used to assist in mopping up was withdrawn.

By 6.30 a.m. the relief was complete, and the disposition of the troops organised.

A great number of the enemy were hit by snipers during the day whilst trying to get away from shell holes and trenches into which they had gone for cover.

9 / -

9 **GENERAL.**

The success of the operation was, in my opinion, entirely due to the dash, determination and fine fighting qualities displayed by the three attacking Companies of the 15th H.L.I., and especially to the way in which the leading platoons of these Companies carried out the role allotted them, namely to push right on to the final objective, close under the barrage, dealing only with machine guns or enemy posts directly obstructing their advance, and leaving all mopping up to be carried out by the rear platoons.

The enemy were, undoubtedly, taken by surprise, the greater part of the garrison, which comprised a Battalion of Infantry with a Machine Gun Company, were asleep in their cellars and dugouts at the time of the attack.

These had not time to offer any organised resistance, and it is, perhaps, as well that this was so, as very determined opposition was encountered from such parties of Infantry and Machine Guns that were posted for the defence of the Village.

It was only after stubborn and prolonged fighting that all these enemy posts were finally disposed of. Those giving the most trouble were situated at the Northern and Southern extremities of the Village where they held out for several hours, their capture causing our troops numerous casualties.

The stubborn nature of the fighting can be gauged from the heavy casualties suffered by the three attacking Companies of the 15th H.L.I. and the two platoons 5/8th Royal Scots, which were operating against the Southern outskirts of AYETTE.

These amounted to 126, including six Officers, or a proportion of 40% of the troops engaged.

It had been estimated, prior to the attack, that the garrison did not exceed one Company of Infantry, with one or two heavy, in addition to several light, Machine Guns.

A close inspection of the Village subsequent to its capture, cannot fail to impress one with admiration of the feat so successfully accomplished by the attacking force of the 15th H.L.I.

This force, as stated above, consisted of 3 Companies only, with an average strength of 85 men each.

The /-

The Village is a long straggling one, extending in length from North to South for over half a mile, with an average breadth from East to West of one quarter of a mile.

The Village was held by a Battalion of Infantry, at least equal and probably superior in numbers to the attacking force, and had the support of a Machine Gun Company. It offered special facilities for defence, and great difficulty for the attack.

The numerous ruined and partially destroyed buildings, scattered lengths of trench and heavy wire entanglements, fallen trees and impenetrable hedges, deep shell craters and mass of debris generally, all tended to break up the cohesion and general direction of the attack, and rendered control by Company and Platoon Commanders very difficult.

The weather conditions were, again, unfavourable, heavy rain fell a few hours prior to the attack, making the ground slippery and difficult to traverse, and the moon was obscured by clouds.

The enemy was flushed with the success of his recent operations, his "morale" was consequently good, and he occupied a position which, if properly organised for defence, could justly be considered impregnable to any but a major operation.

The men made every effort, and successfully, to retain their section organisation throughout the attack, and when separated from their own units, attached themselves to the nearest section, thus greatly facilitating control on the part of subordinate Commanders.

It is not possible to speak too highly of the conduct of all ranks engaged in this operation, and the behaviour and dash shewn by the small party of 5/6th Royal Scots on the Southern flank, was all that could be desired.

Their casualties were heavy, and their work beyond all praise.

I am forwarding a number of names of Officers and men recommended for special recognition, but it is difficult to discriminate, where the gallantry of all engaged was so marked.

Brigadier General,

4th April, 1918. Commanding 14th Infantry Brigade.

VI Corps G.S. 89/4.

Third Army.

I submit a copy of a report received from the 32nd Division on the capture of AYETTE on the night of the 2nd/3rd April. The operation, which was carried out at very short notice, and which presented many difficulties, was completely successful owing to the careful manner in which it was planned, the gallantry and good leading of the assaulting units and the control retained by senior Officers.

The work of the Artillery, Engineers and Machine Gunners was most praiseworthy and greatly contributed to the success obtained.

(Sgd). A. HALDANE, Lieut-Genl.

13th April 1918.

Commanding, VI Corps.

- 2 -

32nd Div. No. G.S. 1719/0/7.

14th Infantry Brigade.
xxx xxx

The Divisional Commander is pleased to forward the attached remarks of the Corps Commander on the operations for the capture of AYETTE.

(Sgd). A.E.McNamara, Lieut-Colonel,
General Staff,
32nd Division.

14/4/1918.

H.Q.
14TH INFANTRY BDE.
No.
Date

- 3 -

14th Inf. Bde. No.G.214/0/14.

5/6th Royal Scots.
1st Dorset Regt.
15th H. L. I.
14th T.M.Battery.

The attached remarks of the Corps Commander are forwarded for information.

Blackburn Capt
for
Captain,
Brigade Major, 14th Infantry Brigade.

15/4/1918.

32nd Division.

VI Corps G.S. 29/6.

The sub-joined remarks of the Army Commander on the operation carried out by the 32nd Division at AYETTE are forwarded for your information.

VI Corps. 14/4/18. (Sgd). R.J.KEARSLEY, B.G.,G.S.

The capture of AYETTE by the 32nd Division was an admirable minor operation.

The preparation by the Staff and the execution by the troops are most commendable. The most noteworthy features appear to be the initiative shewn by subordinate leaders in overcoming the unexpected, and the determination of the leading waves to reach the final objective and to remain there.

I congratulate the Divisional Commander and all ranks on the result of this most satisfactory exploit.

14-4-1918 (Sgd). J. BYNG, General.

32nd Div. No. G.S. 1719/0/8.

14th Inf. Bde. No.G.214/0/18.

5/6th Royal Scots.
1st Dorset Regt.
15th H. L. I.
14th T.M.Battery.

The attached remarks of the Army Commander on the capture of AYETTE are forwarded for the information of all ranks.

M H Gray

17/4/1918.

Captain,
Brigade Major, 14th Infantry Brigade.

No 6 (6)

Map Ref. Sheet 57D. N.E.

To: A.D.J.
PLUMP.

3/4/18.

Gained 1st Objective AAA

Casualities:-

R. D. McArthur Lt.
10 Platoon

Per Runner
TIME.

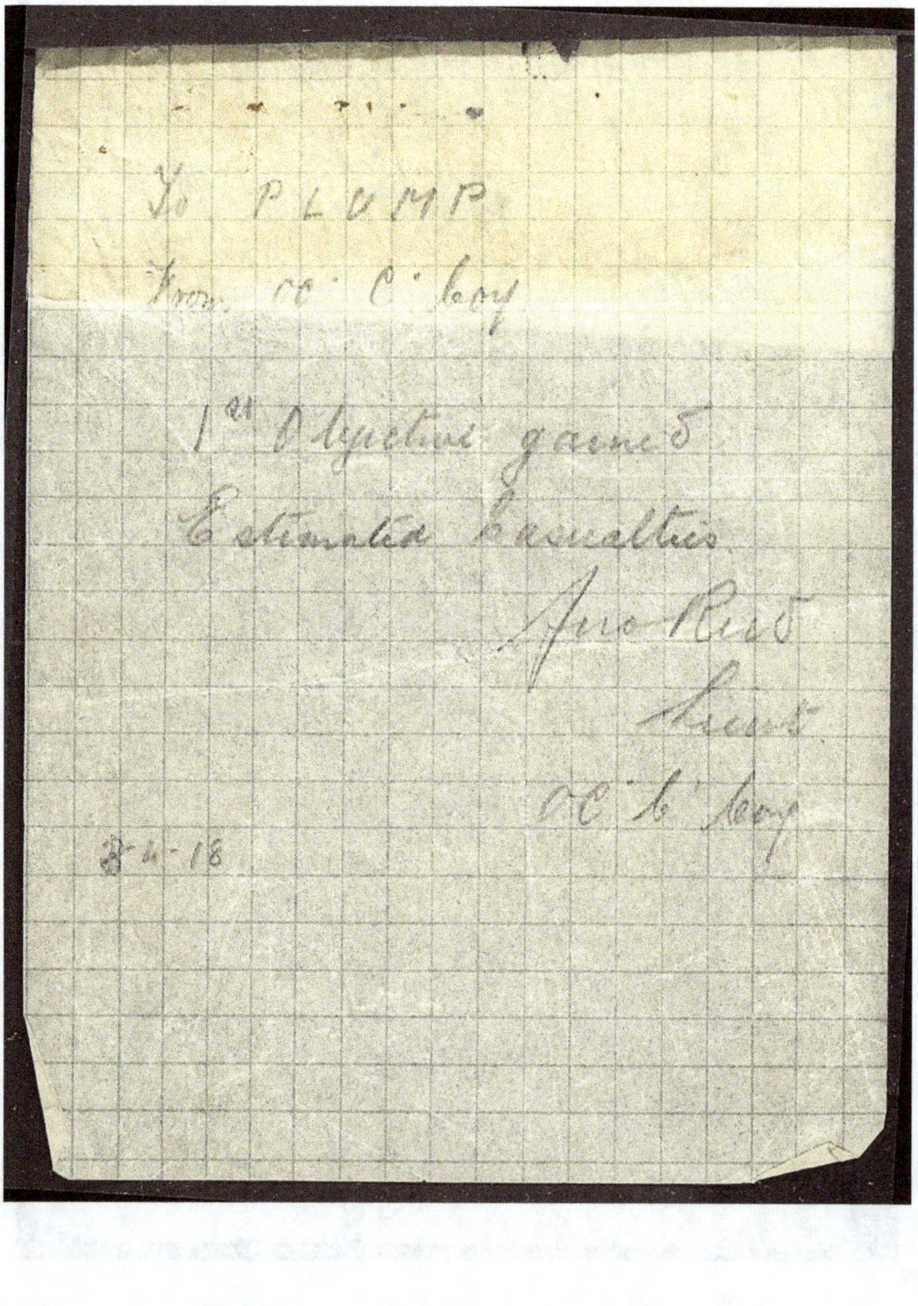

To PLUMP

From OC 'C' Coy

1st Objective gained

Estimated casualties

Jno Reid

Lieut

OC 'C' Coy

3-4-18

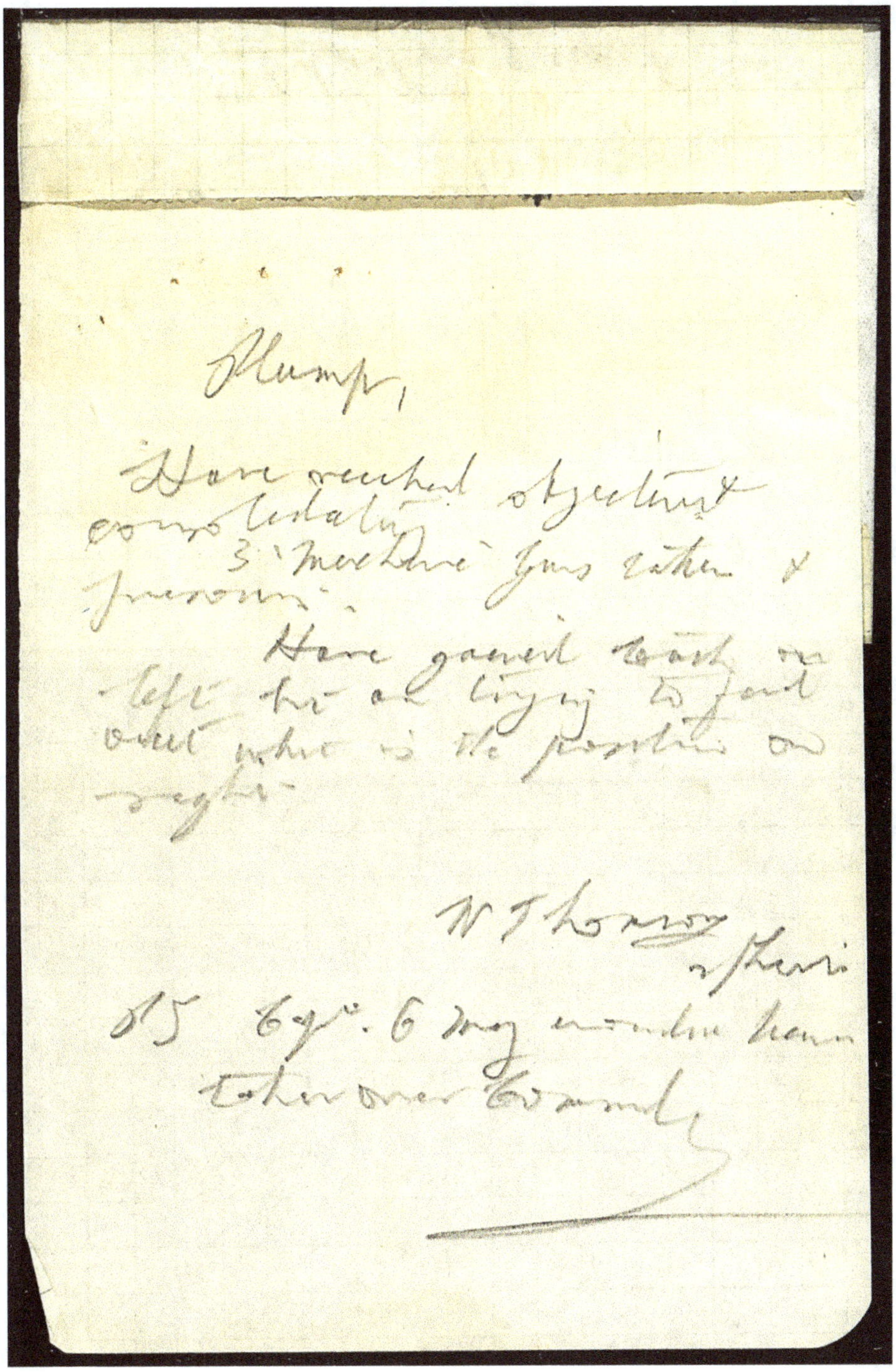

Plumpy,

Have reached objective & consolidating.
3 'Machine' Guns taken & prisoners.
Have gained touch on left but am trying to find out what is the position on right.

[illegible]

85 Coy. 6 [illegible] have taken over command

To PLUMP
From OC "C" Coy

Consolidating on
Final Objective
but left flank held
up by strong enemy
posts on road at RED
HUT
Please send strong
detachment down

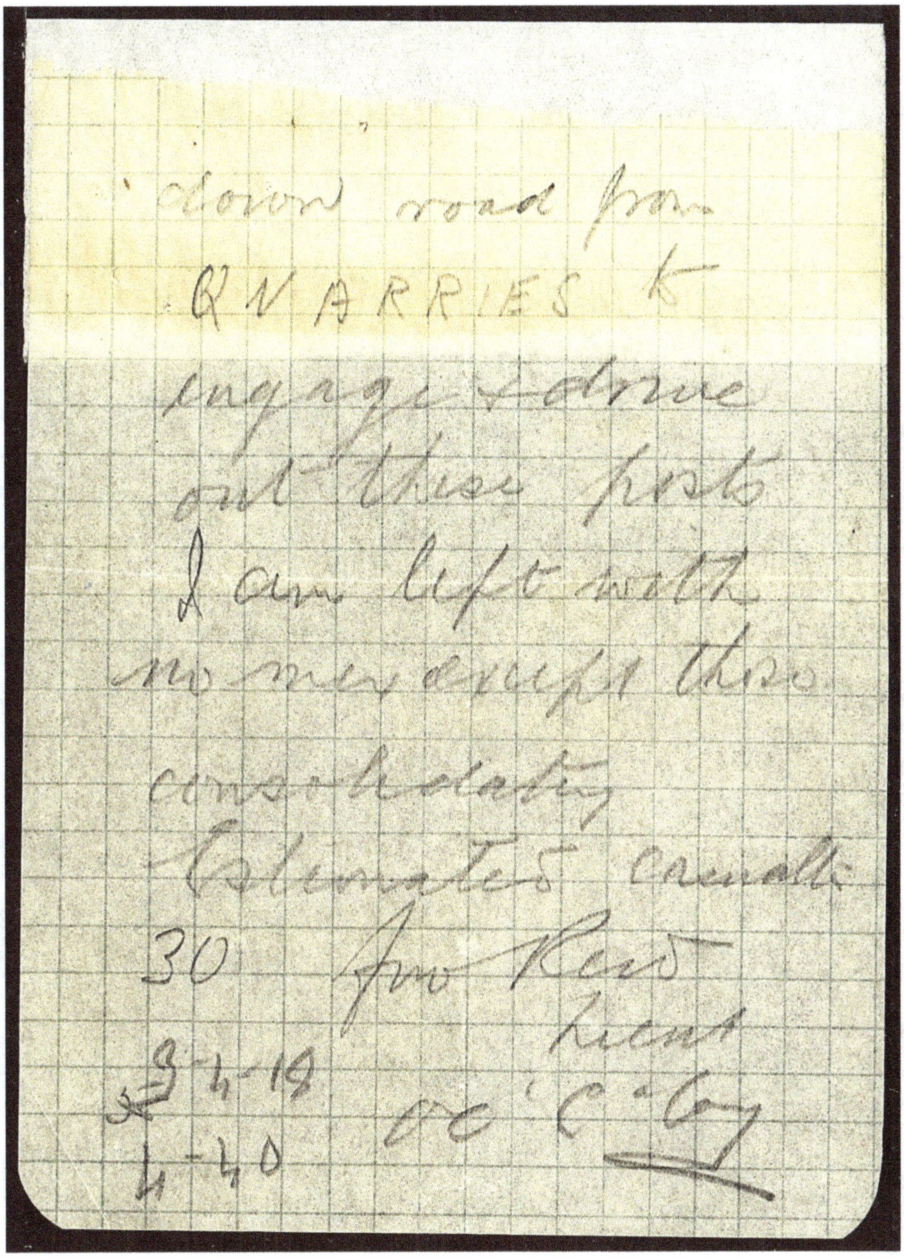

down road from
QUARRIES to
engage & drive
out these posts
I am left with
no men except those
consolidating
Estimated casualties
30 Jno Reid
Lieut
9-4-18 OC 'C' Coy
4-40

From: O/C B Coy

Situation quiet. AAA
Casualties. 10 O.R. AAA
Right flank exposed
AAA. In touch with
C & a weak platoon
D Coy/

W Doughty

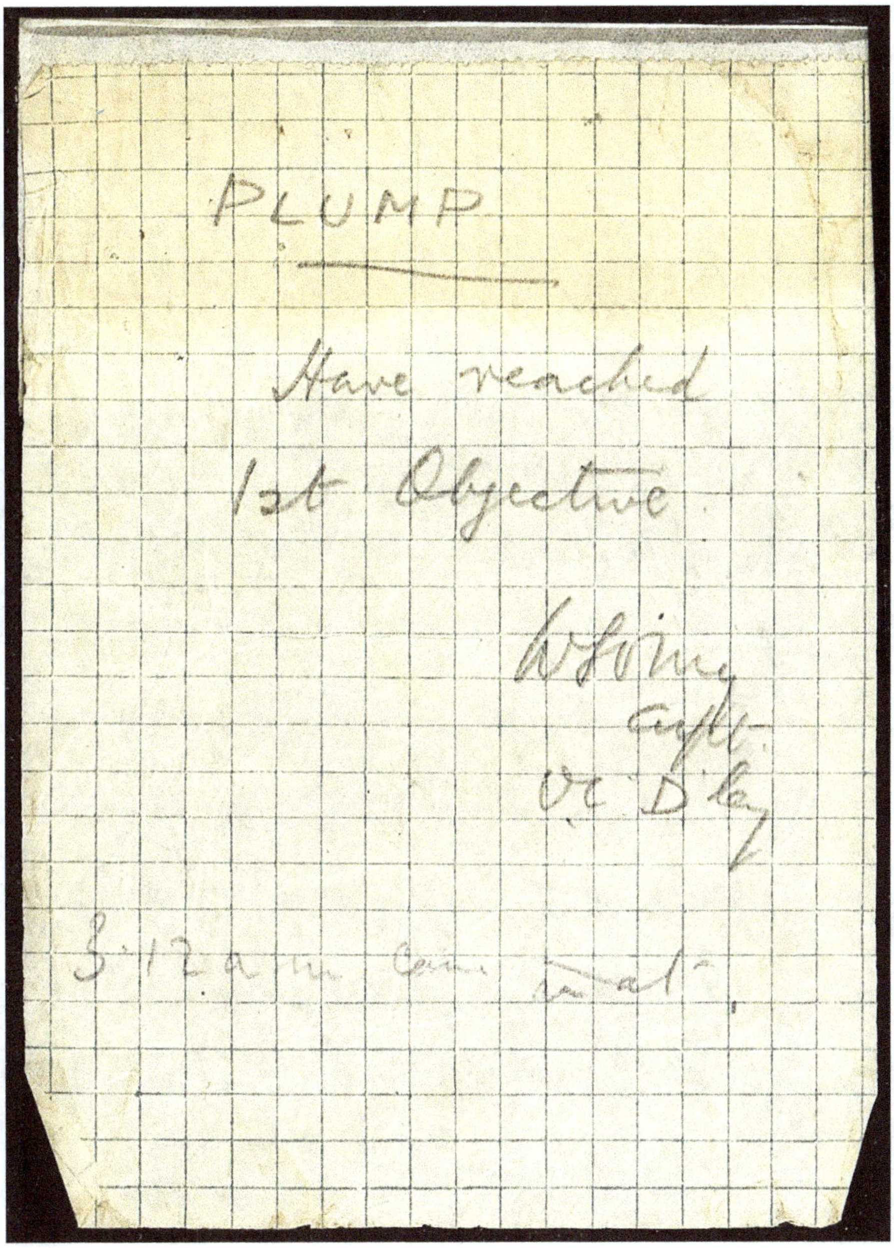
PLUMP

Have reached

1st Objective

W Loring

Capt.

OC D Coy

8.12 am [illegible]

Objectives taken
AAA Casualties
slight AAA
Prisoners 10

W D Capt

2-45 AM

Recd. 4.30

To PLUMP
From O.C. C Coy

2nd Objective gained
Estimated casualties

Jno Reed
Lieut
3-4-18 O.C. C Coy

Recd. 6.0m

"A" Form. Army Form C. 2121.
(In pads of 100.)

MESSAGES AND SIGNALS.

No. of Message..........

Prefix......... Code......... m	Words.	Charge.	This message is on ...... of:	Recd. at .... m.
Office of Origin and Service Instructions.	Sent		No. 6	Date..........
	At.........m.		Service.	From..........
	To..........			
	By..........		(Signature of "Franking Officer.")	By..........

TO PLUMP

Sender's Number.	Day of Month.	In reply to Number.	AAA
* 549	3		

Hearty congratulations on successful operation. Have heard your men driving from Eastern edge of village. The two sections left you are still in your position and I will leave them there for the present but I consider that you should gain touch with me as soon as possible as I have not got touch at present and have been unable to do so

From

Place PRINT

Time 7.15 Am

W. [illegible] Capt Adjt Lt Col

The above may be forwarded as now corrected. (Z)

Censor. Signature of Addressor or person authorised to telegraph in his name.

* This line should be erased if not required.

(3198.) Wt. W 12952/M1294. 375,000 Pads. 1/17. H. W. & V., Ld. (E. 616.)

"C" Form.

Army Form C. 2123,
(In books of 100.)

MESSAGES AND SIGNALS.

No. of Message 15

Prefix SM Code [illegible] Words 36

£ s. d.

Charges to Collect

Service Instructions

Received. From PLATE By [illegible]

Sent, or sent out. At ____ m. To ____ By ____

Office Stamp. H D1 3/4/18

Handed in at H D C Office 11·15A m. Received 11·30A m.

TO Plump and Please

* Sender's Number	Day of Month.	In reply to Number	AAA
D33	3rd		

all	ranks	of	PLATE
offer	their	heartiest	congratulations
to	PLUMP	and	PLEASE
and	trust	their	losses
were	slight	and	that
this	is	only	the
first	of	many	such
successes			

FROM PLATE (1st DORSETS 14th Brigade)

PLACE & TIME

* This line should be erased if not required.

[illegible]

Secret.

Operation Order No 19. No 7
By Lt/Colonel V.B. Ramsden M.C.
Comdg. the 15th Batt H.L.I.

Map Reference.
Sheet: 27.d. N.E.
1/10000.

(7)

(1).a. The 15th H.L.I will be relieved on the night of 4/5th April 1918 by 1st Dorset Regt.
On completion of Relief the Batt will withdraw into position in Purple Line, vacated by 1st Dorset Regt and will become responsible for defence of Purple Line.

b) Companies will be relieved & will move into positions as under.

H.L.I. Companies.	Relieved by 1st DORSET Coys.	Moves to position in purple Line
A	A	Left.
B	B	Right
D	C	Centre.
C.	D	Reserve.
H.Qs.	H.Qs.	F.7.c.8.5.

(2). Advance parties.
The 1st Dorset Regt will send forward 1 Officer per Company and 1 representative per platoon and 1 N.C.O. for Bn. H.Qs. to report at Bn. H.Qs at 3.A.M.
The 15/H.L.I. will send forward to H.Qs 1st Dorset Regt. 2 N.C.O's per Coy. and 1 N.C.O for Bn. H.Qs. to report at Batt H.Qs. 15th H.L.I at 12 midnight.

(3) Guides.
One guide per platoon, and one for Coy. H.Qs. will be at Ration dump. Batt. H.Qs. at 7.30 pm. to meet the first Dorset Regt Company. Commanders will arrange that their advance parties guide their companies to new positions on relief.

No. 4.

No. 4. All available information about the line will be carefully handed over.
Trench store lists will be carefully prepared & a receipt for stores obtained. Duplicate copies of these lists will be forwarded to Batt. Hqrs. by 9 AM. 5th Inst.

No. 5. The greatest care will be taken in handing over, & no officer will leave his post until the relieving officer is satisfied that he knows his post, its position, & role.

No. 6. No transport will be available to take Men's stores etc. to the Paper Line.

No. 7. Rations & Water are brought up nightly at dusk by limber and water cart respectively.

No. 8. Completion of relief will be notified by quickest means available in code as under:-

Relief complete. — WHAT
Little Shelling — ABOUT
Much Shelling — IT.

No. 9. Acknowledge.

4. 4. 18.

B. C. Hitchen, Lt for Major
A/Adj 15th Bn. H.L.I.

Secret. **No 8** (8)

Operation Order No. 20
by Lt/Colonel V. B. Ramsden M.C.
Comdg. the 15th Batt H. L. I.

Map Reference
Sheet. 57 D. N. E.
1/10,000.

No. 1. The 15th H. L. I. will relieve the 5/6 Royal Scots in the Forward System, Right Sub Sector, (Centre Bde) to night 9/10 April, 1918.

No. 2. The greatest care will be taken in handing over all posts. The Officer taking over a post, will not report relief complete until he is satisfied that he knows the position, and extent of his post, and its defences, position of adjoining posts, Company & Batt H. Qrs, orders for Defence, and all other information concerning the post he is taking over.

No. 3. Defence Schemes, Maps, Schemes of Work, and all other information about the line will be taken over. Trench Store Lists, taken & handed over will be carefully checked, and duplicate copies forwarded to Bn H. Qrs by 9 A.M. on the 10th Inst.

No. 4. Advance Parties

One Officer & one Runner per Coy. and 1 N.C.O. per platoon will report at H. Qrs. of 5/6 Royal Scots at 3 A.M. 9th inst These will obtain all information possible and will be ready to guide the relieving troops to their posts.

No. 5. One Guide per Coy. H. Qrs., and one per platoon, will be at junction of sunken Road with Purple Line F.2.d.5.2 for Companies as under.

A. Coy.
C " ... 7.45 p.m.
B " ... 8.45 p.m.
D " ... 9.45 p.m.
10.45 p.m.

One guide for Band will be at same place at 7.45 p.m. and the Guide for Bn H. Qrs at 10.45 p.m.

No. 6.

No. 6. On completion of Relief Batt will be disposed as follows.

A. Coy.	Right.
C "	Centre
B "	Left.
D "	Support.
Bn. H. Qs.	F. 9. a 5. 4.

No. 7. Companies will move into the line with Battle Stores complete less S.O.S. Very lights, which will be carefully taken over.

No. 8 Water & Rations.
Companies will send back nightly parties to carry forward Rations & drinking Water

No. 9. Hot Food.
Hot food will be cooked for forward companies in AYETTE. and for Rear Companies near Bn. H.Qs.

No. 10. Completion of Relief will be reported to Bn. H. Qs. in Code as under.

Relief Complete.	Business
Little Shelling.	As.
Much Shelling.	Usual.

No. 11. Companies will report that they are in Touch with Units on their Flanks as under.

Right Flank	Happy.
Left Flank	Glad.

No. 12. Acknowledge.

[signature]
Major
Adjt. 13/ Bn. A.L.

SECRET. No 9 (9)

Operation Order No. 31.
By Major C. M. Cleghorn
Commanding 15th Bn Argyl. L. I.

Map Reference Sheet 54D NE. 1/10000.

1. The 1st Dorset Regt. will relieve the 15th H.L.I. in the Right Batt. front of the Centre Brigade Sector on the night of 19th/20th April 1918.

2. On completion of relief 15th H.L.I. will withdraw into Reserve and take over position vacated by 1st Dorset Regt. in the PURPLE LINE.

3. Coys will be relieved as in the following table.

15th H.L.I.	1st Dorset Regt. Coy. Relieving	LOCATION on Withdrawal
A	B	Old German Line F5 a
B	D	Old German Line F5 a
D	A	PURPLE LINE
C	C	PURPLE RESERVE LINE
H.Q	H.Q	F8 a 07.

4. The greatest care will be exercised in taking and handing over all posts.

The Officer commanding a post will not leave it until he is satisfied that the relieving Officer understands his post, its defence, and location.

Officers commanding A and B. Coys. will take immediate steps to see that Officers and N.C.O.s. are familiar with the routes to Battle positions of their Coys. in the PURPLE LINE.

5. All Defence Schemes. Maps, Schemes of Work and Trench Stores Lists will be most carefully handed over and duplicate copies of receipts obtained forwarded to Batt. Hqrs by 9 a.m. on 20th inst.

6. ADVANCE PARTIES.

(a) 1st. Dorset Regt. will send advance parties of 1 Officer per Coy. and 1 N.C.O. per platoon to report at Batt. Hqrs. at dawn on 19th inst.

6/ (b) 15th H.L.I. will send advance parties of 1 Officer per Coy and 1 N.C.O. per platoon to report at Batt Hqrs. of 1st Dorset Regt at 3 p.m. on 19th inst.

7/ GUIDES.

(a) Each Coy will send one guide per platoon and One for Coy. H.Q. to junction of PURPLE LINE and SUNKEN ROAD as under:-

A. Coy at 8.15 p.m.
B. Coy at 9.15 p.m.
D. Coy at 10.15 p.m.
C. Coy at 11.15 p.m.

Personnel of Batt. H.Q. of 1st Dorset Regt. will arrive at Batt H.Q. of 15th H.L.I. at 10 p.m.

8/ (a) O.C. Coys will ensure that all Battle equipment is brought out of the line. This to include the proper percentage of Tools. Water Tins on hand will be returned to the Water Cart prior to relief.

(b) O.C. Coys will arrange with their advance parties to return and guide relief troops to new positions.

9/ LEWIS GUNS.

Lewis Guns of C and D Coys will be carried by the gun teams to the new positions. Guns of A and B Coys will be loaded on a limber at Batt Hqrs. at 10 p.m and taken back to MONCHY. Two representatives per Coy will accompany this limber.

10. Orderly Room, Signals and Medical Stores will be collected at Batt H.Q. at 10 p.m and taken by limber to new H.Q.

11. RATIONS + WATER.

Rations will be delivered at Batt. H.Q. for C and D. Coys. and at MONCHY for A and B Coys.

12. COOKING.

The Sergeant cook will make all necessary arrangements for cooking in new Area, and will ensure that all cooking utensils are brought out of the line.

13. In the Reserve Area Personnel for Straggler posts will be detailed as under:-

Each post to consist of 1 L/cpl and 2 O.R.

A Coy at F1 a 51
A. Coy at E12 b. 87.
B Coy at E12 b 87.

These posts will be reconnoitred at once and personnel held in readiness to move to them immediately S.O.S is fired.

14. Completion of relief to be notified in code as under.

RELIEF COMPLETE :- BYNG.
LITTLE SHELLING :- BOYS.
MUCH SHELLING :- HERE.

15. Acknowledge.

W White
Major
a/Adjt 15th H.L.I

1st Dorset Regt Relief Orders. Copy No. 11.

1. Coys will be disposed as stated in my O.R. No. 133. of 18/4/18.
2. Guides from 15th H.L.I. will be at junction of the PURPLE Line with the sunken road about F. 2. d. 3. 2. at the following hours:-
   - B Coy at 8. 15pm.
   - D " " 9. 15pm.
   - A " " 10. 15pm.
   - C " " 11. 15pm.

   There will be 5 guides from each Coy - 1 for Coy H.Q. and 1 for each platoon.
   No guides will be provided for Bn H.Q.
   Battalion Headquarters will take over 15th H.L.I. Battalion Headquarters at 10pm.
3. Q.M. will make his own arrangements for moving camp kettles, & officers kits of coys to their new cookhouses.
   2 front Coys have 2 cookhouses in AYETTE.
   Support, Reserve & Bn H.Q. cookhouses are together.
   8 Hot Food containers will be used for carrying food to Support & Reserve coys & Bn H.Q.
4. All Coy Lewis guns will be carried by the men.
   Everything to be conveyed by transport will be ready stacked at the place where rations are unloaded nightly by 8. pm.
5. Coys will report relief complete in code word by wire and runner:-
   - Relief complete - FORD
   - Much Shelling - STAYNER
   - Little Shelling - THWAYTES.
6. ACKNOWLEDGE.

D. S. Taylor
Captain
Adjutant 1/Dorset Regt.

19. 4. 18.

Copies to:-
No. 1. C. O.
2. Adjt.
3. OC. A Coy.
4. OC. B Coy.
5. OC. C Coy.
6. OC. D Coy.
7. Signals.
8. Q.M.
9. RSM.
10. [illegible]
11. 15th H.L.I.
12. File.

SECRET.

No 10

10

Operation Order No. ~~22~~

by Major G. W. Clapham D.S.O.

Commanding 15th Batt. High. L. I.

MAP REF. 57D N.E. 1/10000.

LENS SHEET 11 1/10,000

1. (a) The 14th Inf. Bde. will be relieved by the 1st Guards Brigade on the night 24/25th April 1918.

(b) The 15th H.L.I. will be relieved by the 2nd Grenadier Guards on the night 24/25th April 1918.

(c) On relief the Battalion will withdraw to SAULTY. The Division then being in the THIRD ARMY RESERVE. Details of moves in TABLE A.

2. All Defence schemes, defensive arrangements, information about the line, and the various lines of defence will be carefully handed over on relief.
The greatest care must be taken to ensure that every post and locality is carefully handed over.

3. Lists of Trench Stores will be carefully prepared and receipts obtained. Duplicate copies of these lists to be forwarded to this Office by 9 A.M. on 25th inst.

4. Battle Stores, i.e. S.A.A. Grenades and Tools will not be taken out of the line, but will be stored in the line, and included in trench stores lists.

5. Lewis Guns and ammunition will be carried by L.G. sections.

6. One limber will be at Batt. H.Q. at 4.30 P.M. to collect cooking utensils. It will collect those of A and B Coys on its return.
A second limber will be at Batt. H.Q. at 4.30 p.m. to collect Orderly Room, Medical, Signal, and Mess Stores. Officers Mess Stores of A and B Coys will be collected on returning.

7. All Water Tins will be handed over full.

8. Completion of relief to be reported at once by wire and runner in code as under:-

RELIEF COMPLETE	–	BLACK
LITTLE SHELLING	–	AND
MUCH SHELLING.	–	WHITE.

9. Acknowledge.

Copies issued to.

1. C.O.
2. O.C. A. Coy.
3. " B "
4. " C "
5. " D "
6. Signal Officer
7. Q.M.
8. File
9. War Diary
10. 14th Inf. Bde.

mwhite Major
a/adjt 15th/13th H.L.I.

24. 4. 18.

APPENDIX A.

1.

DATE	UNIT	FROM	TO	RELIEVING UNIT
April 24/25th	15TH H.L.I.	RESERVE (No. 3 Bn.)	SAULTY	2ND. GRENADIER GUARDS

2. GUIDES.

At rate of 1 per Platoon and 1 per Coy and Batt. H.Q. to report at 14th Inf. Bde. H.Q. (E 4 a 5 7.) at 9 A.M. on 24th inst. and await arrival of relieving troops. Relieving Batt. will debus at approximately 4 p.m.

3. MOVEMENT OF COYS ON RELIEF.

To be notified later

4. ADVANCE PARTIES.

The Q.M. will arrange to take over billets at SAULTY and to have platoon guides at debussing point to guide Platoons to new billets.

5. Cross country routes will be used where possible.

SECRET

[illegible]

G.W. 1

Preliminary Orders.

1. With reference to No. G.W. 2 of this unit, every endeavour must be made to have the work detailed therein completed by 12 noon tomorrow 21st inst.

2. A and B Coys will form a dump of tools at their Coy H.Q. and will not carry these to Batt. H.Q. Dump.

3. Each Coy will detail guides as under -

1 per Platoon

1 per Coy H.Q.

to report at H.Q. Inf. Bde H.Q. by 9 a.m. on 21st inst.

They will be accomodated at Bde H.Q. until incoming Batt. (3rd Batt. Grenadier Guards) arrives.

Rations for the day will be taken.

Clean, smart intelligent men must be sent.

M White

Major & Adjt.

Instructions regarding War Diaries and Intelligence Summaries are contained in F. S. Regs., Part II. and the Staff Manual respectively. Title pages will be prepared in manuscript.

WAR DIARY
or
INTELLIGENCE SUMMARY.
(Erase heading not required.)

15 H. L. I.

Map Reference Sheet 51^C SE 1/20,000

Army Form C. 2118.

Vol 31

Place	Date May	Hour	Summary of Events and Information	Remarks and references to Appendices
SAULTY.	1.		The Battalion carried out training as per programme. Lectures & Manoeuvres on the Battalion Range. 2nd Lt HEPBURN with the Lewis Gun class fired on range in the afternoon. The Commanding Officer and Company Commanders attended the Lecture on Gas by the DIVISIONAL GAS OFFICER. Weather dull & cold.	[illegible]
	2.		B Company carried out Musketry on the Battalion Range. The Battalion carried out practices in Open Warfare. The Gas N.C.O.s & Pioneer Sergeant attended Lecture on construction of Gas Proof Shelters & Entrances. The Battalion turned out on a practice Alarm the message being received at 6.15 pm. they were inspected by BRIGADIER GENERAL LUMSDEN. V.C. DSO. in the CHATEAU GROUNDS. Weather warm.	[illegible]
	3		The Battalion carried out a Tactical Scheme in Open Warfare up till mid-day the afternoon being spent bathing & cleaning equipment. The weather was warm & bright. CAPT J.M. DAWSON C.F. posted to the Battalion for duty.	[illegible]
	4.		The Battalion had the Brigade Range allotted to them for the day. A+B Companies carried out a Musketry Programme in the forenoon and C+D Companies in the afternoon. The Officers Dinner was held to celebrate the victory of AYETTE. Weather Dull.	
	5.		Church service was held in the CHATEAU GROUNDS under CAPT DAWSON. In the afternoon the second in commands of companies reconnoitred the route to the line in case of Alarm. The Officers played the Sergeants at football the result being Officers 2 Sergeants 1. The [illegible] weather prevailed.	[illegible]

A5834 Wt. W4973/M687 750,000 8/16 D. D. & L. Ltd. Forms/C.2118/13.

81.0

15 sheets

Instructions regarding War Diaries and Intelligence Summaries are contained in F. S. Regs., Part II. and the Staff Manual respectively. Title pages will be prepared in manuscript.

WAR DIARY
or
INTELLIGENCE SUMMARY.
(*Erase heading not required.*)

15th H. L. I.

Army Form C. 2118.

Map Reference Sheet 51C SE 1/10000

Place	Date May	Hour	Summary of Events and Information	Remarks and references to Appendices
SAULTY.	5.		The Battalion was drawn up in Mass formation in the CHATEAU GROUNDS and inspected by BRIGADIER GENERAL LUMSDEN. VC DSO. after the inspection the Inspecting General gave an address to the Battalion complimenting them on their past work in the Line. In the afternoon an Investiture for decoration was held at BAVINCOURT by the CORP. COMMANDER. The number of recipients from the BATTALION was OFFICER'S 5. NCOs & Men 9.	
	6,		Battalion carried out training as per programme of work C & D companies in the forenoon and A & B Companies on the BRIGADE RANGE in the afternoon. In the evening the BATTALION played the 1ST DORSET REGT at football and after a very fast and thrilling game the 15TH H.L.I. at the finish of the game was ten goals up. Final result being 15TH H.L.I. 10. 1ST DORSET REGT NIL. Weather showery.	
	7.		The Battalion carried out in the forenoon a small scheme on Open Warfare returning about 1.15 pm. In the afternoon the COMMANDING OFFICER lectured to the OFFICER'S & NCO'S in the CHATEAU GROUND'S Weather fine & warm.	
	8.		The Battalion carried out a small scheme on Open Warfare returning in time for lunch. In the afternoon the Officers & NCOs attended a demonstration on the BRIGADE RIFLE RANGE by CAPT NICOL of the 3rd Army Musketry Camp showing them how you can get the competitive spirit into the men when carrying out work on the range. Weather very warm.	
	9		The Battalion carried out training as per programme. In the evening A Coy played B Coy at football in the CHATEAU GROUNDS. the final result being one goal each. Weather warm.	

A5834 Wt. W4973/M687 750,000 8/16 D. D. & L. Ltd. Forms/C.2118/13.

Instructions regarding War Diaries and Intelligence Summaries are contained in F. S. Regs., Part II. and the Staff Manual respectively. Title pages will be prepared in manuscript.

WAR DIARY
or
INTELLIGENCE SUMMARY.
(Erase heading not required.)

15th H L I.

Map Reference Sheet 51c SE 1/10,000

Army Form C. 2118.

Place	Date May	Hour	Summary of Events and Information	Remarks and references to Appendices
SAULTY.	10.		The Battalion carried out Musketry on the BRIGADE RANGE all day A & C Coy's in the forenoon B & D Coy's in the afternoon. In the evening the Battalion team played the 92nd FIELD AMBULANCE at football on the SAULTY GROUND and after a very exciting & fast game the final result saw the H.L.I. 3 goals up. Final Score H.L.I. 3 AMBULANCE 0. Weather cold & dull.	
Map Refce BOISLEUX.	11		The Battalion spent the day cleaning up and getting ready for going into the line in the evening it moved up and took over from the 2nd Ox's & Buck's. Operation orders No 23 issued. The Battalion embussed at 7.15 pm and at BOIRVILLE where they debussed each man was served out with tea & Biscuits accompanied by music from the DIVISIONAL BAND. They then proceeded on their way and carried out the relief with the Ox & Buck's. There was very little shelling during the relief and it passed off very quiet.	Appendix 1
	12.		All companies settled down in the line in respective positions of trench system. During the day there was very little shelling. Enemy's aircraft was very active. Weather warm good observation	
	13.		Enemy T.M's busy on right Battalion front, Aircraft on both sides busy. The Companies worked on their trenches making T. bays & firing positions. Our aircraft very busy at night and set a Dump on fire at BOISELLE Weather very warm.	

A5834 Wt. W4973/M687 750,000 8/16 D. D. & L. Ltd. Forms/C.2118/13.

Instructions regarding War Diaries and Intelligence Summaries are contained in F. S. Regs., Part II. and the Staff Manual respectively. Title pages will be prepared in manuscript.

WAR DIARY
or
INTELLIGENCE SUMMARY.
(*Erase heading not required.*)

Army Form C. 2118.

15 HLI.

Map Reference BOISLEUX. 51c S.E. 1/10000.

Place	Date	Hour	Summary of Events and Information	Remarks and references to Appendices
Front Line	14		Our artillery fired Gas Shells into HAMLINCOURT but owing to the wind changing the effects of same was felt in the front line. Artillery & aircraft very quiet all day. At night MAJOR WHITE sited a series of new posts. Weather very warm.	RB
	15		A few T.M's fell near the support line. The evening passed very quiet.	WM
	16		Operation orders issued No 24. The companies carried out Intercompany reliefs. A Coy was relieved by B & C. by D Coy. There was little or no shelling while the relief was being carried out. 2nd Lt A. HUBBARD posted to B Coy for duty. Weather warm, observation good.	WM Appendix 2
	17.		Enemy's artillery versus our own had one or two duels through the day. At night the enemy laid down a Trench Mortar Barrage on the Right Brigade front and tried to raid the left post of the K.O.Y.L.I's from the start to the finish it only lasted about thirty minutes. Wiring and digging the new posts was carried out during the evening. Weather warm. Slight breeze.	WM

A5834 Wt. W4973/M687 750,000 8/16 D. D. & L. Ltd. Forms/C.2118/13.

Instructions regarding War Diaries and Intelligence Summaries are contained in F. S. Regs., Part II. and the Staff Manual respectively. Title pages will be prepared in manuscript.

WAR DIARY
or
INTELLIGENCE SUMMARY.
(*Erase heading not required.*)

15 H.L.I.

Army Form C. 2118.

Map France BOISLEUX 51c SE 1/10,000

Place	Date	Hour	Summary of Events and Information	Remarks and references to Appendices
Front Line	18		Operation Orders issued No 25. The Battalion was relieved by 1st DORSET REGT. The relief was carried out without any disturbance by the enemy on the completion of the relief the Battalion moved back for four days to the reserve line's at HENDECOURT.	Appendix 3. RB
	19		The day was spent cleaning up equipment Rifles after coming out of the line. The Company Platoon & Section commanders in the afternoon reconnoitred their respective battle positions in the PURPLE LINE for defence. In the evening an inspection of Gas Helmets was carried out under company arrangements. Weather very warm.	RB
	20		Inspection parades was carried out by companies also started bathing at RANSART. Enemy's artillery very active on the back area's.	RB
	21		Aerial activity on both sides The Battalion played the 2nd BATTALION H.L.I at football at BAVINCOURT. The ground was not in the best condition owing to the grass being long which made the game heavy but after a very enjoyable game the final result was in a draw one goal each. A practice stand too in their respective battle positions at 10-45 pm was held and the companies were inspected by MAJOR. CLEGHORN. D.S.O.	RB
	22.		The day was spent cleaning preparatory for going into the line operation orders No 26. issued The Battalion relieved the 5/6th ROYAL SCOTS on the left sector. The first platoon moved off	Appendix 4 RB

contd

A5834 Wt. W4973/M687 750,000 8/16 D. D. & L. Ltd. Forms/C.2118/13.

Instructions regarding War Diaries and Intelligence Summaries are contained in F. S. Regs., Part II. and the Staff Manual respectively. Title pages will be prepared in manuscript.

WAR DIARY
or
INTELLIGENCE SUMMARY.
(Erase heading not required.)

Map Reference Sheet BOISLEUX 51^{B}SE 1/20000

Army Form C. 2118.

Place	Date	Hour	Summary of Events and Information	Remarks and references to Appendices
Front Line	22.		at 10 pm and the relief was completed at 1.45 a.m.	
	23.		Enemy aircraft busy in the morning the day passed very quiet. Mild Wind Visibility good.	
	24		A very miserable day was spent in the line owing to the inclemency of the weather No aircraft to be seen also very little shelling. The night passed very quietly.	
	25.		Aerial activity all day one of the enemys planes flew over our lines & dropped a parachute His artillery proceeded to shell our support & reserve lines & back area's Weather mild visibility good.	
	26		The enemys artillery active at different times all day. From our O.P. parties of men were seen walking towards St LEGER. The largest party was about 25 in number. The night was very quiet, aircraft very active. Major G. CLEGHORN proceeded on a COMMANDING OFFICER'S course. Weather warm & good for observation.	
	27.		Enemys artillery very active all day from early morning till evening both in forward & back area's The Battalion carried out inter-company reliefs without being harassed by artillery or Machine Gun fire. The evening passed very quiet. Weather mild & cloudy but good for observation.	

A5834 Wt. W4973/M687 750,000 8/16 D. D. & L. Ltd. Forms/C.2118/13.

Instructions regarding War Diaries and Intelligence Summaries are contained in F. S. Regs., Part II. and the Staff Manual respectively. Title pages will be prepared in manuscript.

WAR DIARY
or
INTELLIGENCE SUMMARY.

(*Erase heading not required.*) Map Reference BOISLEUX Sheet 51c SE 1/10,000

Army Form C. 2118.

Place	Date	Hour	Summary of Events and Information	Remarks and references to Appendices
Front Line	28		Early in the morning our artillery laid down a barrage on the left DIVISIONAL FRONT and the enemy put up a large number of single & double green lights & single & double red lights; as on the day previous the enemy's artillery was very active and from 2-30 am to 6 am put over a large number of Gas Shells into BOISLEUX AU MONT, & back area's Weather warm, Wind mild, observation good.	[illegible]
	29.		Very little shelling all day. At night our planes were very active over the enemy's lines & back area's and the dropping of bombs could be heard quite distinctly, about 12 Midnight two large white flares were dropped from our planes, At one time 14 search lights were observed searching for our planes at once. A large number of Observation balloons were up on both sides. Weather warm, Observation good.	[illegible]
	30.		The morning was very quiet about 1-30 pm the enemy's artillery was very active on the road round about the Battalion Headquarters and Railway in rear, Aerial activity on both sides active, Operation Orders No 24 issued. The 1st DORSET REGt relieved the Battalion in the line. After the relief being completed the Battalion withdrew to the BRIGADE PURPLE RESERVE. There was very little shelling and the relief was carried out without a hitch. ~~The enemy's artillery active from~~ ~~[illegible] Aerial activity on both side~~, Weather warm, Observation good.	[illegible] Appendix 5 [illegible]

A5834 Wt. W4973/M687 750,000 8/16 D. D. & L. Ltd. Forms/C.2118/13.

Instructions regarding War Diaries and Intelligence Summaries are contained in F. S. Regs., Part II. and the Staff Manual respectively. Title pages will be prepared in manuscript.

WAR DIARY
or
INTELLIGENCE SUMMARY.

(*Erase heading not required.*) Map Reference ~~[illegible]~~ 1/10,000

Army Form C. 2118.

Place	Date	Hour	Summary of Events and Information	Remarks and references to Appendices
PURPLE RESERVE	31		Enemy's artillery active on rear batteries all day. Bathing was carried out by the companies at BLAIRVILLE. 2 American Officers & 8 O.R. posted to the Battalion for tuition.	[illegible]

	1st MAY		31st MAY	
	OFF	ORs	OFF	ORs
Commanding Officer's Strength	31	895	28	863
FIGHTING STRENGTH.				
Officers	38		37	
Other Ranks	991		969	

TOTAL CASUALTIES for the MONTH.	OFFICERS	ORs.
Killed and Died of Wounds	-	10
Wounded	1	46
Missing	-	-

[illegible] May
O. [illegible] 15th H.L.I.

A5834 Wt. W4973/M687 750,000 8/16 D. D. & L. Ltd. Forms/C.2118/13.

(2)

1/ [illegible]
[illegible]
(a) D Coy [illegible] A [illegible]
[illegible]
[illegible] complete. A Coy [illegible]
[illegible]
Coy
(b) D Coy [illegible] C Coy [illegible]
[illegible] Relief [illegible]
[illegible]

2/ A, B and C Coys [illegible] their present positions [illegible] 2 AM (D Coy [illegible] at 1. AM).

3/ [illegible] and properly [illegible] out.

4/ [illegible] of Relief to be arranged by Coy. Commanders concerned.

5/ C Coy [illegible] their rations [illegible] a Guard [illegible] their ration [illegible] Quarter [illegible]

6/ On completion of Relief it will be reported by Wire and Runner [illegible]

RELIEF COMPLETE — ANOTHER
LITTLE SHELLING — LITTLE
MUCH SHELLING — DRINK

7/ ALKNOWLEDGE

SECRET **Operation Order No. 25.** 5

By Lieut-Colonel [illegible] D.S.O. M.C.
Commanding 15th Battn. The Highland L.I.
18th Aug 1918.

[illegible]

1/ The 1st Dorset Regt. will relieve the 15th H.L.I. in the Right Battalion Sector of the Brigade Front on the night of 18/19th inst.

2/ On completion of relief the 15th H.L.I. will withdraw into Support in the PURPLE LINE.

3/ Inter-Company reliefs will take place as under

15th H.L.I. Coy.	Relieved by 1st Dorset Coy	Takes over Position vacated by 1st Dorset Coy
D.	C.	C.
B.	A.	A.
A.	B.	B.
C.	D.	D.
H. Qrs	H. Qrs.	H. Qrs.

2 Sections of Battn. H.Qrs L.G. platoon in the Reserve line will be relieved by 2 sections of 1st Dorset Regt. The 1st Dorset Regt. will take over one A.A. position at Battn. H.Q.

4/ Relieving Coys. will arrive in order;
LEFT FRONT C Coy, RIGHT FRONT A Coy,
SUPPORT D Coy, and RESERVE D Coy.

5/ The greatest care will be taken in handing over the line.
All available information including that gained by our patrols, instructions for defence, schemes of work, and trench stores will be most carefully handed and taken over.
Duplicate copies of trench store lists to be forwarded to Battn. H.Qrs. by 9 A.M. on 19th inst.

SECRET.

4

Operation Order No 26.
by Lieut-Colonel N.B. Ramsden D.S.O. M.C
Commanding 15th Bn. High. L. I.

1. The 15th H.L.I. will relieve the 5/6th Royal Scots in the left Sub. Sector tonight 22nd. inst as under.

A Coy. (plus 2 Bn. L.G. Sections)		relieve	A. Coy. Royal Scots		in front line.
C. Coy	15th H.L.I.	do.	B. Coy	do.	in support
D Coy	do	do.	C. Coy	do.	in reserve.
B. Coy.	do.	do.	D. Coy.	do.	in defended locality.

2. Guides at the rate of 1 per Coy. H.Q. and 1 per Platoon will be supplied by 5/6th. Royal Scots who will report at Bn. H.Q. 15th H.L.I this evening. These guides will be sent up to reconnoitre areas occupied by 15th. H.L.I. and will then guide platoons to their new positions.

3. There will be no movement from present positions until orders are received from Bn. H.Q. approximately 9.30 p.m.

4. Rations will be issued before moving. Lewis Guns of A. C and D. Coys. will be carried on ration limber and drawn at Batt. H.Q.

5. Defence Schemes, Trench Stores and all information about the line to be carefully taken over on relief and copy of all Stores taken over to be sent to Bn. H.Q. at 10 a.m. 23rd. inst.

6. Completion of relief will be reported by wire and runner to Bn. H.Q. in the following code:-

RELIEF COMPLETE	-	GIN
LITTLE SHELLING	-	AND
MUCH SHELLING	-	BITTERS.

7. Acknowledge.

[signature] 2nd. Lieut
for O.C. 15th. H.L.I.

SECRET

5.

Operation Order No 27.

By Lieut-Colonel V. B. Ramsden D.S.O. M.C.
Commanding 15th Battn The Highland Light Infantry.

Map Sheets 51 B S.W.
51 C S.E.

---

1. The 1st DORSET Regt will relieve the 15th Battn H.L.I. in the left sub. sector of the Brigade Front tonight the 30th/31st inst.
On completion of relief the Battalion will withdraw into Brigade Reserve in the PURPLE LINE and take over positions vacated by 1st DORSET Regt.

2. Inter Company reliefs will take place as under

15th Battn H.L.I. COMPANY.	1st DORSET Regt. COMPANY RELIEVING	1st DORSET Regt COMPANY TAKEN OVER FROM IN PURPLE LINE
B. and 2 Sections of H.Q. L.G. Platoon	B. and Battn H.Q. L.G. Platoon (4 Guns)	C.
D.	C.	D.
C. and 1 Section of H.Q. L.G. Platoon	D. and 1 L.G. Section	A.
A.	A.	B.
BATTN. H.Q. and 2 A.A. Guns	BATTN. H.Q. and 2 A.A. Guns	BATTN. H.Q. (H.Q. L.G. Platoon will be located at Battn H.Q.)

3. ADVANCE PARTIES. The 1st DORSET Regt. will send forward advance parties of 1 Officer & 1 N.C.O. per Coy at 3 P.M. These advance parties to be given all possible information about the line.
Advance parties of 1 Officer per Coy and 1 N.C.O. per platoon & Coy. H.Q. will report at H.Q. of 1st DORSET Regt. at 4 P.M. at X 12 d 2 6. This advance party less A Coy, will return to present Battn H.Q., after having taken over all information at 10.30 P.M., to guide relieved platoons to new locations.
'A' Coy. advance party to return to present Coy. H.Q.

4. GUIDES. B, D, C, and H.Q. Coys. will send reliable guides to Battn. H.Q. at 9 P.M., at the rate of 1 per platoon, 1 per Coy. H.Q., and 1 per Battn. H.Q.

5. All available information about the line, its defences, enemy attitude etc will be most carefully handed over to relieving Officers. No Officer will leave his line until the relieving Officer is satisfied that he is fully cognisant with his line and the role of its garrison.
Trench Stores will be carefully handed over and duplicate lists forwarded to Battn. H.Q. by 9 A.M. on 31st inst.
Defence Schemes, Schemes of Work, Air Photos etc. to be handed over.

6. Completion of Relief will be reported at once by wire and runner to Battn. H.Q. in code as under;

RELIEF COMPLETE	______	GIN
LITTLE SHELLING	______	AND
MUCH SHELLING	______	VERMOUTH.

7. Three limbers will be at Battn. H.Q. at 10.30 P.M. One half limber will be available for Lewis Guns and Magazines of each of B. D., and C. Coys and one half limber for Battn H.Q. Lewis Guns and Magazines. (A Coy will carry back Lewis Guns and Ammunition.)
One limber will transport Orderly Room, Mess, Medical and Signal Stores

8. RATIONS AND WATER. These will be dumped at new locations under Coy. Q.M. Sergts.

9. ACKNOWLEDGE

30th May 1918.

W. White Major,
A/Adjutant

Instructions regarding War Diaries and Intelligence Summaries are contained in F. S. Regs., Part II. and the Staff Manual respectively. Title pages will be prepared in manuscript.

WAR DIARY
or
INTELLIGENCE SUMMARY.
(*Erase heading not required.*)

5th A. & S. H.

Army Form C. 2118.

Map Reference Sheet 51c 51B SW 1/20000

Place	Date	Hour	Summary of Events and Information	Remarks and references to Appendices
FRONT LINE	6th		The Companies carried out work as per programme. The day was very quiet except for one or two shells in front of the reserve line. BRIGADIER GENERAL LUMSDEN V.C. D.S.O. was buried at BERLES AU BOIS large turnout attended representatives from Corps & Division attended the funeral. Massed pipe & brass bands from the Brigade. 2nd Lt D.W. KEITH proceeded to 3rd ARMY MUSKETRY SCHOOL to undergo three weeks training.	B
	7th		Operation Orders issued No. 29. Intercompany reliefs were carried out without any interruption reliefs being completed by 11 pm. 2nd Lt H.L. FREW 2nd Lt J.F. WEBSTER joined the company's in the line for duty. Weather good, observation fair.	Appendix 2 B
	8th		MAJOR CLEGHORN DSO returned from Commanding Officers course. The enemy's artillery was very active on our Support Line with small calibre shells. Enemy aeroplane flew about 1000 feet up over our lines at 4 am. At 10.30 pm a test S.O.S. signal was fired from our front line to see if same could be picked up by artillery. Weather warm. Observation good. 2nd Lt D. PRYDE proceeded to 3rd ARMY SCHOOL to undergo 14 days general training	B
	9th		The weather continuing to be good the trenches got into a good condition and the companies were able to make themselves more comfortable. The enemy shelled the back of BOIRY ST MARTIN with pretty heavy shells. Large patrol of our planes crossed the enemy's lines flying at a great height. Observation fair. Wind Field	B

A5834 Wt. W4973 M687 750,000 8/16 D. D. & L. Ltd. Forms/C.2118/13.

Instructions regarding War Diaries and Intelligence Summaries are contained in F. S. Regs., Part II. and the Staff Manual respectively. Title pages will be prepared in manuscript.

WAR DIARY
or
INTELLIGENCE SUMMARY.
(Erase heading not required.)

15th H. L. I.

Army Form C. 2118.

Map Reference Sheet 51^C 51^B S.W. 1/20000

Place	Date	Hour	Summary of Events and Information	Remarks and references to Appendices
FRONT LINE.	10		BRIGADIER GENERAL, L. P. EVANS. VC. DSO. arrived to take over 14TH BRIGADE to replace GENERAL LUMSDEN VC. DSO. COL RAMSDEN. DSO. MC. returned to the Battalion to resume duty. The day passed very quietly the companies carried out work on their own lines.	B
"	11		The enemy's artillery was very active on our Support Line with 77 m.m. shells resulting in 2nd Lt A FLETCHER being wounded in the face otherwise the other part of the line was very quiet. 2ND LT. P.C.L. TIMONY. rejoined the Battalion for duty.	B
"	12		The companies were preparing to being relieved and Operation Orders No. 30. issued. The 1st DORSET REGT relieved the Battalion in the line the Battalion moving back to the PURPLE RESERVE for four days rest. The relief carried out without any interruption.	Appendix No 3. B
PURPLE RESERVE	13		The day was carried out the companies bathing at RANSART and BLAIRVILLE under the supervision of Medical Officer. Weather warm. Observation good.	B
"	14		The companies carried out Inspections, and Musketry & Gas Drill in the trenches where the platoons were billeted.	B
	15		The company commanders reconnoitred the Purple Reserve Line. The companies again cleaning up preparing to go into the line.	B

A5834 Wt. W4973 M687 750,000 8/16 D. D. & L. Ltd. Forms/C.2118/13.

Instructions regarding War Diaries and Intelligence Summaries are contained in F. S. Regs., Part II. and the Staff Manual respectively. Title pages will be prepared in manuscript.

WAR DIARY
or
INTELLIGENCE SUMMARY.
(*Erase heading not required.*)

Army Form C. 2118.

5th H.L.I.

Map Reference Sheet 51c 51B S.W. 1/20,000

Place	Date	Hour	Summary of Events and Information	Remarks and references to Appendices
PURPLE LINE	16.		The Battalion moved up into the line and relieved the 5/6th ROYAL SCOTS. Operation Orders No. 31 issued. The first company moved off at 10 pm and the relief took place without any interruption whatever the relief being completed at 12.30 am.	Appendix B4
FRONT LINE	17.		The companies carried out work on their different sections. 2nd Lt JC AIRNE proceeded to England. Observation from the line reported movement in the rear areas at night our planes carried bombing raids on the rear areas. Weather warm, observation good.	
"	18.		The front line companies were busy carrying out the wire organisations required building blocks in the trenches also making Lewis Gun posts. Patrols were busy trying to ascertain the posts and if held by the enemy preparatory to raid. Enemy planes very active also artillery on rear areas. Meritorious Medals awarded to RQMS. LOCHRIE J. C.S.M. SWINDLEY C, SERGT STEVENSON A. SERGT RIPPON. T.	
	19.		Operation Orders issued No 32. A fighting patrol under 2nd Lt A.M. BROWN to penetrate into enemy's line of posts and if possible to capture and secure identifications every arrangements made to make the raid a success the zero hour was at 1 am. and when the patrol left and moved through the lane of wire cut on that evening they encountered an unknown belt so could not proceed as they would be late for the artillery barrage lifting. much to the annoyance of both to the leader of the patrol and also the men. Weather good. Observation good. Wind fitful	Appendix A5

A5834 Wt. W4973 M687 750,000 8/16 D. D. & L. Ltd. Forms/C.2118/13.

Instructions regarding War Diaries and Intelligence Summaries are contained in F. S. Regs., Part II. and the Staff Manual respectively. Title pages will be prepared in manuscript.

WAR DIARY
or
INTELLIGENCE SUMMARY.
(Erase heading not required.)

15th H.L.I.

Army Form C. 2118.

Map Reference Sheet 51C & 51B SW 1/20000

Place	Date	Hour	Summary of Events and Information	Remarks and references to Appendices
FRONT LINE	20.		Work carried on as per programme laid down. Wiring being carried out by the reserve companies. Aerial activity was nil owing to it being very cloudy and threatening to rain. Observation fair; cloudy wind fresh.	[initials]
	21.		Reconnaissance patrol sent out preparatory to raid and located enemy holding posts about 300yds in front of our line after being bombed & fired on returned with the information required. Enemy artillery active on reserve line & rear area. Our aeroplanes very active from 11pm over the enemy back area. A large number of search lights seen. 2Lt. P.C.L. TIMONY proceeded to England on 14 days leave.	[initials]
	22 } 23 }		Operation Orders issued No 33. A fighting patrol left our lines on the night of 22/23rd to raid enemy posts and get if possible identifications. 2nd Lt. J. CROMBIE & CSM McGARVA M.M. & 19 OR left the trench at 1.45 am and proceeded to the point where they were to line up and await the barrage. A party of Lewis Gunners & Bombers were arranged about 200 yds to the left as a ruse party to fire their guns & discharge bombs to attract the attention of the enemy, as soon as the barrage came down. At 2 am prompt the artillery, Machine Guns, Stokes, Lewis Guns, and bombing party started	Appendix 6 [initials]

A5834 Wt. W4973 M687 750,000 8/16 D. D. & L. Ltd. Forms/C.2118/13.

Instructions regarding War Diaries and Intelligence Summaries are contained in F. S. Regs., Part II. and the Staff Manual respectively. Title pages will be prepared in manuscript.

WAR DIARY
or
INTELLIGENCE SUMMARY.
(Erase heading not required.)

15th H.L.I.

Army Form C. 2118.

Map Reference Sheet 51C 51B S.W. 1/20000

Place	Date	Hour	Summary of Events and Information	Remarks and references to Appendices
FRONT LINE	23		firing the artillery barrage was perfect and the alignment of the bursting of shells perfect: after the barrage lifted the party rushed the objective and in the interval a late shell fell among 2Lt CROMBIE'S party wounding four including 2Lt CROMBIE. CSM McGARVA realising the position at once returned and took charge of the whole party and assisted by Sergt. TWEEDIE led the patrol to the objective after searching and bombing dugouts the party returned to the line with a coat, helmet & equipment owing to the enemy not being there no prisoners were taken. The rest of the day passed very quiet except for a little shelling on the support & reserve lines. Observation good visibility fair. Wind fresh. 2nd Lt A.M. BROWN proceeded to VIth Corps School to undergo three weeks training	att. to Appendix 6 Report on Raid.
"	24		The day was not so quiet as days previous owing to the enemy shelling our support & reserve lines with shells of a heavy calibre. The Battalion learned of the news of 2Lt J. CROMBIE at Casualty Clearing Station DOULLENS which from the Commanding Officer downwards was very much regretted. 2Lt O PAYDE returned to the Battalion from 3rd Army General course.	
	25		Operation Orders No. 34 Issued The Battalion spent the day cleaning up the line and getting ready for the relief. The 5/6th ROYAL SCOTS relieved the Battalion in the line owing	Appendix 7

A5834 Wt. W4973/M687 750,000 8/16 D. D. & L. Ltd. Forms/C.2118/13.

Instructions regarding War Diaries and Intelligence Summaries are contained in F. S. Regs., Part II. and the Staff Manual respectively. Title pages will be prepared in manuscript.

WAR DIARY
or
INTELLIGENCE SUMMARY.
(*Erase heading not required.*)

Army Form C. 2118.

15th H.L.I.

Map Reference Sheet. 51c 51 B SW 1/20000

Place	Date	Hour	Summary of Events and Information	Remarks and references to Appendices
FRONT LINE			to the moon being at its height. the relief was pretty late before being completed. It was under the new organisation and took more time handing over positions. The relief complete was reported at 1-10 am. The Battalion moving back to Divisional Reserve near RANSART.	
PURPLE LINE	26.	"	The Battalion carried out Inspections also repairing shelters all day. In the morning the Companies bathed at RANSART and BLAIRVILLE and also had their clothes ironed under the supervision of the Medical Officer Lt. P.W. McLAUGHLAN. Weather good. In the evening MAJOR G CLEGHORN and two officers per company reconnoitred the PURPLE RESERVE LINE on the RIGHT BRIGADE. Transport competition was held in the Brigade the winner being entered for the Divisional Competition. Order of Winners 1st 15. H.L.I. 2nd 1st DORSETS 3rd 5/6th ROYAL SCOTS.	
	27.	"	The Battalion carried out Training & Musketry for one hour at a time near RANSART. The men returning to their respective lines feeling fit and looking forward to a rest.	
	28	"	Operation Order No. 35 issued Owing to 1st DORSET REGt. relieving the 5/6th ROYAL SCOTS it necessitated the Battalion moving up from the Divisional Reserve to the PURPLE RESERVE. The relief was	Appendix 8

Instructions regarding War Diaries and Intelligence Summaries are contained in F. S. Regs., Part II. and the Staff Manual respectively. Title pages will be prepared in manuscript.

WAR DIARY
or
INTELLIGENCE SUMMARY.
(*Erase heading not required.*)

15th A. F. I.

Map Reference Sheet 51c 51B SW.

Army Form C. 2118.

Place	Date	Hour	Summary of Events and Information	Remarks and references to Appendices
PURPLE LINE			completed by 11-30 pm. Visibility good. Observation good. Wind mild	B
"		29.	The day was warm with a mild breeze blowing the companies carried out training Musketry & Gas Helmet Drill in the trenches where the platoons were stationed. Weather warm observation fair Visibility good.	B
"		30	The day was very warm with a mild breeze blowing. The companies in the forenoon carried out their usual training. 2Lt D.W. KEITH returned to the Battalion from the 3rd ARMY MUSKETRY SCHOOL, Lt H.A. AGNEW left the Battalion on being transferred to the 16th H.L.I. Observation good. Visibility good. Aerial activity on both sides	B

A5834 Wt. W4973 M687 750,000 8/16 D. D. & L. Ltd. Forms/C.2118/13.

Army Form C. 2118.

Instructions regarding War Diaries and Intelligence Summaries are contained in F. S. Regs., Part II. and the Staff Manual respectively. Title pages will be prepared in manuscript.

WAR DIARY
or
INTELLIGENCE SUMMARY.
(Erase heading not required.)

Place	Date	Hour	Summary of Events and Information	Remarks and references to Appendices

	1ST JUNE		30TH JUNE	
	OFF	ORs	OFF	ORs
Commanding Officer's Strength	28	869	29	849
FIGHTING STRENGTH				
Officers	37		37	
Other ranks	969		921	

TOTAL CASUALTIES for the month.

	OFF	ORs
Killed and Died of Wounds	1	11
Wounded	1	61
Missing	–	–

R B Herbert Capt for Lieut-Colonel,
Comm'dg. 15/HIGH. L. I.

A5834 Wt. W4973 M687 750,000 8/16 D. D. & L. Ltd. Forms/C.2118/13.

13. Relief to be notified to this office in the following code:—

RELIEF COMPLETE — BLAST.
LITTLE SHELLING — HIS.
MUCH SHELLING — EYES.

14. ACKNOWLEDGE.

J G Stephen Captain A/Adj
15th Bn. H.L.I.

7. Completion of relief will be notified in code as under:-

RELIEF COMPLETE	-	PORT
LITTLE SHELLING.	-	AND
MUCH SHELLING.	-	LEMON.

8. Acknowledge.

W.D. White
Major.
Commanding 15th Bn. High. L.I.

7.6.18.

Addendum

These orders are subject to alteration in the event of the projection of gas to-night.

W.D. White Maj.

SECRET

OPERATION ORDER No. 30

by Major C. S. M. Gleghorn D.S.O.

commanding 15th Bn High. L. I.

MAP REF SHEET 51B S.W. } 1/20000
51C S.E. }

[illegible] Dorset Regt. will relieve the 15th H. L. I. in the right Battn. sub-sector on the night 12/13th June 1918.

On completion of relief, the 15th H. L. I. will withdraw into Brigade reserve and be responsible for the defence of the PURPLE LINE

2/ Inter-Company reliefs and moves will be carried out as under.

H. L. I. COMPANY	RELIEVED BY 1st DORSET COY	POSITION ON COMPLETION OF RELIEF
C and 3 L. G. SECTIONS	D and 3 L. G. SECTIONS	CHATEAU WOOD
B	B.	TRENCH IN X15 a.
A.	A.	TRENCH IN X 9 c.
H.Qrs.	H.Qrs.	X 10 d. 1. 5.
D	C.	TRENCH IN X 16 a. AND b.

3/ The greatest care will be taken in handing over all posts and lines.

No officer will report his relief complete until the relieving officer is satisfied that he understands his line, its defences and the role of its garrison. ~~[illegible]~~ All defence schemes, schemes of work etc. will be carefully handed over. Duplicate copies of trench store lists to reach this office by 9 a.m. on 13th inst.

4. Guides will report at Battn. H.Qrs. at 10.30 p.m. on 12th inst. as under:-

1 per Platoon and 1 per Coy. H.Qrs. for C. B. and A Coys. the reliefs for which will arrive in this order.

D. Coy. will arrange to have 2 Platoon guides and 1 for Coy. H.Qrs. at road junction S.11 d 5. 2 at 10.30 p.m. and will send 2 guides to report at Battn. H.Qrs. of 1st Dorset Regt. at 3 p.m. These latter guides will take the two Platoons of C Coy. 1st Dorset Regt. direct to billets in trench in S 13 a and b.

5 ADVANCE PARTIES.

1st Dorset Regt. will send the following advance parties to report at Battn. H.Qrs at 7 p.m.

Front Line Company - 1 Officer and 1 N.C.O

Remainder - 1 Officer and 1 N.C.O per Platoon and Coy. H.Q.

15th H.L.I. will send advance parties of 1 Officer and 1 N.C.O per Platoon and Coy. H.Qrs. to report at Battn. H.Qrs. at 8 p.m. (C Coy's N.C.Os. will be sent down before dawn on 12th inst. These advance parties will be given instructions to return to Battn. H.Qrs at 11 p.m and guide relieved platoons to their new positions.

6/ Coy Commanders will ensure that all trenches are handed over in a clean and sanitary condition. Special attention being paid to latrines.

7/ Limbers will be available at Battn. H.Qrs. from 11.30 p.m on 12 inst. for use as under.

1 Limber - For Battn. H.Qrs. Orderly Room, Mess, Signal and Medical Stores.

1 Limber - For Lewis Guns and Magazines of A and B Coys.

1 Limber - For Lewis Guns and Magazines of C Coy. and Battn. H.Qrs. Platoon.

1 Limber - For cooking utensils

8/ All water tins to be brought out, and hot food carriers left at cook house.

9/ Completion of relief will be notified by wire and runner to Battn. H.Qrs. in code as under:-

RELIEF COMPLETE - VERY
LITTLE SHELLING - NEAR
MUCH SHELLING - HOME

10 ACKNOWLEDGE.

11.6.18

[signature] Lt.
for Major
Commanding 15th Bn. H.L.I.

SECRET

Operation Order No. 31
by Major G. M. Cleghorn D.S.O.
Commanding 15th Battn. Highland Light Infantry

4

Map Ref. Sht 51B S.W.
1/20,000

1/ The 15th Battn. High. L.I. will relieve the 5/6th Royal Scots in the left Battn sector tonight the 16/17th inst

2/ Inter-Company reliefs will take place as under;-

H.L.I. Coy.	5/6th Royal Scots Coy.	Positions on Completion
1½ Platoons "A" (including 2 L.G. sections) + 3 H.Q. L.G. section & A Coy H.Q.	"C"	Front Line
"D."	"A"	Support Line
"C."	"D"	Reserve Line
"B"	"B"	Defended Locality
2½ Platoons "A" Coy	—	Positions in Sunken Roads in B. 16 Central

Note;- "A" Coy will establish Coy. H.Q. at B 23 d.16 and will be disposed in the line with Coy H.Q. and 2 Battn. H.Q. L.G. Sections on the right in close touch with the 1st Dorset Regt and 5 Section posts on the left in close touch with the 2nd Manchester Regt. The remaining rifle section will be used at night as a trench and wire patrol. The 2½ platoons near Battn. H.Q will be given orders direct from Battn. H.Q. Officer in charge of these will report his relief complete direct to Battn. H.Q.

3. Advance Parties.

Companies will send advance parties to report at Battn. H.Q. for instructions at 5 P.M. 16th inst as follows;-

B. and C. Coys — 1 Officer & 1 N.C.O. per platoon and Coy. H.Q.
D. Coy — 1 Officer & 1 N.C.O.
A. Coy — 1 Officer & 1 N.C.O. to take over in front line and 2 N.C.O.'s to take over position at Battn. H.Q.

4/ Times and Guides.

"A" Coy will move off from present positions at 9.30 P.M. as under;-
1 Platoon + 1 Coy. L.G. Section + 1 Battn. H.Q. Section
Coy. H.Q. + 1 Rifle Section + 2 Battn. H.Q. Sections,
1 Platoon + 2 Rifle Sections,
and 1 Platoon.

Remaining Coys. will follow on with 200 Yards interval between platoons.

"B" Coy will proceed direct to positions in the defended locality.

Guides will be at new Battn. H.Q. from 10.30 P.M.

5/ The greatest care will be observed in taking over all posts and lines.

An Officer will not report his relief complete until he is satisfied that he is conversant with his position, and the role of his command.

5/ Continued
Office schemes, schemes of work and all information about the line will be most carefully taken over.
Trench store lists in duplicate, both taken and handed over will be at these H.Q. at 9 A.M. on 17th inst.

6/ Rations and Water.
Rations will be issued and carried on the man before leaving.
All water bottles will be full.
Water for daily consumption will be taken as far as Battn. H.Q. by limber and will be carried forward by relieving troops from there

7 Lewis Guns and Ammunition.
Limbers will be at Battn H.Q. at 7.30 P.M. for these as under:—
One Limber — For A. and Battn. H.Q. L.G's
One Limber — For C. Coy and D Coy
One Limber — For Orderly Room, Signal and Medical Stores.
Representatives from each Coy will proceed with these to arrange to hand them out to relieving platoons on arrival at new Battn. H.Q.
"B" Coy will carry forward its own L.G's and ammunition

8/ Hot Food.
This will be supplied to Front Line and Support once only tonight and twice nightly thereafter.
"D" Coy will supply its own carrying party for this and a party will be supplied from the rear portion of "A" Coy to carry up to the front line.
All others will draw their food at usual times daily.

9 Completion of Relief will be reported in code as

RELIEF COMPLETE — ARE
LITTLE SHELLING — YOU
MUCH SHELLING — DRY

10. ACKNOWLEDGE

16th June 1918

W White Major,
Adjt. 15th Bn. Highl. L.I.

S E C R E T.

OPERATION ORDER No. 23
by Lieut.-Colonel V.B. RAMSDEN, DSO. MC.,
Commanding 15th Bn. THE HIGHLAND LIGHT INFANTRY,

Map Reference. Sheets 51c S.E.
51b S.W.

1.(a) The 32nd Division (less Artillery) will relieve the 2nd Division in the centre sector of the 6th Corps front on the nights 11/12th May and 12/13th May 1918.

(b) The 14th Infantry Brigade will relieve the 5th Infantry Brigade in the line on the night of 11/12th May 1918.

(c) The 97th Bde. will be on the right and the 96th Bde. will be on the left of the 14th Bde. on completion of Divisional Relief.

2. The 15th Bn. H. L. I. will relieve the 2nd Oxford and Bucks Light Infantry in the Right Sub-sector of the 14th Infantry Bde.

Boundaries are as follows:-
Right Bde. Boundary. S.28.b.6.4. - S.22.d.3.1. - S.14.d.9.2.
Left Bde. Boundary. S.18.c.2.1. - S.17.c.0.5. - S.10.c.1.0.

Right Bn. Boundary S.28.b.6.4. - S.22.d.3.1. - S.14.d.9.2.
Left Bn. Boundary. S.23.c.8.1. - S.23.a.1.7. - S.16.c.2.2.

The 1st Dorset Regt. will be on the left of the 15th H. L. I. and the 5/6th Royal Scots in Support.

3. The Bn. will be disposed in the line as under:-
No. 1. (Right Front) Coy. - "A" Coy.
No. 2. (Left Front) Coy. - "C" Coy.
No. 3. (Support) " - "B" Coy.
No. 4. (Reserve) " - "D" Coy.
The Bn. L.G. Platoon will be in the reserve line held by No. 4 (D) Coy.

4. Details of move from present location are shown in appendix 1.

5. All defence schemes, defensive arrangements, information about the line etc. will be taken over on relief.
Officers taking over defences will ensure that they obtain the fullest possible details as to positions of Units on their flanks, enem's attitude etc. before reporting relief complete.
Duplicate copies of Trench Store Lists taken over to be forward to Bn. H.Qrs. by 9 a.m. on 12th inst.

6. Completion of relief will be reported by wire and Runner to Bn. H.Q. in code as under:-
Relief complete - [illegible].
Little shelling - SHORT
Much shelling. - SPELL.

7. The Transport Lines and Q.M. stores will be in BAILLEULMONT.
The Q.M. will arrange to take over all billets occupied by 2nd Oxford and Bucks Light Infantry.

8. The Q.M. will arrange to issue before 12 noon tomorrow sandbags at the rate of 3 per man to be carried into the line as battle stores.

9. RATIONS & WATER.
24 hours rations plus the Iron Ration will be carried into the line on the man.
All water bottles will be filled, four tins of water per Coy. will be carried forward on the Lewis Gun Limbers.
Water will be brought up with rations from BAILLUEMONT nightly. Coys. will make their own arrangements as to provision of carrying parties for rations and water each night.

10. COOKING.
At present all cooking is done on Tommy Cookers.

11. Lewis Guns.
1 Limber will be provided for the Lewis Guns and ammunition, 24 magazines per gun, of "A" and "C" Coys. and one for "B" and "D" Coys. These will proceed to the dump at S.21.b.4.1. An N.C.O. per Coy. will accompany these Limbers and will see that all guns and ammunition are collected by the L.G. Sections on arrival at this point. Lewis Guns and ammunition of Hqrs. Platoon will be carried in limber of "B" and "D" Coys.
Guns and ammunition to be loaded in limbers by 5 p.m. on 11th inst.

12. ORDERLY ROOM, MESS, and MEDICAL STORES.

1 Limber will be provided to convey Orderly Room, Mess, and Medical Stores to the new Bn. Hqrs.
A second limber will be available to convey Coy. Mess Stores and Officers Kits to the dump at S.21.b.4.1.
These limbers to be loaded by 5 p.m.

13. Greatcoats in bundles of 5 and blankets in bundles of 10 will be dumped at Q.M. Stores at 7.30 a.m. tomorrow morning.
Haversacks to be clearly labelled and dumped at Q.M. Stores at 10 a.m.

14. OFFICERS VALISES.

Officers valises will be dumped outside billets at 12 noon. The Q.M. will arrange for the transferance of all stores dumped.

15. ACKNOWLEDGE.

L. C. Hodgson(?) Lt-Col
Lieut-Colonel,
Commanding 15th Bn. High. L. I.

10/ 5/18.

Copies issued to:-
C.O.
2nd In Command.
"A" Coy.
"B" Coy.
"C" Coy.
"D" Coy.
Signal Officer.
Q.M.
T.O.
War Diary.
File.
14th Infantry Brigade.

APPENDIX 1.

1. ADVANCE PARTY.
An advance party consisting of 1 Officer, 1 N.C.O., 1 Lewis Gunner, 1 Signaller and 1 Runner per Coy., and of 1 N.C.O., 1 Signaller and 5 Runners for Bn. H.Qrs. will report to the 5th Bde. H.Qrs. at RANSART X.8.d.0.4. at 5 p.m. on 10th inst.

2. The Battalion will parade in Battle order in CHATEAU GROUNDS SAULTY at 6.30 p.m. and will march to embussing point, CHAPEL V.2.d.9.2. in order "C" "A" "B" "D" and Hqrs.
Time of embussing - 7.15 p.m.
debussing point - BLAIRVILLE. X.4.a.9.3.

3. O.C. Coys. will detail an Officer or senior N.C.O. to be in charge of each bus. No. man is to leave the bus without permission from the Officer or N.C.O. in charge.

4. GUIDES. Coy. guides will be provided at debussing point and will lead Coys. to point S.21.b.4.1., where guides at the rate of 1 per Coy. H.Qrs. and 1 per platoon will be obtained.
Movement from debussing point to be by platoons at 100 yards interval.

5. The 1st Line Transport will move to the new lines under orders to be issued separately.

Report on fighting Patrol of the 15th H.L.I on night of 23rd/24th inst.

Strength: 1 Officer (2/Lt CROMBIE J.)
1 C.S.M. (Mc GARVA J)
419 O.Rs.

Object: To attack the known enemy posts on the Sunken Road from S 24 c 25 to S 24 c 28 and kill or capture the garrisons of these and secure identifications.

Detail of progress

(a). At 12.30 am. a party of 1 N.C.O. and 6 O.Rs. proceeded along the trench to S 23 d 52 and there took up position to watch the right flank of the attack. This party was in position by 1 am.

(b) A rifle Grenade Section, firing No 36 Grenades, moved out into old trench at S 23 b 83 and was ready to fire at 1 am.

Similarly a LEWIS GUN at S 23 b 74 was ready to fire on posts at 1 am.

These cooperated with the STOKES MORTARS in creating a diversion by firing on the enemy posts about S 24 a 32.

(c) At 12.15 am. a party of 1 Off and 1 O.R. laid a tape through the gaps in the wire, and 50 yds beyond from Road ind. S 23 d 55 75 in which the whole assembly party were collected. 1 N.C.O. and 2 O.Rs. were then posted at the end of this tape to ensure that the route to the assembly point was clear.

(d) At 1.20am. the first party of 1 Off. and 6 O.Rs. moved out and took up position on the bank at S 23 d 65.

At 1.25 am. the second party of 1 Sgt & 6 ORs moved out and took up position 20 yds to the left of first party.

At 1.30 am. the third party of 1 C.S.M. and 10 O.Rs. moved out and took up position 20 x to the right of the first party.

All three parties were assembled by 1.45 am.

At 1.50 am. a supporting party of 1 Off. (Lt THOMSON) and 8 O.Rs. (1 L.G. Team + 2 stretcher bearers) moved out and proceeded direct to the Lone Tree at S 23 d 8550 ....

(c) At Zero – 30 secs the artillery firing on the left of the objective opened fire, and at zero the remainder of the artillery and the M. Guns joined in.

The Assaulting Party moved forward at once to within 30 yds of the barrage which was very accurate indeed.

At zero + 5' on the artillery lifting on to the road beyond the attackers rushed the road at about S 24 c 2 4. On reaching it, a very late round from one of our guns landed just between the right and centre parties causing us 6 casualties including the O.C. Raid (2/Lt CROMBIE). C.S.M. McGARVA saw that 2/Lt CROMBIE was a casualty and took charge leading the men down the road. He personally examined every post and shelter up to and including the trench at S 24 c 28 and the the post immediately on the left of this. He then took both the right and left parties back up the road to ascertain what had happened to the centre party and found that it had been put out of action by the "late" shell as above. The wounded were all brought in with the assistance of the supporting party.

Information Gained.

The enemy did not retaliate in any way whatever.

No artillery action, machine gun fire nor very lights were noted on his part.

At this time it is practically certain he had no troops in front of the road

Secret 15th Battalion The Highland Light Infantry

Amendment to O. O. No 33

Para III. Delete and Substitute;–

Assaulting Party

2/Lieut. Crombie, C.S.M. McGarva M.M., Sgt Goodie & 18 O.R. in 3 Columns

Strength of Columns from Left to Right;–

Sgt Goodie & 4 O.R.
L/Cpl Rae & 4 O.R.
C.S.M. McGarva M.M. & 10 O.R. } 2/Lieut. Crombie

Supporting Party

Lieut. Thomson & 8 O.R. (including 4 C.S. Stretcher)

Para IV. Add;–

At Zero – 5

The Supporting Party will leave our F.L.T. and will move to the Assembly position occupied by the Assaulting Party and will take up position just in rear of same.

Para V. At Zero;

The Supporting Party will move along the bank to the Lone Tree and remain there until the return of the Assaulting Party. They will cover the withdrawal of the Assaulting Party and will themselves withdraw on the signal of 2 Very Lights put up at Raid H.Q. in quick succession.

Para VI. Substitute;–

Centre Column

The centre party will be back about 25x from the 2 wing parties and will not enter the Sunken Road until the flank parties have dealt with any Enemy seen therein.

Para VII. Delete and Substitute;–

Having mopped up the objective the Assaulting Party will withdraw across country to the Lone Tree, where the O.C. & O.i/c Supporting Party will check them and withdraw to our F.L.T. covered by the Supporting Party.

Additional Para XIX Listening Post

"C" & "D" Coy will place a listening post at S.23.d.5.2. at Zero – 60. This post will withdraw at Zero + 30.

Para XX. Dress

S.D. Steel Helmets (dulled). Rifles & Bayonets (blacked)

S.B.Rs. slung on the back. 2 Bombs & Ammunition in pocket.

Each column to take 2 pairs of wire cutters.

23rd June 1918

Major,
[illegible]

Copies Issued to all Recipients of O.O. No 33 of 22nd June 1918

O. O. No. 33 contd.

IX **Diversion.** In order to distract the enemy's attention from his left flank the following "Ruse" will be carried out.

(a) Two 18 Pdrs will spray the Sunken Road from S. 24. c. 05. 90 – 28 from Zero to Zero + 4.

(b) Two Stokes Mortars (from approx. S. 23 d. 4. 8.) will engage the enemy post at S. 24 a. 3 2 and the huts in that vicinity. This fire will commence at Zero + 3 and will be maintained at the rate of 6 rounds a minute till Zero + 20.

(c) One Lewis Gun firing from our F.L.T. at about S. 23. b. 6. 2. will fire bursts of fire into the post at S. 24. a. 3. 3. and the huts in that vicinity from Zero + 3 to Zero + 20.

(d) A Rifle Grenade Section consisting of one Sgt. & 6 O.R. will be posted in the old trench in S. 23. b. 7. 4. and will fire No. 36 Grenades in salvoes and singly in the direction of the huts about S. 24 a. 3. 3. This fire will be maintained from Zero + 3 to Zero + 8.

X **Co-operation.** R.F.A., Stokes, and M.G's, otherwise than already laid down, as per sketch specially issued.

XI **Prisoners.** Prisoners will not be searched until their arrival at Battn. H.Q. O.C. "D" Coy will detail men, other than the raiding party, as escort.

XII **Identification.** All Maps, Correspondence, Identity Discs, and Marks on the clothing will be removed and left at Battn. H.Q. O.C. "D" Coy will send in to Battn. H.Q. a nominal role of the raiding party.

XIII **Code.** The following code will be in operation;

Prisoners Captured	=	P. 1, 2, 3, etc
Casualties K.	=	K. 1, 2, 3, etc
W.	=	W. 1, 2, 3, etc
M.	=	M. 1, 2, 3, etc
M.G's Captured	=	X. 1, 2, 3, etc
Assaulting Party	=	A.

eg. Assaulting party returned, 3 prisoners & 1 M.G. captured, one wounded = Aaaa P3aaa X1aaa W1

XIV **Communications.** Cpl. Anderson will lay two new lines from the Support Coy to the Front Line H.Q.

XV **General.** 2/Lieut. Brough will be responsible for the party mentioned in para IX (c) & (d) & will ensure that sufficient drums & bombs are taken up.

XVI **H.Q.** Raid H.Q. will be at old front line Coy H.Q. S. 23. d. 35. 75.

XVII **Zero Hour.** This will be notified later.

XVIII **Acknowledge.**

Major
A/Adjt.

22nd June 1918.

Copies to;
No. 1 O.C. A Coy
No. 2 O.C. B Coy
No. 3 O.C. C Coy
No. 4 O.C. D Coy
No. 5 14/Inf Bde
No. 6 14/T.M.B.
No. 7 Centre Group R.F.A.
No. 8 15th L.F.
No. 9 5/6 Royal Scots
No. 10 } WAR DIARY.
No. 11 }
No. 12 FILE, LOBE (REAR).

SECRET 15th Battalion The Highland Light Infantry

Addendum to Operation Order No. 5. Copy No. 12.

Zero Hour will be 2 A.M. on 24th June 1918

Acknowledge

23rd June 1918

M White Major

Acting Adjt.

SECRET

15th Battalion Highland Light Infantry

Operation Order No. 33

Copy No. 12

I. General. The 15th H.L.I. will carry out a Minor Enterprise to harass the enemy & gain identifications.

II. Intention. A fighting patrol will attack the enemy's position in the Sunken Road from S.24.c.2.4, destroy any posts and bomb dug-outs.

III. Troops Allotted. Assaulting Party.
2/Lieut [illegible], C.S.M. McGowan M.M., Sgt [illegible] and 18 O.R. in 3 columns.
Strength of Columns from L – R.
1 Lt. & 4 O.R., 1 Officer & 7 O.R., 1 C.S.M. & 7 O.R.

IV. Assembly. At Zero – 15. The assaulting party will form up in 3 columns in single file on the embankment at S.23.d.7.6, columns being 10x apart.

V. Method of Attack. At Zero. A shrapnel barrage will commence on the objective. The assaulting party advancing in 3 columns at 30x interval in single file and will approach as close as possible to the barrage on the line from the point of assembly to S.24.c.2.5.
At Zero +5. The barrage will lift and the assaulting party will rush the Sunken Road & will left wheel down the line of the objective.

VI. Action on Reaching Objective. Left Column
The left party will attack N.wards along the top & the W. side of the Road, deal with any opposition encountered & co-operate with the centre party.
Centre Column.
The centre party will attack up the Road (N. wards) deal with any opposition encountered & bomb dug-outs.
Right Column
The right party will attack up the E side of Road, deal with any opposition encountered & cooperate with the Centre party.

VII. Withdrawal. On completion of their task the assaulting party will withdraw up the Sunken Road thence left handed along the embankment to the aeroplane at S.23d.75.70 and thence to our F.L.T.

VIII Wire Cutting. A lane in the wire belts will be cut from point of exit on the night of the 22/23rd.
A tape will be laid through the gap cut on the night of the operation and the last belt (or point of exit from [illegible] wire) will be marked by white paper tied on the post.

7. COOPERATION. Artillery. M.G's and Stokes will cooperate as arranged.

8. PRISONERS. Prisoners will not be searched before their arrival at Bn. H.Q.

9. IDENTIFICATIONS. No Maps. documents or letters etc. are to be carried by any of the patrol or supporting party.

10. CODE. The following code will be in operation.

PRISONERS captured	=	P-----1, 2, 3 etc.
CASUALTIES K.	=	K.------1.
CASUALTIES W.	=	W.------1.
CASUALTIES M.	=	M.------1.
M.G's captured	=	Z------1.
ASSAULTING PARTY returned.	=	A.
SUPPORTING PARTY "	=	B.

eg. Assaulting party returned. 3 prisoners and 1. M.G captured and wounded =

A. aaa P.3 aaa Z1 aaa W1

11. RAID H.Q. OLD FRONT LINE H.Q.

12. SYNCHRONISATION. Watches will be synchronised at RAID H.Q. at 10.15 p.m

13. DRESS. Steel Helmets, box respirators, rifle and bayonet, bandolier. Each man will carry 2 Mills hand grenades.

14. ACKNOWLEDGE.

John [signature]

Captain & a/adjt.
for O.C. 15th. Bn. High. L. I.

SECRET. War Diary

Copy No. 5

15TH Bn. The Highland Light Infantry

Operation Order No 32.

19th June 1918

1. GENERAL. The 15th H.L.I. will carry out a minor enterprise to assist in diverting the enemy's attention from operations on its left flank.

2. INTENTION. A fighting patrol will investigate the enemy's posts from S.24. a 5.4. – 8.7. to kill Bosch and gain identifications and information.

3. TROOPS ALLOTTED.

ASSAULTING PARTY.

2/Lt. A.M BROWN. Sgt. Morrow and 15 O.R.

SUPPORTING PARTY.

1 Sgt. and 8 O.R. and 1 L.G.

4. FORMING UP.

AT ZERO – 25 The assaulting party will leave the front line at about S.23 b.5.2. and proceed to about S.24 a 4.3.

The covering party will follow about 100 yds. in rear and will remain in valley about 100 yds. in rear of assaulting party.

5. METHOD OF ATTACK.

ASSAULTING PARTY.

AT ZERO. The Artillery will commence an intense barrage on the objective.

AT ZERO + 3 The four guns firing on the right of the objective will lift, and the patrol will attack the SOUTHERN end of the objective.

AT ZERO + 7 The remaining four guns will lift and the patrol will attack the NORTHERN end of the OBJECTIVE.

SUPPORTING PARTY.

AT ZERO + 3 The SUPPORTING party will move into the position originally occupied by the assaulting party, and will cover their right flank.

6. WITHDRAWAL.

ASSAULTING PARTY.

On completion of mopping up at final point S.24 a.8.7. the party will withdraw.

SUPPORTING PARTY.

Will withdraw at ZERO + 40 or on a red VERY LIGHT going up from front line.

SECRET.

2

Operation Order No 29
by Major W. White M.C.
commanding 15th Bn. High. L. I.

Map Ref. Sheet 51B. S.W 1/20,000.

1. The following inter-company relief will take place tonight the 7/8th June 1918.

C. Coy plus 3 H.Q. L.G. sections will relieve D. Coy plus 3 H.Q. L.G. sections in the front line.

D. Coy will withdraw on completion to positions vacated by C. Coy. B. Coy will relieve A. Coy in Support Line
A. Coy will withdraw on completion to Reserve Line.

2. All Defence Schemes. Schemes of work, and information about the various lines will be most carefully handed over.

3. Advance parties and guides.

(a) On receipt of these orders C. Coy. will send forward to D. Coy one Officer and one N.C.O.

(b) D. Coy. will send one Officer and one representative per platoon and Coy H.Q. to C Coy.

(c) A. and B. Coys. will each send advance parties of 1 Officer per Coy. and 1 N.C.O. per platoon and Coy H.Q.

The special duties of these advance parties will be to become thoroughly acquainted with the work in progress.

The advance party sent forward by D. Coy. will guide the platoons of C. Coy to the front line, and guide out the relieved platoons of D. Coy.

4. Rations and Water.

C. and B. Coys. will issue rations and water before moving off.
A. and D. Coys. will issue these on completion.

5. Wiring Squads.

A and D Coys. will each leave two wiring squads to work on continuation of wiring scheme till dawn on 8th inst when these will withdraw to rejoin their coys.

These squads will be augmented by squads from C and B Coys. immediately on completion.

6. All other details will be arranged by Coy Commanders concerned.

SECRET

REPORT on Fighting Patrol of the 15th H.L.I. on night of 23rd/24th inst.

9/17/9/26/3

Strength: 1 Officer (2/Lieut. CROMBIE. J.)
1 C.S.M. (McGARVA J.)
and 19 O.R.

Object: To attack the known enemy posts on the sunken road from S.24.c.2.5. to S.24.c.2.8. and kill or capture the garrisons of these and secure identifications.

Detail of Progress:

(a) At 12.30 a.m. a party of 1 N.C.O. and 4 O.R's. proceeded along the trench to S.23.d.5.2. and there took up position to watch the right flank of the attack. This party was in position by 1 a.m.

(b) A Rifle Grenade Section, firing No.36 Grenades, moved out into old trench at S.23.b.8.3. and was ready to fire at 1 a.m.
Similarly a Lewis Gun at S.23.b.7.4. was ready to fire at 1 a.m.
These co-operated with the Stokes Mortars in creating a diversion by firing on the enemy posts about S.24.a.3.2.

(c) At 12.15 a.m. a party of 1 Officer and 1 O.R. laid a tape through the gaps in the wire and about 50 yards beyond, from raid H.Q., S.23.d.35.75. in which the whole assaulting party were collected. 1 N.C.O. and 2 O.R. were then posted at the end of this tape to ensure that the route to the assembly point was clear.

(d) At 1.20 a.m. the first party of 1 Officer and 4 O.R. moved out and took up position on the bank at S.23.d.6.5.
At 1.25 a.m. the second party of 1 Sergt. and 4 O.R. moved out and took up position 20 yards to the left of 1st party.
At 1.30 a.m. the third party of 1 C.S.M. and 10 O.R. moved out and took up position 20 yards to the right of first party.
All three parties were assembled by 1.45 a.m.
At 1.50 a.m. a supporting party of 1 Officer (Lt. THOMSON) and 8 O.R. (1 L.G. team and 2 stretcher bearers) moved out and proceeded direct to the Lone Tree at S.23.d.85.80.

(e) At Zero minus 30 seconds the artillery firing on the left of the objective opened fire, and at Zero the remainder of the Artillery and the Machine Guns joined in.
The assaulting party moved forward at once to within 30 yards of the barrage which was very accurate indeed.
At Zero plus 5, on the artillery lifting on to the road beyond, the attackers rushed the road at about S.24.c.2.4. On reaching it, a single <u>late</u> round from one of our guns landed just between the right and centre parties causing us 6 casualties including the O.C. Raid (2/Lt. CROMBIE).
C.S.M. McGARVA saw that Lieut. CROMBIE was a casualty and took charge leading the men down the road. He personally examined every post and shelter, up to and including the trench at S.24.c.2.8. and the hut immediately on the left of this. He then took both the right and left parties back up the road to ascertain what had happened to the centre party and found that it had been put out of action by the late shell as above.
The wounded were all brought in with the assistance of the supporting party.

Information /

Information gained.

The enemy did not retaliate in any way whatever.

No artillery action, Machine gun fire nor Very Lights were noted on his part.

At this time it is practically certain he had no troops in front of the road, running from S.30.a.1.0. to S.24.b.3.0.

No enemy were discovered in any of the posts on the sunken road. An overcoat, set of equipment and helmet were found in the post at S.24.c.2.7. and these were brought in. This post is the only one showing any signs of recent occupation.

The small trench at S.24.c.2.8. was quite clear except for one of our own shovels.

There is a short belt of concertina wire about S.24.c.2.6. just across the road.

The shelters on the East side of the road showed no traces of occupation.

(Sd) W. WHITE, Major,
for Lt.-Col. Comdg. 15th HLI.

24/6/18.

6027

32nd DIV. No. GS 1719/26 24 JUN 1918 GENERAL STAFF

H.Q. 14TH INFANTRY BDE. No. G176/8/6 Date 24.6.18

TO/ 32nd Div

Herewith report by OC 15th HLI on last night fighting patrol

The party were well handled and I consider Company Sergeant Major J McGARVA showed considerable initiative in searching a larger area than was allotted to him by visiting the hut East of the road.

L Rowans Brig Gen.

June 24th 1918

14th Inf Bde

G. S. O.	
G. S. O. I.	
G. S. O. II.	[illegible]
G. S. O. III.	

I concur. A very well executed raid, creditable to all concerned, including the Artillery, though the one late round was unfortunate. The raiding parties were very well led and C.S.M. McGarva showed great initiative and powers of command.

T.S.L.

at VLAMERTINGHE at 1.10 p.m. 22nd inst.

12. TRANSPORT.

The following Transport will go on Omnibus Train and will report to a representative from Brigade Hqrs. at 7 a.m. Four cookers, two watercarts, 1 Mess Cart, C.O's. Chargers. The remainder of Transport will proceed by march route passing Brigade Starting Point at 8.38 a.m. 21st inst. Detailed instructions will be issued to Transport Officer. Signalling Officer will arrange to load all Signalling equipment on afternoon of 20th inst.

13. AREA STORES.

R.E. Stores used for Training purposes, billet stores, palliases, basins etc., will be collected by Q.M. by 20th inst., and return to Area Commandant, RENOQUE, and receipts obtained.

[signature] for - Lieut-Colonel,
Commanding 15th Bn. High. L. I.

Report on fighting Patrol of the 15th H.L.I on night of 23rd/24th inst.

Strength: 1 Officer (2/Lt CROMBIE. J.)
1 C.S.M. (McGARVA J)
& 19 O.Rs.

Object:

To attack the known enemy posts on the Sunken Road from S24 c 25 to S24c 28 and kill or capture the garrisons of these and secure identifications.

Detail of progress.

(a). At 12.30 am. a party of 1 N.C.O. and 4 O.Rs. proceeded along the trench to S23d52 and there took up position to watch the right flank of the attack. This party was in position by 1 am.

(b) A rifle Grenade Section, firing No36 Grenades, moved out into old trench at S23b83 and was ready to fire at 1 am.

Similarly a LEWIS GUN at S23b74 was ready to fire ~~a few~~ at 1 am.

These cooperated with the STOKES MORTARS in creating a diversion by firing on the enemy posts about S24a.32.

(c) At 12.15 am. a party of 1 Off and 1 O.R. laid a tape through the gaps in the wire, and 50 yds beyond from Raid Hd., S23d35 75, in which the whole assembling party were collected. 1 N.C.O and 2 O.Rs. were then posted at the end of this tape to ensure that the route to the assembly point was clear.

(d). At 1.20 am. the first party of 1 Off. and 4 O.Rs. moved out and took up position on the bank at S23d65

At 1.25 am. the second party of 1 Sgt + 4 O.Rs moved out and took ~~out~~ up position 20yds to the left of first party.

At 1.30 am the third party of 1 C.S.M and 10 O.Rs. moved out and took up position 20x to the right of the first party.

All these parties were assembled by 1.45 am.

At 1.50 am the fighting party of 1 Off. (Lt THOMSON) and 8 O.Rs. (L.G. Team + 2 stretcher bearers) moved out and proceeded direct to the Lone Tree at S.23d 8580

(c) At Zero - 30 secs the artillery firing on the left of the objective opened fire, and at Zero the remainder of the artillery and the M Guns joined in.

The Assaulting Party moved forward at once to within 30 yds of the barrage which was very accurate indeed.

At Zero + 2 on the artillery lifting on to the road beyond the attackers rushed the road at about S.24c 24. On reaching it, a single late round from one of our guns landed just between the right and centre parties causing us 6 casualties including the O.C. Raid (2/Lt CROMBIE). C.S.M. McGARVA saw that 2/Lt CROMBIE was a casualty and took charge leading the men down the road. He personally examined every post and shelter up to and including the trench at S.24c 38 and the hut immediately on the left of this. He then took both the right and left parties back up the road to ascertain what had happened to the centre party and found that it had been put out of action by the "late" shell as above. The wounded were all brought in with the assistance of the supporting party.

Information Gained

The enemy did not retaliate in any way whatever.

No artillery action, machine gun fire nor very lights were noted on his part.

At this time it is practically certain he had no troops in front of the road running from S 30 a 10 to S 24 b 30.

No enemy were discovered in any of the posts on the Sunken Road. An overcoat, set of equipment and helmet were found in the post at S 24 c 27 and these were brought in. This post is the only one showing any signs of recent occupation.

The small trench at S 24 c 28 was quite clear except for one of our own shovels.

There is a short belt of concertina wire about S 24 c 26 just across the road.

The shelters on the E. side of the road showed no traces of occupation.

24.6.18.

Wm White Maj for
Lt. Col. Cmdg. 15th H.L.I.

The attached report on the action of a strong patrol of the 15 HLI (14th Bde) on the night of June 23/24 is forwarded. I consider the enterprise was well conducted & that CSM McGARVA showed sound judgement & powers of command.

SECRET

#7

Operation Order No. 34
by Major G M Clegeon D.S.O.
Commanding 15th Bn. High. L.I.

Map Ref. Sheets 51 B. SW
51. C. SE.

1/ The 5/6th Royal Scots will take over the Sub-Sector at present held by the 15th H.L.I. on the night of 25/26th June 1918.
On completion of relief 15th H.L.I will withdraw into Div. Reserve in trenches, E. of RANSART.

2/ Companies will be relieved as follows:-

POSITION	H.L.I. COY	RELIEVED BY
FRONT LINE	D. Coy.	2 Platoons D. Coy R. Scots
SUPPORT LINE	B. Coy.	D Coy less 2 Platoons R. Scots
RESERVE LINE	C. Coy	2. Platoons A Coy R. Scots
BN HQrs.	BN HQrs.	A. Coy HQrs R. Scots
DEFENDED LOCALITY	1 A Coy	2 Platoons C. Coy R. Scots.

3/ ADVANCE PARTIES
No advance parties will be sent by 5/6th Royal Scots.
Advance parties of 15th H.L.I will be sent from personnel presently at Transport lines to the Reserve Area, and will arrange accomodation there.

4/ GUIDES
D. Coy. will send 2 guides - 1 per platoon to junction of support line with road at S23 a 2.2. at 10.15 pm.
B. Coy will send 3 guides - 1 per platoon and 1 for Coy HQrs. at same place and time.
No guides will be required for A & C. Coys.

Guides from advance parties will be at and Reserve. Bn. HQrs. (X10 d 2 5) at 11.30pm and will guide companies to their new billets.

5/1 All details about the line, scheme of work, etc, will be most carefully handed over.

6. C. Coys. will take the greatest care to ensure that relieving units understand clearly the new disposition and exact posts to be occupied by their two platoons taking over frontage previously held by a company.

Duplicate copies of Trench stores lists handed over, will be forwarded to this office by 9am 26th inst.

6/1 Four limbers will be at Bn. HQrs at 11pm for use as follows:-

Bn HQrs	—	1 Limber
B & C Coys. Lewis Guns and Magazines	—	1 Limber
D & HQrs. Coys Lewis Guns and Magazines	—	1 Limber
Water Tins and Cooking utensils	—	1 Limber.

A Coy will carry their Lewis Guns & Magazines.

7/1 Completion of relief will be notified by wire (DARLING permitting) and runner in code as under:-

RELIEF COMPLETE	-	BRING
LITTLE SHELLING	-	ALL
MUCH SHELLING	-	TINS

8/1 Acknowledge.

John L. [signature]
Capt.
A/adj 15th H.L.I.

629

SECRET.

32nd DIVISION
No. G1719/26/2
25 JUN 1918
GENERAL STAFF

Headquarters,

VI Corps.

The attached report on the action of a strong patrol of the 15th H.L.I. (14th Infantry Brigade) on the night of June 23/24th is forwarded.

I consider the enterprise was well executed and that C.S.M. McGARVA showed much initiative and power of command.

A. L. McNamara Lt Col
for Major-General,
Commanding 32nd Division.

25th June 1918.

32nd DIVISION
No. G1719/26
27 JUN 1918
GENERAL STAFF

32 Div
Yes very creditable particularly the initiative shown by C.S.M. McGarva
[illegible]

running from S 30 a 10 to S 24 b 30.

No enemy were discovered in any of the posts in the Sunken Road. An overcoat, set of equipment and helmet were found in the post at S 24 c 27 and these were brought in. This post is the only one showing any signs of recent occupation.

The small trench at S 24 c 28 was quite clear except for one of our own shovels.

There is a short belt of concertina wire about S 24 c 26 just across the roads.

The shelters on the E. side of the road showed no traces of occupation.

24.6.18.

M White Maj for
Lt. Col. Cmdg. 15th H.L.I.

Report on Rand

Copy No.....

SECRET.

15th Bn. THE HIGHLAND LIGHT INFANTRY.

OPERATION ORDER No. 58.

app I

Map Reference - Sheet 19 1/40,000. 6th AUGUST, 1918.

1. The 14th Infantry Brigade will entrain at WAAYENBERG (K19.a.8.9.) and detrain at VILLE LEMARCHET, (Sheet LENS 11 1/100,000)

2. Moves will be carried out in accordance with Table A. attached.

3. (a) ENTRAINMENT.
D. Coy. will report to the entraining Officer, Captain J.D. DUNN, M.C. at 9.30 p.m. tonight, 6th inst. at the entraining station. This Coy. will proceed by the last train for the Brigade Group.

(b) The Transport Officer will supervise the entrainment of all horses and mules. Breast ropes for horse trucks must be provided by the Battalion. Ropes for lashing vehicles will be on the train.

(c) The entrainment must be completed by 3.30 p.m.

4. BILLETING PARTIES.
2/Lieut. HORNE and the C.Q.M.Sgts. from each Coy. will meet at the Orderly Room at 9 p.m. tonight. This party will report to the Staff Captain of the 14th Infantry Brigade at the entraining station at 11.30 p.m. with bicycles.

5. (a) DISCIPLINE.
All doors of covered trucks and carriages on the right side of the train are to remain shut during the course of the journey.

(b) No personnel stores will be allowed in the brake van at each end of the train or on the roof of trucks.

(c) No covered trucks will be used for baggage as it restricts the space available for personnel.

(d) Watercarts and all waterbottles will be entrained full.

6. ENEMY AIRCRAFT.
Headquarters will arrange to mount two A.A. L.G.S. on the train.

7. (a) RATIONS.
Rations for the 8th inst. will be distributed amongst the men prior to moving off. Dinners on the 7th inst. will be served at the station prior to entrainment.

(b) D. Coy's. Cooker will proceed with it to the station and will entrain with the Coy. also Lewis Gun Limber. Rations for the 9th will be taken to the station in limber.

8. LOADING.
All loading is to be completed by 9.30 a.m. Mess cart and one limber will be at Bn. Hqrs. at 9 a.m. at which time all officers mess kit is to be ready for loading. 1 Limber will be at Bn. Hqrs. at 9 a.m. to collect the Orderly Room boxes and all Signal Stores.
The Transport Officer will arrange to collect all Lewis Gun Limbers which are to be loaded by 9 a.m.
Watercarts will go round the Coys. at 8 a.m. at which time all men must fill their waterbottles.
Arrangements for carrying Officers valises will be issued later.
The Medical cart will be at Bn. Hqrs. at 9 a.m.

J.G. Stephen
Captain,
A/Adjt., 15th B

Sent		Recd. at ....m.
At ....m.	.... Service.	Date ....
To		From ....
By	(Signature of "Franking Officer.")	By ....

TO: A, B, C, D, HQ Coy, TO & QM.

Sender's Number.	Day of Month.	In reply to Number.	AAA
O.O. 39			

1/ 1 Brigade group will move to DOMART area [illegible] 12th [illegible]

2/ The Batt will parade in the same place as this morning at 7.10 pm. One quarter [illegible] platoon [illegible] 4 pm. [illegible] these [illegible].

Between [illegible]

[illegible]

3. Route D22 a 5 [illegible] D [illegible] c 1.3

4/ Distances [illegible] Distances between [illegible]

From

Place

Time

The above may be forwarded as now corrected. (Z)

Signature of Addressor or person authorised to telegraph in his name

* This line should be erased if not required.

[illegible] Wt. W3 [illegible] (E. 318)

MESSAGES AND SIGNALS. No. of Message..........

......Code............m. / ...ace of Origin and Service Instructions	Words	Charge.	This message is on a/c of:	Recd. at......m.
	Sent		..........Service.	Date..........
	At ....m.			From ....
	To			
	By		(Signature of "Franking Officer")	By..........

TO

Sender's Number.	Day of Month.	In reply to Number.	AAA

units as follows:—

Between	units	200 yds
"	Companies	100 yds
"	transport & unit	100 yds.

5/ Brigade starting point

The Batt will pass the Brigade starting point at D9C13 at 4 49. pm

6/ Inform

A	B
C	D
TO.	QM.
RSM.	

From 5th HLI.

Place

Time

The above may be forwarded as now corrected. (Z) ....

.... Censor. Signature of Addressor or person authorised to telegraph in his name

* This line should be erased if not required.

Order No. 1625 Wt. W3253/ P 511. 27/2 H. & K., Ltd. (E. 2634).

5 (contd.)
C. Coys rations will be dumped at X 4. L 6.4 and a guard provided by Batt. Hqrs.

(6) COOKING.
A, B, & D. Coys will cook about X 4. a 6.0.

(7) WATER.
A, B, & D. Coys. will draw their cooking water at the well in the quarry. A water cart will be kept at Batt. Hqrs. & sent round Coys. once daily so that men can fill their water bottles.

8 TRENCH. STORES
Coys. will hand over all trench stores and obtain receipts. These will be sent to this office by 12 noon tomorrow, in duplicate.
Coys. will also hand over the extra battle stores issued to them before coming into the line (viz 2 bombs per man & extra bandolier per man, also red flares and very lights.)
Picks & shovels brought in the line & 10 petrol tins will be handed over by each Coy. Coys. will form these into dumps.
The Royal Scots will leave their battle stores in the billets that the Batt is taking over.

9 BATTLE STORES.
Coys. must also make sure now, that there are no deficiencies in the permanent battle stores and equipment. If any deficiencies do exist, they must be made up by salvage.

10 L.G MAGAZINES
Coys. will salve as many Lewis Gun magazines & magazine boxes as possible & send them down to present Batt. Hqrs.

11 DEAD
O.C. Coys will be held personally responsible that all dead are either sent to Batt Hqrs. if British, & buried if German.

12 All information about the line will be carefully handed over. No officer will leave the line until the relieving Officer is satisfied that he is thoroughly cognisant of all positions and defences.

SECRET.

Operation Order No. 62 App V

By Major G. M. Clyhams. D.S.O.

Commanding 15th Batt. High. L.I.

Ref. French message map

---

1 The 5/6th ROYAL SCOTS will relieve the 15th H.L.I. in the left Batt. sector on the night 26/27th inst.

2 Coys. will be relieved by the ROYAL SCOT companies as follows:—

Royal Scot will relieve	H.L.I.	
C Coy.	B. Coy.	RIGHT FRONT.
A Coy.	A Coy.	LEFT FRONT
D. Coy.	C. Coy.	SUPPORT
B. Coy.	D. Coy.	RESERVE

3 GUIDES.

My 57. of today is cancelled.
Coys. will send guides to meet their relieving Coys. of the Royal Scots to the following places, to be there at 8.30pm.

B. Coy guides meet Royal Scots at X4 d 6.3.
A Coy " " " " at Batt. Hqrs.
C Coy " " " " at X5 a 00.35
D. Coy " " " " at Batt. Hqrs.

B & C. Coys. will send out an Officer with the guides, which will be used this evening, to reconnoitre the route to their points this afternoon.

4 On relief Coys. will move back & take up position as follows:—

A Coy	take from	A Coy	ROYAL SCOTS about	X4 a 6.0.
B. Coy	" "	B. Coy	" "	X9. b 7.6
C. Coy.	" "	C. Coy.	" "	X4 d 7.2.
D Coy (2 platoons)	"	D Coy (2 platoons)	"	X4 d 5.8
D Coy (2 platoons)	"	D Coy (2 platoons)	"	X4 c 6.3.
Batt. Hqrs.	"	Batt. Hqrs.	"	X9. b 8.8.

Coys. will send one guide per platoon to Batt. Hqrs. at 4pm. today. They will be shown where their Coys. are going, & will then return to their Coys.

5 RATIONS.

Rations for Batt. Hqrs. & B. Coy. will be dumped at the new Batt. Hqrs. X9. b.8.8. Both these Coys. will cook there.
Rations for A & D Coys. will be dumped at X4. c.6.7. & a guard on them provided by Batt. Hqrs.

Secret.

OPERATION ORDER. No. 41

App IV

MAJOR G.M. CLEGHORN. D.S.O.

Commanding 15th. Battalion Highland Light Infantry.

REF. SHEET. 62D. S.E.1/20,000

1. The 97th. Inf. Brigade will attack HERLEVILLE on the morning of 23r inst. in conjunction with the 1st. Australian Division on the left.
The 6th. Australian Battalion, 2nd. Australian Brigade will be on the left of the 97th. Inf. Bde.

2. The 97th. Inf. Bde. will attack on a two battalion frontage.
On the right - 2nd. K.O.Y.L.I. with one Coy. 1/5th. BORDER REGT. attached.
On the LEFT - 10th. A.& S.H. with two Coys. 1/5th. BORDER REGT attached.

3. The 2nd. K.O.Y.L.I. attack on two Coy. frontage.
The 10th. A.& S.H. on a three Coy. frontage.
Map showing final objective, Battalion, and Coy. frontages is attached.
1/5th. BORDER REGT. less 3 Coys. are in Brigade reserve to the 97 Inf. Bde. and move to position in X 8 a. on Y/Z night.

4. Strong points will be constructed in the vicinity of X6 central and R 36 c 7.6. under Divisional arrangements.

5. During the attack the following liasson posts are to be permanent established by the 10th. A.& S.H.:-
S. E. corner of wood R 36 a o.o.
M 31 b 5.0. on final objective line.

6. Forward prisoner collecting station will be Quarry X 4 a 5. 0.

7. The 15th. H.L.I. will occupy by Zero the positions in X 1 b & d mormally occupied by the reserve Battalion 97th. Inf. Bde. When this has been done the Battalion will be prepared to move at half hours motice.
Further details regarding this move will be issued later.

8. With reference to the above the 14th. Inf. Bde. will be prepared to relieve the 97th. Inf. Bde. in the line on the night of 23/24th. inst.

9. When the move takes place the 1st DORSET REGT. will relieve the 2nd. K O Y L I on the right. The 15th. H L I will relieve the 10th. A& S H on the left . The 5/6th. ROYAL SCOTS will be in Brigade reserve.

10. Each Coy. will send 2 N C Os to report at Batt. H/Q at 9 am. 23rd. inst. to Lieut. D.W. KEITH. who will take them forward to get into touch with the 10th. A &S H.

11. In all probability when the Battalion go into the line;-
A Coy. on the right, and B Coy. on the left will relieve the three Coys. of the 10th. A & S H. in the front line. C Coy. will be in support, and D Coy. in reserve.

12. ACKNOWLEDGE.

G Stephen

Captain.

A/ Adj. 15th. Bn. HIGH L. I.

SECRET. COPY No......

15th Bn. THE HIGHLAND LIGHT INFANTRY.

OPERATION ORDER No. 40

17th AUGUST, 1918. A.H. III

Map Reference - Sheet 62d 1/40,000.

1. The 32nd Division less Artillery will relieve the 2nd AUSTRALIAN Division in the line on the nights 17/18th and 18/19th AUGUST 1918.

2. Flanking Divisions will be :-

Right - 4th AUSTRALIAN Division.
Left - 5th AUSTRALIAN Division.

3. The sector will be taken over by :-

96th Infantry Brigade on the Right
97th Infantry Brigade on the Left.
14th Infantry Brigade in Divisional Reserve.

4. The Bn. will take over from the 10th A.& S.H. in O.35.d.1.9.

5. One sergeant from each Coy. will report to 2/Lieut. R.B.C. BROUGH at 7.40 a.m. at the Orderly Room. These N.C.Os. will act as an Advance Party to take over billets and will proceed by a lorry leaving Bde. H.Qrs. at 8 a.m.

This party will, when it has taken over billets, return to the debussing point to guide the Bn.

6. The Bn. will move by bus tomorrow, embussing at about C.3.d.1.4. at 8 p.m. It will debus at W.11.b.4.2.

The Bn. will parade at D. Coy's. Lines at 7.30 p.m. ready to march to embussing point. One marker per platoon to report to the R.S.M. at 7.15 p.m.

7. The Transport will be Brigaded and will march under the Bde. Transport Officer.

Order of march :- Bde. Hqrs., 5/6th Royal Scots, 1st Dorset Regt. 15th Bn. H. L. I., 14th T.M. Battery etc.

The head of the column will pass the starting point - Road junction C.3.d.8.9. - at 9 a.m. BOURGES on AMIENS - ROYE Road. A distance of 500 yards to be maintained between Units.

8. Lewis Guns will be carried in L.G. Limbers. These will meet the Bn. at the debussing point.

9. Coys. will keep sufficient Camp Kettles for use tomorrow. These will be carried by lorry. All fresh meat will be cooked tonight or early tomorrow.

10. All stores are to be loaded by 8 a.m. sharp.

All men will fill their waterbottles in the morning and keep them full.

ACKNOWLEDGE.

[signature]
Captain,

A/Adjt., 15th Bn. High. L. I.

15th H.L.I.

Vol 33

Instructions regarding War Diaries and Intelligence Summaries are contained in F. S. Regs., Part II. and the Staff Manual respectively. Title pages will be prepared in manuscript.

WAR DIARY
or
INTELLIGENCE SUMMARY.
(*Erase heading not required.*)

Army Form C. 2118.

Place	Date	Hour	Summary of Events and Information	Remarks and references to Appendices
PURPLE LINE	July 1st.		Bathing was carried out by companies at RANSART in the forenoon. Competitions on the miniature range was carried out under the supervision of CSM. STRACHAN Weather very warm. Observation good.	B M
"	2nd.		During the day company officers reconnoitred the HENDECOURT DEFENCES with MAJOR. CLEGHORN. D.S.O.	B M
"	3rd.		Enemy aircraft busy all morning. The companies carried out training in a small scale. Observation good	B M
"	4		Official word received that the Division was being relieved by the GUARD'S DIVISION. Companies commenced looking forward for stores for training. Weather fair, Wind Mild.	B M
"	5		Operation Orders No36 issued. The Battalion would be relieved by the 1st Battn IRISH GUARDS after relief being completed the Battalion moved back to SAULTY, entraining at RANSART and detraining at CHAPEL DUMP. the last party arrived in SAULTY at 5.30 am.	Appendix B M

33.0
11 sheets

A5834 Wt. W4973 M687 750,000 8/16 D. D. & L. Ltd. Forms/C.2118/13.

Instructions regarding War Diaries and Intelligence Summaries are contained in F. S. Regs., Part II. and the Staff Manual respectively. Title pages will be prepared in manuscript.

WAR DIARY
or
INTELLIGENCE SUMMARY.
(*Erase heading not required.*)

5th H L I

Trench Reference 51C S.E. 1/10,000

Army Form C. 2118.

Place	Date	Hour	Summary of Events and Information	Remarks and references to Appendices
SAULTY	6.		The day was spent cleaning up and checking battle stores. In the afternoon the companies played football. CAPT. E. McLEAN rejoined the Battalion for duty as chaplain.	BM
	7th		Church service was held in the CHATEAU GROUNDS. The service was conducted by CAPT. DAWSON. The praise being led by the 5/6th ROYAL SCOTS BAND. CAPT. HERBERT held a sports meeting to discuss the chances of having Battalion sports.	BM
	8th		The Battalion started on training as per programme of work. A Coy on the range at P.33.a. The remainder of the companies carried out training in the CHATEAU GROUNDS. The afternoon was devoted to sports.	BM
	9th		Musketry carried out on the Range by B Coy. The Battalion Lewis Gunners carried out range practice under 2LT. HEPBURN.	BM
	10th		The training was carried out as per programme. Musketry on the range. Drill Lewis Gun classes etc. The Pipe Band played in the CORP. COMPETITION and after a very close result obtained second place. The 2nd HLI obtaining first place. The five a side football competitions started all being played in the afternoons.	BM

A5834 Wt. W4973 M687 750,000 8/16 D. D. & L. Ltd. Forms/C.2118/13.

WAR DIARY
or
INTELLIGENCE SUMMARY.
(*Erase heading not required.*) 15th H.L.I. Map Reference 51G S.E. 1/10000

Army Form C. 2118.

Instructions regarding War Diaries and Intelligence Summaries are contained in F. S. Regs., Part II. and the Staff Manual respectively. Title pages will be prepared in manuscript.

Place	Date	Hour	Summary of Events and Information	Remarks and references to Appendices
SAULTY	11		The morning was very wet and parades were delayed after which the programme as near as possible was carried out. CAPT. J.F. MOIR M.C. and other two officers reconnoitred the HENDECOURT DEFENCES. The Battalion carried out Bathing parades in the afternoon.	BM
	12		Training carried out as per Programme. In the afternoon all Subaltern officers paraded under 2nd Lt HEPBORN for instruction in Lewis Guns. A lecture was given by 3RD ARMY. PT. and B.F. Instructor to the Battalion. At 6 pm a Set turnout was held by the DIVISION and the Battalion was inspected by BRIG. GEN. EVANS. V.C., D.S.O.	BM
	13		The day was spent without doing any work owing to heats to being ran off in connection with the Battalion Sports which were being held that day. The sports commenced at 1-30 pm and continued up till 4-30 pm. The running was closely contested also the football. The Tug of War final A Coy v H.Q. Coy. was very exciting but after a long and strenuous pull A Coy beat Headquarters Coy. Side shows caused great amusement and attracted a large number of the spectators. After a very enjoyable day which was due to the hard work by CAPT. R. HERBERT. The spectators enjoyed a two and a half hour's programme	BM

A5834 Wt. W4973 M687 750,000 8/16 D. D. & L. Ltd. Forms/C.2118/13.

Instructions regarding War Diaries and Intelligence Summaries are contained in F. S. Regs., Part II. and the Staff Manual respectively. Title pages will be prepared in manuscript.

WAR DIARY
or
INTELLIGENCE SUMMARY.
(*Erase heading not required.*) 5th H.L.I.

Army Form C. 2118.

Map Reference Sheet 57c SE 1/20,000

Place	Date	Hour	Summary of Events and Information	Remarks and references to Appendices
SAULTY	13.		by the Divisional Concert Party "The Pedlars"	
"	14		The Battalion carried out Training. Three officers proceeded to reconnoitre the back area's & defences. A Gas Lecture was given by the Divisional Gas Officer to Officers & NCO's in the CHATEAU GROUNDS.	B.M.
	15		The Battalion carried out a small scheme on Open Warfare at La BAZEQUE in the forenoon and after dinners had been served on the field they proceeded to watch a demonstration of Cooperation of TANKS with Infantry in the attack.	B.M.
	16.		The Battalion carried out Bathing per companies two in the forenoon and two in the afternoon.	B.M.
	17.		There was no training carried out owing to the Division moving north. Packing of Stores and Inspection of Battle Stores was carried out per company arrangements.	B.M.
	18.		Operation Order No. 34. issued The Battalion would parade in CHATEAU GROUNDS at 11 pm and proceed	Appendix 2. RB

A5834 Wt. W4973 M687 750,000 8/16 D. D. & L. Ltd. Forms/C.2118/13.

Instructions regarding War Diaries and Intelligence Summaries are contained in F. S. Regs., Part II. and the Staff Manual respectively. Title pages will be prepared in manuscript.

WAR DIARY
or
INTELLIGENCE SUMMARY.
(Erase heading not required.) Map Reference Sheet HAZEBROUCK 5A 1/20000

Army Form C. 2118.

Place	Date	Hour	Summary of Events and Information	Remarks and references to Appendices
			to MONDICOURT where they entrained for the NORTH. After being 12 hours on the way arrived at WAYENBERG. After unloading the train the Battalion had tea and marched to billets at BAMBECQUE where everything was arranged by CAPT MOIR, MC.	RB M
BAMBECQUE	19		The Battalion carried out inspection parade and scrubbing equipment.	RB M
"	20.		Owing to no training area being available the Companies carried out Musketry & Gas Drill on their own lines.	RB M
"	21		The Battalion ~~paraded~~ for Church Service under CAPT E MacLEAN. After church parade the companies carried out Musketry & Arm Drill.	RB M
"	22.		A & C Companies marched to OOS-CAPPELL to have their Gas masks tested by the BRIGADE GAS Officer. In the afternoon CAPT STEVEN. MC. reconnoitred the line in front of KEMMELL.	RB M
"	23.		The companies carried out training as per programme of work. A & C Companies Bathing in the forenoon. B & D Companies also marched in the afternoon and had their respirators tested by the BRIGADE GAS Officer at OOS CAPPELL.	RB M

Instructions regarding War Diaries and Intelligence Summaries are contained in F. S. Regs., Part II. and the Staff Manual respectively. Title pages will be prepared in manuscript.

WAR DIARY
or
INTELLIGENCE SUMMARY.
(*Erase heading not required.*) 15th H.L.I.

Army Form C. 2118.

Map Reference sheet HAZEBROUCK 5A 1/20000

Place	Date	Hour	Summary of Events and Information	Remarks and references to Appendices
BAMBECQUE	24.		COL. V.B. RAMSDEN DSO MC. conducted a party of officers from the BRIGADE and reconnoitred the tracks WEST of POPERINGHE	B M
			The Companies carried out musketry under MAJOR. CLEGHORN. DSO. at HOOTKERQUE. Three officers reconnoitred the line in front of KEMMELL.	B
	25		Owing to the broken weather training was cancelled MAJOR. CLEGHORN DSO. attended a GENERAL COURT MARTIAL of which he was PRESIDENT. Four officers from the Battalion attended a exhibition given by aeroplanes dropping of boxes of SAA. at Proven.	B M
	26.		The Battalion watched a Demonstration given by four platoons on the Open Warfare attack on a post & strong point. In the forenoon the companies carried out Bathing at BAMBECQUE. Three officers from the Battalion reconnoitred the KEMMELL FRONT.	B M
	27.		Two Companies carried out Musketry at HOOTKERQUE under MAJOR CLEGHORN. DSO. cookers accompanied the parties and dinners were served on the Range.	B M
	28.		The Battalion paraded for Church parade under CAPT. F. McLEAN. Three officers reconnoitred the KEMMELL FRONT.	B M

A5834 Wt. W4973 M687 750,000 8/16 D. D. & L. Ltd. Forms/C.2118/13.

Instructions regarding War Diaries and Intelligence Summaries are contained in F. S. Regs., Part II. and the Staff Manual respectively. Title pages will be prepared in manuscript.

WAR DIARY
or
INTELLIGENCE SUMMARY.
(Erase heading not required.)

15 H. L. I.

Army Form C. 2118.

Map Reference Sheet HAZEBROUCK 5A 1/20000

Place	Date	Hour	Summary of Events and Information	Remarks and references to Appendices
BAMBECQUE	29		Two companies carried out Musketry at HOUTKERQUE the other two companies carried out Bathing at BAMBECQUE.	[illegible]
"	30.		The Bathing of the Battalion was completed in the forenoon, The two companies who bathed yesterday carried out training under company arrangements.	[illegible]
"	31		The Battalion paraded for one hours' Battalion parade in the morning. afterwards the men were marched to field where an elaborate sports programme had been arranged by 14th Brigade, Cookers were taken and dinners and tea served, despite the fact that the 15th H.L.I. failed to win any of the events, a most enjoyable afternoon was spent.	[illegible]

A5834 Wt. W4973/M687 750,000 8/16 D. D. & L. Ltd. Forms/C.2118/13.

Army Form C. 2118.

Instructions regarding War Diaries and Intelligence Summaries are contained in F. S. Regs., Part II. and the Staff Manual respectively. Title pages will be prepared in manuscript.

WAR DIARY
or
INTELLIGENCE SUMMARY.
(Erase heading not required.)

Place	Date	Hour	Summary of Events and Information	Remarks and references to Appendices

	1st JULY		31st JULY	
	OFF	ORs	OFF	ORs
Commanding Officer's Strength	29	844	26	892
FIGHTING STRENGTH				
Officers	37		38	
Other ranks	921		963	

TOTAL CASUALTIES for the month

	OFF	OR.
Killed and Died of Wounds	-	1
Wounded	-	2
Missing	-	-

[signature] Lieut-Col
Commdg. 15/HIGH L.I

A5834 Wt. W4973 M687 750,000 8/16 D. D. & L. Ltd. Forms/C.2118/13.

SECRET.

Copy No. 8.

Operation Order No 35.
By Major G.M. Cleghorn D.S.O.
Commanding 15th Bn. High. L.I.

Map Ref. 51 B. SW
51 C SE

1/ The 1st DORSET REGT will relieve the 5/6th ROYAL SCOTS in the Brigade front on the night of the 28/29th inst.
The 15th H.L.I. will take over the defences of the PURPLE LINE from the 1st DORSET REGT. on their vacating these.

2/ On completion of move Coys. will be located as under:-

B COY in CHATEAU WOOD.
A COY in trenches in X16. b.
C. COY in trenches in X16 d.
D COY in trenches in X15 a.

3/ B. Coy. will move from its present location at 10.15 pm. and Coys. will follow in above order by platoons at 200 yds. intervals.
D. Coy. will occupy its new position as soon as this is vacated by Coy of 1st DORSET REGT.

4/ Advance parties (less D. Coy) will report to Bn. HQrs. of 1st DORSET REGT at 7. pm. tonight. These to consist of 1 Officer per Coy. and 1 NCO. per platoon and Coy. HQrs.

5/ All details about the defences to be carefully taken over. Copies of trench store lists in duplicate to reach this office by 9 am. on 29th inst.

6/ Lewis Gun sections will carry their guns and ammunition. 1/2. limber per Coy. will be available for transport of cooking utensils, water, etc.

7/ Position at present occupied by 15th H.L.I. will be taken over by 5/6th ROYAL SCOTS.

8/ Completion of move to be reported in code as under:-

RELIEF COMPLETE - SALVAGE
LITTLE SHELLING - MUCH
MUCH SHELLING - REQUIRED

9 Acknowledge.

W W White
Major
A/Adj 15th H.L.I.

No 1

[illegible]

I. (a) [illegible]

[illegible] DEFENCES

II [illegible]

III [illegible]

IV [illegible]

V [illegible]

[illegible] DEFENCES [illegible]

[illegible]

IX [illegible]

RELIEF COMPLETE — BLACK
LITTLE SHELLING — AND
MUCH SHELLING — WHITE

[illegible]

ACKNOWLEDGE.

[illegible signature]

[illegible]

FILE

No. 2

OPERATION ORDER No. 37.
by,
Lieut-Colonel V.B. RAMSDEN, D.S.O., M.C.,
Commanding 15th Bn. Highland Light Infantry.

---

1. Bn. will move by strategic trains on the 19th JULY entraining at MONDICOURT and detraining at WAYENBERG.

2. MOVES. Moves will be carried out according to attached Table "A".

3. ENTRAINING. A party of 2 Officers and 100 O.Rs. from "A" Coy. will report to Major WHITE, M.C. at MONDICOURT Station at 2.30 p.m. today to act as a loading party. This party will be relieved by a similar party from the 1st Dorset Regt. at 2 a.m. 19th inst., and will travel by No. 12 train moving off at 3.32 a.m.

4. DETRAINING. O.C. "C" Coy. will detail 2 Officers and 100 O.Rs. to report to Lieut. A.B. STEWART on arrival at detraining station. They are required to relieve a similar party of the 5/6th Royal Scots.

5. TRANSPORT. 2/Lieut. J.U. McGILL and the P.W. Platoon will proceed with the Transport to the station for loading purposes.
Breast ropes for horse trucks must be provided by the Bn. Ropes for lashing vehicles will be provided by the railway.

6. The quartermaster will arrange to have as many lanterns as possible at the station during the entrainment.

7. DISCIPLINE. All doors of the covered trucks and carriages on the right hand side of the train, when on the Main Line must be kept closed.
The usual Bn. entraining discipline will be carried out. Coy. guides will report to the Adjutant on arrival at the station, these will be placed opposite the right carriage of each Coy. O.C. Coys. will find out from them how many carriages have been allotted their Coys. Coys. will then be split up as required according to the carriage accommodation. Before the order is given to advance and entrain, the bugler will sound the advance from the place of assembly. Then when Coys. are ready and standing opposite their carriages in two ranks in depth, the bugler will sound one "G" upon which the train will be boarded.
The same procedure will be adopted on detraining.

8. All Coys. and the Transport will render marching out states in duplicate to the Orderly Room by 6 p.m. today. These will show the number of men, horses, G.S. Wagons, Limbered G.S. Wagons and bicycles moving by train, the number of the train being stated.

9. BILLETING PARTY. A billeting party consisting of Captain J.F. MUIR, MC, and 1 N.C.O. per Coy. will report to the Orderly Room at 4 p.m. today where they will draw bicycles. They will then proceed to the new area by No. 3 train leaving MONDICOURT at 6.32 p.m. Captain J.F. MUIR, M.C. will report to the Staff Captain at detraining station.

10. BAGGAGE & LEWIS GUNS. All Lewis Guns will be loaded in Coy. Limbers by 6 p.m. today.
All Officers valises are to be dumped at Q.M. Stores at 4.30 p.m. today. The Mess Cart will collect Officers Mess Kit at their Messes at 9 p.m. tonight.

11. ACKNOWLEDGE.

J.G. Stephen

Captain,
A/Adjt., 15th Bn. High. L. I.

TABLE "A".

Serial No.	Date.	Coy.	Starting point.	Times of passing starting point.	Route.	Time train departs.	No. of train.	Order of march.
7.	18 & 19	"A" "C" "B" H.Q.	V.1.d.9.6.	12 mn.	V.8.c.6.1. DOULLENS - ARRAS ROAD. C.2.a.3.7.	3.32 am.	12	Band,H "A" "C" "D".
7a	do;	Trans. less "B" Coy. & Cooker.	do:	11 pm.	do;	3.32 am.	12	
7b.	19th	"B" Coy. & Cooker.	do:	2.50 am.	do:	6.32 am.	15	

REMARKS:-

Dress - F.S.M.O. Steel Helmets will be worn.

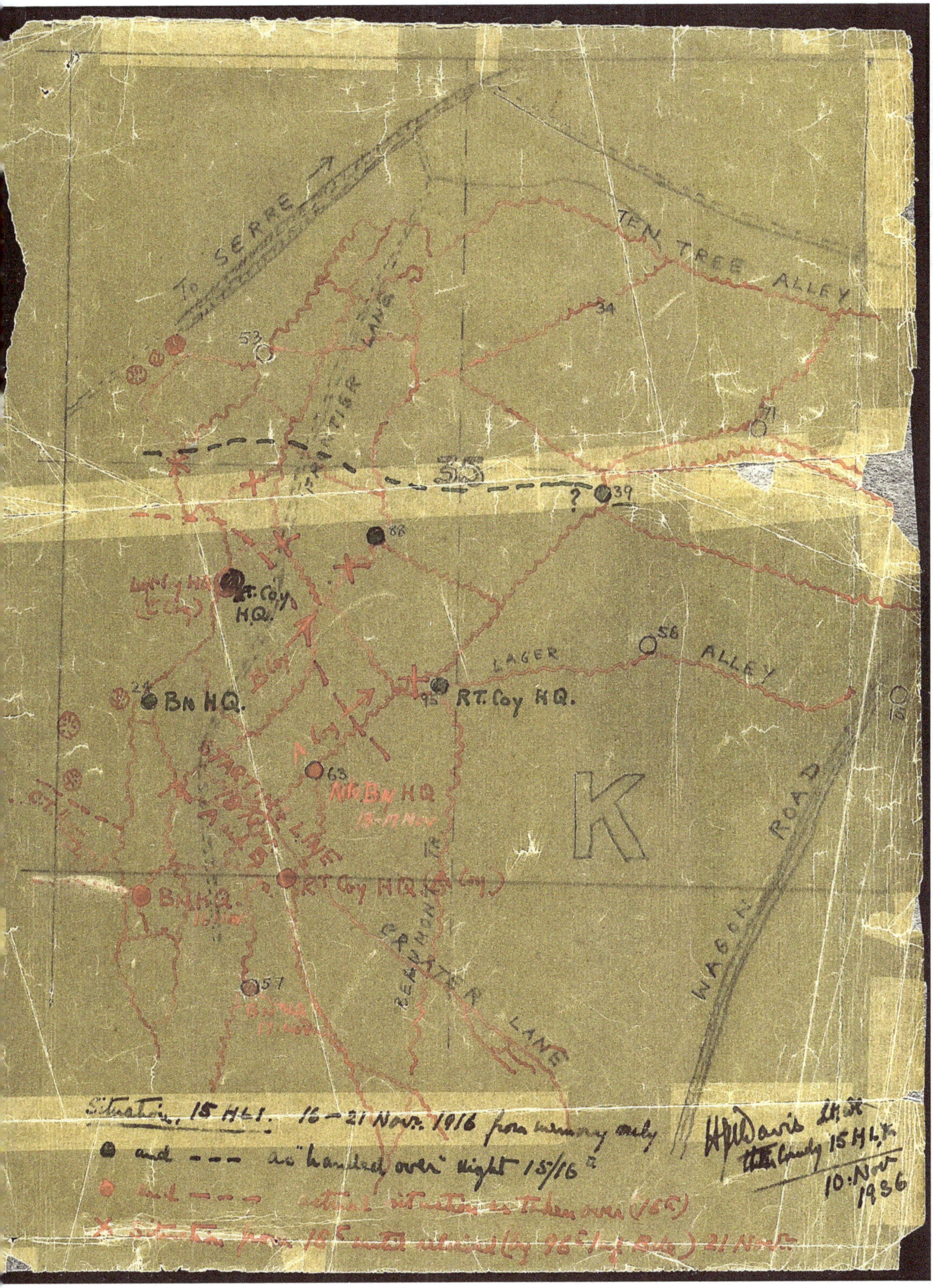

To SERRE
TEN TREE ALLEY
FRONTIER LANE
LAGER ALLEY
RT. Coy HQ.
BN HQ.
K
WAGON ROAD
STARTING LINE
CRATER LANE
RT Coy HQ
BN HQ
Situation, 15 HLI. 16 – 21 Nov. 1916 from memory only
and - - - as "handed over" night 15/16th
and - - - actual situation as taken over (16th)
X Situation from 18th until relieved (by 96th Inf Bde) 21 Nov.
10: Nov 1936

Lt Col. H. J. N. Davis
6, The Park, Cheltenham

Situation in Black ink as taken over from 1 Dorset [illegible] 1917 [illegible] 1 Dorset Regt) chiefly
Blue Posts etc as occupied Jan Feb 1917

1:5,000

REDAN

EDITION 2.
CANCELLING ALL PREVIOUS ISSUES.

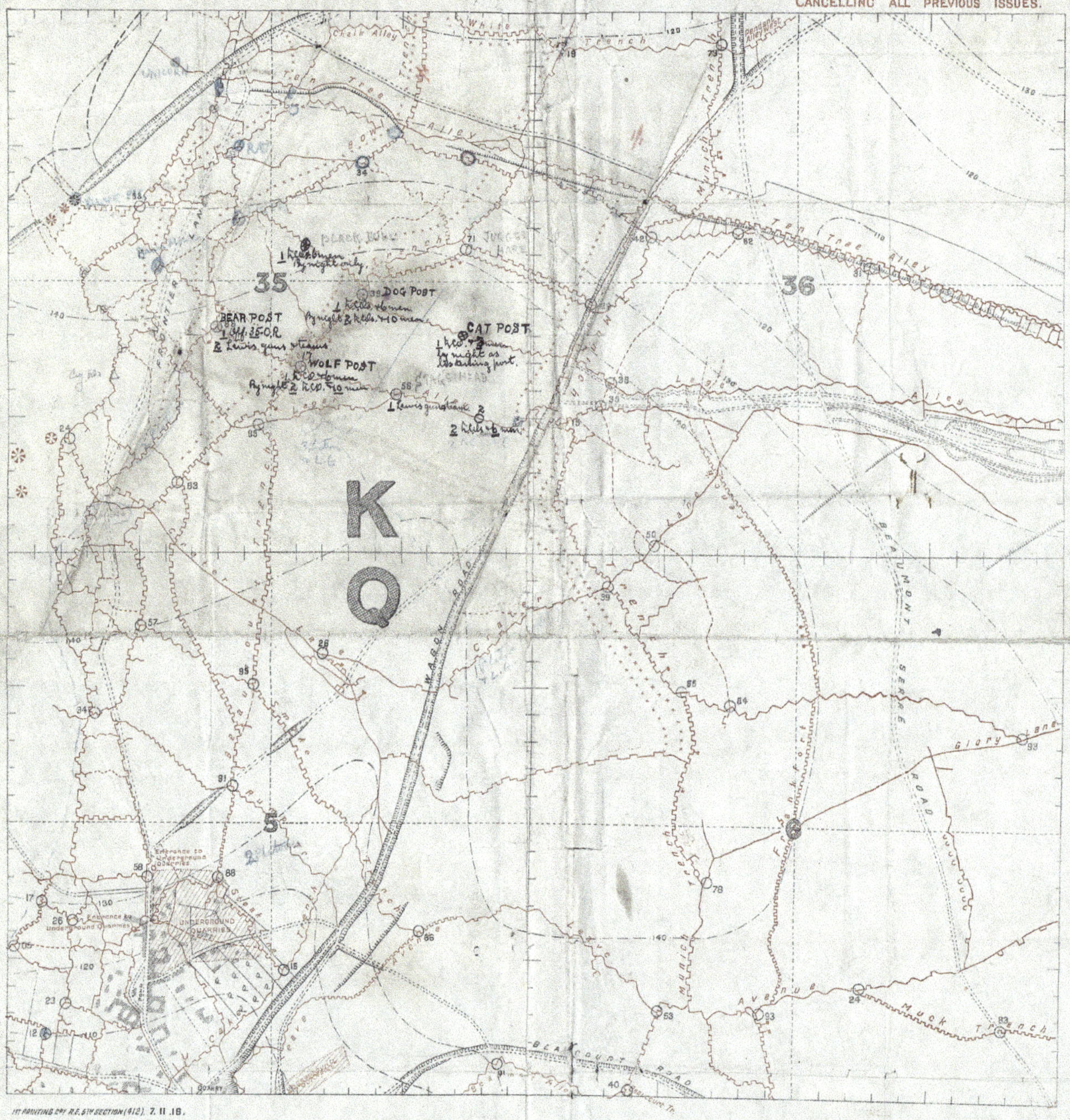

1st Printing Coy R.E. 5th Section (612). 7.11.16.

TRENCHES CORRECTED TO 12-11-16

Scale 1:5,000

From the fact that an obstacle is not represented on the map it is not to be taken for granted that one does not exist.

This map differs in certain detail from current maps of smaller scales.

The numbers against circles are approximate co-ordinates. When used as a means of reference the square also must in all cases be indicated.

(383)

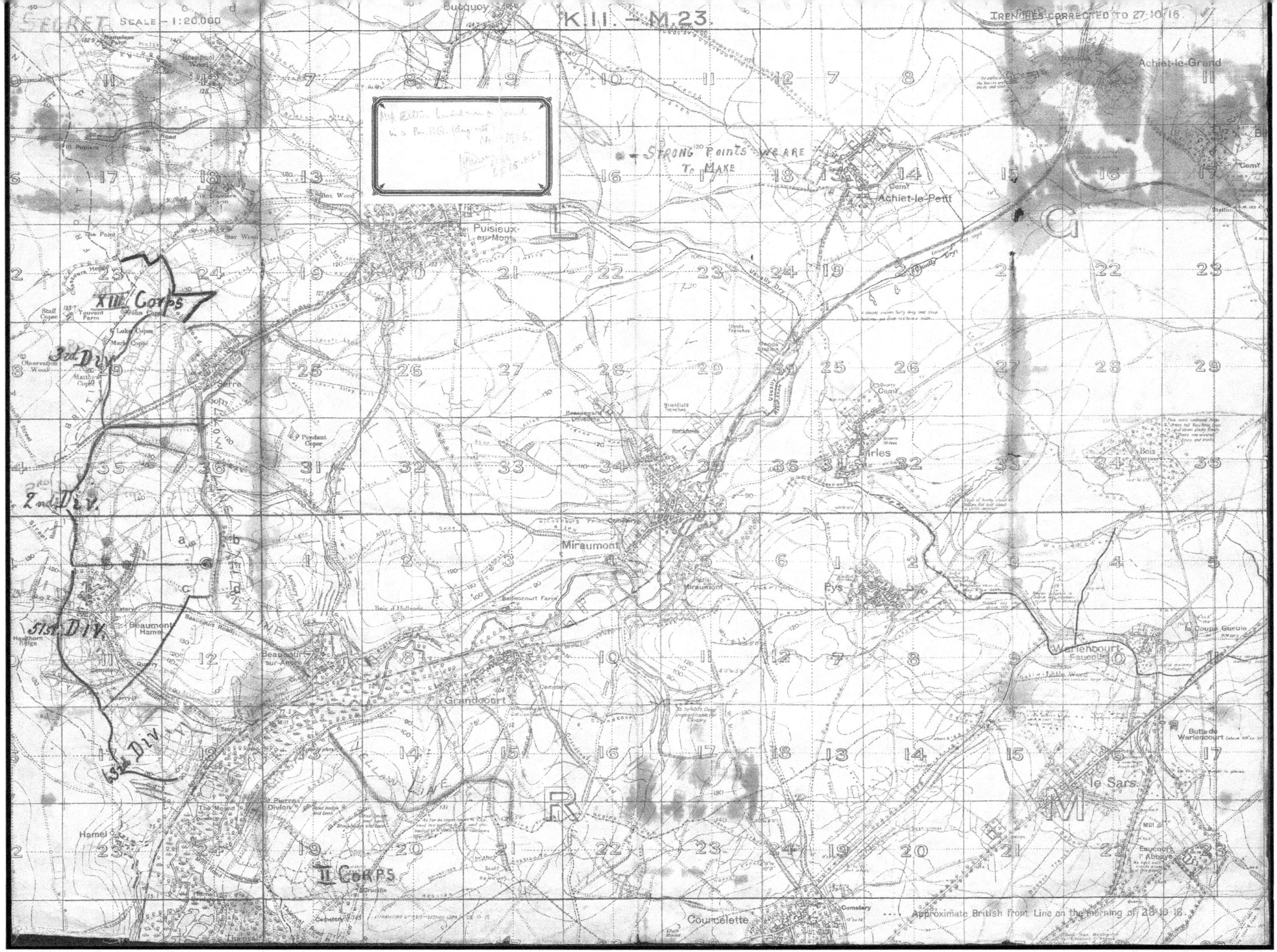
SECRET
SCALE – 1:20,000
K.11. – M.23.
TRENCHES CORRECTED TO 27-10-16
Bucquoy
Achiet-le-Grand
Achiet-le-Petit
Puisieux-au-Mont
STRONG Points WE ARE To MAKE
XIII Corps
3rd Div
2nd Div
51st Div
63rd Div
II Corps
Serre
Miraumont
Petit Miraumont
Irles
Pys
Beaumont Hamel
Beaucourt sur-Ancre
Grandcourt
Warlencourt-Eaucourt
le Sars
Butte de Warlencourt
Eaucourt l'Abbaye
Courcelette
Hamel
The Point
Hawthorn Ridge
Observation Wood
Pendant Copse
Baillescourt Farm
Bois d'Hollande
Box Wood
Star Wood
YELLOW LINE
Approximate British Front Line on the morning of 28-10-16

Instructions regarding War Diaries and Intelligence Summaries are contained in F. S. Regs., Part II. and the Staff Manual respectively. Title pages will be prepared in manuscript.

WAR DIARY
or
INTELLIGENCE SUMMARY.
(Erase heading not required.)

Army Form C. 2118.

15 H.L.I.

14/37

WO 34

34. O

17 sheets

Place	Date	Hour	Summary of Events and Information	Remarks and references to Appendices
	1918			
BAMBECQUE	Thurs. Aug. 1		Frequent showers of rain during the day which interfered somewhat with the training of the Battalion in the forenoon. Training was carried out under Company arrangements.	WC
do	Fri. Aug 2		Another day of heavy rain showers owing to which the forenoon training programme was cancelled. Night operations were also cancelled for the same reason.	WC
do	Sat. Aug 3		Training again interfered with by rain. Orders were received in the afternoon from Brigade that the Battalion, along with the rest of the Brigade Group, were to proceed on Monday to an area outside ST. OMER for special training. Transport are to leave tomorrow morning by road, taking two days to the journey. C. Coy are to proceed by train tomorrow ahead of the remainder of the Battalion.	WC
do	Sun. Aug 4		A Brigade Church Service in commemoration of the outbreak of the war was held in the forenoon. The Battalion, less 'C' Company, was present. 'C' Coy. entrained at ROUSEBRUGGE and proceeded to ST OMER from where they marched to new area at CORMETTE. A billeting party consisting of 2/Lt D C HODGE and five N.C.O.s travelled by bus motor lorry from Bde Headquarters to CORMETTE where arrangements were made	WC

A5834 Wt. W4973/M687 750,000 8/16 D. D. & L. Ltd. Forms/C.2118/13.

Instructions regarding War Diaries and Intelligence Summaries are contained in F. S. Regs., Part II. and the Staff Manual respectively. Title pages will be prepared in manuscript.

WAR DIARY
or
INTELLIGENCE SUMMARY.
(Erase heading not required.)

Army Form C. 2118.

Place	Date	Hour	Summary of Events and Information	Remarks and references to Appendices
	1918		to accommodate the Battalion when it arrived tomorrow. In the afternoon orders were received from Brigade countermanding the move to CORMETTE. Instructions were sent to the details already at CORMETTE to rejoin Battalion at BAMBECQUE. The transport were also advised of the alteration in the orders.	b.e.g. [illegible]
BAMBECQUE	Mon. Aug 5		The forenoon was spent in cleaning up lines preparatory to moving off to another area. The transport arrived back at BAMBECQUE about 1 p.m. and the Billeting party and 'C' Coy. returned from ST. OMER late in the afternoon.	b.e.g. [illegible]
BAMBECQUE	Tues. Aug 6		In the afternoon orders were received from Brigade that the 32nd Division were leaving their present area for a new area South of the SOMME. The battalion entrains at WAYENBERG rail head tomorrow at 4 p.m. Billeting party of 2/Lt HODGE and four N.C.O.s went on ahead leaving WAYENBERG at 11-30 p.m. tonight. Operation Order No. 38 was issued for the move (App. I)	b.e.g. [illegible] (O.O. 38 App. No. I)
BAMBECQUE	Wed. Aug 7.		Battalion, including Transport, marched from BAMBECQUE to WAYENBERG rail head and entrained there. Train left for new destination at 4 p.m. and the remainder of the day was occupied by the journey.	b.e.g. [illegible]

A5834 Wt. W4973 M687 750,000 8/16 D. D. & L. Ltd. Forms/C.2118/13.

Instructions regarding War Diaries and Intelligence Summaries are contained in F. S. Regs., Part II. and the Staff Manual respectively. Title pages will be prepared in manuscript.

WAR DIARY
or
INTELLIGENCE SUMMARY.
(Erase heading not required.)

Army Form C. 2118.

Place	Date	Hour	Summary of Events and Information	Remarks and references to Appendices
GENTELLES	1918 THURS. Aug. 8		Battalion arrived at FLEXICOURT about 5 a.m. and detrained there. Arrangements had been made by the Billeting party, according to orders, to billet the Battalion at PICIGNY. These orders were countermanded and fresh ones issued by Brigade to the effect that the Battalion were to proceed up the line at once. The Battalion embussed at 1.30 p.m. and debussed late at night outside GENTELLES. Billets were found in an open field. Transport proceeded by road and arrived at new area about 3 a.m. on the 9th inst.	L.C.H. [illegible]
BEAUCOURT	FRI. Aug 9		The forenoon was spent in cleaning up and resting. Fresh orders were received and in the afternoon the Battalion marched from GENTELLES to field outside BEAUCOURT where they bivouaced for the night.	L.C.H. [illegible]
BOUCHOIR	SAT. Aug 10		Battalion and transport moved off from bivouacs at 6 a.m. Details to be left out of the line remained behind under Lt FRASER. Transport proceeded as far as FOLIES where they remained. The remainder of the Battalion took up its position outside BOUCHOIR, the 15th H.L.I. being in Brigade Reserve. The details left behind proceeded to join the Transport lines in the evening. During the march they came under hostile aircraft bombing and suffered a few casualties.	L.C.H. [illegible]
BOUCHOIR	Sun Aug 11		An attack on the village of PARVILLERS was undertaken by Brigade. The 1st Dorset Regt and 5/6th Royal Scots were in the front line with the 15th H.L.I. in reserve. The village was not captured. Both the attacking Battns. suffered casualties in officers and men. Only "D" Coy. of the	L.C.H. [illegible]

A5834 Wt. W4973/M687 750,000 8/16 D. D. & L. Ltd. Forms/C.2118/13.

Instructions regarding War Diaries and Intelligence Summaries are contained in F. S. Regs., Part II. and the Staff Manual respectively. Title pages will be prepared in manuscript.

WAR DIARY
or
INTELLIGENCE SUMMARY.
(Erase heading not required.)

Army Form C. 2118.

Place	Date	Hour	Summary of Events and Information	Remarks and references to Appendices
BOUCHOIR	1918		H.L.I. were engaged, being sent up to support the 1st Dorset Regt. Casualties were slight. Capt. J. BRODIE, M.C., was wounded. Transport remained at FOLIES.	
BOUCHOIR FOLIES BEAUCOURT	Mon. Aug. 12		The 14th Brigade were relieved in the early morning by the 9th Canadian Brigade. The 15th H.L.I. moved back to Transport lines at FOLIES arriving there about 4 a.m. In the afternoon the Battn. with Transport marched to BEAUCOURT where they bivouaced in a field on the outskirts of the village. Weather exceptionally fine and very warm. Capt. J F MUIR, M.C. and 2/Lt. J. U. McGILL proceeded on leave to England. 2/Lt. H. C. DUFF joined the Battn. to-day for duty.	[illegible]
BEAUCOURT DOMART	Tue. Aug. 13		The Battn. were paraded in their lines in the forenoon and were addressed by the Divisional Commander on the recent operations. In the afternoon the whole 14th Brigade group marched to new area outside DOMART where the 15th H.L.I. bivouaced in the open by the roadside. It is expected that we remain here for a few days to rest. Weather very fine and warm	[illegible] O.O. 39 (App. 11)
DOMART	Wed. Aug. 14		Battle order fixed. The Commanding Officer inspected the lines in the forenoon after which Coys. did [illegible] arm drill. The men were [illegible] in the evening. In the afternoon the four Coys bathed in the River LUCE.	[illegible]
DOMART	Thur. Aug. 15		The Battalion paraded at 5 a.m. and did open warfare practice over ground in the vicinity of the camp. Returned to camp about 10 a.m. 2/Lt. R S C BROUGH rejoined from Intelligence Course also Capt. J R ROBERTSON, M.C. and 2/Lt. HEPBURN rejoined from leave at TROUVILLE.	[illegible]
DOMART	Fri. Aug. 16		Fine weather continues. The Battalion did another early morning practice returning to camp about 11 a.m. 2nd Lt. T. W. HEPBURN took over command of "D" Coy vice Capt. BRODIE, M.C. wounded.	[illegible]

A5834 Wt. W4973/M687 750,000 8/16 D. D. & L. Ltd. Forms/C.2118/13.

Instructions regarding War Diaries and Intelligence Summaries are contained in F. S. Regs., Part II. and the Staff Manual respectively. Title pages will be prepared in manuscript.

WAR DIARY
or
INTELLIGENCE SUMMARY.
(Erase heading not required.)

Army Form C. 2118.

Place	Date	Hour	Summary of Events and Information	Remarks and references to Appendices
DOMART	1918 Sat. Aug. 17		The weather was much cooler and looked like rain. The Battalion again carried out an open warfare scheme in the morning.	[illegible]
DOMART HARBONNIERES	Sun. Aug. 18		Open air church parade service was held in the forenoon. The Transport left at 8 a.m. and proceeded by road to new area at BOIS de TAILLEUX, north of WARFUSEE. Details to be left out of the line left at 4 p.m. and marched to same place where accommodation was found for them in old German dugouts. The remainder of Battalion embussed at 9 p.m. and debussed at a point W. of HARBONNIERES where they occupied billets taken earlier in the day by 2/Lt. R.S.C. BROUGH. MAJOR JAGER, TANK CORPS, reported at DOMART for a period of duty and proceeded with Battn. to HARBONNIERES. Operation Order No 240 attached. (App. III)	b.e.d. [illegible] OO No 40 App III
HARBONNIERES	Mon Aug. 19		Quiet day. Battalion was reorganised in depth. Wiring parties were sent out at night. Capt. J. SHIRLEY, M.C., reported at Transport lines for duty with the battalion. Weather very warm and fine.	b.e.d. [illegible]
HARBONNIERES	Tues. Aug. 20		Lt.Col. V.B. RAMSDEN, D.S.O., M.C., went down to Transport lines and Major C.M. CLEGHORN took over command. Battn. Headquarters were moved to a more central position. 2nd Lt. WEBSTER reported back from 2nd Army Musketry School. Both he and Capt. SHIRLEY joined the battalion in front, Capt. SHIRLEY taking over command of A. Company. Capt. R.B.H. ALEXANDER proceeded to Divisional Depot Battn.	b.e.d. [illegible]
HARBONNIERES	Wed. Aug. 21		Battalion still remained in the same position and work was limited to several working and wiring parties. Situation quiet. 2/Lt. W. RITCHIE reported for duty, and was posted to B. Coy. 2/Lt. R.S.C. BROUGH proceeded on leave to England.	b.e.d. [illegible]

Army Form C. 2118.

Instructions regarding War Diaries and Intelligence Summaries are contained in F. S. Regs., Part II. and the Staff Manual respectively. Title pages will be prepared in manuscript.

WAR DIARY
or
INTELLIGENCE SUMMARY.

(Erase heading not required.)

Place	Date	Hour	Summary of Events and Information	Remarks and references to Appendices
HARBONNIERES	1918 Thurs. Aug 22		Battalion moved forward into Divisional Reserve, Transport lines were also moved forward to area outside BAYONVILLERS. Operation Order No. 41 was issued. (App. IV)	6 c Q OO No. 41 App (IV)
HARBONNIERES	Fri. Aug 23		In the morning Lt Col RAMSDEN was ordered to proceed to [illegible] Brigade H.Q. and remained there during the day while operations were proceeding. The Battalion remained in reserve. In the afternoon the Brigade took over a portion of the line, the 15th H.L.I. taking over from the 10th Argyll & S Highlanders. The enemy was not very active and the day passed quietly.	6 c Q
HARBONNIERES	Sat. Aug 24		The Colonel returned to Transport Lines from Brigade in the forenoon. Battalion took over another 500 yards more trench to the right. In the afternoon heavy enemy shelling of our line took place and A Coy suffered some casualties, 2/Lts P.C.L. TIMONY and J. WEBSTER being killed.	6 c Q
HARBONNIERES	Sun. Aug 25		A quiet day with a change in the weather. Heavy rain in the evening. Operation Order No. 42 re relief by Royal Scots tomorrow was issued. (App. V)	6 c Q OO No. 42 (App V)
HARBONNIERES	Mon. Aug 26		Another quiet day. The Commanding Officer visited the Battalion in front [illegible] returned to the transport lines late in the day. In the evening the Battalion was relieved by the Royal Scots.	6 c Q
HARBONNIERES	Tues. Aug 27		Showery day. Situation very quiet in front. The Commanding Officer took over command of the Battalion in the afternoon.	6 c Q

A5834 Wt. W4973/M687 750,000 8/16 D. D. & L. Ltd. Forms/C.2118/13.

Instructions regarding War Diaries and Intelligence Summaries are contained in F. S. Regs., Part II. and the Staff Manual respectively. Title pages will be prepared in manuscript.

WAR DIARY
or
INTELLIGENCE SUMMARY.

(Erase heading not required.)

Army Form C. 2118.

Place	Date	Hour	Summary of Events and Information	Remarks and references to Appendices
HARBONNIERES	1918 Wed Aug 28		During the retreat of Germans in front the Battalion moved forward from its position in the Harbonnières area without getting into touch with the enemy & proceeded via FRAMERVILLE and SOYECOURT to a position 2,000 yards east of DENIECOURT. The transport also moved forward and billeted for the night at SOYECOURT. During the day CAPT J. SHIRLEY M.C. was wounded. Capt A. G. McNAUGHTEN rejoined Battn from Instruction Course ALDERSHOT.	[illegible]
DENIECOURT	Thur Aug 29		In the morning the pursuit was continued and the Battalion advanced to a position south of the main road to VILLERS CARBONNEL. A few casualties were suffered through enemy shelling.	[illegible]
VILLERS CARBONNEL	Fri Aug 30		The Battalion remained in its position throughout the day. At night the Brigade moved southward and the 10th H.L.I. took up its position near BARLEUX where they were in reserve to the 1st Dorset Regt. which formed an Outpost Battn to the Brigade. Capt J. F. MUIR, M.C. reported for duty off Course. 2/Lt I. R. HAWKE joined the Battn for duty. Later in the evening, this officer was slightly wounded and was taken to hospital. The transport moved in the afternoon to [illegible] ESTREES.	[illegible]
BARLEUX	Sat Aug 31		A quiet day. Except shelling and bombing at night. Transport was moved to DENIECOURT. Lt. J. V. [illegible] GILL rejoined from leave.	[illegible]

A5834 Wt. W4973 M687 750,000 8/16 D. D. & L. Ltd. Forms/C.2118/13.

Instructions regarding War Diaries and Intelligence Summaries are contained in F. S. Regs., Part II. and the Staff Manual respectively. Title pages will be prepared in manuscript.

WAR DIARY
or
INTELLIGENCE SUMMARY.
(Erase heading not required.)

Army Form C. 2118.

Place	Date	Hour	Summary of Events and Information	Remarks and references to Appendices

	1st August OFF	1st August ORs	31st August OFF	31st August ORs
Commanding Officers Strength	27	880	25	729
FIGHTING STRENGTH				
Officers	38		34	
Other Ranks	964		804	

TOTAL CASUALTIES for the month

	OFF.	OR
Killed and Died of Wounds	2	12
Wounded.	3	128
Missing.	-	2

[Signature] Lieut Col,
Commdg. 15th Bn HIGH. L. I.

A5834 Wt. W4973/M687 750,000 8/16 D. D. & L. Ltd. Forms/C.2118/13.

TABLE "A" TO ACCOMPANY 15th Bn. H. L. I.
OPERATION ORDER No. 38.

Serial No.	Train.	Date	Coy.	Starting Point.	Time of passing starting point.	Route.	Time train departs.	Order of march.
13	16	7th	A.B. C. H.Q. Trans. Q.M. Stores.	Entrance to A. Coys. billet.	10.45 am.	BAMBECQUE. KRUISTRAAT W.20.c.9.6. Military Rd. W.21.b.1.3. W.22.c.6. MOLENWAL.	4 p.m.	H.Q. A.B.C. Transport.
19	19	7th	D. Cooker.	BN. H.Q.	6.30 pm. 6th inst.	do:	7 p.m. 7th inst.	

<u>NOTES</u>:- (a) The strictest march discipline will be maintained on the march to and from the station.

(b) The following distances will be maintained on the march:-

Between Coys. 100 yards.
" Bns. 500 yards.
" Transport and other Units - 100 yards.
" Sections of 6 vehicles - 25 yards.

(c) 4 Pipers and 2 drummers will march with each Coy. (A.B.C. and H.Q.)

Instructions regarding War Diaries and Intelligence Summaries are contained in F. S. Regs., Part II. and the Staff Manual respectively. Title pages will be prepared in manuscript.

WAR DIARY
or
INTELLIGENCE SUMMARY.
(Erase heading not required.)

Army Form C. 2118.

14/32 15 HLI 14/32 48 35

Place	Date	Hour	Summary of Events and Information	Remarks and references to Appendices
BARLEUX	1918 Sun 1 Sept		Battalion remained in their posts in BARLEUX area with the Transport still at DENIECOURT. Weather still continues fine and very warm. Everything quiet.	[illegible]
do	Mon 2 Sept		Battalion still in the same place, the pursuit of the enemy having temporarily ceased. Exceptionally warm day.	[illegible]
do	Tues 3 Sept		During the day the Battalion by Companies marched to baths at ESTREES where the men bathed and had clean change of clothing, afterwards returning to BARLEUX. Orders were received for the Battalion to move forward and hold a line on the West Bank of the SOMME. During the night of the 3/4th "A" and "B" Companies moved forward to the position indicated.	[illegible]
BARLEUX } SOMME }	Wed 4 Sept		The positions taken up during last night and this morning were held throughout the day. Quiet day with the weather still continuing fine and warm.	[illegible]
BRIE AREA	Thurs 5 Sept		During the morning the Battalion crossed the SOMME, the crossing being made in the neighbourhood of EPERTIGNY. "D" Company were the first to cross	[illegible]

35-0
11 sheets

A5834 Wt. W4973/M687 750,000 8/16 D. D. & L. Ltd. Forms/C.2118/13.

WAR DIARY
or
INTELLIGENCE SUMMARY.
(Erase heading not required.)

Instructions regarding War Diaries and Intelligence Summaries are contained in F. S. Regs., Part II. and the Staff Manual respectively. Title pages will be prepared in manuscript.

Army Form C. 2118.

Place	Date	Hour	Summary of Events and Information	Remarks and references to Appendices
			Considerable opposition was met with from the enemy, chiefly from machine gun fire, and many hand to hand encounters took place. During the course of the fighting 54 prisoners were captured by the Battalion and several machine guns. The enemy withdrew and the Battalion took up a position in trenches about 1000 yards east of the river SOMME. The casualties sustained were practically nil. Transport advanced to VILLERS CARBONNEL	G.O.D.
BRIE AREA	Fri. Sept 6		During the succeeding day the Battalion pursued the enemy still further, finally occupying the village of BOUVINCOURT, with Battalion Headquarters established at ST. CREN. Transport advanced from VILLERS CARBONNEL and parked for the night about two kilos west of ATHIES.	G.O.D.
BOUVINCOURT	Sat. Sept 7		In the morning a move was made from BOUVINCOURT in a southerly direction to ~~[illegible]~~ TERTREE where accommodation in huts was obtained.) The Transport also advanced and rejoined the Battalion at this place. Weather very warm.	G.O.D.
TERTREE	Sun Sept 8		Church parade was held in the forenoon. 2/Lt. BROUGH rejoined from leave. Heavy showers throughout the day.	G.O.D.
do	Mon Sept 9		The day was spent in refitting the men and general cleaning up.	G.O.D.

Instructions regarding War Diaries and Intelligence Summaries are contained in F. S. Regs., Part II. and the Staff Manual respectively. Title pages will be prepared in manuscript.

WAR DIARY
or
INTELLIGENCE SUMMARY.
(Erase heading not required.)

Army Form C. 2118.

Place	Date	Hour	Summary of Events and Information	Remarks and references to Appendices
TERTREE	1918 Tues Sept 10		Very showery day. Battalion carried out training under Company arrangements. Lieut. W. J. YOUNGER rejoined from Signalling Course and took up duties as Signalling Officer. 2/Lieut. A. McCREDIE joined the Battalion for duty.	MM 6 e.D.
TERTREE	Wed Sept 11		The Battalion with Transport left the camp at TERTREE and marched to TREFCON where they occupied billets in ruined houses and huts.	MM 6 e.D.
TREFCON	Thurs Sept 12		An attack scheme which was arranged for the morning was cancelled by Brigade. Training under Company arrangements was carried out instead. Weather rather unsettled with frequent showers of rain.	MM 6 e.D.
TREFCON	Fri Sept 13		A scheme, similar to that arranged for yesterday morning, was carried out by the Battalion this morning.	MM 6 e.D.
TREFCON	Sat Sept 14		The Battalion, with transport, left TREFCON during the day and proceeded back to CORBIE area, billets for the battalion being allotted at BUSSY-LES-DAOURS. The transport went by road, leaving about 5 in the morning. The rest of the Battalion proceeded by lorries and arrived at BUSSY about 6 p.m. Excellent billets were obtained.	MM 6 e.D.

A5834 Wt. W4973/M687 750,000 8/16 D. D. & L. Ltd. Forms/C.2118/13.

Army Form C. 2118.

Instructions regarding War Diaries and Intelligence Summaries are contained in F. S. Regs., Part II. and the Staff Manual respectively. Title pages will be prepared in manuscript.

WAR DIARY
or
INTELLIGENCE SUMMARY.
(Erase heading not required.)

Place	Date	Hour	Summary of Events and Information	Remarks and references to Appendices
BUSSY-LES-DAOURS	1918 Sun Sept 15		Church parade was held in the forenoon. In the afternoon the men were paid. The weather was very fine throughout the day.	G.E.D. MM
do	Mon Sept 16		Another warm day. Orders were received during the day that the Battalion were to move off to-morrow to the front area. The transport preceded the rest of the Battn., moving off by road at 4 in the afternoon. A halt was made for the night at BAVINCOURT. Operation Order No. 42 was issued.	G.E.D. MM O.O. No. 42 (App. I) MM
do	Tue Sept 17		The Battalion embussed at 9 a.m. from DAOURS to where they marched from BUSSY. The new area just outside ATHIES was reached early in the afternoon. The Commanding Officer went to the 32nd Divisional Reception Camp at CORBIE prior to proceeding on leave on the 20th inst. Major G. Clayton, D.S.O. took over command of the Battalion.	G.E.D. MM
ATHIES	Wed Sept 18		Training under company arrangements was carried out in the forenoon. Weather very fine and warm.	G.E.D. MM
do	Thurs Sept 19		Battalion training was carried out in the forenoon. Another fine day.	G.E.D. MM

A5834 Wt. W4973 M687 750,000 8/16 D. D. & L. Ltd. Forms/C.2118/13.

Instructions regarding War Diaries and Intelligence Summaries are contained in F. S. Regs., Part II. and the Staff Manual respectively. Title pages will be prepared in manuscript.

WAR DIARY
or
INTELLIGENCE SUMMARY.
(Erase heading not required.)

Army Form C. 2118.

Place	Date	Hour	Summary of Events and Information	Remarks and references to Appendices
ATHIES	1918 Fri. Sept 20		Training by Companies was carried out in the forenoon. The afternoon was spent in recreational training, inter-company football matches being played.	6 c.D. [illegible]
do	Sat Sept 21		An attack scheme was carried out by the battalion in the forenoon in presence of the Brigadier.	6 c.D. [illegible]
do	Sun Sept 22		Church parade was held in the forenoon. In the evening orders were received that the Battalion would move forward to new area tomorrow.	6 c.D. [illegible]
do	Mon Sept 23		The Battalion moved at 11 am. to LARRIS WOOD where the men were bivouaced.	6 c.D. [illegible]
LARRIS WOOD	Tues Sept 24		The morning was spent in training, each platoon doing a platoon scheme. In the afternoon A Coy. played B. Coy at football.	6 c.D. [illegible]
do	Wed Sept 25		Battalion bathed at ATHIES. Wet day. The afternoon was spent in cleaning up.	6 c.D. [illegible]
do	Thurs Sept 26		Training was carried out till 12-30 pm. In the afternoon A Coy. again played B Coy at football.	6 c.D. [illegible]

A5834 Wt. W4973 M687 750,000 8/16 D. D. & L. Ltd. Forms/C.2118/13.

Army Form C. 2118.

Instructions regarding War Diaries and Intelligence Summaries are contained in F. S. Regs., Part II. and the Staff Manual respectively. Title pages will be prepared in manuscript.

WAR DIARY
or
INTELLIGENCE SUMMARY.

(Erase heading not required.)

Place	Date	Hour	Summary of Events and Information	Remarks and references to Appendices
LARRIS WOOD	1918 Fri. Sept. 27		Training was carried out under Company arrangements. In the afternoon the Battalion played the R.E.s at football.	Mr
LARRIS WOOD	28th		The morning was spent in preparing for the coming attack and issuing stores. At 5 pm the Batt moved to COOKER QUARRY AREA where it bivouaced for the night.	OO No 43 App II Mr
COOKER QUARRY	29th 30th	}	See attached narrative	App III Mr

A5834 Wt. W4973/M687 750,000 8/16 D. D. & L. Ltd. Forms/C.2118/13.

Instructions regarding War Diaries and Intelligence Summaries are contained in F. S. Regs., Part II. and the Staff Manual respectively. Title pages will be prepared in manuscript.

WAR DIARY
or
INTELLIGENCE SUMMARY.
(Erase heading not required.)

Army Form C. 2118.

Place	Date	Hour	Summary of Events and Information	Remarks and references to Appendices

	1st SEPT.		30th SEPT	
	OFFs	ORs	OFFs	ORs
Commanding Offr's Strength	25	724	22	640
FIGHTING STRENGTH				
Officers	34		30	
Other Ranks	811		745	

TOTAL CASUALTIES for the month

	OFFs	ORs
Killed & Died of Wounds	1	12
Wounded	2	72
Missing	.	.

[illegible] Lieut. Colonel,
Comdg. 13th Bn HIGH. L. I.

A5834 Wt. W4973/M687 750,000 8/16 D. D. & L. Ltd. Forms/C.2118/13.

Copy No.....

SECRET.

15th Bn. THE HIGHLAND LIGHT INFANTRY.

OPERATION ORDER No. 42.

App I

1. The 14th Infantry Brigade will move by bus on 17th inst. to ATHIES AREA. The Transport will move on 16th and 17th inst.

2. The Battalion Transport will leave the present billets at 3.10 p.m. today.

3. All loading must be completed by 2.30 p.m.

4. The following will be dumped at the Q.M. Stores by 1.30 p.m. without fail:-

Signal Stores.
Orderly Room boxes.
Officers valises.
Officers Mess Kit.

Only sufficient Mess Kit to last for two days is to be retained as it will have to be carried to and from the buses.

5. Coys. will retain sufficient Camp Kettles for cooking purposes.

6. Lewis Guns will be carried by the men also 12 magazines per gun.

7. Battle details will parade at the Orderly Room at 4 p.m. today to proceed to the Reception Camp. They should have their rations for 17th inst. on them. Nominal rolls to be forwarded to Orderly Roomx as soon as possible.

J.G. Stephen

Captain,

16-9-18.

A/Adjt., 15th Bn. High. L. I.

Wo 1.
Sego
Reuge
[illegible]
Yates : McEwan
Rich shavels

SECRET. Copy No......

War Diary 28/9/18 App II

15th Bn. THE HIGHLAND LIGHT INFANTRY.

OPERATION ORDER No. 43.

Reference Sheets 62c S.E., 62c N.E., & THORIGNY 1/20,000.

1. On a date to be notified later the 4th Army will attack the HINDENBURG LINE, cross the Canal and exploit its success up to the RED LINE.

2. The 11th American Division and Australian Corps will be on the left of the 9th Corps. The former, after crossing the CANAL TUNNEL at BELLECOURT will open out the breach made in the HINDENBURG LINE, and the latter will pass through and join up with the 9th Corps.

3. The 9th Corps will attack as follows:-
The 46th Division will capture the first objective - GREEN LINE, and the 32nd Division will ~~xx~~ then pass through and push forward at least as far as the RED LINE.

4. The 1st Division may exploit South of the Canal if there are signs of the enemy weakening.
The 6th Division may cross the Canal at LETRONQUOY when the RED LINE has been reached by the 32nd Division.

5. During Y/~~Night~~ night the 14th Infantry Brigade on the right and 97th Infantry Brigade on the left will move into the old trench system on the LEVERGUIER RIDGE..
Dividing line between 15th Bn. H. L. I. and 1st Dorset Regt. will be the road cutting trench system through R.5.a.0.0.
5/6th Royal Scots will assemble in CAUBRIERES Woods No. 2.

6. Route to assembly area will be POUILLY-Q.30.c.05.55.-SOYECOURT -GRANGE-R.8.a.5.8.-R.3.c.0.5.

7. Order of march - H.Q. Coy. B.C.A.D. and 1st line Transport.

8. Time of starting will be notified later.

9. On Z day the advance through the 46th Division will be carried out by 15th Bn. H. L. I. on the RIGHT, 1st Dorset Regt., on the LEFT and 5/6th Royal Scots in RESERVE.
Inter Bn. Boundary will be a line parallel to and 500 yards distant from the Canal.

10. In the advance B. Coy. will be on the LEFT, C. Coy. on the RIGHT, A. Coy. in SUPPORT and D. Coy. in RESERVE.
Bn. H.Qrs. will move in advance of D. Coy.

11. One Coy. of Tanks will operate with the 14th Infantry Brigade, three Tanks being allotted to 15th H. L. I.
It is not intended that the Infantry or Tanks should wait for one another, but when the situation developes into open warfare the Infantry should point out to the Tanks, which may be near them, any positions which are giving trouble. When the Tanks are in front of the Infantry platoon Commanders must detail parties to mop up every machine gun nest etc. which is being dealt with.

12. The following signals will be used by the Tanks to communicate with the Infantry:-
(a) Tanks to Infantry.
Green and White flag denotes COME ON.
Red and Yellow flag denotes OUT OF ACTION.
Tri coloured ~~xxxxxxx~~ flag denotes COMING BACK.

(b) Infantry to Tanks.
Helmets raised on rifles indicates - TANKS ASSISTANCE REQUIRED.

App II

NARRATIVE of EVENTS from
29th SEPTEMBER 1918 to 6th OCTOBER 1918.

About 10 a.m. on the 29th SEPTEMBER 1918, the Battalion moved forward from COOKER QUARRY Area, crossed the canal at BELLENGLISE and followed up the 46th Division till just behind the GREEN LINE. At 5.30 p.m. orders were received that the Bn. were to attack at 6 p.m. and capture the RED LINE including the Tunnel and the Trench System to the South of it.

At 6 p.m. the attack started and before progress could be made the GREEN LINE had to be captured and mopped up, three machine guns and about thirty prisoners being taken in it. B. and C. Coys. went right through the village of LE TRONQUOY and consolidated about 200 yards in advance of the RED LINE. Two platoons of A. Coy. took and consolidated the Trench System to the South of the Tunnel, while the other two platoons mopped up the Tunnel assisted by two platoons of D. Coy.

The enemy was found in very large numbers in the Tunnel and in the Trenches round it.

The whole line was captured and consolidated by 8.30 p.m. but mopping up continued all night.

On the morning of the 30th inst. the 1st Division on our right, attacked and drove about 30 of the enemy into our lines. Later about 8.30 a.m. the enemy attempted a counter attack on the left of our position but this was frustrated by Lewis Gun fire before it reached our lines.

After this counter attack had failed a day light patrol was sent out to ascertain if the enemy was in strength in the valley below our position. The patrol was fired on by two machine guns continuously from the moment it left the trench, and after going forward 200 yards was forced to retire having lost half its numbers.

During the whole of this operation the Bn. captured over 650 prisoners, 15 Howitzers and Field Guns, one Trench Mortar and 28 Machine Guns, with the loss of 3 Officers and 70 Other Ranks.

13. Tanks working with 32nd Division will be marked with a large II in Roman Figures and 32nd Divisional sign.

14. Zero hour will be notified later.

ADMINISTRATIVE PORTION.

1. (a) There will be no Brigade Dumps, the mobile reserve will be used where necessary. It will be refilled by the [illegible] section [illegible].
The Mobile Reserve will move with Bn. H.Qrs.

(b) 50 boxes of S.A.A. and 50 Lewis Gun magazines buckets have been sent to the Tank Corps to be carried forward by them. They will be dumped at [illegible] and can be drawn by Coys. when required.

RATIONS. 2. The unconsumed portion of the days rations will be carried on the man (in the mess tin) on the 29th inst. when moving off. Rations for the 30th inst. and iron rations will be carried in the haversack.

WATER. 3. The OMIGNON RIVER can be used as far as [illegible]. Forward of [illegible] wells will have to be used after being examined by the medical officer. Water carts will accompany the Battn. to the assembly position.
Mens water bottles must be full before moving today and again tomorrow by 10 a.m. without fail.

TRANSPORT. 4. (a) A Echelon 1st line Transport will accompany the Bn. tonight. It less cookers and watercarts will break off from the column and park at [illegible].
Cookers and watercarts will be left with the Bn., horses returning to [illegible].

(b) B. Echelon will be brigaded under the Brigade Transport Officer and park at [illegible].
Pack Animals will go with 1st Line Transport.

BREAKFAST. 5. Coys. will ensure that the men get a good hot meal tomorrow morning.

6. On the morning 30th inst. the following will rejoin the Bn. at an hour to be notified later;-

Lewis Gun Limbers.
Cooker Horses.
Watercart Horses.
Pack animals.
Tool wagon.
Mobile Reserve of S.A.A. and Bomb wagon.
Signal Limber.
Mess Cart Horse.
Maltese Cart.

7. All Officers valises, Signal Stores, Orderly Room Boxes will be dumped at the Q.M. STORES by 5 p.m. today.
Instructions for Mess Kits will be issued later.

8. Medical arrangements will be as follows;-
A wounded dressing station will be established at VADENCOURT CHATEAU R.11.c.1.1.
As soon as the 32nd Division crosses the Canal two advanced dressing stations will be established one of them behind each leading infantry brigade on the LEVERGIES - [illegible] and JONCOURT - [illegible] Roads respectively. When the advanced dressing stations have been established a Main Dressing Station will be established at R.11.c.1.1.

Acknowledge.

Captain,
A/Adjt., 15th Bn. High. L. I.

Instructions regarding War Diaries and Intelligence Summaries are contained in F. S. Regs., Part II. and the Staff Manual respectively. Title pages will be prepared in manuscript.

WAR DIARY
or
INTELLIGENCE SUMMARY.
(*Erase heading not required.*)

Army Form C. 2118.

15 HLI
Vol 36

Place	Date October	Hour	Summary of Events and Information	Remarks and references to Appendices
LE TRONQUOY	1st		At 4 am the battalion was relieved by the 1st Cameron Highlanders and withdrew to trenches in the vicinity of the canal tunnel in rear of the village of LE TRONQUOY. At 2.30 pm the battalion moved to positions in support to the 5th/6th Royal Scots just south of LEVERGIERS. At 4 pm the 5th/6th Royal Scots attacked the village of SEQUEHART. A Coy also advanced to join up their right flank with the 1st Division. D Coy was later sent up to assist A Coy. B and C Coys remained in reserve.	J.G.S.
SEQUEHART	2nd		During the night the enemy attacked and retook the village of SEQUEHART. ~~and~~ B & C Coys were then ordered up into close support to the ROYAL SCOTS. At 6 am that battalion again attacked SEQUEHART supported by B and C Coys. During this attack these two Coys were both reduced to roughly 20 strong, the remnants establishing themselves in and on the outskirts of the village. During the morning the enemy again counter attacked retaking the village, our line being once more established just west of the village. Major Cleghorn, 2nd Lts Pryde, Ritchie, McGill & Lt Thomson were wounded during this operation.	J.G.S.
SEQUEHART	3rd		At dawn the 1st Dorsets attacked SEQUEHART but were later caused to retire. Our patrols then finding the village to be unoccupied A and D Coys went forward and established themselves on the eastern edge of the village. That evening the enemy once more counter attacked but this failed with heavy casualties.	J.G.S.

36.0
9 sheets

A5834 Wt. W4973/M687 750,000 8/16 D. D. & L. Ltd. Forms/C.2118/13.

Army Form C. 2118.

WAR DIARY
or
INTELLIGENCE SUMMARY.
(Erase heading not required.)

Instructions regarding War Diaries and Intelligence Summaries are contained in F. S. Regs., Part II. and the Staff Manual respectively. Title pages will be prepared in manuscript.

Place	Date	Hour	Summary of Events and Information	Remarks and references to Appendices
LIAHCOURT	Fri. Oct 4 1918		The Battalion was relieved in the line by the 1st Sherwood Foresters and moved back to LIAHCOURT. The relief was carried out without any casualties being suffered by shelling.	bcg
VENDELLES	Sat Oct 5th 1918		The Battalion moved from LIAHCOURT to the vicinity of VENDELLES. Major W. WHITE, M.C., was recalled to Division	bcg
BOUVINCOURT	Sun Oct 6		The Battalion moved from VENDELLES to BOUVINCOURT to rest, arriving there at 2 p.m. in the afternoon. Brig. Gen. L.P. EVANS V.C. congratulated the Battalion on the good work they have done in the recent operations	bcg
BOUVINCOURT	Mon Oct 7		Companies carried out inspection parades etc. Lt. Col. V.B. RAMSDEN, D.S.O., M.C., returned from leave and assumed command of the 14th Brigade during the absence on leave to U.K. of Brig. Gen. L.P. EVANS, V.C. 2Lt. T.W. HEPBURN returned from leave from U.K.	bcg
do	Tues Oct 8		Battalion paraded in the forenoon and were addressed by Major General T.W. LAMBERT who thanked them for their successful fighting during the past fortnight. 2/Lt GAGE proceeded on leave to PARIS.	bcg

A5834 Wt. W4973/M687 750,000 8/16 D. D. & L. Ltd. Forms/C.2118/13.

Instructions regarding War Diaries and Intelligence Summaries are contained in F. S. Regs., Part II. and the Staff Manual respectively. Title pages will be prepared in manuscript.

WAR DIARY
or
INTELLIGENCE SUMMARY.
(Erase heading not required.)

Army Form C. 2118.

Place	Date 1918	Hour	Summary of Events and Information	Remarks and references to Appendices
BOUVINCOURT	Wed. Oct 9		Training was carried out in the forenoon under company arrangements. During the afternoon an inter-company football match was played between A and B Companies in which the former proved successful. Capt. R.B. HERBERT proceeded on leave to the U.K.	G.C.B.
do	Thurs Oct 10		In the forenoon the Battalion went for a route march. C and D Companies played a football match in the afternoon resulting in a win for D. Coy. 2/Lt. J.B. MUIR and 2/Lt. A.M. PICKEN reported to the Battalion for duty.	G.C.B.
do	Fri. Oct 11		A tactical scheme was taken part in during the forenoon. The afternoon was spent in recreational training. 2/Lt J. McEWAN reported to the Battalion for duty. Notification was received of the promotion to the rank of Capt. of Lt. B.C. FLETCHER and 2/Lt. T.W. HEPBURN, M.C.	G.C.B.
do	Sat Oct 12		The forenoon was again spent in carrying out a tactical scheme. Wet weather interfered with the recreational training in the afternoon.	G.C.B.

A5834 Wt. W4973/M687 750,000 8/16 D. D. & L. Ltd. Forms/C.2118/13.

Instructions regarding War Diaries and Intelligence Summaries are contained in F. S. Regs., Part II. and the Staff Manual respectively. Title pages will be prepared in manuscript.

WAR DIARY
or
INTELLIGENCE SUMMARY.
(Erase heading not required.)

Army Form C. 2118.

Place	Date	Hour	Summary of Events and Information	Remarks and references to Appendices
BOUVINCOURT	1918 Sun. Oct 13		Church parade was held in the forenoon. Lt. E. LYALL reported to the Battalion for duty and was posted to A. Coy.	bcg
do	Mon. Oct 14		Practice in attack formation was carried out in the forenoon. Notification of promotion to the rank of Major was received in the case of Capt. J.F. MUIR M.C.	bcg
do	Tues. Oct 15		Training under company arrangements was carried out in the forenoon. In the afternoon a Rugby football match was played between teams of the 14th and 97th Bdes. in which the former proved successful. An enjoyable concert was held by A. Coy. in their billet.	bcg
do	Wed. Oct 16		A tactical scheme was arranged and carried out during the forenoon. The afternoon was spent in recreational training. C. Coy. organised a concert which was successfully ~~arranged~~ held in the evening.	bcg

Instructions regarding War Diaries and Intelligence Summaries are contained in F. S. Regs., Part II. and the Staff Manual respectively. Title pages will be prepared in manuscript.

WAR DIARY
or
INTELLIGENCE SUMMARY.
(Erase heading not required.)

Army Form C. 2118.

Place	Date	Hour	Summary of Events and Information	Remarks and references to Appendices
BOUVINCOURT	1918 Thurs Oct. 17		The Battalion went for a route march in the forenoon. In the evening orders were received from Brigade that the Battalion, along with the rest of the Brigade group, were to move from their present billets to BELLENGLISE.	6 e.g.
BELLENGLISE	Fri. Oct. 18		According to orders the Battalion left BOUVINCOURT at 9-30 a.m. and marched to new area at BELLENGLISE, a distance of 12 kilos. BELLENGLISE was reached about 4 p.m. Accommodation was found in old German trenches and dugouts. The weather was fine during the day.	6 e.g.
do	Sat. Oct 19		The day was spent in cleaning up and resting. The day kept fine till the evening when some rain fell. Orders were received from Brigade for another move forward to-morrow to BOHAIN. 2/Lt. GAGE returned from leave in PARIS. Capt. J.R. ROBERTSON, M.C. returned from leave to U.K.	6 e.g.
BOHAIN	Sun. Oct 20		The Battalion left BELLENGLISE at 9 a.m. and marched to BOHAIN which was reached about 4-30 p.m. The day was very wet which made the marching very heavy. Excellent accommodation was found in the town. Lt. A.W. CAVE, and Lt. W.J. YOUNGER and 2/Lt GAGE proceeded on leave to U.K	6 e.g.

Instructions regarding War Diaries and Intelligence Summaries are contained in F. S. Regs., Part II. and the Staff Manual respectively. Title pages will be prepared in manuscript.

WAR DIARY
or
INTELLIGENCE SUMMARY.
(Erase heading not required.)

Army Form C. 2118.

Place	Date 1918	Hour	Summary of Events and Information	Remarks and references to Appendices
BOHAIN	Mon Oct. 21		The morning was spent in cleaning up. In the afternoon the Battalion along with the rest of the Brigade was paraded and medal ribbons were presented to the various recipients of awards in the recent fighting.	[illegible]
do	Tues Oct 22		The Battalion went out in the forenoon to carry out an attack scheme but owing to heavy rain the practice had to be abandoned and the men returned to their billets. The weather cleared up in the afternoon.	[illegible]
do	Wed. Oct 23		Some shelling of the town took place in the early morning but no damage was done to the area occupied by the Battalion. A tactical scheme was carried out during the forenoon. Lt. Col. V. B. RAMSDEN, D.S.O., M.C., resumed command of the Battn. on the return from leave of Brig. Gen. L. P. EVANS, V.C. Lt. J. W. M. PATERSON and Lt. J. B. PATON reported to the Battn. for duty.	[illegible]
do	Thurs Oct 24		Training under company arrangement was carried out during the forenoon. In the evening a Battalion concert was held in the local cinema theatre. The entertainment proved most successful. There was some shelling of the town at night but no damage was done.	[illegible]

A5834 Wt. W4973/M687 750,000 8/16 D. D. & L. Ltd. Forms/C.2118/13.

Instructions regarding War Diaries and Intelligence Summaries are contained in F. S. Regs., Part II. and the Staff Manual respectively. Title pages will be prepared in manuscript.

WAR DIARY
or
INTELLIGENCE SUMMARY.
(Erase heading not required.)

Army Form C. 2118.

Place	Date 1918	Hour	Summary of Events and Information	Remarks and references to Appendices
BOHAIN	Fri. Oct 25		Commanding Officer's parade was held in the morning. The rest of the forenoon was spent in Company training. Lt. HODSON and 2/Lt. M BARR reported for duty and were posted to A and C Company respectively.	[illegible]
do	Sat. Oct 26		A tactical scheme was arranged and carried out in the forenoon. In the afternoon the Battn. played the 10th A+S.H at football. The match resulted in a win for the 10th A+S.H by two goals to none.	[illegible]
do	Sun Oct 27		Church parade was held in the forenoon. The weather remains fine but rather cold.	[illegible]
do	Mon. Oct 28		The Battn. went for a route march in the forenoon. Night operations were held in the evening.	[illegible]
do	Tues. Oct. 29		Training under Company arrangements was carried out in the forenoon. In the afternoon orders were received that the Battalion was to move from BOHAIN to ST. SOUPLET.	[illegible]

Instructions regarding War Diaries and Intelligence Summaries are contained in F. S. Regs., Part II. and the Staff Manual respectively. Title pages will be prepared in manuscript.

WAR DIARY
or
INTELLIGENCE SUMMARY.
(Erase heading not required.)

Army Form C. 2118.

Place	Date 1918	Hour	Summary of Events and Information	Remarks and references to Appendices
ST. SOUPLET	Wed Oct 30		The Battalion along with the rest of the Brigade group left BOHAIN and marched to ST. SOUPLET where they remained during the night.	[illegible]
LE QUENOPLET	Thurs Oct 31		The Battalion, less transport, left their billets at ST. SOUPLET and marched to LE QUENOPLET Farm, 2000 yards N.E. of ST. SOUPLET, where they relieved the 9th Norfolks. The Commanding Officer along with Company Commanders reconnoitred the front area.	[illegible]

A5834 Wt. W4973/M687 750,000 8/16 D. D. & L. Ltd. Forms/C.2118/13.

Instructions regarding War Diaries and Intelligence Summaries are contained in F. S. Regs., Part II. and the Staff Manual respectively. Title pages will be prepared in manuscript.

WAR DIARY
or
INTELLIGENCE SUMMARY.
(Erase heading not required.)

Army Form C. 2118.

Place	Date	Hour	Summary of Events and Information	Remarks and references to Appendices

	1st OCT		31st OCT.	
	Off	ORs	OFF	ORs
Commanding Officer's Strength	22	664	23	573
FIGHTING STRENGTH				
Officers	30		35	
Other Ranks	774		437	

TOTAL CASUALTIES for the month

	OFF	ORs
Killed & Died of Wounds	.	32
Wounded	6	151
Missing	.	4

W Wanosk[?] Lieut. Col.
Comm'dg. 15/HIGH. L. I.

A5834 Wt. W4973/M687 750,000 8/16 D. D. & L. Ltd. Forms/C.2118/13.

War Diary

Appendix IV

Copy........

THE 15th BN. HIGHLAND LIGHT INFANTRY.

Operation Order No. 15 A.

Reference Sheet 27 1/40,000 and special enlargements issued.

1. INFORMATION.
(1) The enemy is holding strongly a line running through B.23.d.4.4 - B.24.c.3.2. - B.24.d.5.5. - C.19.c. central, with an advanced crater line through B.29 central and B.30 central approx.
(2) Enemy concrete strong points are known to exist at B.3o.a.2.0. B.30.a.6.6. b.24.c.9.2.
(3) This advanced defended Zone is held by approx. 2 Coys. a third is held in support at B.24.c.1.9.

2. INTENTION.
(1) The 14th Infantry Brigade in co-operation with Brigades on either flank will attack on a four Battalion frontage, the enemy's position and establish itself ultimately on a GREEN LINE running from B.24.a.1.1. - C.9.8. to C.19.b.7.4.
(2) The 15th H. L. I. will attack on the left of the Brigade frontage and will consolidate finally on the GREEN LINE from B.24.a.1.1. - B.24.c.9.8.

3. OBJECTIVES.
The first objective.
A line running from B.30,a.0.9. - 9.7. BLUE LINE (2
2nd Objective
A line running from B.24a.1.11 - c.9.8. (GREEN LINE)

4. DISTRIBUTION.
(a) "C" and "D" Coys. will capture the 1st objective, each Coy. occupying 200 yards frontage.
(b) "A" and "B" Coys. will capture the 2nd Objective.

5. ASSEMBLY.
"C" and "D" Coys. will assemble on a tape line running from B.30.c.0.8. - c.9.4.
"A" and "B" Coys. will assemble 50 yards in rear of above line

6. FORMING UP
(1) "C" and "D" Coys.
Will form up ("C" on left and "D" on right on a 2 platoon frontage Each platoon frontage will be covered by 2 half sections (i.e. extended to about 14 paces) the remaining half of those sections will be formed up 5 yards in rear and will cover the intervening spaces.
The remaining sections of these leading platoons will be formed up on sections columns 5 yards in rear of the line in front at 40 yards in terval.
The remaining platoons will be formed up in rear of each attacking platoon in section columns at 5 yards distance and 40 yards interval. Each half platoon forming the 3rd and 4th line in rear of each respective front line platoon
(2) "A" COy. will form up in rear of "C" Coy.
"B" Coy. will form up in rear of "D" Coy.
Each Coy. will form up in half platoon columns at 30 yards interval, and each platoon at 10 yards distance.
(i.e. each Coy. will form a 3rd and 4th Supporting Line for each attacking front line Coy).

7. METHOD OF ATTACK.
"C" and "D" Coys. will capture and consolidate the BLUE LINE.
"A" and "B" Coys. will leap-frog "C" and "D" Coys. on the BLUE LINE.

BLUE LINE and capture and consolidate the GREEN LINE, for which purpose the creeping barrage will form a protective barrage for 15 minutes at 100 yards in front of th e BLUE LINE.

8. RESPONSIBILITY.

The front platoons of "C" Coy, will be responsible for the capture of the strong points at B.30,a.2.0. and B.30.a.0.6. The sections detailed for the capture of the latter strong points will consolidate it. The platoons of "B" Coy. detailed to capture the strong point at B.24.c.9.1. will consolidate it. Throughout the advance the leading platoons will rush any opposition which may unexpectedly arise.

9. ARTILLERY TIMETABLE.

At Zero (i.e. 9.30 a.m.) and intense shrapnel barrage will commence under cover of which the whole Battalion will move forward as close to the barrage as possible. After the barrage has crept forward 100 yards lines will open out to the usual distance.

The barrage will creep forward at the rate of 4 minutes per 100 yards.

At Zero plus 25 minutes the barrage will remain 100 yards in front of the 1st objective for 15 minutes. (to demonstrate this white ground flares will be lit)

At Zero plus 38 minutes the barrage will commence to move forward at the same rate until Zero plus 62 when it will lift 100 yards and form a protective for ¾ hour (imaginary)

10 MACHINE GUNS.

One section of 14th Coy. M.G. Coy. will co-operate. O.C. section will arrange to subject the farm buildings in B.24c.1.9. to heavy fire throughout the operation.

Two mobile guns will g o forward with the attacking troops.

11. CONSOLIDATION.

Each objective must be consolidated in depth. The Coys. responsible for the consolidation of the first objective will immediately with draw at least one platoon to about 200 yards in rear. These platoons will be held in readiness as immediat e counter-counter attacking troops.

Sections must be told off to consolidate definite strong points . All other troops will be withdrawn to meet any contingency.

All Lewis Gun sections must be told off to definite strong points to break up counter attacks.

12. COMMUNICATIONS.

TAPES. Tapes must be laid out during the advance to Coy. Hdqrs.
RUNNERS Forward Relay Posts will be established at B.30c.8.8. and B.3 0.a.0.5

Each Coy. will send 2 runners to above posts.

SIGNALS. SHUTTER COMMUNICATION will be established whenever possible. Lines (for practice) will be laid from Coy. Hdqrs to Bn. Hdqrs. and to Brigade Forward Station.

13. HDQRS.

Bn. Hdqrs. at Zero at B.30.c1.0.
"C" Coys. hdqrs. after first Objective has be gained at B.30 a.3.6
"D" Coys. " " " " " " " B.30 a.7.5.
Bn. Hdqrs. " " " " B.30.a.8 .2.
"A" Coys. Hdqrs.-after 2nd Objective " " B.24.c.3.7.
"B" Coy. " " " " " " B.24 c.8.5.
Bn. Hd qrs. " " " " " B.30.a.8.2.
Brigade Forward Station B.29.d.5.5.

14. WATCHES. To be synchronized at 8.45 a.m.

15. REPORTS.
Every $\frac{1}{4}$ hour to Bn. Hdqrs. by runner and visual.

16. ACKNOWLEDGE.

NOTE.
(1) Coys. must keep close liaison with troops on either flank. (imaginary)
(2) There will be an enemy.

R M Grant
Captain,
A/Adjt. 15th Bn. High. L.I.

Appendix I

TRAINING PROGRAMME for Thursday 1st November 1917.

Coys.	Time	Nos on parade	Nature of Training	Locality	Remarks.
All Cos. & Hdqrs.	6.45 - 7.15 am.	22 Off. 700 O.R.	B.F.	Billets.	
Bn.	10-1 pm.		Bn. Attack Scheme	Area H.5.	Co-operation of Vickers & T.M. Btys. Scheme to be submitted later.

R M Grant Captn & Adjt
for Lieut-Colonel,
Commanding 15th Bn. High. L. I.

TRAINING PROGRAMME FOR FRIDAY 2nd November 1917.

Coys.	Time	Nos on parade.	Nature of Training	Locality	Remarks.

B R I G A D E   O P E R A T I O N S.

R M Grant Captn & Adjt
for Lieut-Colonel,
Commanding 15th Bn. High. L. I.

TRAINING PROGRAMME for Saturday 3rd November 1917.

Coys.	Time	Nos on parade.	Nature of Training	Locality	Remarks.
	Battalion Route March.				Route to be submitted later.

R M Grant Capt & Adj
for Lieut-Colonel,
Commanding 15th Bn. High. L. I.

Appendix II

15th Bn The Highland Light Infantry.

TRAINING PROGRAMME for Monday 5th November 1917.

Coys.	Time.	Nature of Training	Locality	Remarks.
Bn.	6.45 - 7.15 a.m.	P.T.	Billets	
"A" & "B" Coys.	9.30 - 10.30 a.m.	Platoon Training Platoons in attack on strong points.	B.29.c.24	2 Platoons attacking. 2 Platoons watching in each case
"C" & "D" Coys.	"	do:	B.28.d.central.	
	10.30 - 11 a.m.	Coy. Commanders criticisms.		
"A" & "B" Coys.	11 a.m. 12.30 p.m.	Coys. in attack on Strong Points.	do:	Each Coy. to attack 2 Strong Points. affiliated Coy. to find barrage, and counter-attack party & counter-counter attacking troops
"C" & "D" Coys.	do:	do:		do:
"A" & "B" Coys. Off. & N.C.Os.	5.30 - 6.30. p.m.	Lecture.		Coy. Schemes on model.

Lieut-Colonel,
Commanding 15th Bn. Highland L. I.

15th Bn. THE HIGHLAND LIGHT INFANTRY.

TRAINING PROGRAMME for Tuesday 6th November 1917.

Coys.	Time	Nature of Training	Locality	Remarks.
Bn.	6.45 – 7.15 a.m.	B.F.	Billets	
Bn.	9.15 a.m.	Rendezvous at B.29.d.7.7. (a) Drill deployment for attack formation on taped line		
	12.30 pm.	(b) Bn. in attack on enemy position organised in depth. (c) Repetition.	B.30.c.	
"C" & "D" Coys. Off.& N.C.Os.	5.30 – 6.30 pm.	Coy. Schemes on model.		

[signature]

Lieut-Colonel,
Commanding 15th Bn. Highland L. I.

15th Bn. THE HIGHLAND LIGHT INFANTRY.

TRAINING PROGRAMME for Wednesday 7th November 1917.

Coys.	Time.	Nature of Training	Locality	Remarks.
Bn.	9 a.m. 12 noon.	Route March.	Route to be submitted later.	Dress F.S.M.O.

[signature]

Lieut-Colonel,
Commanding 15th Bn. Highland L. I.

15th Bn. THE HIGHLAND LIGHT INFANTRY.

TRAINING PROGRAMME for Thursday 8th. November 1917.

Coys.	Time.	Nature of Training	Locality	Remarks.
Bn.	6.45 am. 7.15 am.	B.F.	Billets	
"A" Coy.	9 - 1 pm.	Musketry. Close Order Drill Gas Drill. Extended Order Drill.	Billets.	
"B","C" & "D" Coys.	9.15 am. 10 am.	Coy. Close Order Drill		
	10.10 am. 10.30 am.	Gas Drill.		
	10.30 - 11 a.m.	Extended Order Drill.	B.30.a.	
	11.15 - 12 noon.	Open warfare Formations		
	12.10 - 1 p.m.	Open warfare Drill. Attack Practice.		
Bn.	6 p.m. 10. p.m.	Night Operations (a) Rendesvous (b) Forming up in Gas Helmets on a taped line.	B.30.a.5.5. B.30.c.8.5. 48.	Platoons to march to rendesvous on a compass bearing.

REGIMENTAL CLASSES:-

SIGNALLERS under Bn. Signalling Officer.

LEWIS GUNNERS under Lewis Gun Officer.

ALL

(1) Stoppages and Mechanism 1 hour.
(2) Immediate Action 1 "
(3) Tactical Handling 1 "

[illegible]
Lieut-Colonel.
Commanding 15th Bn. Highland L. I.

15th. Bn. HIGHLAND LIGHT INFANTRY.

TRAINING PROGRAMME FOR FRIDAY 9th. November 1917.

Coys.	Time.	Nature of Training.	Locality.	Remarks.
Battn.	6.45 a.m.- 7.15 a.m.	P.T.	Billets.	
Battn.	9.30 a.m. - 12.30 p.m.	(a) Battn deploying from Col. of route into Attack formation. (b) Battn in Attack on enemy position organised in depth.	B.24.c.	
All Officers.	5.30 p.m.	War Game in Model.	Hd.Qrs.	

Captain,
A/Adjt. for O/C. 15/H.L.I.

15th. Bn. HIGHLAND LIGHT INFANTRY.

TRAINING PROGRAMME for SATURDAY, 10th. November 1917.

Coys.	Time.	Nature of Training.	Locality.	Remarks.
Battn.	6.45 a.m. -7.15 a.m.	P.T.	Billets.	
"B" Co.	9 a.m. - 1 p.m.	Musketry.	?	
"A", "C" & "D" Cos.	9.15 a.m - 10.15 a.m.	Ceremonial.	B.3.d.Central.	
	10.15 a.m.- 10.45 a.m.	March to Area. Practice Advanced Guard and Rear Guard Formations.	B.5.a.	
	11 a.m. - 12.15 p.m.	Movements in Open Warfare Formation.		

Captain,
A/Adjt. for O/C., 15/H.L.I.

SECRET. Appendix III Copy No........

War Diary

15th Bn. THE HIGHLAND LIGHT INFANTRY.

Operation Order No. 16 A.

Reference Sheet 27 1/40,000 & Sketch Map attached special enlargement of B.29 & 30.

---

1. INFORMATION.
   (a) As a result of our operations during the last few weeks the enemy has been driven back from his main defensive positions, and now holding a series of shell-hole positions, disposed in depth, and supported by numerous Strong Points, roughly on the line WOLMERINCKHOVE – WORMHOUDT.
   (b) In conjunction with "X" Division on the right and "Y" Division on the left, the 32nd Division will attack and capture the enemy's position on a front of 1,600 yards from the railway in B.30.d. to HARDROOCKSTRAATE (B.29.c.) and to a depth of 750 yards.
   (c) Enemy strong points known to exist are located in right Bn. frontage at B.30.c.4.5., 80.85., a.60.25 a.1.3.

2. INTENTION.
   (1) The 14th Infantry Brigade with one Battalion "Z" Brigade attached, will attack at Zero hour on "Z" day, enemy's position from about the WINDMILL in B.30.d. to H.5.a. central.
   Only two Battalions will take part in the attack.
   Remaining troops are imaginary.
   (2) The 15th H.L.I will attack the enemy's position from B.30.d.1.2. – B.30.c.5.0.

3. OBJECTIVES.
   1st Objective. The area B.30.d.1.2. – B.30.a.8.2. – B.30.c.2.8. – B.30.c.5.0. and the Green Line inclusive on a frontage of 370 yards.
   2nd Objective. The area B.30.a.8.2. – B.30.a.6.8. – B.29.b.9.4. – B.30.c.2.8. and the RED LINE inclusive on a frontage of 370 yards.
   For objectives see also Sketch "A" attached.

4. DISTRIBUTION OF TROOPS.
   (a) The 15th H. L. I. will attack on the right and 1st Dorsets on the left.
   (b) Troops to capture 1st Objective.
   "A" and "B" Coys. will capture the GREEN LINE from B.30.a.8.2. to B.30.c.2.8. and the area B.30.d.1.2. – B.30.a.8.2. – B.30.c.2.8. – B.30.c.5.0. Frontage of attack 370 yards.
   (c) Troops to capture 2nd Objective.
   "C" and "D" Coys. will capture the RED LINE from B.30.a.6.8. to B.29.b.9.4. and the area B.30.a.8.2. – B.30.a.6.8. – B.29.b.9.4. – B.30.c.2.8. Frontage 370 yards.
   (d) The dividing line between the Battalion and the 1st Dorsets on the LEFT will be B.30.c.5.0. – B.30.c.2.8. – B.29.b.9.4. as shewn on Sketch "A".

5. FORMING UP.
   The Battalion will form up "A" on the left "B" on right, "C" behind "A" "D" behind "B" on a taped line by Zero – 20 minutes in the usual formation as per Sketch already issued, the leading wave on a line from B.30.d.2.3. – B.30.c.5.0. Each attacking Coy. will form up on 185 yards frontage. The leapfrogging Coys. i.e. "C" and "D" Coys. will form up 100 yards in rear of the rear lines of their front line Coys.

6. DIRECTION OF ADVANCE.

General direction of the advance will be N.E.N.

7. METHOD OF ATTACK.

At Zero the Battalion will advance maintaining as nearly as possible their original formation of assembly , the leading waves following closely under the barrage. Artillery barrage table is attached A.P.F. 2.

The leading Coys. will reach the 1st OBJECTIVE at Zero plus 17 at which time the leap-frogging Coys. "C" and "D" will continue their advance until they reach the line of the 1st OBJECTIVE which will be at Zero plus 21 minutes. They will immediately extend into their attacking formation and be prepared to carry on the advance at Zero plus 23.

NOTE.

"C" and "D" Coys. must move as quickly as possible from Zero plus 17 as they have to travel 190 yards and get extended in 6 minutes. During this interval the barrage will be placed 100 yards in front of the GREEN LINE.

To show Coys. when they have reached their 1st OBJECTIVE coloured smoke (represented by white flares on the line of the objective) will be interspersed with the barrage.

At Zero plus 23 "C" and "D" Coys. will continue the advance to the RED LINE which will be reached at Zero plus 34 minutes.

8. RESPONSIBILITY.

The right leading section of left platoon "A" Coy. supported by 1 section will capture mop up and consolidate the strong point at B.30.c.4.5.

The left leading section of right platoon "B" Coy. supported by 1 section will capture mop up and consolidate the strong point at B.30.c.80.85.

The left leading section of right platoon "D" Coy. supported by 1 section will capture mop up and consolidate the strong point at B.30.a.60.25.

The right leading section of left platoon "C" Coy. supported by 1 section will capture mop up and consolidate the strong point at B.30.a.1.3.

In each of the above instances 1 section only will be left to garrison and consolidate the posts, the 2nd sections will immediately form up and follow up the barrage or remainder of its Coy.

Any unknown strong points which may become disclosed will be immediately rushed by the leading waves. All gaps found in the general line must be immediately filled in by sections in rear working round the flank of the strong points, and forming up under the barrage.

9. CONSOLIDATION.

Consolidation of both objectives will be carried out in depth.

10. ACTION ON REACHING THE OBJECTIVE.

As soon as an objective is secured the Coy. detailed for its capture will tell off sufficient troops to hold it against counter attacks, remainder, at least 1 platoon will be withdrawn and held in readiness in some selected place to meet any eventuality.

Two Mobile Vickers Guns will be placed in each of the strong points, B.30.a.60.25. and B.30.a.1.3. O.C. "A" and "B" Coys. will detail one Lewis Gun for each of the strong points B.30.c4.5. and B.30.c.80.85.

At least two other Lewis Guns should be placed in the front line of each Coy. frontage, one being held in reserve.

11. MACHINE GUNS.
4 (FOUR) Vickers Guns will be attached to the Battalion.
These will form up in rear of "C" and "D" Coys. respectively in pairs and will closely follow their Coys. and will eventually establish themselves in pairs at S.P.'s B.30.a.60.25. and B.30.a.1.3.
2 Machine Guns will barrage points in rear of the 2nd Objective. When this has been gained two of the above guns will take up a position in the vicinity of the WINDMILL and await opportunity.

12. STOKES GUNS.
Four Stokes Guns will support the attack of the Battalion. 1 section i.e. 2 guns will form up in the centre behind "A" and "B" Coys. and will keep close touch with the O.C. Coys. concerned. 1 section(2 guns)will form up in the centre ~~xx~~ behind "C" and "D" Coys. and will keep close touch with the O.C. Coys. concerned. Both sections will be ready to give immediate support to the attack in ~~xxx~~ case of necessity.

13. DRESS.
Battle Order. Packs will be carried in place of the haversack on the back. 20 shovels per Coy. will be carried. Each man will carry 2 days rations (imaginary) and the iron rations in the pack.
S.A.A. and Bombs will be carried as follows:-

	S.A.A.	Bombs.	Rifle Grenades.
Riflemen.	220	1	-
Bombers.	220	2	-
Rifle Bombers.	170	1	6
Lewis Gunners.	70 S.A.A. and 4 Lewis Gun Magazines		

(additional ammunition will be imaginary for this exercise)

14. COMMUNICATIONS. The Brigade Signalling Officer will arrange for
Wire (a) communication from Brigade FORWARD Station - Bn. Hq.
Brigade FORWARD Station ~~xxxx~~ will move forward with the rear waves and establish an advanced Report Centre at B.30.c.2.5.
The Battalion Signalling Officer will be responsible for maintaining communication between the ~~xxxxxx~~ Command post and the advanced Report Centre after the first objective has been captured.
(b) For the sake of practice wires will be laid from Bn. Command Post to Coy. Hqrs.
SHUTTER COMMUNICATION to Bn. Hqrs. will be practiced.
Tapes. During the advance men must be told off to lay tapes to Coy.Hqrs
Runners. FORWARD RELAY POSTS will be established at B.30.a.4.1. and B.30.a.55.50.

15. LIAISON. O.C. "A" Coy. will detail 1 Cpl. and 4 men for Liaison with 1st Dorsets along road in B.30.d. central.

16. WATCHES. O.C. Signals will arrange to synchronise watches at 7 a.m. "Z" day.

17. REPORTS. Reports to Bn. Hdqrs. at Zero - 15 and every hour subsequently

18. HDQRS.

Advanced Brigade Hdqrs.	H.6.c.7.9.
Bn. Hdqrs.	H.6.b.8.3.
1st Dorsets.	H.5.d.8.9.
Bde. FORWARD Station.	B.30.c.1.3.
Bn. C. P.	B.30.a.5.5.
"A" Coy. Hdqrs.	B.30.c.35.70.
"B" Coy. "	B.30.c.75.95.
"C" Coy. "	B.30.a.1.3.
"D" Coy. "	B.30.a.5.2.

19. ZERO 10.30 a.m.
20. ACKNOWLEDGE.

Captain,
A/Adjt. 15th Bn. High. L. I.

Appendix V

Fil

~~30~~

War Diary

Copy........

THE 15th BN. HIGHLAND LIGHT INFANTRY.

Operation Order No. 15 [illegible].

Reference Sheet 37 1/40,000 and special enlargements issued.

---

1. **INFORMATION.**
   (1) The enemy is holding strongly a line running through B.23.d.4.4 - B.24.c.3.2. - B.24.d.5.5. - C.19.c. central, with an advanced crater line through B.29 central and B.30 central approx.
   (2) Enemy concrete strong points are known to exist at B.30.a.2.0. B.30.a.6.6. B.24.c.9.2.
   (3) This advanced defended Zone is held by approx. 2 Coys. a third is held in support at B.24.c.1.9.

2. **INTENTION.**
   (1) The 14th Infantry Brigade in co-operation with Brigades on either flank will attack on a four Battalion frontage, the enemy's position and establish itself ultimately on a GREEN LINE running from B.24.a.1.1. - C.9.8. to C.19.b.7.4.
   (2) The 15th H. L. I. will attack on the left of the Brigade frontage and will consolidate finally on the GREEN LINE from B.24.a.1.1. - B.24.c.9.8.

3. **OBJECTIVES.**
   The first objective.
   A line running from B.30.a.0.9. - 9.7. BLUE LINE (2
   2nd Objective
   A line running from B.24a.1.1. - c.9.8. (GREEN LINE)

4. **DISTRIBUTION.**
   (a) "C" and "D" Coys. will capture the 1st objective, each Coy. occupying 200 yards frontage.
   (b) "A" and "B" Coys. will capture the 2nd Objective.

5. **ASSEMBLY.**
   "C" and "D" Coys. will assemble on a tape line running from B.30.c.0.8. - c.9.4.
   "A" and "B" Coys. will assemble 50 yards in rear of above line

6. **FORMING UP**
   (1) "C" and "D" Coys.
   Will form up ("C" on left and "D" on right on a 2 platoon frontage Each platoon frontage will be covered by 2 half sections (i.e. extended to about 14 paces) the remaining half of those sections will be formed up 5 yards in rear and will cover the intervening spaces.
   The remaining sections of these leading platoons will be formed up on sections columns 5 yards in rear of the line in front at 40 yards in terval.
   The remaining platoons will be formed up in rear of each attacking platoon in section columns at 5 yards distance and 40 yards interval. Each half platoon forming the 3rd and 4th line in rear of each respective front line platoon
   (2) "A" Coy. will form up in rear of "C" Coy.
   "B" Coy. will form up in rear of "D" Coy.
   Each Coy. will form up in half platoon columns at 30 yards interval, and each platoon at 10 yards distance.
   (i.e. each Coy. will form a 3rd and 4th Supporting Line for each attacking front line Coy).

7. **METHOD OF ATTACK.**
   "C" and "D" Coys. will capture and consolidate the BLUE LINE.
   "A" and "B" Coys. will leap-frog "C" and "D" Coys. on the BLUE LINE.

Duplicate
copy.

BLUE LINE and capture and consolidate the GREEN LINE, for which purpose the creeping barrage will form a protective barrage for 15 minutes at 100 yards in front of the BLUE LINE.

8. RESPONSIBILITY.

The front platoons of "C" Coy, will be responsible for the capture of the strong points at B.30.a.2.0. and B.30.a.0.6. The sections detailed for the capture of the latter strong points will consolidate it. The platoons of "B" Coy. detailed to capture the strong point at B.24.c.9.1. will consolidate it. Throughout the advance the leading platoons will rush any oppositions which may unexpectedly arise.

9. ARTILLERY TIMETABLE.

At Zero (i.e. 9.30 a.m.) and intense shrapnel barrage will commence under cover of which the whole Battalion will move forward as close to the barrage as possible. After the barrage has crept forward 100 yards lines will open out to the usual distance.

The barrage will creep forward at the rate of 4 minutes per 100 yards. At Zero plus 25 minutes the barrage will remain 100 yards in front of the 1st objective for 15 minutes. (to demonstrate this white ground flares will be lit)

At Zero plus 38 minutes the barrage will commence to move forward at the same rate until Zero plus 62 when it will lift 100 yards and form a protective for ½ hour (imaginary)

10 MACHINE GUNS.

One section of 14th Coy. M.G. Coy. will co-operate. O.C. section will arrange to subject the farm buildings in B.24c.1.9. to heavy fire throughout the operation.

Two mobile guns will go forward with the attacking troops.

11. CONSOLIDATION.

Each objective must be consolidated in depth. The Coys. responsible for the consolidation of the first objective will immediately with draw at least one platoon to about 200 yards in rear. These platoons will be held in readiness as immediate counter-counter attacking troops.

Sections must be told off to consolidate definite strong points. All other troops will be withdrawn to meet any contingency.

All Lewis Gun sections must be told off to definite strong points to break up counter attacks.

12. COMMUNICATIONS.

TAPES. Tapes must be laid out during the advance to Coy. Hd qrs.

RUNNERS Forward Relay Posts will be established at B.30c.8.8. and B.30.a.0.5

Each Coy. will send 2 runners to above posts.

SIGNALS. SHUTTER COMMUNICATION will be established whenever possible. Lines (for practice) will be laid from Coy. Hd qrs to Bn. Hdqrs. and to Brigade Forward Station.

13. HDQRS.

Bn. Hdqrs. at Zero at B.30.c1.0.		
"C" Coys. hdqrs. after first Objective has been gained	at	B.30 a.3.(
"D" Coys.	"	B.30 a.7.5.
Bn. Hdqrs.	"	B.30.a.8 .2.
"A" Coys. Hdqrs. after 2nd Objective	"	B.24.c.3.7.
"B" Coy.	"	B.24 c.8.5.
Bn. Hd qrs.	"	B.30.a.8.2.
Brigade Forward Station		B.29.d.5.5.

14. WATCHES. To be synchronized at 8.45 a.m.

15. REPORTS.
Every ¼ hour to Bn. Hdqrs. by runner and visual.

16. ACKNOWLEDGE.

NOTE.
(1) Coys. must keep close liaison with troops on either flank. (imaginary)
(2) There will be an enemy.

R M Grant
Captain,
A/Adjt. 15th Bn. High. L.I.

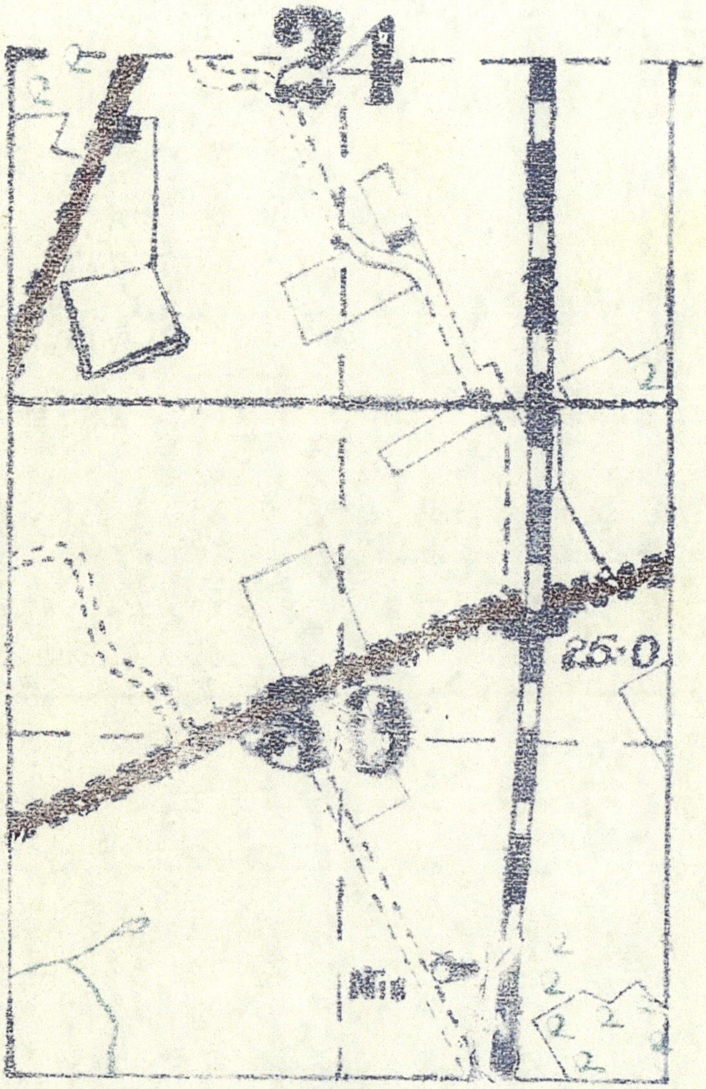

B

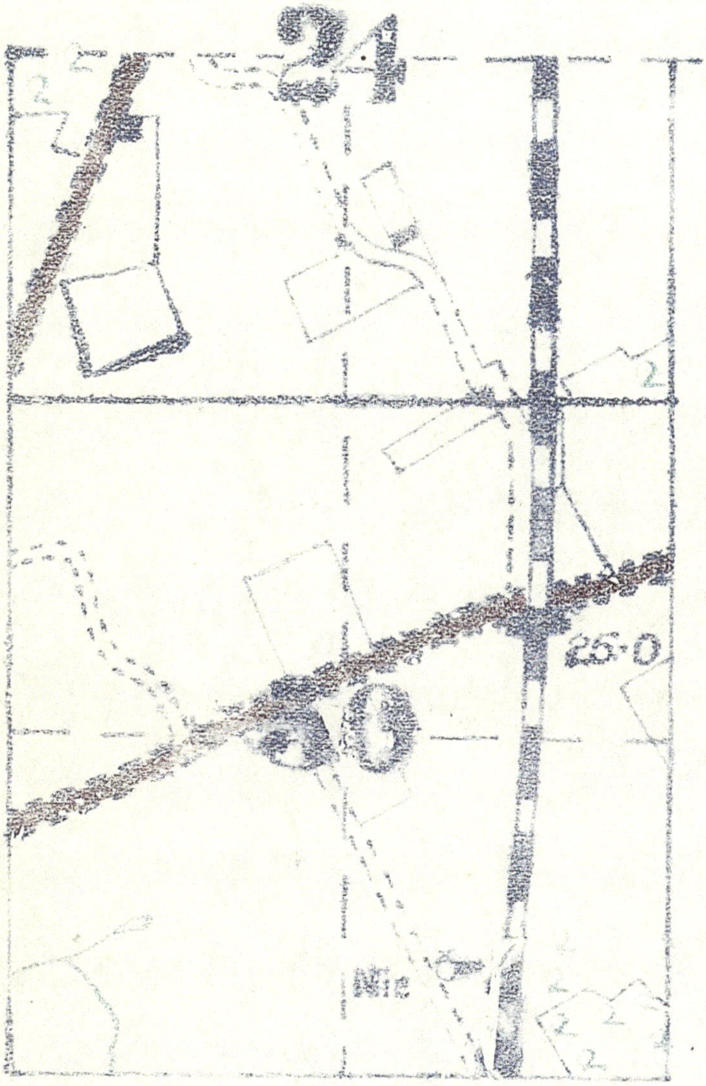

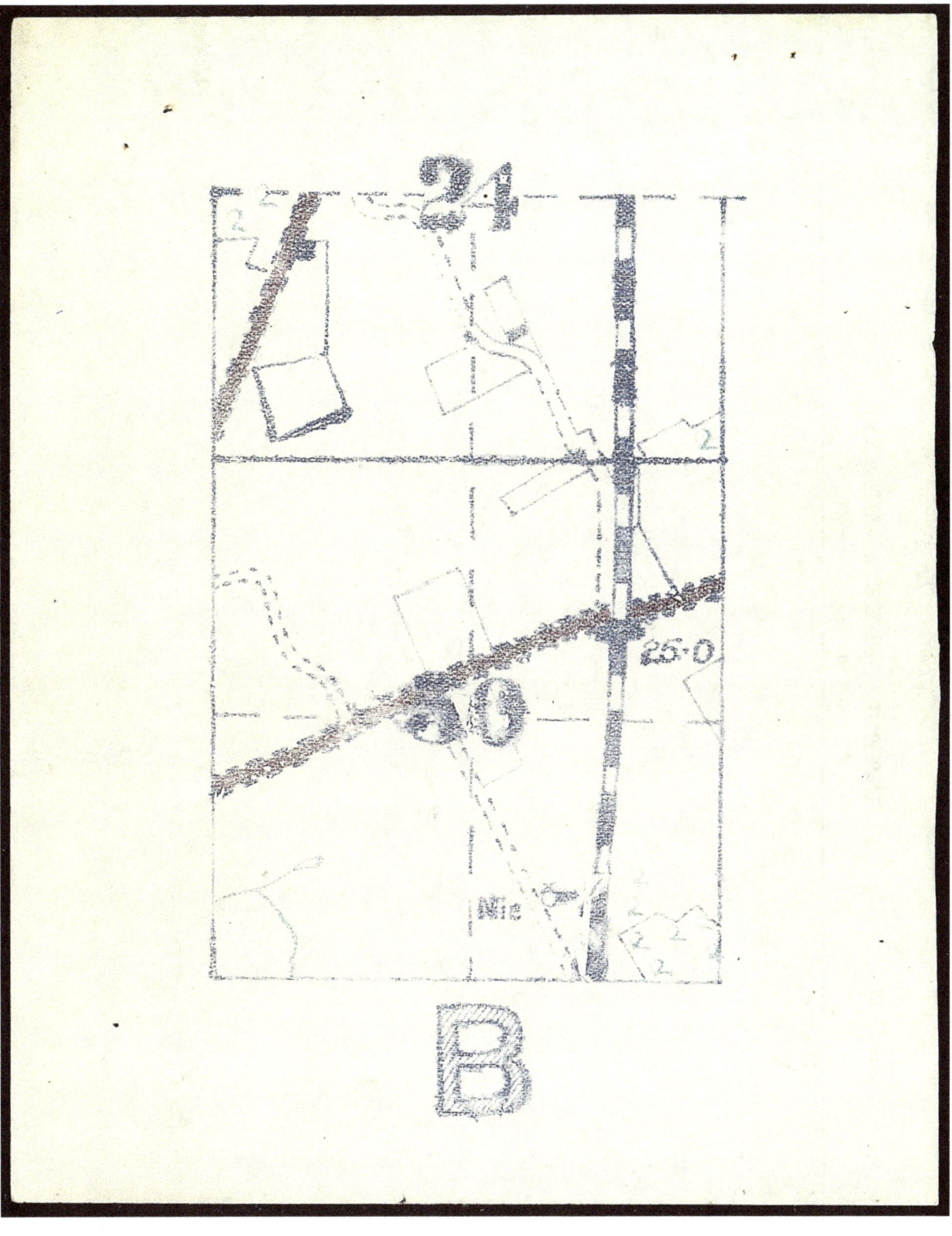

B

Instructions regarding War Diaries and Intelligence Summaries are contained in F. S. Regs., Part II. and the Staff Manual respectively. Title pages will be prepared in manuscript.

WAR DIARY
or
INTELLIGENCE SUMMARY.
(*Erase heading not required.*)

15 ~~#~~ H L I

Army Form C. 2118.

Vol 37

Place	Date Novr.	Hour	Summary of Events and Information	Remarks and references to Appendices
LE QUENELLET FARM.	1st		The battalion completed the consolidation of the area. The forward areas were also reconnoitred & plans for the coming attack commenced. Cold & wet.	J.H.S.
"	2nd		The forward areas were again reconnoitred and assembly positions etc. chosen. Fine.	J.H.S.
"	3rd		The day which was wet was spent in preparing for the crossing of the OISE CANAL. During the night the battalion moved to an assembly position about 1000 Yards NORTH WEST of the village of ORS where it remained in Brigade reserve during the crossing of the CANAL.	J.H.S.
ORS	4th		During the morning the remainder of the Brigade forced a crossing at ORS and at 13.30 hrs. the battalion followed and formed up on the EASTERN BANK. It then advanced to the DOTTED BLUE line which was reached at 15.00 hrs. Passing through the 1st Dorset Regt. on this line the advance was continued to the BLUE LINE where the leading companies were held up by machine gun fire from LOCQUIGNOL FARM and WALLEHEIN FARM which was later overcome and the farms captured. During this operation 30 prisoners and 8 guns were captured.	J.H.S.
EAST OF ORS	5th		At 05.30 hrs. the battalion advanced without opposition to the RED LINE during which 4 guns were captured. At about 09.00 hrs. the 46th Division passed through our line to continue the advance, and the companies withdrew to a rendezvous at BEAUREVOIR FARM from which the battalion marched to FAVRIL where it was billeted for the night. During the evening the village was shelled, one of the billets being struck by a shell which caused 20 casualties.	J.H.S.
FAVRIL	6th		Very wet. In the afternoon the battalion marched to LA BASSE HAROILLES and billeted there for the night.	

A5834 Wt. W4973 M687 750,000 8/16 D. D. & L. Ltd. Forms/C.2118/13.

37.0

14 sheets

Instructions regarding War Diaries and Intelligence Summaries are contained in F. S. Regs., Part II. and the Staff Manual respectively. Title pages will be prepared in manuscript.

WAR DIARY
or
INTELLIGENCE SUMMARY.
(Erase heading not required.)

Army Form C. 2118.

Place	Date	Hour	Summary of Events and Information	Remarks and references to Appendices
LA BASSE HAROILLES }	7th		In the morning the battalion marched via Gd FAYT to LE FOYAUX. Very damp. JHS	App. 1. OO No 48
LE FOYAUX	8th		Wet. The day was spent in drying clothes and tending feet.	JHS
LE FOYAUX	9th		Marched to a field just west of AVESNES where dinners were served. From there C and B Companies marched off independently to take over the front and support areas from the 97th Inf. Brigade. A and D Companies and Battn. H.Q. established themselves in AVESNELLES. Very fine.	JHS OO No 50 issued App 2.
AVESNELLES	10th		Fine. Companies cleaned up and held inspections. In the afternoon A and C companies moved into SEMERIES.	JHS
AVESNELLES	11th		At 7.10 a.m. a message was received to the effect that hostilities would cease at 11. a.m. The Commanding Officer addressed the battalion and told them the great news which was immediately followed by three cheers for the King. The day was most ably celebrated later in conjunction with the ROYAL SCOTS.	JHS
AVESNELLES	12th		Fine. The day was spent very peacefully.	JHS
AVESNELLES	13th		Fine and frosty. The battalion marched to SAINS DU NORD and had dinners in a field just north of the village, marching into billets about 2 p.m.	JHS App No 3
SAINS DU NORD	14th		Fine. Companies spent the day cleaning up.	JHS
"	15th		The G.O.C. 14th Inf. Brigade inspected the battalion.	JHS
"	16th		The G.O.C. 32nd Division presented medal ribands to those members of the 14th Inf. Brigade who had gained them during the fighting at SEQUEHART. In the afternoon part of the battalion bathed.	JHS

A5834 Wt. W4973/M687 750,000 8/16 D. D. & L. Ltd. Forms/C.2118/13.

Instructions regarding War Diaries and Intelligence Summaries are contained in F. S. Regs., Part II. and the Staff Manual respectively. Title pages will be prepared in manuscript.

WAR DIARY
or
INTELLIGENCE SUMMARY.
(Erase heading not required.)

Army Form C. 2118.

Place	Date	Hour	Summary of Events and Information	Remarks and references to Appendices
SAINS DU NORD	17th		A Brigade thanks-giving service was held in the morning. In the afternoon the bathing was completed. Fine. Capt. E. Maclean C.F. rejoined. OO No 1 Issued	J.H.S. App No 4
"	18th		The day was spent in preparing for the long march to Germany and in dumping surplus stores.	J.H.S.
"	19th		The march to Germany was commenced. After dinners had been served at a mid-day halt the battalion marched to SIVRY, where it was billeted for the night. Fine. Addendum to OO No 1 Issued	J.H.S. App No 5
SIVRY	20th		The battalion marched to FROID CHAPELLE. Fine. OO No 2 Issued.	App No 6 J.H.S.
FROID CHAPELLE	21st		A and B companies work on the road just east of RANCE. C and D companies cleaned up and held inspections.	
"	22nd		C and D companies worked on the roads during the morning. The Commanding Officer lectured to A and B companies in the morning and to all N.C.Os. in the afternoon.	J.H.S. J.H.S.
"	23rd		Battn. H.Q. furnished a party to complete the work on the roads. The Commanding Officers ceremonial parade was held for the remainder of the battalion, after which companies trained under their own arrangements.	J.H.S.
"	24th		The battalion marched to DAUSSOIS. Fine. OO No 3 Issued	App. No 7 J.H.S.
DAUSSOIS	25th		The day was spent in cleaning up. Fine	J.H.S.
"	26th		All companies bathed and carried out parades under their own arrangements.	J.H.S.
"	27th		Wet parades were cancelled. Bathing was completed. The Commanding Officer lectured to all officers and N.C.Os on demobilization. This was followed by a lecture by Rev. E. Maclean C.F. on the educational scheme.	J.H.S. J.H.S.

A5834 Wt. W4973/M687 750,000 8/16 D. D. & L. Ltd. Forms/C.2118/13.

Army Form C. 2118.

Instructions regarding War Diaries and Intelligence Summaries are contained in F. S. Regs., Part II. and the Staff Manual respectively. Title pages will be prepared in manuscript.

WAR DIARY
or
INTELLIGENCE SUMMARY.
(Erase heading not required.)

Place	Date	Hour	Summary of Events and Information	Remarks and references to Appendices
DAUSSOIS	28th		R.S.M's parade was followed by a route march, the men being made to run home across country. Wet. The educational classes commenced.	MS
"	29th		The whole battalion bathed and received a clean change of clothing.	MS
"	30th		St. Andrews Day. The men were presented with St. Andrews flags which they wore on their tunics. Battalion parade was held in the morning after which companies worked on the roads.	MS

Instructions regarding War Diaries and Intelligence Summaries are contained in F. S. Regs., Part II. and the Staff Manual respectively. Title pages will be prepared in manuscript.

WAR DIARY
or
INTELLIGENCE SUMMARY.

(Erase heading not required.)

Army Form C. 2118.

Place	Date	Hour	Summary of Events and Information	Remarks and references to Appendices

	1st Nov Off	1st Nov ORs	30th Nov Off	30th Nov ORs
Commanding Officer's Strength	23	570	30	672
FIGHTING STRENGTH				
Officers	35		36	
Other Ranks	744		770	

TOTAL CASUALTIES for the month	OFFs	ORs
Killed & Died of Wounds	.	2
Wounded	.	15
Missing	.	-

Hansch Lieut Col.
Comm'dg. 15/HIGH. L. I.

A5834 Wt. W4973 M687 750,000 8/16 D. D. & L. Ltd. Forms/C.2118/13.

Z.T6

SECRET. Copy No......

OPERATION ORDER No. 48.

App No.1

Reference Sheet 57a.

Unless contrary Orders are received, the following move and operation will take place tomorrow morning :-

1. The Bn. will move at 0730 Hrs. passing the Starting Point, road junction H.22.b.4.4. at that hour.

2. Order of march :- C.B.D.A. H.Q. Coys.

3. **ROUTE.** Through MAROILLES - Road junction H.17.b.3.4. - H.18.c.95.95. - I.13.c.9.5. where detailed orders will be issued.

4. Coys. will move at 100 yards interval accompanied by their Lewis Gun Limbers.
Cookers and Pack Animals will move in rear of Bn. Hqrs.

5. **OPERATION.** The Bn. will operate on the Left Flank of the 97th Inf. Bde. and will consolidate on the GREEN LINE (which runs North and South along the line of the road in I.24.d. and I.30.b. and d.)
The Bn. will consolidate on this line from road junction in I.24.b.8.1. to I.24.d.3.0.
The actual situation is uncertain, but the 2nd K.O.Y.L.I. are attacking the GREEN LINE on our right and it is quite probable that they will attack before us on the whole front, in which case we shall relieve them on our portion of the line when the leading Coy. arrives there.
C. Coy. will attack on the whole front and take over and consolidate this line.
B. Coy. will be in Support, 200 to 300 yards in rear and will consolidate on a line about the GRID LINE between I.23. and I.24.
D. Coy. will be in reserve and will consolidate about the line of the GRID LINE between I.22. and I.23.
A. Coy. will be held in Bn. Reserve about the wood in I.21.d.
Bn. Hqrs. will be in the Farm House in I.21.b.8.3.

6. The Bn. Northern Boundary is the 9th Corps Northern Boundary already issued. The Bn. Southern Boundary runs East and West along the GRID LINE between I.21. and 27. and I.30. and 34.

7. Os.C. B. and C. Coys. will meet the Commanding Officer mounted at Bn. Hqrs. at 0645 Hrs. for reconnaissance.

8. Sick Parade - 6.45 a.m. at Bn. Hqrs. Billet.

J. G. Stephen
Captain,
A/Adjt., 15th Bn. High. L. I.

6-11-18.

Copies issued to :-

1. O.C. A. Coy.
2. O.C. B. Coy.
3. O.C. C. Coy.
4. O.C. D. Coy.
5. O.C. H.Q. Coy.
6. 14th Inf. Bde.
7. Adjt.
8. War Diary.

SECRET. War Diary

Copy No......

15th Bn. THE HIGHLAND LIGHT INFANTRY.

OPERATION ORDER No. 50.

App 2.

1. The 14th Infantry Brigade will relieve the 97th Brigade today 9th inst on the Divisional Front.

2. The Bn. will take over the Front Line south of the river running through squares K.19., K.20., K.21.
The 1st DORSET Regt. will take over the line North of this.
Details as to the Line will be issued later.

3. The Brigade will rendezvous at J.28.b. and J.29.a. where dinners will be served at 1100 Hrs.

4. The Bn. will pass the Starting Point I.30.c.3.1. at 0930 Hrs.

5. Order of March - C.B.D.A.H.Q. Coy. Transport. The usual interval to be maintained. Cookers and Lewis Gun Limbers will march in rear of their Coys.

6. The Transport and Q.M. Stores will move with the Bn.

7. All loading to be completed by 0830 Hrs.
(a) All Officers valises will be stacked outside their Hqrs. by 0730 Hrs.

(b) All Officers Mess Kit will be stacked outside Coy. H.Q. by 0845 Hrs.

8. Dress - Battle Order except for Details who will wear F.S.M.O.

9. Coys. will break step while crossing bridge and the Transport will cross at a walk.

J.G. Stephen

Captain,

A/Adjt., for O.C. 15th Bn. H. L. I.

Issued to :-

1. O.C. A. Coy.	2. O.C. B. Coy.
3. O.C. C. Coy.	4 O.C. D. Coy.
5. O.C. H.Q. Coy.	6. Q.M.
7. ADJT.	8. War Diary.

Battalion Orders by
Lieut. Col. [illegible], [illegible]
Commanding 15th Battalion The Highland Light Infantry.
12th Nov., 1916.

- - - - - - - - - - - - - -

	1.	Reveille and Breakfast.....Under Coy. Arrangements.
MOVE.	2.	The Battalion will move to SAINS-DU-[illegible] area tomorrow as detailed below unless orders to the contrary are received.
STARTING POINT.	3.	The Battalion will pass the starting point - Road junction X 29 d 0.7 at 09.[illegible].
ORDER OF MARCH.	4.	The Order of March will be as follows:- Band, A, C, B, D, H.Q. Coys. and Transport.
DRESS.	5.	Dress will be Battle Order with steel helmets strapped to haversacks. Those men who have packs will wear F.S.M.O. with steel helmets strapped to packs.
INTERVALS.	6.	The usual distances will be maintained.
LOADING.	7.	(a). Officers' Valises will be stacked outside their Coy. Messes by 08.30 hrs. These will be picked up by the baggage wagon which will follow in its own time. (b). Officers' Mess Kit will be put on the Coy. Lewis Gun Limbers. (c). Lewis Gun Limbers and Cooker Horses will report to B. & D. Coys. at 08.15 hrs.
BILLETING PARTY.	8.	O/C. Coys. will earmark one N.C.O., & the Q.M. one man from Transport and one from Q.M. Stores to act as billeting party. 2/Lieut. [illegible] will be in charge. Orders as to when and where this party meets will be issued later.
DINNERS.	9.	It is probable that the Battalion will have to halt outside the new area for dinners.
	10.	The Band will stack their packs at the Transport Lines at 08.30 hrs.

[illegible]
Capt.,
A/Adjt., 15th High. L.I.

SECRET. Copy No. 11

App No 4

BATTALION OPERATION ORDER No. 1.

17th Nov., 1918.

1. At an early date the 32nd. Division will march into Germany. The average length of march will be 10 miles per day. The Division is expected to reach the Line of the MEUSE about 22nd - 23rd. inst. and the German frontier about Dec., 2nd.
The country and roads between MARCHE and VIELSALM are bad and very hilly. There is also very little accommodation.

2. The 32nd. Division will follow the 66th. Division.
The Battalion will follow the 1st. Dorset Regt.
1st. Line transport will accompany the Battalion. Baggage wagons will be brigaded and march in rear of the 14th Infantry Brigade.

3. No. grenades will be carried. 60 rounds S.A.A. only will be carried on the man during the march. The extra accommodation then provided on the Transport will be used to carry jerkins.

4. As the supplies will be received by lorry during the night, the road along which the Battalion moves must be kept absolutely clear of all traffic from the moment of the arrival of the Battalion in billets until that of its departure in the morning.

5. All stores dumped prior to the march will be brought forward later by rail.

6. Steel Helmets and box respirators will be carried on the man. Caps will be worn on the march.

7. All blankets will be carried by either 4 G.S. Wagons or 2 lorries.

8. There will be no ten minute halts on the way to starting points, but they will be rigidly adhered to once the battalion has reached the main line of march.

9. In order to give space on the road the band will march in sections of threes and not in sections of fours.

10. For the purpose of cooking and rationing H.Q. Coy., Transport and Q.M. Stores will be attached to companies as under:-

H.Q. Coy.	will be	attached to	A. Coy.
Transport	do.	do.	B. Coy.
Q.M. Stores	do.	do.	C. Coy.

This will take effect from the 1st day of the march (inclusive). O.C. H.Q. Coy. & the Q.M. will notify the Coy., to which their commands are to be attached, of the numbers that will be attached to it. O.C. A, B & C Coys. will then add these numbers to their ration strengths and draw rations accordingly. It will be attempted to make future billets fit in with the above scheme.

11. O.C. A, B, C, D & H.Q. Coys will each detail one man or N.C.O. to act as billeting party throughout the march. If possible they should be able to talk French. The Q.M. will also detail one man or N.C.O. from the transport. The names of these N.C.O's. or men will be notified to the Orderly Room by 12.00 hrs on 18th inst. This party will be known as the BILLETING PARTY, and no change is to be made in it without reference to the Orderly Room. The members of this party, with the exception of the Transport N.C.O., will be given cycles which they will keep and look after throughout the march. The Transport N.C.O. will be mounted.

Each/

Each member of the Billeting party must find out daily before leaving the ration strength of his company and that of each platoon.
Major B.M. JAGER will be in charge and when allotting billets will do so with a view to keeping the billets H.Q. Coy. & A. Coy., Transport & B. Coy., Q.M. Stores & C. Coy. as close together as possible.
C.Q.M.S's. will not be chosen as members of the billeting party.

12. Throughout the march companies will furnish the battalion guard in rotation as at present. These guards must be turned out clean and smart and should be warned at least three days before the day on which they will mount, and if possible be given half an hour's guard drill on each of these three days.

13. Leave will continue as at present. Those going on leave will proceed to the reception camp in the supply lorries.

14. The restrictions on the use of cameras are cancelled.

15. Regulations as to censorship will be relaxed. Men will be allowed to describe where they are and the nature of their surroundings.

Capt.,
A/Adjt., 15th Bn. The High. L.I.

Issued to

Commanding Officer......	No.	1	Copy.
2nd. in command.........	"	2	"
O.C. A. Coy.............	"	3	"
O.C. B. Coy.............	"	4	"
O.C. C. Coy.............	"	5	"
O.C. D. Coy.............	"	6	"
O.C. H.Q. Coy...........	"	7	"
Q.M......................	"	8	"
Transport Sgt...........	"	9	"
Adjutant................	"	10	"
War Diary...............	"	11	"
File....................	"	12	"

SECRET. Copy No. 11

15th BATTALION THE HIGHLAND LIGHT INFANTRY.

App: No. 5

ADDENDUM to Battalion Operation Order No. 1.

1. The Battalion will commence the march to Germany to-morrow 19th inst.

2. In future the maps which will be referred to in order will be:- NAMUR No. 8 $\frac{1}{100,000}$

MARCHE No. 8 $\frac{1}{100,000}$.

3. Companies will carry their Jerkins on their Coy. Lewis Gun Limbers, also Officers' Mess Kit.
H.Q. Coy. Jerkins will be carried on the rear half of H.Q. Lewis Gun Limber.

4. The Band packs and spare instruments will be loaded on half the T.M.B. limber. The band will put their jerkins in their packs.
The other half of this limber is allotted to the Q.M. for surplus stores.

5. Three Cooks will march in rear of each Coy. Cooker. These cooks will put their packs on their Coy. Lewis Gun Limber. H.Q. Coy., Transport & Q.M. Stores Cooks. will march with H.Q. Coy. but will put their packs in H.Q. L.G. Limber. They will join the Cooker of the Company to which they are attached immediately on arrival at billets or when a dinner halt is given.

6. Rations will be kept on the Cooker and only sufficient for each meal issued at a time.

7. Water bottles must be filled daily before marching off.

8. Blankets must always be rolled tightly in bundles of ten. Rope or other material has been issued for this purpose.. This must be carefully kept as no further supply will be available during the march.

9. Punctuality in every detail is essential; this applies especially to limbers and cookers which are with Coys.

10. No man will be allowed to fall out on the line of march without a "chit" from his company commander or 2nd. in Command.

11. The whole of the Q.M. Stores personnel will march with H.Q. Coy.

12. At halts all men must take off their equipment and pack animals will be off loaded. As only a minute and a half is allowed for putting on packs and falling in men must do this smartly or halts will have to be curtailed.

13. An inspection of feet also foot rubbing must be carried out daily by companies. A supply of soap and powder may be drawn from the medical Corporal on application.

14. Reveille. . . . . .06.00 hrs.
Breakfast. . . . . 07.00 hrs.
Sick Parade. . . . . 08.00 hrs.

15. Company on Duty...........C. Coy.
Battalion Orderly Officer.....2/Lieut. A. ROSS.

16/

16. The Battalion will pass the starting point - road junction 100 yds. SOUTH EAST of Church - at 09.30 hrs.

17. Order of March :- H.Q., A,Band, B,C & D. Coys. & Transport.

18. DRESS:- F.S.M.O.

19. The Guard will dismount at 8 a.m. and join its company. The police will take over the prisoners at 8 a.m. The new guard will mount at an hour to be notified later (i.e. roughly two hours after arrival in billets.)

20. Blankets will be stacked outside billets by 06.30 hrs. The Q.M. will arrange to collets them. Sgt. BEATTIE will be in charge of blankets throughout the march and will be responsible that they are drawn as soon as possible on arrival in billets and are collected punctually in the mornings.

21. Officers' Valises will be stacked outside their billets by 07.30 hrs. The Q.M. will arrange to collect them.

22. Lewis Gun Limbers will be loaded by 08.00 hrs.

23. One Limber will report to the O. Room at 07.45 hrs. to pick up signal stores and O.Room boxes.

24. Half of the T.M.B. Limber will be loaded at the Q.M. Stores and will then report to H.Q. Coy. at 08.00 hrs. to pick u p the band's packs.

25. All water-bottles must be filled to-night.

26. The Mess cart will report to the mess at 08.00 hrs.

27. Billets will be inspected by the Commanding Officer at 08.30 hrs.

28. Marching out states will be handed to the Adjutant at the starting point. These will show the numbers catually marching with each coy.

29. The Battalion will be billeted in SIVRY Area to-morrow. ROUTE:- RAMOUSIES - LIESSIES - MOSTRIMONT.

30. Throughout the march a mid-day halt will be observed from 11.30 hrs to 13.00 hrs. daily.

31. The following distances will be observed at all times:-

Between UNITS:- 50 yds.
do. Companies:- 10 yds.

In order to prevent the column becoming unduly long offir & N.C.O's. will march in the sections of fours. In each platoon there will not be more than one incomplete section of fours.

32. No compliments will be paid on the march.

33. Instructions for the Billeting party will be issued later

34. A C K N O W L E D G E.

J. F. Stephen
Capt.
A/Adjt., 15th Bn The High L.I.

Issued to all recipients of Battalion Operation Order No 1.

<u>SECRET.</u> <u>15th H.L.I.</u> Copy No....4....

Battalion Operation Order No. 2. 19th Nov., 1918.

App No 6.

1. Reveille. . . . . .06.00 hrs.
   Breakfast . . . . .07.00 hrs.
   Sick Parade . . . . .18.00 hrs.

2. The Battalion will march to FROID CHAPELLE to-morrow 20th inst. passing starting point - Battn. H.Q. Mess - at 08.17 hrs. (Facing

3. Order of March same as after dinner to-day.

4. The Billeting party will meet Major R.M. JAGER at 07.30 hrs. at Battn. H.Q. Mess. They will put their packs on their Coy. Lewis Gun Limbers.

5. All packs must be as carefully packed as to-day.

6. Coy. Commanders are reminded that they are responsible for the cleaning of their Lewis Gun Limbers & cookers throughout the march. It was noticed that the Lewis gun limbers were not up to the usual standard to-day.

7. Blankets & Officers' Valises <u>must</u> be stacked on the side of the road at their billets at 07.00 hrs. Only one Officer's Valise was in time to-day. This will not happen again.

8. All other loading as per Operation Order No.1 will be completed by 07.30 hrs.

9. There will be no dinner halt.

Capt.,
A/Adjt., 15th Bn. The High. L.I.

Copies issued as in B.O.O. No.1.

SECRET

Copy No. 11 ...

15th Battalion The Highland Light Infantry.

OPERATION ORDER No. 3. 23rd., Nov., 1916.

App. No. 4

1. Reveille.......................06.00 hrs.
Breakfast.......................06.30 hrs.
Sick Parade.....................10.30 hrs.

2. Company on Duty...............B. Coy.
Battn. Orderly Officer.......2/Lieut. P.R.H. LONGLEY.

3. The Battalion will move to the [illegible] AREA to-morrow, 24th inst.

4. The Battalion will pass the starting point - ROAD JUNCTION beside Battalion Headquarters Mess - at about 08.30 hrs. (Exact time will be notified later.).
DRESS:- F.S.M.O.

5. Order of March. . . .H.Q. Coy., C. & D. Coys., BAND, A. & B. Coys. and Transport.
Ten yards distance to be maintained between companies.

6. All blankets will be rolled in bundles of Ten and stacked outside billets by 07.00 hrs.
All loading to be completed by 07.30 hrs.
The T.M.B. Limber will report at H.Q. Coy. at 07.00 hrs. to collect the Band's packs.
The Mess cart will report to Battn. H.Q. Mess at 07.15 hrs.
Officers' Valises to be outside their billets by 07.00 hrs.

7. Orders for the Billeting party will be issued later.

Capt.,
A/Adjt., 15th Bn. The High. L.I.

Copies issued as per Battn. Operation Order No. 2.

AFTER ORDER.

It has been noticed that men of this Battalion have been walking about in the village without belts on. This practice must cease. This order is to be read out on parade to all ranks.

Instructions regarding War Diaries and Intelligence Summaries are contained in F. S. Regs., Part II. and the Staff Manual respectively. Title pages will be prepared in manuscript.

WAR DIARY
or
INTELLIGENCE SUMMARY.
(Erase heading not required.)

Army Form C. 2118.

15 HLI

38

Place	Date Dec	Hour	Summary of Events and Information	Remarks and references to Appendices
DAUSSOIS	1st		Battalion attended Devine Service forenoon. In the afternoon A & D Coys played Football. Result A - 3 goals D 1 goal. Weather fine.	[initials]
"	2nd		Wet - Companies in Billets. In the afternoon Battalion played the 168th Brigade R.F.A at Football and won by 3 goals to one Goal. French and Book-keeping Classes held in the evening.	[initials]
	3rd		Captain J G Stephen MC proceeded on Leave. Battalion out on route march in the morning - YVES. GOMEZEE - FAIROUL. WALCOURT - VOGENEE. DAUSSOIS. Weather showery. Afternoon A. Coy played B. Coy at football. B Coy winning by 6 goals to NIL. Composition & Arithmetic Classes held in the evening.	[initials]
"	4th		Wet - Coys carried on training in Billets. French and Book-keeping Classes held. NCOs Drill Class under Sgt [illegible] commenced. Battalion HQrs played 14th Brigade Headquarters at Football and won by 5 Goals to NIL. C Coy played inter-platoon games at football. Evening Short-hand Class cancelled.	[initials]
	5		Fine - Battalion under R.S.M for one hour then from 10.30 am - 12-30 pm engaged in sweeping roads. Arithmetic and French Classes held. Afternoon C & D Companies played football. Result C 5 goals D Coy NIL	[initials]
	6		Fine. Officers and NCOs [illegible] Battalion under RSM and cleaning Village. Headquarters played B Coy at football. Result Headquarters 2 Goals. B Company 1. Goal. French and Book-keeping & English Composition Classes held.	[initials]

38-0
5 sheets

A5834 Wt. W4973/M687 750,000 8/16 D. D. & L. Ltd. Forms/C.2118/13.

Instructions regarding War Diaries and Intelligence Summaries are contained in F. S. Regs., Part II. and the Staff Manual respectively. Title pages will be prepared in manuscript.

WAR DIARY
or
INTELLIGENCE SUMMARY.

(Erase heading not required.)

Army Form C. 2118.

Place	Date	Hour	Summary of Events and Information	Remarks and references to Appendices
DAUSSOIS	7th		Fair. Inspection by Brigadier and Company Training R.F.A. Race meeting Lt Col Ramsden DSO MC Lt Keith 2/Lt J.U. McGill represented Battalion in Brigade Race meeting by C.O. at 5.30 pm on Extension of Service	[initials]
	8th		Church Parade in forenoon. Weather fine Afternoon Right half Battalion played Left half Battalion Result Right half Battalion 7 Goals Left half Battalion 1 Goal	[initials]
	9th		Wet. In Billets Training. Book keeping, French & English Composition Classes held. Afternoon Brigade Shield Cup; Battalion versus Brigade. Result Battalion 9 Goals Brigade NIL	[initials]
	10th		Fair. Battalion Route March in morning. Route SOUMOY — SENZEILLE - VILLERS DEUX EGLISES — DAUSSOIS. French Classes held during the evening.	[initials]
	11th		Wet. Parades off on account of weather. Cleaning up for march next day. French, Book-keeping and English Composition Classes held in the evening	[initials]
	12th		Very Wet. Battalion moved to BIESMEREE and billeted there for the night 12/13th. Route - DAUSSOIS - YVES GOMEZEE - FRAIRE - DONVEAU CROSS ROADS BIESMEREE (15 miles) O.O No 4 issued	[initials]
BIESMEREE	13th		Very Showery — Battalion moved from BIESMEREE to DENEE — Route, BIESMEREE, FURNAUX — DENEE. O.O. No 5 issued	Appendix No 1 [initials]
DENEE	14th		Fair. Cleaning up and re-adjusting of Billets. 2/Lieut D. C. Hodge returned from Leave	Appendix No 2 [initials]

A5834 Wt. W4973 M687 750,000 8/16 D. D. & L. Ltd. Forms/C.2118/13.

Instructions regarding War Diaries and Intelligence Summaries are contained in F. S. Regs., Part II. and the Staff Manual respectively. Title pages will be prepared in manuscript.

WAR DIARY
or
INTELLIGENCE SUMMARY.
(Erase heading not required.)

Army Form C. 2118.

Place	Date	Hour	Summary of Events and Information	Remarks and references to Appendices
DENEE	15th		Church Parade. Weather Fair.	
	16th		Wet. R.S.M. Parade and Company Training. English Composition Class held in the evening	
	17th		Fair. Commanding Officer's Parade. Company Training - preparing for move. O.O. No 6 issued	Appendix No 3
	18th		Wet. Battalion moved from DENEE to GODINNE - Route:- DENEE - BIOUL - ANNEVOIE - ROUILLON - RIVIERE - GODINNE (10 miles) arrived in Billets about 1 PM	
GODINNE	19th		Fair. Cleaning up and readjusting of Billets	
	20th		Very Wet. In Billets - First Leave allotment granted to Namur. English Composition Class held during evening	
	21st		Fair. Commanding Officers Parade and Company Parades. Two Arithmetic Classes held	
	22nd		Fine. Church Parade in morning:- B Company played D Company at football in the afternoon, B Coy winning by 2 goals to one goal. First Draft of Miners (6) proceeded to Concentration Camp for Demobilization. Men (about 150) arrived from Reception Camp. Lieut J B Longlands and 2/Lieut J Brown joined Unit.	
	23rd		Wet. In Billets. Second batch of Miners (30) left for Concentration Camp.	
	24th		Fair - Re-adjustment of Billets - Cross Country Race	

A5834 Wt. W4973 M687 750,000 8/16 D. D. & L. Ltd. Forms/C.2118/13.

Army Form C. 2118.

Instructions regarding War Diaries and Intelligence Summaries are contained in F. S. Regs., Part II. and the Staff Manual respectively. Title pages will be prepared in manuscript.

WAR DIARY
or
INTELLIGENCE SUMMARY.
(Erase heading not required.)

Place	Date	Hour	Summary of Events and Information	Remarks and references to Appendices
GODINNE	25th		Christmas Day - Fine - Commanding Officer visited men at Dinner. Brigadier General visited Officers mess in the forenoon	[illegible]
"	26th		Fine. Battalion bathed at ANHEE - Football match between 15th H.L.I. and 5/6th Royal Scots was played at HUN - Result H.L.I. 6 goals Royal Scots NIL	[illegible]
	27th		Fair but Cold - Battalion Parade under R.S.M. and Company Training - Rugby trial match played on our ground, Royal Scots and 15th H.L.I. - 5 points - Dorsets & Brigade H.Qrs - NIL	[illegible]
"	28th		French (6 Corp) Book keeping - English Composition Classes [illegible] very well - Battalion in Billets - 2 Arithmetic Classes held	[illegible]
"	29th		Football match for Shield Competition was played between 1st Dorsets and 15th H.L.I. on the ground of the latter. Result H.L.I. 11 goals, Dorsets 2 goals	[illegible]
"	30th		Rugby match between 14th Brigade and 97th Brigade - Result 14th Bde 45 points - 97th Bde NIL	[illegible]
"	31st		Route March Route LUSTIN STATION - RIVIERE YVOIR - GODINNE.	[illegible]

A5834 Wt. W4973 M687 750,000 8/16 D. D. & L. Ltd. Forms/C.2118/13.

Instructions regarding War Diaries and Intelligence Summaries are contained in F. S. Regs., Part II. and the Staff Manual respectively. Title pages will be prepared in manuscript.

WAR DIARY
or
INTELLIGENCE SUMMARY.
(Erase heading not required.)

Army Form C. 2118.

Place	Date	Hour	Summary of Events and Information	Remarks and references to Appendices
	25th		Bn in billets. Bgd. training programme carried out. Men were bathed at Douilly. 2/Lieut Macqueen joined for duty. Weather fine.	
	26th		Bn in billets. Bgd. training programme carried out. Work started on Bn Rifle Range. Weather fine.	
	27th		Bn in billets. Inspection at Douilly of Brigade by Brigadier. The Bn paraded in the afternoon for gas instruction by Div. Gas officer. Weather fine.	
	28th		Bn in billets. Training according to Bgd. programme. Weather fine.	
	29th		Bn in billets. Church parade held at Toulle. Weather fine. Lecture by M.O. on Sanitation. Bn Baths started. Football. Headquarters v D coy. result win for headquarters.	
	30th		Bn in billets. Inspection at Douilly by Divisional Commander. Football. Headquarters v A coy. Win for Headquarters. Weather very fine.	

A5834 Wt. W4973/M687 750,000 8/16 D. D. & L. Ltd. Forms/C.2118/13.

Army Form C. 2118.

Instructions regarding War Diaries and Intelligence Summaries are contained in F. S. Regs., Part II. and the Staff Manual respectively. Title pages will be prepared in manuscript.

WAR DIARY
or
INTELLIGENCE SUMMARY.
(Erase heading not required.)

Place	Date	Hour	Summary of Events and Information	Remarks and references to Appendices
GODINNE	31st		Recreational Training Class on Parade Ground. Book keeping Class held in evening.	

	1st DEC		30th DEC	
	Off	ORs	Off	ORs
Commanding Officer's Strength	30	673	28	618
FIGHTING STRENGTH				
Officers	37		34	
Other Ranks	772		784	

Casualties NIL

John S. Allein Major
Commdg. 15/H.L.I.

A5834 Wt. W4973 M687 750,000 8/16 D. D. & L. Ltd. Forms/C.2118/13.

Army Form C. 2118.

Instructions regarding War Diaries and Intelligence Summaries are contained in F. S. Regs., Part II. and the Staff Manual respectively. Title pages will be prepared in manuscript.

WAR DIARY
or
INTELLIGENCE SUMMARY.

(Erase heading not required.)

Place	Date	Hour	Summary of Events and Information	Remarks and references to Appendices

	Officers	O R
Killed	2	30
Died of Wounds	–	12
Wounded	2	122
Wounded at duty	1	1
Wounded accidentally		1
Missing.		4
Total	5	170

A Gillon Major,
Comm'dg, 15/HIGH L.I.

A5834 Wt. W4973 M687 750,000 8/16 D. D. & L. Ltd. Forms/C.2118/13.

Appendix VI

War Diary

Battalion Orders
by Lieut-Colonel V.B.RAMSDEN, M.C.,
Commanding, 15th.Bn.Highland Light Infantry,
1st November 1917.

---

1. Reveille...............................6 a.m.
Breakfast - under Co. arrangements.
Sick Parade...............................8 a.m.
C.O's Orderly Room........................3 p.m.

2. No P.T. or B.F.

3. All Cos. and Hd.Qrs. will rendezvous at H.5.b.2.0. (scene of night operations) at 9 a.m.
Cos. will parade as strong as possible.- including Stretcher Bearers who will fall out at rendezvous and fall in behind the Band.

4. T.O. will arrange to send a limber with 80 shovels to report to Sergt.BEATTIE at Q.M.Storesat 8 a.m. Sergt. BEATTIE will load up all available tape, 4 red flags, Battalion flag, rattles, 8 smoke bombs (with detonators, but without rods or cartridges) and proceed with limber to parade ground.

5. Reference to to-morrow's operations - Cos will draw shovels, bombs, tape, etc., on the ground; small red flags will represent relay posts, battalion flag will be at Bn.Hd.Qrs.

6. Dress for Barrage Party:- Walking Out Dress with Waterproof Sheets and Tins.
2/Lieut. McCAIG will be in charge.

R.M. Grant Captain,

A/Adjt., 15th.Bn. High. L. I.

SECRET

Copy No..............

BATTALION OPERATION ORDER No. 5.

Map Reference:- NAMUR 8.

12th Dec., 1918.

app 2

1. Reveille. . . . . .07.00 hrs.
   Breakfast . . . . .08.15 hrs.
   Sick Parade . . . . .09.00 hrs.
   Guard Mounting. . . . .~~XXXXXXXXXX~~
   Retreat . . . . .16.00 hrs.
   Staff Parade. . . . . .21.00 hrs.

2. Company on Duty . . . ."A". Coy.
   Battalion Orderly Officer . . . . . .2/Lieut. J.A. DUNLOP.

3. The Battalion will move to DENEE to-morrow, 13th inst.
   Route:- FURNAUX - DENEE.
   Battalion will pass the starting point - Railway Crossing on BIESMEREE - FURNAUX ROAD - at 10.15 hrs.
   Order of March:- H.Q., D., C., Band, A. & B. Coys. & Transport.
   Dress:- F.S.M.O.

4. Marching out States will be handed to Adjutant at the Starting Point.

5. Blankets will be dumped at Q.M. Stores as follows:-
   H.Q., A & B. Coys. at 07.45 hrs.
   C. & D. Coys. & Transport at 08.00 hrs.
   All loading to be completed by 09.00 hrs.
   Officers' Valises will be outside their billets by 08.45 hrs

6. The Commanding Officer will inspect Billets at 09.30 hrs.

7. Company Cookers with cooks and C.Q.M.S's. will move to New Area at 09.15 hrs. under the Quartermaster.

[signature] Lieut.,
A/Adjt., 15th Bn. The High. L.I.

Copies issued as in Battn. Operation Order No. 4.

SECRET.

Copy No. 10

BATTALION OPERATION ORDER NO 6.

Map Ref:- NAMUR 8.

17th Dec., 1918.

App 3

1. Reveille. . . . . .06.30 hrs.
Breakfast . . . . .07.30 hrs.
Sick Parade . . . . .08.30 hrs.
Retreat . . . . .16.00 hrs.
Staff Parade. . . . . .21.00 hrs.

2. Company on Duty . . . . "B". Coy.
Battalion Orderly Officer . . . 2/Lt. F.R.H. LONGLEY.

3. The Battalion will move to GODINNE to-morrow, 18th. inst.
Route:- BIOUL - ANNEVOIE ROUILLON - RIVIERE - GODINNE.
The Battalion will pass the starting point - 8th. Kilometre Stone on main BIOUL Road - at 09.15 hrs.
Order of March:- H.Q., A. & B. Coys., Band, C. & D. Coys., Transport.
Dress:- F.S.M.O.
2/Lieut. J.A. DUNLOP will report to O.C. C. Coy. for duty on the march.

4. Marching out states will be handed to the adjutant at the Starting Point.

5. Blankets will be stacked at Coy. H.Qrs. by 07.00 hrs,
Officers' Valises will be outside their billets by 07.30 hrs.
The Quartermaster will arrange to collect these.

6. Coy. Lewis Gun Limbers will report to Coy. H.Qrs. at 07.45 hrs
Limber for Band packs will report at Band Billet at 08.00 hrs.
Limber for Orderly Room & Signal Boxes will report at Orderly Room at 08.00 hrs.
Mess Cart will report at H.Q. Officers' Mess at 07.45 hrs.
All loading must be completed by 08.30 hrs.

7. There will be no Mid-day halt. Dinners will be served on arrival in new billets.

8. The Commanding Officer will inspect Billets at 08.30 hrs.

D. Scott
Lieut.,
A/Adjt., 15th Battn. The High. L.I.

Copies issued as in Bn. O.O. No. 5.

SECRET. Copies Issued.......... 11

BATTALION OPERATION ORDER No. 4.

Map Reference:- NAMUR 8. 11th Dec., 1918.

App. 1

1. Reveille. . . . . .06.30 hrs.
   Breakfast . . . . .07.00 hrs.
   Sick Parade . . . . .08.15 hrs.

2. Company on Duty . . . ."D". Coy.
   Battalion Orderly Officer.. . .2/Lieut. J.U. McGILL.

3. The Battalion will move to BIESMERE to-morrow, 12th inst.
   Route:- DAUSSOIS - YVES GOMEZEE - FRAIRE - DONVEAU CROSS ROADS - BIESMERE.
   The Battalion will pass the starting point - C. Coy's. Officers' Mess - at 09.00 hrs.
   Order of March:- H.Q., B, D. Coys., Band, C. & A. Coys., Transport.
   Dress:- F.S.M.O.

4. Marching out states will be handed to the Adjutant at the starting point.

5. Water bottles will be filled prior to marching out.

6. All blankets will be rolled in bundles of TEN and stacked at Q.M. Stores by 07.00 hrs.
   Loading of all Stores, Jerkins, Hand packs &c. must be completed by 08.00 hrs. Officers' Valises will be outside their billets by 07.30 hrs. The Q.M. will arrange to collect them.

7. The Commanding Officer will inspect billets at 08.30 hrs.

8. There will be a mid-day halt from 11.50 hrs. - 13.00 hrs. for dinner.
   For the purpose of cooking H.Q. Coy, Transport and Q.M. Stores will be attached to companies as follows:-

H.Q. Coy.	will be attached to		A. Coy.
Transport	do.	do.	B. Coy.
Q.M. Stores	do.	do.	C. Coy.

   The Quartermaster will make the necessary arrangements for this.

9. The Mess Cart will be at Battalion H.Q. Mess at 07.45 hrs.

10. Orders for billeting party will be issued later.

Lieut. A/Adjt.,
15th Bn. The High. L.I.

Copies issued as in Operation Order No. 3.

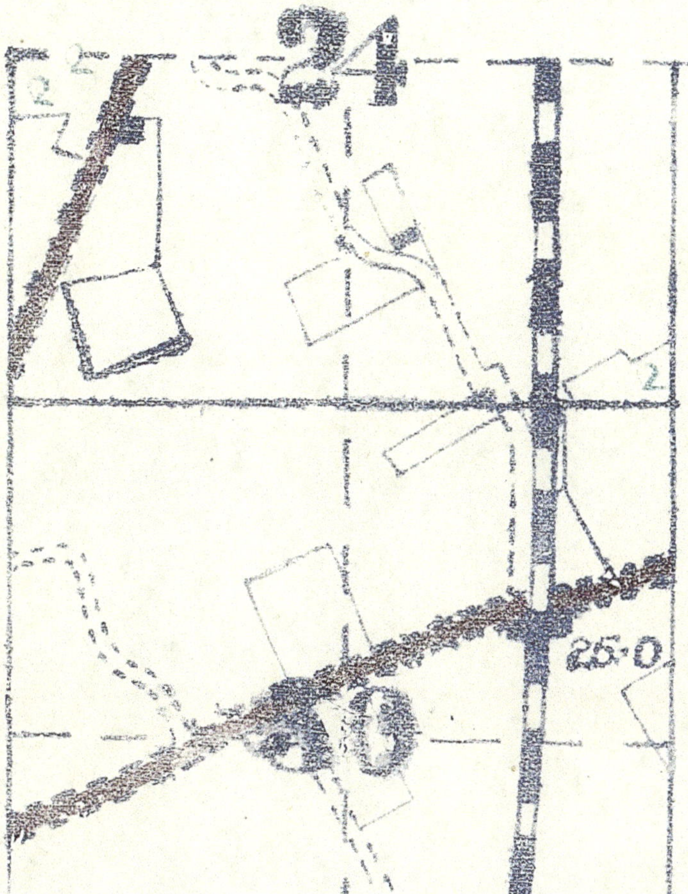

B

LANCASHIRE DIVISION
(LATE 32ND DIVN)

14TH INFY BDE (1ST LANCS INFY BDE)

15TH BN HIGH'D LT INFY

JAN-~~FEB~~ MAR 1919

To LOWLAND DIV (late 9 DIV)

LOWLAND BDE

15th H. L. I.

Army Form C. 2118.

~~WAR DIARY~~
or
INTELLIGENCE SUMMARY.
(Erase heading not required.)

Instructions regarding War Diaries and Intelligence Summaries are contained in F. S. Regs., Part II. and the Staff Manual respectively. Title pages will be prepared in manuscript.

VR 39

Place	Date	Hour	Summary of Events and Information	Remarks and references to Appendices
GODINNE	1919 JAN 1.		Fine - No parades. Commanding Officer visited men at dinner; Coy Concerts held.	
	2.		Fine. R.S.M. and Coy Drills - Battalion Cross Country Race run in order to pick team for Brigade Race. Arithmetic and English Composition Classes held.	
	3.		Fine. The Commanding Officer held inspection of all Companies in the form of a competition, this was won by C Coy 14 Platoon winning the platoon Competition. Classes were again held in the morning and evening.	
	4.		Fair. R.S.M's parade followed by Battalion Physical Training Parade. In the afternoon the Brigade Cross Country Race was run. The Battalion was third in this race	
	5.		Wet. Church parades as usual. In the afternoon Battalion played Brigade Headquarters team at football and won by 6 goals to 1 goal	
	6.		Fine. R.S.M's parade and Battalion Physical Training, then under Company arrangements.	
	7.		Fine but windy. The Battalion went for a Route March in the morning. Company games of football were played in the afternoon. [illegible] training [illegible] held [illegible] evening.	
	8.		Very [illegible] with a little frost. Adjutant's Parade, then under Coy arrangements. Platoon football games were played in the afternoon	
	9.		Fine. R.S.M's parade, Battalion Physical Training Parade & Coy training. Platoon football and a Brigade practice Rugby game were played in the afternoon	

A5834 Wt. W4973 M687 750,000 8/16 D. D. & L. Ltd. Forms/C.2118/13.

39.0
7 sheets

a.o.f.0

Instructions regarding War Diaries and Intelligence Summaries are contained in F. S. Regs., Part II. and the Staff Manual respectively. Title pages will be prepared in manuscript.

WAR DIARY
or
INTELLIGENCE SUMMARY.
(Erase heading not required.)

Army Form C. 2118.

Place	Date	Hour	Summary of Events and Information	Remarks and references to Appendices
[illegible]DINNE	JAN 10		Fine. R.S.M's parade followed by Battalion Physical training. The Battalion played the 5/6 Royal Scots at football, the game was drawn	
	11		Wet. Bathing was commenced, remainder of Battalion paraded under Coy arrangements. 14th Brigade played the South African Brigade at Rugby and won by 15 points to 3 points after an exciting game	
	12		Dull. Church Parades as usual. Bathing continued. C Coy beat B Coy in a Company League Match	
	13		Fine. R.S.M's Parade, then under Coy arrangements. Inter platoon football was played in the afternoon	
	14		Dull. Commanding Officer's Ceremonial Parade after which he addressed the Battalion. Platoon games in the afternoon also Hockey game	
	15		Wet. Morning Parades cancelled. Coys were put through Gas Chamber and [illegible] tested. In the afternoon the Battalion played the [illegible] Regiment in the final of the Brigade Football Competition, [illegible] was drawn. The Shield was presented to the team after [illegible] of the Brigadier. This is the second time in succession that the Battalion has won the Shield.	
	16		Fine. Adjutant's Parade, then under Coy arrangements. The Brigade was to have played the Australians at Rugby but this was cancelled at the last moment. A scratch game of football was played instead.	

Instructions regarding War Diaries and Intelligence Summaries are contained in F. S. Regs., Part II. and the Staff Manual respectively. Title pages will be prepared in manuscript.

WAR DIARY
or
INTELLIGENCE SUMMARY.
(Erase heading not required.)

Army Form C. 2118.

Place	Date JAN	Hour	Summary of Events and Information	Remarks and references to Appendices
GODINNE	17		Fine. Commanding Officers Ceremonial Parade, practising for presentation parade next day. In the afternoon A Company beat D Company at football	[illegible]
	18		Very Wet. Presentation of Medal Ribands and Divisional Monthly Cup by Divisional General	[illegible]
	19		Fine. Church Services as usual. C & D Coys played platoon games in the afternoon	[illegible]
	20		Fine but Cold. Adjutants parade and Company training. B Coy played D Company at football. B Coy winning by 3 goals to 0 goals.	[illegible]
	21		Fine. Frosty. R.S.Ms parade and Company training. B & D Companies played platoon games in competition	[illegible]
	22		Fine Frosty. Commanding Officers practice for Prince of Wales visit. B Coy played D Coy at Hockey. Result B Coy 3 goals D Coy 2 goals	[illegible]
	23		Frosty with slight fall of snow. The Battalion was reviewed by His Royal Highness The Prince of Wales at 10 am. After the Battalion had received the Prince in line, he walked round the ranks. His Royal Highness chatted to a number of the men. All Officers were presented to His Royal Highness. After the Prince had inspected the Battalion the march past took place. At the conclusion of the parade The Prince expressed to the Commanding Officer his pleasure in seeing the Battalion and commented upon the appearance & high standard of efficiency of the Battalion	[illegible]

Instructions regarding War Diaries and Intelligence Summaries are contained in F. S. Regs., Part II. and the Staff Manual respectively. Title pages will be prepared in manuscript.

WAR DIARY
or
INTELLIGENCE SUMMARY.
(Erase heading not required.)

Army Form C. 2118.

Place	Date JAN	Hour	Summary of Events and Information	Remarks and references to Appendices
GOZINNE	24		Frosty and fine Holiday. No parades afternoon Battalion played Royal Scots at Hockey and won by 3 goals to 2 goals.	[illegible]
	25		Fine & frosty. Lewis Gun and Musketry training carried out in Billets. C Coy played 206 Coy Royal Engineers at Football. Result 3-3. A Coy played D Company at Hockey and B Company played final of the platoon competition.	[illegible]
	26		Frost & Snow. Church parade as usual. B Company played 90th Field Ambulance at football and won by 2 goals to 1 goal.	[illegible]
	27		Frost & Snow. preparing for move	[illegible]
	28		Frost & Snow. Battalion moved to NAMECHE and billetted for the night	[illegible] Appendix No 1
NAMECHE [illegible]	29		Frost & Snow. Battalion entrained at NAMECHE en route for BONN	[illegible]
	30		Frost & Snow. Battalion arrived in BONN about 6-45 am and marched to Barracks for the night.	[illegible]
BONN GERMANY	31		Frost and Snow. Battalion moved from BONN Barracks to Billets in BEUEL.	[illegible]

Instructions regarding War Diaries and Intelligence Summaries are contained in F. S. Regs., Part II. and the Staff Manual respectively. Title pages will be prepared in manuscript.

WAR DIARY
or
INTELLIGENCE SUMMARY.
(Erase heading not required.)

Army Form C. 2118.

Place	Date	Hour	Summary of Events and Information	Remarks and references to Appendices
	JAN 31		Battalion supplied numerous guards including the RHINE BRIDGE Guard	

	1st JAN		31st JAN	
	Off	ORs	Off	ORs
Commanding officers Strength	30	623	19	540
FIGHTING STRENGTH				
Officers	34		33	
Other Ranks	784		702	

Casualties NIL

W D White Major
Commdg 15/H. L. I

A5834 Wt. W4973 M687 750,000 8/16 D. D. & L. Ltd. Forms/C.2118/13.

SECRET. Copy No......

15th Bn. The Highland Light Infantry.

OPERATION ORDER No. 7.

Map Reference:- NAMUR 8 1/100,000.
do: [illegible] 1/100,000.

1. The move to [illegible] will commence tomorrow Tuesday 28th. inst. The Battalion will march to NAMECHE tomorrow and billet there for the night. The Battalion will entrain at NAMECHE the following day.

2. Reveille. . . . . .0600 Hrs.
Breakfast . . . . .0[illegible] Hrs.
Sick Parade . . . .[illegible] Hrs.

3. The Battalion will pass the Starting Point - Battalion Orderly Room at [illegible] Hrs.
Route:- [illegible] - [illegible] - [illegible] - [illegible] - GOYET - NAMECHE.
Order of march:- H.Q. and A. Coys., Band, B.C. and D. Coys., Transport.
Dress:- F.S.M.O. - Jerkins will be carried in the pack and Greatcoats carried on Coy. L.G. limbers as far as possible.
Instructions with regard to carrying surplus will be issued later.

4. O.C. D. Coy. will detail a party of [illegible] men under an N.C.O. (Sgt) to march in rear of Transport.

5. Boots will be oiled, greased or dubbined today. On completion of the march tomorrow feet inspection and rubbing will be carried out and dry socks put on.

6. Marching out State will be handed to Adjutant at Starting Point.

7. Water carts and waterbottles must be filled before marching out and again before entraining.

8. Mess Cart will report to H.Q. Mess at 0700 Hrs.

9. Blankets will be rolled in bundles of ten and stacked outside Coy. Billets by 0730 Hrs. The Q.M. will arrange to collect these.

10. Officers valises will be outside billets by 0730 Hrs. The Q.M. will arrange to collect these.

11. All loading must be completed by 0800 Hrs.

12. There will be mid-day halt from 1130 - 1300 Hrs. for dinner.

13. For purpose of cooking during the move:-
H.Q. Coy. will be attached to A. Coy.
Transport do: do: B. Coy.
Q.M. Stores. do: do: C. Coy.
The Sgt. Cook will make the necessary arrangements for this.

14. A billeting party consisting of Lieut. J.B. [illegible] and 1 N.C.O. per Coy. including Transport will proceed to NAMECHE tomorrow morning by motor lorry leaving Q.M. Stores at 0[illegible] Hrs.

15. The Commanding Officer will inspect billets at 0800 Hrs.

16. The time of entraining at NAMECHE on Wednesday 29th inst., is not yet known.

17. Detraining Station is BONN.

18. Time of journey - 15 hours approximately.

19./

19. O.C. D. Coy. will detail a party of 1 Officer and 50 O.Rs. to act as loading party. This party will require to be at entraining station four hours before the train is due to depart.

20. Transport will require to be at Entraining Station four hours before the train is due to depart.

21. On arrival at Entraining Station Os.C. Coys. will be informed the number of trucks at their disposal and Coys. will be divided into parties for each truck. Parties will be marched to the train and formed up in file facing the trucks. No man will enter the train until bugler sounds the "ADVANCE". Coy. Guides will report at entraining station 1½ hours before departure. On arrival of Coys., Guides will be found opposite Coys. First Truck.

22. On arrival at Detraining Station no man will leave the train until the "FALL IN" is sounded by bugler. On this signal, men will detrain fully dressed and Coys. will be formed up facing the train. One marker per Coy. will report to R.S.M. immediately. Coys. will march on markers on advance being sounded. It is essential that entraining and detraining are carried out as expeditiously as possible.

23. Entrainment must be completed half hour before the train is due to depart.

24. No personnel or stores will be allowed in Brake Vans at each end of the train, or on the roofs of the trucks.

25. All horses will be watered at the entraining station before despatch of the train. T.O. will reconnoitre the water supply beforehand.

26. T.O. will provide brest ropes for horses trucks.

27. Great Coats, and at least 2 blankets per man will be drawn on arrival in billets at NAMCHE tomorrow night and if distance permits these will be carried by the men to the station on Wednesday. Men must entrain with blankets.

28. All doors of covered trucks and carriages on the right hands side of the train, when on the main line, must be kept closed.

29. O.C. H. Q. Coy. will detail a picquet for front of train and O.C. D. Coy. will detail a picquet for rear of train to prevent troops leaving at stops.

E. Keith Lieut.,

A/Adjt., 15th Bn. High. L. Infy.

Copies issued as per Battn. Operation Order No. 6.

1/5 H L I

52

Army Form C. 2118.

Instructions regarding War Diaries and Intelligence Summaries are contained in F. S. Regs., Part II. and the Staff Manual respectively. Title pages will be prepared in manuscript.

WAR DIARY
or
INTELLIGENCE SUMMARY.
(Erase heading not required.)

Vol 11

Place	Date Febry	Hour	Summary of Events and Information	Remarks and references to Appendices
BEUEL GERMANY	1		Fine & Frosty. Cleaning of Billets. 10 Guards supplied by Battalion including Rhine Bridge Guard	[illegible]
	2		Fine & Frosty. Church Parade as usual.	[illegible]
	3		Cold & Frosty. Coy Training etc	[illegible]
	4		Frost & Snow. Adjutant's Parade & Company Training	[illegible]
	5		Frost & Snow. Adjutant's Parade. [illegible] [illegible] 1st per Company	[illegible]
	6		Frost and Snow. R.S.M.'s Parade and Company Training	[illegible]
	7		Frost & Snow. R.S.M.'s Parade and Company Training. 2nd Lieut [illegible] rejoined from Brigade	[illegible]
	8		Frost & Snow. Company Training	[illegible]
	9		Frost & Snow. [illegible] Battalion [illegible] [illegible] Prince [illegible] [illegible] Captain [illegible] Robertson [illegible] in charge. Rhine Bridge Guard relieved by 2nd Manchester Regiment [illegible]	[illegible]

A5834 Wt. W4973 M687 750,000 8/16 D. D. & L. Ltd. Forms/C.2118/13.

WAR DIARY
or
INTELLIGENCE SUMMARY.
(Erase heading not required.)

Army Form C. 2118.

Instructions regarding War Diaries and Intelligence Summaries are contained in F. S. Regs., Part II. and the Staff Manual respectively. Title pages will be prepared in manuscript.

Place	Date Febry	Hour	Summary of Events and Information	Remarks and references to Appendices
BEUEL GERMANY	10		Frost & Snow. R.S.M's Parade. Training under Company arrangements & Recreational Training. C Company relieved D. Coy in the outpost line	[illegible]
	11		Companies carried out training under own arrangements. Recreational Training was also continued	[illegible]
	12		R.S.M's Parade and Training under Company arrangements. Classes were held in Arithmetic & English Composition. Lt Colonel V.B. Ramsden D.S.O. M.C. rejoined from Brigade	[illegible]
	13		Adjutants Parade. Companies training under own arrangements. Recreational Training and instruction in [illegible] Board Range finder. Educational Classes were held as usual	[illegible]
	14		Frost & Snow. Adjutants Parade on Football Field. Company [illegible] Specialists Training. Meeting of Sports Committee	[illegible]
"	15		Very Wet. Lecture (Subject Italy her relations with Great Britain) was held in Ober Cassel. A, B & C Companies attended	[illegible]
	16		Dry & Dull. Church Services held in [illegible] Strasse. Voluntary Service held in evening.	[illegible]
	17		Dull & Dry. Adjutants Parade. Arithmetic & Book keeping classes held	[illegible]

A5834 Wt. W4973/M687 750,000 8/16 D. D. & L. Ltd. Forms/C.2118/13.

Instructions regarding War Diaries and Intelligence Summaries are contained in F. S. Regs., Part II. and the Staff Manual respectively. Title pages will be prepared in manuscript.

WAR DIARY
or
INTELLIGENCE SUMMARY.
(Erase heading not required.)

Army Form C. 2118.

Place	Date	Hour	Summary of Events and Information	Remarks and references to Appendices
BEUEL GERMANY	Febry 17		Fair & Dry. 14 Infantry Brigade played Battalion team in the Brigade Shield Competition and won by 4 goals against 2 goals.	[initials]
	18		R.S.M. Parade. Company Training under own arrangements. Recreational Training and instruction on Barr & Stroud Range finder. Educational Classes held as usual. Lt Colonel V.B. Ramsden DSO MC took over temporary command of Brigade	[initials]
	19		Very fair. R.S.M.s Parade. Company Training and Recreational training also instruction in Barr & Stroud Range finder. Arithmetic and Book-keeping Classes held. Brigadier General L.P. Evans VC DSO Commanding Brigade having proceeded to another appointment conveyed his thanks for the magnificent work accomplished by units in Brigade.	[initials]
	20		Fine. Adjutants Parade. Platoon Specialists Training and Recreational Training. Classes held as usual.	[initials]
	21		Fine. Adjutants Parade. Training under Company arrangements also Recreational Training. The Semi-Final of Divisional Cup was played between Divisional Headquarters and the Battalion team. A good game finished Battalion team winning by 4 goals to 1 goal. Novice Boxing Competition held in the evening.	[initials]

Instructions regarding War Diaries and Intelligence Summaries are contained in F. S. Regs., Part II. and the Staff Manual respectively. Title pages will be prepared in manuscript.

WAR DIARY
or
INTELLIGENCE SUMMARY.
(Erase heading not required.)

Army Form C. 2118.

Place	Date Feby	Hour	Summary of Events and Information	Remarks and references to Appendices
BEUEL GERMANY	22		Fine. R.S.M's Parade. Educational Classes in Chemistry, French and English Composition held. Gala Performance was given in STADT THEATRE BONN as a farewell to Battalion before leaving the Division	
"	23		Fine. Church Services held as usual. Battalion Practice for Presentation of Colours.	
	24		Fine. Battalion were presented with Colours on HOFGARTEN Bonn. Lecture on France and Alsace Lorraine in Ober Cassel	
"	25.		Fine. Companies bathed in the morning. Afternoon was spent preparing for move to SOLINGEN. to join 9th Division	
"	26		Fine. Battalion entrained at BEUEL in Route for SOLINGEN	APPENDIX No 1.
			Lt Colonel V. B. Ramsden, D.S.O. M.C. rejoined from 14th Infantry Brigade	
			Special order of the Day received	APPENDIX No 2.
			Divisional Commander Major General T. S. Lambert C.B. C.M.G. visited train before departure, shaking hand with a large number of the Battalion and wishing them every success in New Division	
SOLINGEN GERMANY	27		Dull & cold. Battalion arrived in SOLINGEN. where they were met by Band of the ~~4th Seaforth~~ 5th Cameron Highlanders who played them through the town in route to Billets.	

A5834 Wt. W4973/M687 750,000 8/16 D. D. & L. Ltd. Forms/C.2118/13.

Instructions regarding War Diaries and Intelligence Summaries are contained in F. S. Regs., Part II. and the Staff Manual respectively. Title pages will be prepared in manuscript.

WAR DIARY
or
INTELLIGENCE SUMMARY.
(*Erase heading not required.*)

Army Form C. 2118.

Place	Date	Hour	Summary of Events and Information	Remarks and references to Appendices
SOLINGEN GERMANY	Feby 28		Cold & Dry. B Company relieved one Company of 7th Seaforth Highlanders in outpost line. A C & D Companies went for a short Route march.	

	1st FEB.		28th FEB.	
Commanding officers Strength	OFF	O.R.S	OFF	O.R.S
	19	541	21	513
FIGHTING STRENGTH.				
Officers	33		25	
Other Ranks	703		639	

Casualties Nil.

[signature] Lieut-Col.
Commdg 15/HIGH. L. I.

A5834 Wt. W4973/M687 750,000 8/16 D. D. & L. Ltd. Forms/C.2118/13.

SECRET.   Copy No. 12

15th Battalion The Highland Light Infantry.

OPERATION ORDER No. 8.

Map Reference:- O.L.S. Sheet 59.

1. The Battalion will proceed to join the 9th Division on Wednesday 26th inst., in relief of 7th Battalion SEAFORTH HIGHLANDERS at SOLINGEN.

2. Detail for Wednesday 26th inst.:-

   Reveille. . . . . .07.30 Hrs.
   Breakfast . . . . .08.30 Hrs.
   Sick Parade . . . .09.30 Hrs.
   Dinners . . . . . .12.30 Hrs.

   Tea will be served prior to departure of train.

3. ALL TRANSPORT will be loaded by 12.00 Hrs.

4. Blankets will be rolled in bundles of TEN and stacked outside Coy. Billets by 11.00 Hrs.

5. Officers' Valises will be outside billets by 11.00 Hrs.

6. The Commanding Officer will inspect billets at 11.00 Hrs.

7. Train departs BRUHL at 16.00 Hrs. and arrives SOLINGEN at 19.00 Hrs. (approximately).

8. Companies will be marched to entraining station independently and report there at 14.30 Hrs. Dress:- F.S.M.O. Jerkins will be carried in Company Lewis Gun Limbers. Water-bottles will be carried full.

9. Transport will be at Entraining Station at 13.00 Hrs. Water-carts will be full.

10. O.C. 'B' Coy. will detail a party of 2 Officers & 50 O.Rs. to act as loading party. This party will report at Entraining Station at 13.00 Hrs.

11. Entraining states will be rendered to Orderly Room by 10.00 Hrs.

12. On arrival at Entraining station, Os.C. Coys. will be informed of the number of trucks at their disposal and Companies will be divided into parties for each truck. Parties will be marched to the Train and formed up in file facing the trucks. No man will enter the train until the bugler sounds the "ADVANCE". Coy. Guides will report at Entraining Station 2 hrs. before departure. On arrival of Coys., guides will be found opposite Coys. first truck.

13. Entrainment must be completed half hour before the train is due to depart.

14. No personnel or stores will be allowed in brake vans at each end of the Train, or on the roofs of the trucks.

15. All horses will be watered at the entraining station before despatch of the train.

16. The Transport Sergt. will provide breast ropes for horse trucks.

17. All doors of covered trucks and carriages on the right hand side of the train, when on the main line, must be kept closed.

18./

18. O.C. 'H.Q'. Coy. will detail a picquet for front of train and O.C. 'D' Coy. will detail a picquet for rear of Train to prevent troops leaving at stops.

19. On arrival at detraining station no man will leave the train until the "FALL IN" is sounded by the Bugler. On this signal, men will detrain fully dressed and Companies will be formed up facing the train. One marker per Coy. will report to R.S.M. immediately, Companies will march on marker on ADVANCE being sounded. It is essential that entraining and detraining are carried out as expeditiously as possible.

20. O.C. 'C' Coy. will detail a party of 2 Officers and 50 O.Rs. to act as unloading party on arrival at detraining station.

Lieut.

A/Adjt., 15th Bn. High. L. Infy.

Copies issued as per BATTALION OPERATION ORDER No. 7.

SPECIAL ORDER OF THE DAY.

In bidding farewell to the 16th Battalion The Highland Light Infantry on the 25th February, and to the 15th Battalion, The Highland Light Infantry, on the 26th February, 1919, I desire to thank all ranks for the loyalty, devotion and energy which they have at all times displayed, especially during the last nine months during which I have had the honour to Command the 32nd Division.

It was these qualities which maintained the Spirit of the Division through times of greatest difficulty and trial, and which led us to Victory throughout the great advance from the 8th August till the Armistice in November.

The successful crossing of the SOMME and the rapid advance by the Division on a front of 8000 yards, for several days ahead of all other troops, was due largely to the gallantry and initiative of Officers, N.C.Os., and men of the 15th H.L.I.

At LE TRONQUOY and SEQUEHART, and in the advance beyond ORS to AVESNES, the Battalion showed again and again that spirit of determination and self-sacrifice which has gained for the Division the reputation it holds.

Few Battalions in the British Army can show a finer example of individual heroism than was displayed at BEAUMONT HAMEL on 18th November, 1916, where 60 N.C.Os. and men of the 16th H.L.I. were cut off after reaching their objective, but held out for 8 days, during six of which they were without food.

The entrenching work done by the Battalion, and especially the successful bridging, in conjunction with the Royal Engineers, of the SOMME, the St. QUENTIN Canal, and the SAMBRE and OISE Canal, often under heavy fire, and despite many casualties, showed the highest technical training, and the determination of the Battalion to take its full share in all the victories of the Division.

GLASGOW may well be proud of the troops it has raised and of the men it has so freely given to the Honour of Our King and Country. The presentation of Colours, in PRUSSIA, to the two Battalions on the eve of their departure to join the Lowland Division, forms a fitting termination to the services which both Battalions have rendered during the War to their King and Country, and to the glory of the 32nd Division.

For myself, no honour can be higher than that of having served with them in the Division and of having helped to lead them to final victory.

In the name of the 32nd Division, I ask Lieut. Colonel RAMSDEN, D.S.O., M.C., Commanding 15th Battalion, H.L.I., and Lieut Colonel KYLE, D.S.O., Commanding 16th Battalion, H.L.I., to convey to all ranks my thanks for their services and my best wishes for their happy future in the Army of the Rhine.

T. S. Lambert

24th February, 1919.

Major General,
Commanding 32nd Division.

2188 14 BDE 32 DIV 15th HLI Army Form C. 2118.

Vol 41

Instructions regarding War Diaries and Intelligence Summaries are contained in F. S. Regs., Part II. and the Staff Manual respectively. Title pages will be prepared in manuscript.

WAR DIARY
or
INTELLIGENCE SUMMARY.
(Erase heading not required.)

Place	Date Mar	Hour	Summary of Events and Information	Remarks and references to Appendices
SOLINGEN GERMANY	1st		Fine Cold. Training carried out under Company arrangements.	
"	2nd		Fine - Church Parade held in Protestant Church, Voluntary Service held in evening.	
"	3rd		Fine Companies Bathed in Public Baths Birker Strasse.	
"	4th		Very Wet in morning. Companies training under own arrangements afternoon. Battalion less B Company attended lecture in Kaiser Saal:- Subject America & World Politics	
"	5th		Dull. Companies Training under own arrangements	
"	6th		Dull. Company Training under own arrangements.	
"	7th		Showery Company Training. Battalion less B Company attended Lecture on Industrial Peace after the War in Kaiser Saal	
"	8th		Fair. Companies under Company Commanders carried out training.	
	9th		Cold & Fair. Church Parades as usual	

40.0 6 sheets

Instructions regarding War Diaries and Intelligence Summaries are contained in F. S. Regs., Part II. and the Staff Manual respectively. Title pages will be prepared in manuscript.

WAR DIARY
or
INTELLIGENCE SUMMARY.

(Erase heading not required.)

Army Form C. 2118.

Place	Date March	Hour	Summary of Events and Information	Remarks and references to Appendices
Solingen Germany	10		Fine. Ceremonial Parade in morning. Companies Bathed in Public Baths afterwards.	[illegible]
"	11		Fine. Corps Commanders Inspection on Bismark Strasse, Football Ground. Corps Commander expressed his keen appreciation on the excellent turn-out. Divisional Boxing Competition held in Kaiser Saal Solingen.	[illegible]
"	12		Fine. Morning spent in redistribution of Billets. Divisional Boxing Competition again held in Kaiser Saal.	[illegible]
	13		Very Dull. A.B. & D Companies under Lt J. B Paton proceeded to outpost line to commence wiring of outpost.	[illegible]
"	14		Fine. C & D Companies continued with Wiring of outpost lines. A. Company working on Rifle Range	[illegible]
"	15		Bright Sunshine. Coy Training.	[illegible]
	16		Dull. Church Parades held in Church. Voluntary Service held in Evening. Commanding Officer inspected Billets	[illegible]

Instructions regarding War Diaries and Intelligence Summaries are contained in F. S. Regs., Part II. and the Staff Manual respectively. Title pages will be prepared in manuscript.

WAR DIARY
or
INTELLIGENCE SUMMARY.
(Erase heading not required.)

Army Form C. 2118.

Place	Date March	Hour	Summary of Events and Information	Remarks and references to Appendices
Solingen Germany	17		Dull. Companies Bathed in Public Baths Birker Strasse Thirty men of D Company worked on Rifle Range	[initials]
	18		Snow. A C & D Companies continued Wiring of Outpost line Royal Artillery Band gave a performance in Gymnasium Ohligs. A number of Officers & men of Battalion were present	[initials]
	19		Snow & Sleet Wiring of Outpost line was continued by A & D Companies	[initials]
"	20		Snow & Slush A C & D Companies continued wiring of outpost line Commanding Officer inspected Draft of 157 men who joined Battalion from 1/7 Battalion H L I. The following Officers joined for Duty Captain J. Relgate Stone, 2/Lieut J M Eadie, 2/Lieut W Tait, 2/Lieut R Paton, 2/Lieut R J Douglas 2/Lieut G Park, Lieut W Varley, 2/Lieut J W McLean.	[initials]
"	21		Fair Cold: Training under Company Arrangements. C Company continued wiring of Outpost line, 20 men of A Company working on Rifle Range	[initials]
"	22		Fair & Cold Commanding Officers Parade	[initials]

A5834 Wt. W4973 M687 750,000 8/16 D. D. & L. Ltd. Forms/C.2118/13.

Instructions regarding War Diaries and Intelligence Summaries are contained in F. S. Regs., Part II. and the Staff Manual respectively. Title pages will be prepared in manuscript.

WAR DIARY
or
INTELLIGENCE SUMMARY.
(*Erase heading not required.*)

Army Form C. 2118.

Place	Date Nov	Hour	Summary of Events and Information	Remarks and references to Appendices
SOLINGEN	23		Cold & Fair. Church Parades as usual	[illegible]
"	24		Snow & Frost. C. Company continued wiring of Posts in Outpost Line. D Company working on Rifle Range: Companies Bathed in afternoon	[illegible]
"	25		Snow & Sleet. C. Company wiring Posts in outpost line: A & D Companies Training under Company arrangements.	[illegible]
"	26		Snow & Sleet. Wiring of Posts in Out Post line by C. Company. Party of A. Company working on Rifle Range. Signallers training under Signalling Sergeant. Major J. Z. Muir M.C. and Lieut W. Ferguson proceeded to England for demobilization	[illegible]
"	27		Snow. C. Company wiring of Out Post line: Battalion less B and C Companies attended Lecture on Temperance in Kaiser Saal: Battalion less B. Coy attended Lecture on Germs and Germans in the evening.	[illegible]
"	28		Snow. C Company carried on with Wiring of Out Post Line:- D. Company supplied 20 men for work on Rifle Range, remainder of A and D Companies training under own arrangements. Signallers training under Signalling Sergeant.	[illegible]
"	29		Snow. C and D. Companies continued Wiring of Out Post Line. A Company cleaning up Billets &c: Signallers training under Signalling Sergeant.	[illegible]

A5834 Wt. W4973 M687 750,000 8/16 D. D. & L. Ltd. Forms/C.2118/13.

Army Form C. 2118.

Instructions regarding War Diaries and Intelligence Summaries are contained in F. S. Regs., Part II. and the Staff Manual respectively. Title pages will be prepared in manuscript.

WAR DIARY
or
INTELLIGENCE SUMMARY.
(Erase heading not required.)

Place	Date Mar.	Hour	Summary of Events and Information	Remarks and references to Appendices
SOLINGEN	29.		Battalion Cinema first performance held in Recreation Room, admission free. Very Good Performance.	[illegible]
	30		Heavy Snow. Battalion attended Church Parade, Voluntary Service held in evening. 2/Lieut T. Rule reported for duty and posted to A. Coy.	[illegible]
	31		Heavy Snow. C & D Companies carried on Wiring of Out Post Line. A Company supplied 20 men for work on Rifle Range. Companies bathed in afternoon.	[illegible]

	1st March		31st March	
Commanding Officers Strength	Off	OR	Off	ORs
	20	513	23	551
Fighting Strength				
Officers	25		34	
Other Ranks	639		721.	

W. Ramsden
Lieut. Col.
Commdg 15th Batt. High. L. Inf.

www.ingramcontent.com/pod-product-compliance
Lightning Source LLC
Chambersburg PA
CBHW080802010526
44113CB00013B/2310
* 9 7 8 1 4 7 4 5 2 4 8 5 8 *